Eccentric America

THE BRADT GUIDE TO
ALL THAT'S WEIRD AND WACKY IN THE USA

Jan Friedman

Bradt Travel Guides, UK
The Globe Pequot Press Inc, USA

First published in 2001 by Bradt Travel Guides Ltd,
19 High Street, Chalfont St Peter, Bucks SL9 9QE, England
www.bradt-travelguides.com
Published in the USA by The Globe Pequot Press Inc, 246 Goose Lane,
PO Box 480, Guilford, Connecticut 06437-0480

British Library Cataloguing in Publication Data
A catalogue record for this book is available from the British Library
ISBN 1 84162 023 8

Library of Congress Cataloging-in-Publication Data
Friedman, Jan.
    Eccentric America : the Bradt travel guide / Jan Friedman.—1st ed.
       p. cm.
    Includes bibliographical references and index.
    ISBN 1-84162-023-8
    1. United States—Guidebooks. 2. Eccentrics and eccentricities—
    United States—Guidebooks. 3. Curiosities and wonders—United
    States—Guidebooks. I. Title.

    E158.F69 2001
    917.304'929—dc21

                                                                    2001018791

Photographs
Front cover: Red Stiletto by David Crow, photo © Harrod Blank, www.harrodblank.com
Back cover: Giant creatures line the Enchanted Highway in North Dakota (Rebecca
Penderson/North Dakota Tourism)
Text: American Visionary Art Museum (AV), Harrod Blank (HB), Chad Coppess
Photo/South Dakota Tourism (CC), Dan Curran/Nebraska Division of Tourism (DC), Jan
Friedman (JF), Goggin, Mixed Media (GM), Larry Harris (LH), High Point CVB (HP),
Ohio Division of Travel & Tourism (OH), Nevada Tourism (NT)

Illustrations Dave Colton, www.cartoonist.net
Maps Alan Whitaker

Typeset from the author's disc by Wakewing, High Wycombe
Printed and bound in Italy by Legoprint SpA, Trento

Author

Jan Friedman is no stranger to eccentricity, having spent most of her life in the San Francisco Bay Area. A travel writer, travel photographer and former tour guide, she focused her insightful gaze upon America during a marathon year in which she discovered her own country's eccentric soul. A veteran traveler of 51 countries, Jan finally explored the corners of her own, uncovering proof that Americans have unprecedented freedom to behave in a manner that both shocks and delights foreign visitors.

DEDICATION
This book is dedicated to delightful deviates everywhere who make the world a saner and more interesting place

and

to my friends and family, all of whom listened to endless, hyper descriptions of where I'd just been or what I'd just read, most of which began with some variation of 'You won't believe what I've just seen!'

WWW.ECCENTRICAMERICA.COM WANTS YOU!
If you or someone you know has an eccentricity that belongs in this guide, tell us about it on our website. We also welcome comments about your experiences using this book as well as any updates on the attractions themselves.

Visit eccentricamerica.com for new eccentricities, frequent entry updates, press releases, reviews, and links to related books and websites.

Contents

LIST OF MAPS

Eccentric America	VI–VII	Montana	192
United States of America	inside cover	Nebraska	75
		Nevada	212
		New Hampshire	102
Alabama	164	New Jersey	120
Arizona	263	New Mexico	286
Arkansas	312	New York State	86
California	212	North Carolina	142
Colorado	286	North Dakota	75
Connecticut	102	Ohio	62
Delaware	120	Oklahoma	302
Florida	177	Oregon	192
Georgia	164	Pennsylvania	120
Idaho	192	Rhode Island	102
Illinois	34	South Carolina	164
Indiana	62	South Dakota	75
Iowa	34	Tennessee	142
Kansas	302	Texas	272
Kentucky	142	Utah	263
Louisiana	312	Vermont	102
Maine	102	Virginia	142
Maryland	120	Washington	192
Massachusetts	102	Washington DC	142
Michigan	62	West Virginia	142
Minnesota	34	Wisconsin	34
Mississippi	164	Wyoming	192
Missouri	312		

CANADA

Seattle
WASHINGTON
⬠ 17

Portland ○

OREGON
⬠ 13

Helena ○

⬠ 6
IDAHO
Boise ○

MONTANA
⬠ 10

NORTH DAKOTA
⬠ 11
Bismarck ○

P A C I F I C   O C E A N

San Francisco ○

NEVADA
⬠ 49

Salt Lake City ○
UTAH
⬠ 5

WYOMING
⬠ 5

Cheyenne ○

⬠ 15
SOUTH DAKOTA
Pierre ○

NEBRASKA
⬠ 13
Omaha ○

CALIFORNIA
⬠ 114

Las Vegas ○

Denver ○
⬠ 19
COLORADO

KANSAS
⬠ 11
Topeka ○

Los Angeles ○

San Diego ○

⬠ 10
ARIZONA

Tucson ○

Albuquerque ○
NEW MEXICO
⬠ 26

Lubbock ○

OKLAHOMA
Oklahoma City ○ ⬠ 21

MEXICO

El Paso ○

Fort Worth ○ ○ Dallas
TEXAS
⬠ 31

Houston ●

San Antonio ○

Corpus Christi ○

**KEY TO SYMBOLS USED
ON STATE MAPS**
🎏 Festivals & events
❀ Eccentric environments
♟ Museums & collections
  Attractions:
  🏃 Activity
  🧍 Monument
  ? Curiosity
  🎍 Theme experience
🏢 Cities & towns
👑 Grandiose schemes
✗ Quirky cuisine
! Just plain weird
$ Shopping
🚌 Tours
♠ Quirky quarters
☆ Locations with more than
  one of the above

KEY TO STATE MAPS

State name	**TEXAS**
State capitals	● AUSTIN
	○ SACRAMENTO
Large cities	● Dallas
Other cities	○ Galveston
Major roads	═══════
Other main roads	─────────
International boundary	▬ ▪ ▬ ▪ ▬
State boundary	∙∙∙∙∙∙∙∙∙

ECCENTRIC AMERICA

0 ━━━━━ 200 km
0 ━━━━━ 200 miles

N

CANADA

MINNESOTA
Duluth
17
Minneapolis/
St Paul

Sault Ste Marie

WISCONSIN
22
Milwaukee
Madison

MICHIGAN
13
Lansing
Detroit

Buffalo

VERMONT 11
Montpelier

MAINE
8
Portland

NEW HAMPSHIRE 4

NEW YORK
48
Albany

MASSACHUSETTS 16

Hartford
New York

RHODE ISLAND 8

IOWA 19
Des Moines

Chicago

Toledo

ILLINOIS
19

INDIANA
15
Indianapolis

OHIO
9
Columbus

PENNSYLVANIA
27
Philadelphia

NEW JERSEY 10

CONNECTICUT 12

Kansas City

MISSOURI
17
St Louis

Lexington

WEST VIRGINIA
13

WASHINGTON
■

DELAWARE 5

VIRGINIA
10
Richmond

MARYLAND 14

DISTRICT OF COLUMBIA (DC) 1

KENTUCKY 13

ARKANSAS
14
Little Rock
23

Nashville
TENNESSEE
Memphis

Chatanooga

NORTH CAROLINA
21
Raleigh

S CAROLINA
4
Columbia

ALABAMA
11
10
Montgomery
Jackson

GEORGIA
9
Atlanta
Savannah

MISSISSIPPI
17

LOUISIANA
Mobile
New Orleans

Jacksonville

FLORIDA
38
St Petersburg
Miami

ATLANTIC OCEAN

GULF OF MEXICO

KEY TO THIS MAP

State name	**TEXAS**
Number of mapped sites	14
Capital city	■
Other city	○
International boundary	▬ ▪ ▬ ▪ ▬
State boundary	▪ ▪ ▪ ▪ ▪ ▪

Acknowledgements

A book of this scope never could have been written without the help of hundreds of people who, after they stopped laughing at the nature of my request, threw themselves wholeheartedly into the task of tracking down American eccentricities.

More than 800 tourism bureaus were involved in this project, suggesting sites, confirming details, obtaining photos, marking maps, and providing travel assistance during research trips. I'm eternally grateful for their enthusiastic participation and regret that space considerations prevent me from naming each person and agency individually. I'm also indebted to the Travel Industry Association of America (TIA) and to Travel Publicity Leads, who got the ball rolling by emailing their subscribers with my media request.

I'm especially indebted to Kelly Churchill, my research assistant, who put in hundreds of hours checking and double-checking the entries; to Ellen Rosen and Karen Herzog who patiently read (and reread) the manuscript and gave me their honest opinions; to Joe Bulgatz of New York City who shared his files on eccentric people and places; to Larry Harris of Houston who contributed many photographs of eccentric environments; to Harrod Blank who supplied the cover photo and much information on art car owners and other eccentrics; to Colin Campbell who provided the room with a view in which to write the manuscript, to Traci Shields, Martin Cherry, Marilyn Brandwein, Mike, Don, and Gloria Herzog, and Jack and Ty Brandwein who offered so much support; to Hilary Bradt, Tricia Hayne, Lisa Taylor and the staff at Bradt Travel Guides in the UK; to the staff at Globe Pequot in Connecticut; to Alamo Rental Car for providing a media discount; and to computer geeks everywhere for maintaining the internet, the best thing that ever happened to research.

Introduction

I never thought of myself as eccentric despite being from California, the most eccentric state in the union, and San Francisco which I like to think is the most bizarre city in the country. I grew up thinking a nightly hot tub was a necessity, that everyone needs a hug, and that protest marches were as much a civic duty as voting. With a background like that I came to believe that all Americans are 'free to express their individuality' and I will defend to the bottom of my latte your right to behave outrageously.

I've learned, however, that it's not just Californians who are fiercely proud of their independent heritage and their trailblazing qualities. It's all Americans. It doesn't matter that the rest of the world paints us with an eccentric brush, often dismissing our quirkiness with an attitude that 'all Americans are crazy'. We're a culture based on unprecedented opportunity to achieve individual potential and the freedom to behave in a manner that both delights and shocks foreign visitors. Eccentricity, American style, is both encouraged and enjoyed, at least as long as it doesn't interfere with anyone's schedule.

When I started my research, I worried that people might be offended by the title. It turned out that only four of almost a thousand people I spoke with took offense at the suggestion they – or their attraction – might be eccentric. In fact, dozens of folks went out of their way to convince me of their eccentricity so they could be included in the book. Many even considered it an honor to be so recognized, a validation of their uniqueness.

Personally, I feel privileged to have met so many truly unique people in the course of writing this book, people willing and eager to share their unconventional passions and visions. I've gained a whole new appreciation for those who see our world through slightly skewed glasses. I've been enriched, as I hope you will be, by their stories, activities, and achievements as well as by their unwavering determination to stay their own personal course.

Many theme and regional guides have been published in recent years on various aspects of eccentricity, but none has the scope and perspective of *Eccentric America*. Distilling thousands of pages of research into a portrait of American eccentricity was a daunting task, as was explaining the often unexplainable. The thousand or so entries in this book encompass the quirky people, places, and events that populate the fringes of mainstream tourism; a romp on the wacky side of the American tourist landscape.

I hugely enjoyed the places I visited, and my 'eccentric closet' is filled with mementos and memories. My favorite souvenir is a bottle of Dr Buzzard's

Court Case Bath and Floor Wash; you either put it in your bath water or wash the floor of your business with it when you're facing a court appearance and need to tip the scales of justice in your favor. My most memorable meal included cheddar-flavored worm larvae. Certainly one of my most bizarre activities was skydiving – indoors. But most memorable of all are the people I met through these pages; people I feel honored to know.

I hope you'll enjoy the journey as much as I did.

USING THE GUIDE

Eccentric America is divided into broad geographical regions, with individual states grouped within those regions. Within each state, entries are grouped by the themes described below. Travel details follow each entry. The bibliography, speciality indexes and web directory at the back of the guide can lead you to further information. Nationwide eccentricities are covered in *America's Peculiar Pastimes*, page 7.

Eccentrics aren't always businesslike. Some don't even (gasp!) have a website. Some don't even know what a website is – or have a site that languishes from inattention. Nor are eccentric attractions always predictable. Sometimes the character of a place changes from day to day as folks experiment with different ways of operating, or as their mood changes. Also, check for seasonal variations: many attractions are open only at certain times of the year while operations may be affected by unusual weather.

Every effort has been made to ensure the accuracy of the listings, but mistakes and changes do occur, so you'll still want to confirm the details before you set out. Telephone area codes in America change constantly. Places may close abruptly without notice, or be bought by someone who changes the nature of the attraction. Events may change location from year to year. People die and their quirky contributions can simply vanish. So, please call ahead whenever you can.

That said, it's worth putting up with some uncertainty if you want to experience the unique qualities these eccentrics, attractions and events have to offer.

America's peculiar pastimes

The national section precedes the state listings. Here you'll find a cornucopia of countrywide organizations, passions, and pastimes reflecting American cultural quirks and craziness. To enjoy these national events and activities, you'll need to follow up either by telephone or by visiting the various websites.

Festivals and events

Most of America's festivals, celebrations, and events are unique in that they're based on pop culture, on relatively recent events or on themes created simply as a reason to have fun. With the exception of Native American traditions, American history doesn't go back more than a few hundred years. Our cultural newness explains how we come to celebrate weird festivals like Mike the Headless Chicken Day or the Redneck Games.

But with almost 200 events nationwide, there's never a dull moment, eccentrically speaking. In this category you'll find events like a corn-dog carving contest, a pillow-fighting championship, fruitcake, pumpkin and watermelon tosses, mashed potato wrestling, SPAM™ carving, a chicken-clucking contest, several testicle festivals, a rotten sneaker contest and a downhill furniture ski race. There's even a Nothing Festival when an event-weary tourist town takes a break from its busy season by hanging an empty banner across Main Street, selling T-shirts with nothing on them and holding a parade that no-one enters, but that everyone gathers to watch.

Eccentric environments

People known as 'outsider artists', sometimes referred to as self-taught or visionary artists, created many of the eccentric environments described in this book. An outsider is someone with no formal art training who becomes obsessed with creating one specific kind of art. In this category you'll find more than 50 castles, Holy Lands, futuristic visions, dinosaur parks, bizarre figures, monumental sculptures and houses made from decidedly unconventional materials like paper, bottles or printing plates.

Often these creations are the result of a syndrome called concretia dementia, an excessive compulsion to build using whatever materials are readily available, usually concrete, bottles, cans, scrap metal and other industrial and household junk. This dementia most often strikes people in their later years. The majority of eccentric environments you can visit were built in the early and mid-1900s, before the advent of drugs to control compulsive behavior. Today, if one of your relatives started building a concrete and scrap-iron tower in your backyard, you'd have them on Prozac in no time, squelching their propensity to turn your home into a tourist attraction.

Many of the self-made environments fall into the category of 'God told me to' or 'A little voice told me'. Some of them are built with a specific purpose in mind, usually to share a peculiar 'vision' with the world. Others get built just because it feels good to build them. These environments are often situated on bleak or inhospitable terrain such as desert or swampland, although some can be found in the front or back yards of an outsider's home. Since these installations usually don't do much for property values, their acceptance is pretty much dependent on choosing the right location. So out in the middle of nowhere is where you'll have to go to see many of these remarkable monuments to faith and perseverance.

Most outsiders are solitary folk who just want to be left alone with their ideals and their shovel. The vast majority of them fit the eccentric profile, meaning that they're happy with what they're doing and will continue doing it whether you pay attention to them or not. That their behavior is on the fringe of normality, if not way beyond it, is of absolutely no concern to them. And who knows? Maybe these visionaries know something about fulfillment that we don't.

Museums and collections

Americans are among the world's most skilled and prolific collectors, often creating objects for the sole purpose of collecting them. Throughout the country you'll find quirky museums proudly displaying the odd and curious result of years spent searching for strange or exotic items.

Eccentric America describes almost 200 museums, halls of fame, and collections. While these museums are hardly the kind you'd compare to famous, serious museums, none the less they're still museums, at least in their owner's eyes. Sometimes, while the objects themselves might not be all that strange, their owners might be, making the site worth a visit. Other times, a place might have really weird stuff assembled for non-weird purposes such as notoriety or money.

Collections usually begin by accident or as an occupational sideline, with owners becoming more and more avid over time in the pursuit of their desired objects. The range of collections is astounding and includes: shoes, sandpaper, washing machine mangles, bricks, police insignias, vacuum cleaners, drain tiles and toasters. If more than three of something exists, someone's probably collecting it. Some of the entries in this guide honor themes like sports, the Bible, advertising and medical devices, rather than objects. Others are tributes to various passions and hobbies.

But it doesn't stop with physical collections: the popularity of the internet has created virtual collections as well. On-line you'll find the Museums of Dirt, Toilet Paper, Air Sickness Bags, and Traffic Cones (see the Web Directory, page 335).

Attractions

Here you'll find more than 100 off-beat or wacky attractions, including monuments, Holy Lands, prisons, weird buildings, goofy gardens, and the kind of kitsch roadside attractions for which America is famous: attractions like Corn Palace, Wall Drug, the Crazy Horse Memorial and Graceland. Activities such as indoor sky-diving and trapeze flying are also included here, as well as some unusually off-the-wall entertainment. Wax museums are included in this category because they're generally more commercial than the collections and museums described above.

Most of the attractions listed are commercial, for profit, enterprises which doesn't mean they're not eccentric. While some are professionally designed and managed, others are homemade and quite funky. Wax museums are here because they're generally more commercial than the collections and museums described above. Attractions vary widely in quality and character, but if they're unique, or unique to America, they're included.

Just plain weird

This catch-all category describes 90 people, places or things that defy labels, although it could be said that most of the 1,000 entries in this book could fit in this category. You'll find listings for the toilet-paper tree, a building with furniture hung on the outside, funeral home miniature golf, eccentric grave memorials, a lobster taxi, a woman known as Mother Goose who invented duck diapers, and a man who thinks he's going into space in a homemade rocket. So, if a listing didn't fit naturally into one of the other categories, or if it had a multiple personality, you'll find it here.

Cities and towns

A dozen or so towns are so quirky in character that they deserve a category all to themselves. Here you'll find towns that print their own money, speak their own language, or distinguish themselves in some other way, such as by proclaiming themselves to be the home of Superman or the future birthplace of Captain Kirk.

Grandiose schemes

There aren't many, but they represent exceptionally unrealistic and ambitious undertakings, all perpetrated by visionaries capable of attracting just enough followers to fool themselves into thinking they can actually achieve their grandiose goal. Today, eccentrics like these simply produce their own cable television shows and websites, extending their reach by virtual, rather than just physical, means.

Tours

New York City, Los Angeles, San Francisco, Las Vegas and New Orleans all have their own sections and the distinctive character of these big cities can often be best appreciated by taking tours, especially of – and by – the offbeat. Listed are more than 60 quirky tours led by knowledgeable guides who are themselves quirky characters, or by those who are more normal but lead tours that fit this guide's eccentric theme. Certainly all of these cities could rate an eccentric guidebook on their own. Occasionally, a ghost or haunted tour also appears here.

Shopping

The American consumer culture is famous the world over and we're no slouches when it comes to shopping and gift shops. Certainly there are thousands of unique shopping experiences not listed in this book. The three dozen described here were simply brought to our attention while researching this guide. Shopping for the strange and bizarre is another category that could probably sustain its own guide, and I'd love to hear from readers with suggestions.

Quirky cuisine

The several dozen restaurants you'll find in *Eccentric America* are decidedly curious places, and certainly memorable for their quirky character. They're not rated for quality or price; rather, they're here for their entertainment value, eccentrically speaking, and to give you alternatives to mundane chain restaurants. Most of these establishments are run by highly individualistic people or by corporations who know how to make eccentricity pay.

Quirky quarters

The 70 listings here include an underwater scuba-diving hotel, an Indian hogan, a primitive cave, several former jails, some teepee villages, a sod-house bed and breakfast, a few islands and lighthouses, and a drive-in movie motel where you watch the movie from bed through 'picture' windows. In addition, fantasy/theme rooms are becoming popular in many hotels that are otherwise ordinary. Look for weird decorating themes like 'Alien Invasion', a flying saucer bed surrounded by rock formations; 'Cinderella', a queen-sized, horse-drawn carriage bed and glass slipper whirlpool; or 'Continental', that uses a 1964 Lincoln Continental for the bed. Like the eating establishments above, you can expect to find some very out-of-the-ordinary individuals behind those front desks.

Entertainment

With just a few, long-running exceptions, you won't find music, dance, theater or clubs in this book. Such activities are way too subject to rapid change for inclusion to say nothing of the difficulty of judging their degree of eccentricity.

Maps and travel information

You'll need supplemental road maps for the areas you're visiting. The maps in this book won't always give you the detail you need since the guide covers such a vast area. When you get near your destination, especially to those way off the beaten path, ask a local person to direct you the rest of the way. Most of these attractions are well-known to locals although, occasionally, you may need to ask several people along the way.

KEEPING UP TO DATE

If the contact information given in this book becomes out-of-date, it doesn't mean that the activity or attraction no longer exists. It may have moved, changed contact numbers or websites, been renamed, or been taken over by someone new.

Try searching on line for current information or for the location's chamber of commerce or tourist bureau. Locals will usually be able to track down what you need. Also, log on to eccentricamerica.com; the website will post updated travel information as it comes in. It may take a bit of sleuthing on your part to search out these wayward entries, but you'll usually be rewarded for your efforts. Along the way you might even meet some new eccentrics.

Part One

Eccentric Americans

America is a large, friendly dog in a very small room. Every time it wags its tail, it knocks over a chair.

Arnold Toynbee

Describing the Indescribable

Eccentric America is a walk on the wacky side of American tourism – fun to read, talk about, and follow. It explores the people and places that populate the fringes of mainstream tourism, providing a view of the American psyche as seen through a slightly cracked window. You'll be shocked, surprised, amused and confused.

While the guide is a provocative look at American culture – a place where the outrageous is commonplace and the wacky is indulged – it's not a definitive study of eccentricity. It's difficult enough to describe the indescribable for a lighthearted guide, let alone try to gain expert consensus on the subject from behavioral experts. Eccentricity is one very subjective subject.

Defining eccentricity is like defining beauty: it all depends who's doing the judging. Technically, an eccentric can be defined as someone whose behavior 'varies wildly from the norm', which, depending on circumstances, could even mean you. This definition also allows for society to change its mind from time to time, and from region to region, as to who it labels as deviant, delightful or otherwise. Americans tolerate such a huge range of behaviors that most anything short of picking your nose in public is considered acceptable.

If eccentricity is a term relative only to the behavior of a particular group, how does a cultural group decide who gets to wear the eccentric label and who is dismissed as a crazy old coot? In America, eccentrically speaking, money matters. If you're poor and act bizarre, you're crazy; if you're rich, you're elevated to the status of eccentric. Color matters, too. The whiter you are, the more leeway you have to indulge in eccentric behavior without serious consequence. The darker your skin, the less luxury you have to indulge in strange behavior. The vast majority of eccentrics are middle-class whites.

It's widely believed that Britain, more so than America, is a hotbed of eccentricity, but it turns out that nationality really doesn't matter. A clinical study of eccentrics by Dr David Weeks, whose book, *Eccentrics: A Study of Sanity and Strangeness*, covering both British and American subjects, concluded that approximately one out of every 10,000 people can be considered genuine eccentrics regardless of their country of origin. He also found that full-time eccentrics share a number of traits, particularly those regarding happiness, conformity, and creativity.

Happiness is the key trait that distinguishes an eccentric from someone who's neurotic or mentally ill. Take Leonard Knight of California, for example. For 16 years he's lived alone in a truck, in a remote desert locale, patiently building a mountain in God's honour out of dirt, straw, and paint. That he is happy is obvious as he proudly shows you around his tribute, now 35 feet high. Leonard doesn't suffer from stress and anxiety, doesn't need medication to control his moods, and doesn't need to see a shrink to get through the week. He doesn't even need water, plumbing, or electricity. He gets everything he needs by simply living up to his own expectations.

Like Leonard, most eccentrics have the ability to live in unconventional settings, in unconventional ways, and they don't need other people to affirm their identity. Richard Zimmerman of Idaho, dubbed 'Dugout Dick', likes caves so much that he's spent a good chunk of his life digging them and living in them. Marta Beckett of Nevada opened an opera house in Death Valley and had to paint an audience on the walls so she didn't have to dance by herself. For these loners, solitude is their tool of choice as quiet contemplation fuels their creative fires.

Another eccentric trait is that of flouting convention. Eccentrics are non-conformists, with little or no concern for social convention. They're natural rebels who know they're marching to a different drummer and couldn't care less what tune the band is playing. They know they're different, yet resolutely persist in their passions regardless of the pressure to conform. Tryee Guyton of Michigan painted his blighted neighborhood, including houses, trees, and trash cans, with polka dots. Elvis Aaron Presley McLoud of Mississippi spends every day of his life building a database of every reference ever made to Elvis. John Mikovisch of Texas covered the entire exterior of his house with beer can garlands. As long as eccentrics don't actually do any harm, society will usually let them go on about their business, however bizarre that business may be. Outspoken and out of step, eccentrics are tolerated with good humor, while those considered crazy are whisked out of sight.

True eccentrics have absolute faith that their way is the right one and if you can't see the light, well ... it's your loss. This is especially true of eccentrics who passionately pursue a strange idea or concept. Elizabeth Tashjian, the Nut Lady of Connecticut, worships nuts and her home is a sanctuary to them, a place where she can keep them safe from nutcrackers. Nancy Townsend, also known as Mother Goose, invented duck diapers so people can keep birds as house pets.

Many eccentrics function perfectly well in society even if they do measure success with a crooked yardstick. Brother Joseph, a cleric in Alabama, spent decades building a concrete Holy Land out of cold cream jars, all the while performing his usual duties. John Davis of Kansas spent years building himself a gigantic grave memorial with almost a dozen life-size statues depicting all the phases of his life. Passionate collectors, such as Ken Bannister, the Banana Man from California, and Mildred O'Neil, the Shoe Lady, lead mostly balanced lives despite their obsessions with acquiring particular objects. There's a loopy logic to their thinking; a strange sanity that lets them express themselves more freely than the rest of us without being carted off to the loony bin.

Eccentrics often display brilliant creativity and genius along with their quirks. Unfortunately, modern society too often tries to treat 'aberrant' behavior with drugs, doing a great disservice to those who live on its fringes. Imagine the loss to society if Newton or Einstein had been given Prozac to modify their thinking. Most eccentrics just want to live out their own realities and to leave the world a better place. They want to infect you with their enthusiasm so you, too, can be as happy as they are. *Eccentric America* takes you into their world, giving you the opportunity to come away enriched by the experience.

It has been suggested that as many as one in a thousand of us is a genuine eccentric. If its true, that means you probably know some yourself – and that there could be several more editions of this book!

Perhaps, after all, America never has been discovered. I myself would say that it had merely been detected.

Oscar Wilde

America's Peculiar Pastimes

CAR CULTURE

Nowhere else on earth has the car played such a significant role in shaping a society as it has in America. While other countries had to integrate automobiles into long-established cities and cultures, Americans were able to create a brand new infrastructure based solely on their cars, integrating them so completely into society that the car influenced not only their behavior, but the very architecture of the country itself.

Embracing their cars with a fervor usually reserved for the bedroom, Americans took to the open road. With typical American style, entrepreneurs followed, determined to make the journey as much fun as the destination. During the 1930s and 1940s, billboards, diners, motels and gas stations sprang up, all competing in a mad scramble to get the attention of a Chevy or Ford. Eccentric buildings, in the shape of whatever product was being peddled, proliferated, as did theme attractions and amusement parks. Giant roadside oranges, donuts, chickens, dinosaurs, and mythical figures set you up miles in advance with billboards promising incredible adventures: messages aimed not only at adults, but at the 2.3 children clamoring in the back of a station wagon. While a giant dinosaur might be deemed by the authorities to be out of place near the Eiffel Tower, there were no such restraints along American roads.

In the 1950s, defense fears resulted in the building of a massive, coast to coast, interstate highway system that could also be used to land airplanes. Faster highways, with their limited on-and-off access, paved the way for the rise of the now ubiquitous homogenized franchises. One by one, bits of what became off-road Americana fell into ruin and the roadside, with its quirky facades, lost some of its uniqueness. Today, you can still see the remnants of roadside glory days while meandering down back roads, and now preservationists are rushing to preserve what's left of the odd architecture, gargantuan figures and advertising icons.

Meanwhile, Americans have found new ways to worship their wheels. Besides dozens of museums and restaurant chains devoted solely to cars, trucks, and motorcycles, you'll find an astounding variety of competitions, rallies, races, events, and parades honoring the various sub-cultures of Americans on wheels.

It's a guy thing

Nothing gets the testosterone flowing like a good car crushing which is exactly what you see at **Monster Truck Battles** and **Demolition Derbies**. Events like these symbolize America's worship of motorized power and are, not surprisingly, almost exclusively male domains.

With names like Bigfoot, Grave Digger, and King Krunch, monster trucks are preposterously modified, four wheel drive vehicles that compete by driving off an elevated ramp and seeing how many cars they can crush beneath them before grinding to a stop. The truck body sits way, way up on top of tires six feet high and almost four feet wide. Far too absurd for the road, they're towed to stadium race tracks where they battle it out for superiority. Between 15 and 25 cars are crushed during the average monster truck event that is attended by tens of thousands of rabid fans. The resulting auto carnage leaves the stadium looking like a cross between a battlefield and a junkyard, which is where the soon-to-be crushed cars came from in the first place.

Demolition Derbies are carnage of a different kind: the places to smash, crash, wreck, and otherwise destroy, junk cars that no longer have any business being on the road. Thousands of these events are held in the States each year during which drivers bump, ram, and hammer their car into each other until only one vehicle is left operating. Drivers line up their cars in a circle on a dirt field surrounded by a four-foot high wall of mud. As the siren sounds, the cars begin crashing into each other and the air is filled with the sound of satisfying crunches. Auto parts fly everywhere as, one by one, the cars bite the dust. Helmets and seat belts are the only safety requirements for these modern day gladiators. Good sense is optional.

Part of the entertainment on the drag racing, stock car racing, and monster truck scene is funny cars: cars with eccentric shapes, styles and sizes. Some sport enormous horsepower and hurtle at speeds up to 300 miles per hour. Others are huge, lumbering monsters such as Robosaurun, a 40ft tall, 60,000lb dinosaur that breathes fire while cooking and eating cars. Various bikini and beauty contests are part of this world – are you surprised?

At **School Bus Figure 8 Races**, real-life and race-only bus drivers negotiate the figure 8 course, trying to avoid hitting each other in the crossover, blowing an engine, or tipping over in the turns. The buses are sometimes decorated with graffiti and cartoons of screaming kids painted in the windows.

Common in Southern California and parts of the southwest, **low rider cars** are modified to cruise low and slow. The opposite of hot rods, they use hydraulics to lower the frame to within inches of the ground. Low rider cars are painted with elaborate murals or wild, graffiti-like graphics, costing thousands of dollars, that make personal or political statements. Popular themes include dragons, erupting volcanoes and babes with impossible anatomies. They cruise the streets of Latino neighborhoods and show off at car shows, adding bimbos in bikinis for emphasis. Occasionally they plan 'invasions' by picking a normally quiet town and roaring in, *en masse*, scaring the daylights out of the townsfolk.

Not content with being simply ostentatious, extreme limos are going wacky in a bid for business. Rent a bulletproof, all-terrain stretch Hummer, complete with a hot tub, and you'll be able to soak your way through the most dangerous of neighborhoods. Or get sporty with a Corvette model that has a see through top, get cutsie with the new VW Beetle limo, or get downright modest in a stretch pickup with three bars inside. The most excessive limo has to be the Sheik, a 65ft wonder with four televisions and 30 speakers.

Monster Truck Battles MTRA, 6311 N Lindbergh, Hazelwood, MO 63042; web: www.truckworld.com/mtra

Demolition Derbies DENT; ↘ 716 627 1234; web: www.DENTUSA.com

School Bus Figure 8 Races web: http://members.tripod.com/seat_slasha/f8.html

Low Rider Cars web: www.southweststyles.com

Art cars

America's love affair with the car has some extroverts converting their objects of affection into moving art. **Art cars** are vehicles that have been transformed by their owners into mobile, public folk-art, merging their adoration for their car with their need to express themselves in a very public way. Art car events are quite the opposite of the testerone-enhanced pursuits described above. Driven by highly individualistic and artistic men and women, they slowly cruise the highways on their way to the dozens of art car parades held every year.

There are several hundred art cars nationwide, along with a few art boats and motorbikes. Many have an American flag somewhere on the vehicle as a symbol of personal freedom, the very sentiment that encourages such eccentricity to flourish here

Some artists like to dress like their cars: the 'Button Man' covered his mailbox, toilet, coffin and clothing, as well as his car, in buttons. The 'Ambulance to the Future', by Peter Lochren, has an alien recovering in an oxygen chamber on the roof; its sides are painted with underwater, robotic alien scenes, and he and his co-pilot always wear matching protective gear. Artist Jan Elftmann saved over 20,000 corks while working as a waitress to make her 'Cork Truck'; she has a dress to match.

Other art cars, like the 'Buick of Unconditional Love' owned by Philo Northrup, make a social statement. It features spawning, mummified fish on the hood; a live garden on the back; and Betty Boop making love with a Buddah on the roof. 'Danger', by Reverend Charles Linville (and his dog) is covered with everything that is bad for you, from hazardous industrial equipment to red meat.

Some cars simply reflect their owner's quirky personality. The 'Graffiti Beamer', by Marilyn Dreampeace, invites you to play on her car which is covered with interactive musical toys. The 'Duke', by Rick McKinney, transformed an old 1970s' car into one piled high with antique trunks, a typewriter (reflecting his career as a writer), tons of beads, baubles, bones, robotic arms, graffiti and autographs of celebrities he's come across while driving it. Inside there's a live ferret and a working model train set.

'Cowasaki' is a motorbike converted into a cow; the 'Guitar Cycle' is a rolling guitar. Singer Ray Nelson drove it across the country, singing in honky tonks along the way. And then there's 'Funomena' (fa-nom-en-na – get it?). This mobile museum of the weird and strange also tours with the art cars. Actually, anything on wheels, from unicycles to lawnmowers, can be decked out and join the parades. Log on to the many art car web sites to find out about art car parades and events nationwide.

American Visionary Art Museum; www.avam.org/artcar

HARROD BLANK (Art cars)

Harrod Blank, the photographer and filmmaker who provided the cover photo on this book, owns Cameravan, one of America's most famous art cars. The van is covered with almost 2,000 mostly non-working cameras, a few of which randomly flash and seem to be taking your picture. Several working cameras capture the astonishment and disbelief on people's faces when they see him coming. Not surprisingly, Cameravan has even made folks gawk in amazement in England and Germany.

He also owns Pico De Gallo, a VW Bug transformed into a mini tribute to rock and roll, complete with multimedia and an interactive sound system. Typical of art car owners, Harrod thrives on the attention driving an art car brings. When he drives into a town, he honks the horn just in case people don't notice him. Highly individualistic, art car creators are also open, curious and gregarious: unconventional folk who invite adventure and mystery. 'Time stands still', says Harrod when he's driving one of his art cars; he only drives his regular car when he's in a hurry.

A filmmaker and photographer, he likes to think of himself as a 'conduit to understanding the weird'. In a 1992 film he documented four dozen artists and their cars in a documentary entitled *Wild Wheels*. A book by the same name followed. He's now working on *Wild Wheels II*.

ECCENTRIC SPORTS

Tired of predictable American sports like football and baseball? Consider some of these weird, off-the-wall, or downright wacky sporting events.

The **UX Open** is an alternative golf tour that takes golfing to new heights literally – by transforming ski slopes into never-before-played, rough-terrain, 10-hole golf courses. Up to 72 fit, adventurous golfers can play in each tournament, sometimes riding a chair lift to the next hole. The extreme golfers face hazards like snakes, scorpions, deep ravines, wild turkeys, ice and gnawed flagsticks. Paramedics are thoughtfully provided.

If you have an extremely abrasive personality you'll fit right in at **Belt Sander Drag Racing**. Believe it or not, there's an official International Belt Sander Drag Race Association that helps stage events at hardware and home improvement stores, home shows and lumberyards. The decorated sanders are plugged into long extension cords, then put in a track thirty feet long. When the power goes on, the sanders are off and running; the first one to guide his sander to the end wins.

The American Society of Civil Engineers hosts an annual **Concrete Canoe Competition** for college students. The challenge is to build a canoe sturdy enough to float without sinking, yet light enough to be paddled without exhausting yourself.

BattleBots is the official organization for the emerging sport of **robot combat**. The sport has its origins in the hi-tech alleyways of San Francisco's Silicon Valley where hardcore engineers and designers got their kicks by designing radio-controlled toy robots that bash each other around. By 1994, the underground competitions had become an annual event called the Robot Wars.

In robot combat, every robot is assigned a name, a weight division and a team of handlers who operate it in battle. Combat itself can be one-on-one or a robot free-for-all rumble and takes place inside a specially designed 'battlebox'. Some of the robots are built to destroy while others are designed to disable their opponents. They're not cheap to build, with some of them costing up to $10,000. But with rising sponsorship, prizes are getting bigger as is interest in the sport.

Rivers great and small host thousands of rubber ducks in hundreds of **rubber duck races** held for charity throughout the country. There's even a Great American Duck Race website where you can get all the poop.

Paintball adventures have gone hyper-competitive with complex, role playing scenarios that keep the action and stimulation going longer and farther than do regular paintball games. Competing in scenarios with names like 'Night of the Living Dead' and 'Siege at Cheyenne Mountain', players become part of a historical or fictional plot . Hundreds may participate over a period of many hours – or days – of continuous competition. Some even resort to high tech grenades, global positioning systems and night vision goggles. Be warned, though: those fake bullets leave real dents in your skin.

High tech **night vision goggles** aren't just for paintball, either. They let you do your workout or sporting activity well into the evening, adding a whole new way to break your leg. Mountain biking and rafting are just two of the sports that can be enhanced with night vision goggles.

A sense of humor is helpful in understanding how a weekend chore evolved into yet another wheeled competition. The cutting edge sport of **lawn mower drag** involves guys of ages ranging from 16 to 80 who modify riding lawn mowers so they can accelerate up to 70mph in three seconds and reach top speeds up to 127mph. The only rule is that modifications cannot be made to more than 50% of the original lawn mower.

Dating American-style could be considered a sport, at least as far as **speed dating** goes. It was inevitable that driven singles would find a way to avoid the pick up scene and time-consuming blind dates. Enter speed dating, an instant success in the world of the crazed. Somewhat like musical chairs for grown ups, the women sit at tables, score sheet at the ready. The guys have seven minutes to sit and chat before the bell rings and they have to move on to the next chair. No meaningless small talk is allowed. Participants are encouraged to focus on what the other person is really like. After the event, everyone's cards are analyzed. Two mutual yes's results in telephone contact.

UX Open™ held annually in June; ↘ 973 827 2000; web: www.uxopen.com

Belt Sander Drag Racing held in various locations; web: www.beltsander-races.com

Concrete Canoe Competition held annually. Contact ASCE World Headquarters, 1801 Alexander Bell Dr, Reston, VA 20191-4400; ↘ 800 548 2723 or 703 295 6300

BattleBots web: www.battlebots.com

Great American Duck Race held in various locations. Contact: Great American Duck Races, 16043 N 82nd St, Scottsdale, AZ 85260; ↘ 602 957 3825; fax: 602 954 8217; email: info@duckrace.com; web: www.duckrace.com

Role Playing Scenarios events held in various locations; web: www.jersey.net/~stevec/scenario.htm

Night Vision Goggles. Contact Night Vision ↘ 800 448 8678; web: www.ittnv.com

Lawn Mower Drag Racing, 1812 Glenview Rd, Glenview, IL 60025;
↘ 847 729 7363; fax: 847 729 4208; email: letsmow@aol.com; web:
www.letsmownow.com

Speed Dating, 150 E 52nd St, 10th Floor, New York, NY 10022;
↘ 212 355 7800; fax: 212 355 5855; email:
speeddating_info@speeddating.com; web: www.speeddating.com

ECCENTRIC GROUPS

Nothing beats America's **Gay Pride** events for outrageously flamboyant extravaganzas. Gay Pride parades and celebrations are scheduled in cities and towns all across America. Some of their more renowned events are described in this guide along with tours of premier gay and lesbian communities. A National Coming Out Day was proclaimed in 1988 which led to a rival National Coming Out of Heterosexuals Day, sponsored by right wing religious groups.

'Say it once and say it loud, we are geeks and we are proud.' 'Be there; be square.' Geeks everywhere can break out their fanciest pocket protector, re-tape the bridge on their eyeglasses, and celebrate their geekness at various **Geek Pride** festivals. Speakers you don't have a chance of understanding will be tweaking geek curiosity while 'stump the Geek' trivia contests let them demonstrate their geekness with pride. Non-geeks are welcome, especially if you wear pants several inches too short

'Forward into the past' is the motto of the Society for Creative Anachronism, an organization of members who research and recreate the Middle Ages. Not to be confused with dungeons and dragons role-playing games, these aficionados take their history very, very seriously. From authentic costumes to faking an authentic death on the battlefield, these knights and warriors are exacting in their practice of medieval culture and customs. Feudal society is a lifestyle for its members, many of whom hail from the diametrically opposite high tech field. Events happen almost every weekend around the country which are fascinating, if you like to watch grown-ups playing castle.

Civil War re-enactors are also a zealous bunch, recreating Civil War battles with often fanatical realism. Some re-enactors go so far as to live on a soldier's diet so they'll be appropriately gaunt, or practice bloating out their bodies so they appear to have been dead for a day or two. They sleep outside in the rain, subsist on scavenged food, and have trouble explaining to their loved ones why they do such asinine things.

The **Friends of the Society of Primitive Technology** go back way, way further than the re-enactors above. These folks teach primitive skill workshops where you can learn seven ways to make a fire (flicking your Bik lighter isn't one of them), craft primitive tools and weapons, and make shelters out of natural materials (we're not talking cotton and linen here). Plus, they'll show you how to use all this stuff at their various events. Question: Is being dedicated to 'stone age technology' an oxymoron?

An alliance of 'earth' religious groups, the **Gathering of the Tribes** celebrates both Pagan rituals and Christian traditions, mixing in occasional tarot card readings and massage therapy. Their goal is to 'foster healing relationships with the mother ship we call earth'. An annual gathering takes place in the woods; it's strictly a camping affair.

According to their website, the **Rainbow Nation** is the largest non-organization of non-members in the world. Nobody represents them and the website itself is unofficial. It describes them as 'into non-violence and alternative life styles', which is the same as saying they're still stuck in the 1960s. They hold regional gatherings throughout the year and an annual gathering each summer somewhere in a forest out of sight anyone who doesn't appreciate mind-altering substances. Aging and wanna-be hippies, deadheads, and chickie-poos (young, beautiful things) drink from bliss cups, speak when holding 'the feather', and pray for peace here on earth. Aren't you relieved somebody is looking out for your welfare?

Beware the attack of the closet eccentrics, for they strike when you least expect it. They perpetrate preposterous pranks and instigate infamous insanity, leaving lunatic legacies behind. Who are they? Members of west coast **cacophany societies**, loosely structured groups of people who band together to turn comfort zones inside out and to metaphorically give the finger to the more pompous aspects of American culture. Their pranks, public buffoonery, performance art, and field trips are all about making noisy spectacles of themselves and providing cultural feedback that society hasn't asked for. They're 'nonpolitical, nonprophet, and nonsensical', part time eccentrics creatively misbehaving. According to their website, you may already be a member.

Cacophanists have been seen walking down Beverly Hills' posh Rodeo Drive covered in mud, mounting an assault on city hall dressed as clowns, and publishing a really believable flyer advertising Psychic Car Repair. The San Francisco group held a black tie sewer walk through two miles of underground sewer, dressing in black tie from the waist up and hip high waders below. Absurd protest marches, such as one for the liberation of poultry, a dead dog walkathon, and the Galactic Equality Act (which protests the unfairness of Earth Day to all the other planets) aren't beneath them. In fact, nothing is beneath them as they sacrifice themselves on the altar of public outrage.

Gay Pride Celebrations held in various locations around the country. See www.geocities.com/~alanandsteve/pride.html for a complete listing.

Geek Pride Festivals held annually at various locations; web: www.geekpride.org; ✎ 877 868 4201

Society for Creative Anachronism, PO Box 360789, Milpitas, CA 95036-0789; ✎ 800 789 7486; web: www.sca.org

Civil War Re-enactors. Contact The Civil War Reenactors; web: www.cwreenactors.com; Reenactors of the Civil War: web: http://home.inreach.com/mavgw/racw.htm; First Kansas Civil War Reenactors; web: www.firstkansas.org

Society of Primitive Technology conducts workshops in various locations; web: www.primitiveways.com

Gathering of the Tribes held annually in May in Northern Georgia. Contact GOTT, PO Box 674884, Marietta, GA 30006; ✎ 770 516 6115; web: www.tylwythteg.com

Rainbow Nation Gatherings held annually in regional locations; web: www.welcomehome.org

Cacophony Societies. Contact Los Angeles Cacophony Society; web: www.la.cacophony.org

MISCELLANEOUS ECCENTRICITIES

Shoe trees, not the type you put in your shoes, are the kind you throw your shoes up and into. Shoe trees, and sometimes shoe fences, pop up from time to time on back roads where trees still line the highway. No one really knows how or why a particular tree is selected, but all of a sudden there'll be shoes and boots hanging from it. You won't find many of them listed in this book, though, because nature often has her way with them. So just keep your eyes out or, better yet, start your own shoe tree. Don't trees also deserve their 15 minutes of fame?

If one television programming company has its way, you'll be watching bikini clad anchor men and women deliver the nightly news. Meant to make a mockery of the decline in broadcast morality and mentality, the producers claim people will watch for the excellence of the program. Yea, right. And you read *Playboy* for the articles.

It may have started overseas, but **animal art invasions** have been embraced with typical American enthusiasm and have become big, citywide fund raisers. Beginning in Chicago, they've moo-ved on to Moo York City, Moo Jersey, and Cow-necticut. Bovines such as 'Beach Blanket Esther', wearing a swimsuit, goggles and bathing cap, 'HannuKow', who's Jewish, of course, and a 'Take the Moo Train' subway cow were some of the hundreds of fiberglass cows that took up temporary residence on city streets. Decorated in wacky themes by local artists, they're placed in parks, sidewalks, and outdoor spaces for people to enjoy. How many photographs have been taken of them with their giggling admirers is unknown, but it is known that hundreds of articles have been written about them worldwide. Dubbed 'cows on vacation' and 'cows on parade', the phenomenon has spread to Cincinnati, Ohio where it crossed the species barrier, changing into a 'Big Pig Gig'. Scottsdale, Arizona is following with horses. Can sheep and goats be far behind?

Women do it every day: agonize over what to wear and what to wear with it. Men, traditionally smug owing to their supposed immunity to the whims of fashion, have been thrust into the closet of uncertainty by **dress-down Fridays**. Take pity on the poor guys, for they know not the abyss into which they are falling.

Born out of the casual youth culture of the dot.com and hi-tech business world, the trend dictates that suitable casual attire should be worn on Fridays, throwing men into the same tizzies women have always faced. Nothing so gladdens the heart of a salesman as the sight of a glum looking fellow wandering helplessly round the menswear department. An enterprising tuxedo rental chain store has even begun renting suits and sports jackets.

Art caskets, ocean view plots, and obituaries written by the pre-corpse are becoming common funeral fare as aging baby boomers strive to make their deaths 'meaningful'. New ways to **die in style** include having your ashes blasted from fireworks or being launched into space by a rocket hearse.

Add one more thing you might need a real estate agent for: buying an **underground missile site**. Decades ago, these structures cost several million dollars each to build. Today, these fix-r-uppers are on the market for private and commercial use. If you want to buy one of these 'castles of the 20th century', you'll have to pay on average around half a million dollars to a million plus. You won't find them listed with the Sunday open houses, though. You'll have to fill out an on-line prospect questionnaire before the company, Twentieth Century Castles, will give you any information.

Anybody can create a 'day' in America. You simply proclaim it, then promote it to establish it. You can even register it online at the National Special Events Registry. Ever since the government backed out of the special events business in 1994, it's been open season for holidays. For example, we have Sneak Some Zucchini Onto Your Neighbor's Porch Night, Buy a Musical Instrument Day, National Juggling and Kitchen Klutzes of America Day, Cuckoo Warning Day, and National Nude Day.

Take Our Daughters to Work Day spawned Take Your Dog to Work Day. If a day isn't enough, your can name a week or even a month. March is

National Noodle Month, April belongs to Welding, while May is Fungal Infection Month. For thousands of curious, nutty, and peculiar holidays, log on to **Chase's Calendar** or **Celebratetoday.com**.

Half-a-dozen grown men in the United States make a living blowing bubbles. We're not talking about the baby bubbles you get from those little bottles that come with their own wand. We're talking *bubbles*, bubbles the size of elephants and automobiles, square bubbles, bubbles within bubbles, even bubbles with people in them. A bubblehood of bubblemen perform at festivals and events all over the country, delighting children of all ages with their off-the-wall – and educational – antics.

Gary Golightly got his professional start while practicing his art at a duck pond. When a man asked if he performed at weddings, Gary replied, 'I do now.' When asked how much he charged, Gary said 'A thousand dollars an hour, with a nine-hundred dollar discount.' He has since blown bubbles all over the world.

Louis Pearl weaves comedy and magic into his act, explaining the physical science behind bubble blowing while performing. Sterling Johnson uses only his hands, juggling bubbles and making rolling bubbles, bubble chains, and vibrating bubbles. Tom Noddy, who uses all kinds of utensils in his act, created the cubic bubble and was instrumental in bringing bubble festivals to science centers. Captain Bubbles floats strange objects through the crowds while Kelly O'Neil specializes in the really big bubbles. You can find all these bubble artists, along with their specialties, on their web sites.

There's big money in bubble blowing, at least for kids. Each spring 2,500 Wal-Marts sponsor the National Bubble Blowing Contest. The top six finalists go to the big 'blow-off' to compete for a $10,000 bond and a trip to Disney World.

Guys who make a living blowing bubbles, Gary Golightly; web: www.bubbleman.com; Sterling Johnson; web: www.handblownbubbles.com; Louis Pearl; web: http://tangenttoy.com/lpearl.htm; Kelly O'Neill; web: www.wetrock.com/bbm.html; Richard Faverty; web: http://bubbles.org; Frank Noddy; ➘ 408 423 1021

Buy an underground missile site. Contact 20th Century Castles, Box 4, Dover, KS 66420; ➘ 785 256 6029; email: edpeden@cjnetworks.com

National Special Events Registry, Open Horizons, PO Box 205, Fairfield, IA 52566; ➘ 641 472 6130; fax: 641 472 1560

CURIOUS COLLECTIONS AND PASTIMES

Tattoo conventions vary in size and length, but most of them include body art contests along with an exhibit floor where artists can sell their merchandise and tattooing skills. Unadorned folks attend for many reasons, but the main one is the opportunity to be immersed in a strange, foreign

TOTALLY ABSURD INVENTIONS

Eccentric inventors, convinced of the brilliance and marketability of their individual creations, spend big money to get a patent. Totally Absurd Inventions explores the funnier side of America's inventive nature on a delightfully daft website at **www.totallyabsurd.com**. Some of the stranger inventions include the following:

- A nose wipe for skiers that controls irritating nose drip without having to resort to cumbersome tissues that are never available when you need them. This nifty wrist attachment protects your sleeves without any trouble or bother, preventing interruption of or delay in your sporting activity. Snot a bad idea.

- An easy on, easy lift 'hospital happiness flap' covers that embarrassing part of your anatomy exposed by the diabolical, rear-opening hospital gown. Think what a favor you're doing the hospital staff.

- A motorized ice cream cone. Using your tongue for repeated licking actions can become tiresome. Modern technology saves you the bother: simply put your cone into a holder, flip a switch, and *voilà!* – your tongue stays still while your cone spins around.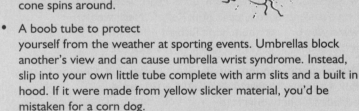

- A boob tube to protect yourself from the weather at sporting events. Umbrellas block another's view and can cause umbrella wrist syndrome. Instead, slip into your own little tube complete with arm slits and a built in hood. If it were made from yellow slicker material, you'd be mistaken for a corn dog.

Other genius inventions on the site include bulletproof buttocks, a thumb-sucking inhibitor, toilet landing lights, a kissing shield and a hat tether.

Ted VanCleave, originator of the site, came upon the idea by accident when he was applying for a patent in 1997 for his inflatable greeting cards.

world while having the freedom to stare at other people's tattoos without being considered rude. You also get a unique chance to ask someone with dozens of body piercings or tattoos all over their bodies why on earth they do it. Tattoo contest categories include the best black and white, most unusual, best tribal, best portrait, and best overall. Bring binoculars: it makes it easier to appreciate the body art up close.

Anyone with an interest in rats and mice – other than exterminators – can join the **American Fancy Rat and Mouse Association**. Devoted to the breeding and showing of fancy rats and mice, the group holds shows in various locales across the country. These misunderstood and much maligned rodents, now bred in over 30 varieties, actually make wonderful pets that can do more tricks than your average dog. At AFRMA conventions the critters compete in a best tricks event and show off their winning personalities for the judges.

Americans are among the world's most skilled collectors, freely indulging their passion for bizarre and ludicrous collectibles. But it's one thing to have a hobby, and quite another to have an obsession. The peculiarity of some of the activities Americans like to share is reflected in the existence of associations for love addicts, Saquatch watchers, wrist wrestlers, time capsule enthusiastists, stilt walkers, polka dancers, green and red chile connoisseurs, ghost researchers, impersonators,  and a group dedicated entirely to absurd special interests. This guide describes a lot of festivals around the country celebrating some mighty strange pastimes.

Scattered all over the states, **Ripley's Believe It or Not Museums** can be found in heavily touristed areas. Each museum's displays, housed in 27 museums in ten countries, are 90% unique and different. Robert Ripley, a modern day combination of Marco Polo and Indiana Jones, collected the unbelievable, inexplicable, and one-of-a-kind oddities over a period of 40 years.

Body Art. ASC Tattoo Directory; web:www.tattoodirectory.com ; Inslingers Ball; web: www.inslingers.com; Agony and Ecstasy Tattoo Convention; web: www.excalevents.com/expo2000

American Fancy Rat and Mouse Association, 9230 64th St, Riverside, CA 92509; web: www.afrma

Ripley's Believe It or Not Museums are located in Wisconsin Dells, WI; St Augustine, Key West and Orlando, FL; San Francisco, Hollywood and Buena Park, CA; Myrtle Beach, SC; Jackson Hole, WY; Atlantic City, NJ; Branson, MO; Grand Prairie, TX; Gatlinburg, TN

CORPORATE ECCENTRICITY

Weirdness pays. Disney discovered this 50 years ago with its mouse ears and big business has been emulating that success ever since. While individual eccentrics do what they do because it feels good, business plays the eccentric card strictly for profit. Such 'designer eccentricity' has a predictable, well-executed outcome, whereas individual eccentricity evolves gradually and without any clear idea of where it might lead.

In Las Vegas you experience the most excessive extremes of corporate eccentricity. Southern California and Florida also go to incredible lengths to get your attention and your dollars. Theme parks across the country are competing to build the biggest, the highest and the most extreme of rides and experiences. Even restaurants play the game, with theme eateries exploiting the wacky for profit. 'Weird, wild, loony, silly and strange' usually adds up to a rewarding bottom line. The American public is so accustomed to excessive behavior that it's becoming commonplace and even mundane.

In this new millenium economy, retaining workers is harder than ever. Corporate **team building** adventures for business are in great demand because they capture employees' imaginations in ways no motivational speaker can. Imagine being strapped inside a human bowling ball and thrown down an inflatable lane into six-foot tall foam pins. Or becoming a human slingshot by hooking yourself on a bungee cord and running down an inflatable runway until the tension snaps you back. Try wearing a velcro jumpsuit, then bouncing off a trampoline and sticking yourself to a wall. Companies like Total Rebound create these types of complex, interactive games that build team spirit and enhance problem solving abilities. Structured competitions, along with 'brain and body fun', appeal to today's cubical bound workers.

POLITICAL CORRECTNESS

Americans are famous for the linguistic lunacy referred to as political correctness. The ability to bend their tongues over backwards to avoid offending even an animal has reached new heights of absurdity. A shoplifter is a 'non-traditional consumer', a prostitute becomes a 'sex care provider', a mute is 'orally challenged', and a hamburger is 'mutilated animal flesh'. Loggers, or 'tree slayers', aren't held in very high esteem nor are fishermen who are considered 'rapers of the oceans'. If you have a learning disability, you have 'self-paced cognitive ability'. Even white trash, proverbially the lowest-ranking butt of jokes, have now become 'PC unaware' and are probably eligible for some kind of government grant.

JUST PLAIN WEIRD

Eccentricity, feminist style, is behind the Anti-Tampon Conference, aka the Mid-Atlantic Feminist Conference, aka the Let Blood Flow Fest. According to the website, the conference is about women's empowerment, radical change, and activism. Apparently, some organizers believe that tampon use contributes to rainforest devastation.

While on the subject, the Museum of Menstruation and Women's Health is looking for a permanent home. Planned displays include an actual menstrual hut, the history of menstrual objects, customs and advertising, and current women's health issues. Until recently the museum was in the private home of a bachelor, but folks were reluctant to visit the museum in that location.

'Puzzling adventures for creative minds' is **Dr Clue**'s motto. Taking team-building activities to city streets, Dr Clue creates team building treasure hunts that are real brain busters. The hunts use cryptic, punny, and word-play clues to get you to off-beat and irreverent places to pick up the next clue. After following a number of clues, cameras are used to take creative group photos at designated spots. Past hunt winners have solved their puzzles and posed as a re-creation of the Beatles' Abbey Road album cover and as a human pyramid against the backdrop of the Transamerica Pyramid building in San Francisco.

The difference between men and boys is the price of their toys. **Incredible Adventures** offers truly outrageous pursuits to people (mostly guys) with enough money to satisfy their every whim. At their Covert Ops weekend, any James Bond wannabe can buy 72 hours of clandestine excitement. Espionage techniques, explosives, booby traps, evasive driving, self-defense and shooting are all part of the adventure. You get to learn ambush, hostage rescue and search-and-destroy techniques as if they were the real thing.

If you prefer the sky to the ground, you can join **Air Combat, USA** where you actually get to fly a light attack fighter aircraft. Outside of the country, they offer MIGS over Moscow, a Wings over Cape Town plus Safari extravaganza, as well as a real-life go-up-in-space adventure.

Team building adventures. Contact Total Rebound, 6610 Goodyear Rd, Benicia, CA 94510; ☎ 707 748 2475; fax: 707 748 0116; web: www.totalrebound.com

Team building treasure hunts, Dr Clue Treasure Hunts, 495 Frederick St, #5, San Francisco, CA 94117; ☎ 415 566 3905; fax: 415 777 0675; web: www.drclue.com

Incredible Adventures, 6604 Midnight Pass Rd, Sarasota, FL 34242; ☎ 800 644 7382; email: migsetc@packet.net; web: www.incredible-adventures.com

No one ever went broke underestimating the taste of the American public.

Henry Louis Mencken

The Eccentric Year

One of the characteristics of eccentricity that makes it so entertaining is its unpredictability. This is especially true for festivals and events. Usually lacking in big corporate sponsorship, events like these tend to thrive on the efforts of dedicated volunteers. This means possible new contact information every year – new websites, new area codes and, sometimes, new dates and locations.

Visit eccentricamerica.com for updated festival and event information. Let us know how you enjoy these wacky festivals and if you have a funny photo to share with others on *Eccentric America's* website.

JANUARY

Fruitcake Toss, Manitou Springs, CO. Contact Manitou Springs Chamber of Commerce, 384 Manitou Ave, Manitou Springs, CO 80829; ✆ 800 642 2567 or 719 685 5089; web: www. manitousprings.org

Ice Box Days at Voyageurs National Park is located in north central Minnesota on the northern border of Minnesota, about 15 miles east of International Falls, MN and 300 miles north of Minneapolis–Saint Paul, MN. International Falls Area Chamber of Commerce; ✆ 800 325 5766 or 218 283 9400; web: www.internationalfallsmn.com

Oatman Bed Races, Oatman, AZ. Contact Oatman-Gold Road Chamber of Commerce, PO Box 423, Oatman, AZ 86433; ✆ 520 768 6222; fax: 520 768 4274; email: oatmanaz@ctax.com; web: www.route66azlastingimpressions.com

Snowdown, Durango, CO. Contact SNOWDOWN Durango, Inc., PO Box 1144, Durango, CO 81302; ✆ 970 382 3737; web: www.snowdown.org

White, White World Week at Sugarloaf Ski Resort RR1 Box 5000, Carrabassett Valley, ME 04947; ✆ 800 THE LOAF or 207 237 2000; fax: 207 237 3768; email: infosugarloaf.com; web: www.sugarloaf.com

FEBRUARY

Cardboard Box Derby, Arapahoe Basin, CO. Contact Arapahoe Basin Resort, Arapahoe Basin, CO 80435; ✆ 970 468 0718; email: abasin@colorado.net.

Elm Farm Ollie Day, Mt Horeb, WI. Contact Mt Horeb Mustard Museum, 109 E Main St, Mt Horeb, WI 53572; ✆ 800 438 6678; email: curator@mustardweb.com; web: www.mustardweb.com. Located about 20 miles west of Madison.

Gasparilla Parade and Pirate Fest Festival, Tampa, FL. Contact Tampa Bay Visitor Bureau; ✆ 813 223 1111 extension 44; web: www.visittampabay.com

Ice Tee Golf Tournament, Lake Wallenpaupack, PA; ✆ 570 226 3191

International Water Tasting Competition, Berkeley Springs, WV. Contact Travel Berkeley Springs; ℸ 800 447 8797; web: www.berkeleysprings.com/water

Joe Cain Day, Mobile, AL. Contact the Mobile Convention and Visitors Corp, PO Box 204, Mobile, AL 36601; ℸ 800 5 MOBILE; fax: 334 208 2060; web: www.mobile.org

Mardi Gras, New Orleans, LA. Contact New Orleans Metropolitan Convention and Visitors Bureau, 1520 Sugar Bowl Dr, New Orleans, LA 70112; ℸ 504 566 5011 or 800 672 6124; web: www.neworleanscvb.com

Moose Stompers Weekend, Houlton, ME. Contact Greater Houlton Chamber of Commerce; ℸ 207 523 4216; email: chamber@houlton.com

Mystery Weekend in Langley, WA. Contact Langley Chamber of Commerce; ℸ 360 221 5676

National Date Festival and The Blessing of the Dates, Riverside County, CA; ℸ 800 811 FAIR or 760 863 8247; web: www.datefest.org

Outhouse Classic, Trenary, MI. Contact Outhouse Classic, PO Box 271, Trenary, MI 49891; ℸ 906 446 3504

Renaissance Fair, Apache Junction, AZ. Fairgrounds are located 9 miles east of Apache Junction on US Route 60; ℸ 520 463 2700; web: www.thegoosemother.com

San Francisco Zoo Valentine's Day Sex Tours, San Francisco, CA. Contact San Francisco Zoo, 1 Zoo Rd, San Francisco, CA 94132; ℸ 415 753 7080; web: www.sfzoo.org

World Snow Shovel Race, Angel Fire, NM. Contact Angel Fire Resort, Angel Fire, NM; ℸ 505 377 4237; email: events@angelfireresort.com; web: www.angelfireresort.com

MARCH

Cardboard Classic Red Lodge Winter Carnival, Red Lodge, MT; ℸ 406 446 2610

Dirt Bag Day, Bozeman, MT. Contact Big Sky Resort, PO Box 160001, 1 Lone Mountain Trail, Big Sky, MT 59716; ℸ 800 548 5000; email: info@bigskyresort.com; web: www.bigskyresort.com

Odor-Eaters International Rotten Sneaker Contest, Montpelier, VT. Contact Montpelier Recreation Department; ℸ 802 223 5141; web: www.mps.l12.vt.us/rec/rec.htm

Rattlesnake Round-up and Cook-off, Sweetwater, TX. Contact Rattlesnake Roundup, PO Box 416, Sweetwater, TX 79556; ℸ 915 235 5488 or 915 235 8938; email: rattle@rattlesnakeroundup.com; web: www.rattlesnakeroundup.com

Renaissance Fair, Apache Junction, AZ. Fairgrounds are located 9 miles east of Apache Junction on US route 60; ℸ 520 463 2700; web: www.thegoosemother.com.

Skijoring, Red Lodge, MT. Contact Skijorama; web: www.skijorama.com

APRIL

Anvil Shooting Contest, Laurel, MS. Held during the Mississippi Forestry and Wood Products Exposition. Contact Economic Development Authority of Jones County, PO Box 527, Laurel, MS 39441; ℸ 601 428 0541; email: PEM@LMFCO.com

Conch Republic Independence Celebration, Florida Keys, FL. Contact Office of the Secretary General of the Conch Republic; ℸ 305 296 0213; fax: 305 296 8803; web: www.conchrepublic.com

Furniture Races, Whitefish, MT. Contact Big Mountain Ski and Summer Resort, PO Box 1400, Whitefish, MT 59937; ➤ 800 858 3913 or 406 862 1900; fax: 406 862 2955; email: bigmtn@bignmtn.com; web: www.bignmtn.com

Kinetic Sculpture Race, Baltimore, MD. Contact American Visionary Art Museum, 800 Key Highway, Baltimore, MD 21230; ➤ 410 244 1900; fax 410 244 5858; web: www.avam.org/kinetic

Mule Day, Columbia, TN. Contact Mule Day Office, 1018 Maury Co Park Dr, Columbia, TN 38401; ➤ 931 381 9557; web: www.muleday.com

Rose Bud Parade, Thomasville, GA. Contact Rosebud Parade Committee, Thomasville Main St, PO Box 1540, Thomasville, GA 31799; ➤ 912 227 7020.

Spalding University's Running of the Rodents, Louisville, KY; ➤ 800 896 8941 extension 2422; fax: 502 585 7158; web: www.spalding.edu/events/ratrace.htm

St Stupid's Day Parade, San Francisco, CA. Contact First Church of the Last Laugh; web: www.saintstupid.com/parade.htm

World Cow Chip Throwing Contest, Beaver, OK. Contact Beaver County Chamber of Commerce, PO Box 878, 33 W 2nd St, Beaver, OK 73932; ➤ 580 625 4726

World Grits Festival, St George, SC. Contact Granny Grits at ➤ 843 563 4366 or the tourist bureau at ➤ 800 788 5646

World's Largest Trivia Contest, Stevens Point, WI. Contact University of Wisconsin–Stevens Point Student Radio Station; ➤ 715 346 3755; web: www.easy-axcess.com/trivia

MAY

The Blessing of the Bikes, Litchfield, CT. Lourdes in Litchfield Shrine, Rte 118, Litchfield, CT; ➤ 860 867 1041

Calaveras County Fair and Jumping Frog Jubilee, Calaveras County, CA; web: www.frogtown.org. Contact Calaveras County Chamber of Commerce, 1211 S Main St, PO Box 1145, Angels Camp, CA 95222; ➤ 209 736 2580; fax: 209 736 2576; web: www.calaveras.org

The Cowboy Trade Day, Claremore, OK. Located north of the city on Historic Route 66; watch for the Git 'N Go Store, turn east onto Blue Starr Drive, go 1 mile to Round Up Club. Contact Cowboy Trader; ➤ 800 553 0353 or 918 341 6985; web: www.cowboytrader.com

Horned Toad Derby, Coalinga, CA. Contact Coalinga Chamber, 380 Coalinga Plaza, Coalinga, CA 93210; ➤ 559 935 2948 or 800 854 3885; fax: 559 935 9044; email: exec@coalingachamber.com; web: www.coalingachamber.com

Kinetic Sculpture Race, Boulder, CO. Contact Boulder Visitor Bureau; ➤ 303 442 2911, or the sponsors, KBCO radio; ➤ 303 444 5600; web: www.kbco.com

Mike the Headless Chicken Days, Fruita, CO; ➤ 877 680 7379; email: mike@miketheheadlesschicken.org; web: www.miketheheadlesschicken.org

O Henry Pun-Off World Championships, Austin, TX. Contact O Henry Museum, Fourth St at Neches in Brush Park; ➤ 512 472 1903 or 512 453 4431; web: www.puny.webjump.com

Pickle Fest, Atkins, AR. Contact Chuck ➤ 501 641 1993; or People for a Better Atkins, Box 474, Atkins, AR 72823; ➤ 501 641 7210

Rat Race, New York City, NY. Contact Carey International, 575 Lexington Ave, Suite 2840, New York, NY 10022; ↘ 212 980 1490

San Francisco Examiner **Bay to Breakers Race**, San Francisco, CA. Contact Examiner Bay to Breakers, PO Box 429200, San Francisco, CA 94142; ↘ 415 808 5000; email: breakers@examiner.com; web: baytobreakers.com

Toad Suck Daze, Conway, AR. Contact Conway Area Chamber of Commerce, 900 Oak St, Conway, AR 72032; ↘ 501 327 7788; fax: 501 327 7790; web: www.toadsuck.org

York Bar's Go Nuts Testicle Festival, York, MT; ↘ 406 475 9949

JUNE

Bug Bowl, South Durham, NC. Contact North Carolina Museum of Life and Science 433 Murray Ave, Durham, NC 27704; ↘ 919 220 5429; fax: 919 220 5575; email: pr.ncmls@mindspring.com

Do-Dah Parade, Kalamazoo, MI. Contact Kalamazoo County Convention and Visitors Bureau, 346 W Michigan Ave, Kalamazoo, MI 49007; ↘ 800 530 9192; or Cumulus Broadcasting WKFR; ↘ 616 344 0111; web: kazoofun.com

Duncan Hines Festival, Bowling Green, KY. Contact Bowling Green Convention and Visitors Bureau; ↘ 270 782 0800; web: www.duncanhinesfestival.com

Elfego Baca Shoot, Socorro, NM. Located on I-25 approx 65 miles south of Albuquerque. Contact New Mexico Institute of Mining and Technology; ↘ 505 835 5725; to register ↘ 505 835 1550

The Great American Think-off, New York, NY. Contact New York Mills Regional Cultural Center, 24 North Main Ave, New York Mills, MN 56567; web: www.think-off.org

Haight-Ashbury Street Fair, San Francisco, CA; ↘ 415 661 8025; email: pabloji@earthlink.net; web: www.haightstreetfair.org

Hillsborough Hog Day, Hillsborough, NC. Contact Hillsborough Chamber, 960 Corporate Dr, Suite 101, Hillsborough, NC 27278; ↘ 919 732 8156; web: www.hillsboroughchamber.com

Mermaid Parade, Coney Island, Brooklyn, NY; ↘ 718 372 5159; web: www.whirl-I-gig.com/mermaid.html

Mustard Family Reunion, Mt Horeb Mustard Museum, 109 E Main St, Mt Horeb, WI 53572; ↘ 800 438 6678; email: curator@mustardweb.com; web: www.mustardweb.com.

National Hollerin' Contest, Spivey's Corner, NC; ↘ 910 567 2600

National Oldtime Fiddlers' Contest, Weiser, ID; ↘ 800 437 1280; web: www.fiddlecontest.com

Pier 39's Street Performers' Festival, Pier 39, San Francisco, CA; ↘ 415 705 5500; fax: 415 981 8808; web: www.pier39.com

Roswell UFO Encounter Festival and Intergalactic Fashion and Food Extravaganza, Roswell, NM. Contact Roswell UFO Encounter, PO Box 2587, Roswell, NM 88202; ↘ 505 624 6860; fax: 505 6224 6863; email: info@RoswellUFOEncounter.com; web: www.roswellufoencounter.com

Ryegate Testicle Festival, Ryegate, MT; ↘ 406 568 2330

Story Telling Festival, Omaha, NE. Contact Storytelling Festival of Nebraska,

1803 S 58th St, Omaha, NE 68106; ℄ 402 551 4532 or 800 551 4532; email: storygalore@home.com; web: www.storygalore.com

Superman Celebration, Metropolis, IL. Contact Metropolis Chamber of Commerce, 607 Market St, Metropolis IL 62960; ℄ 800 949 5740 or 618 524 2714; email: info@hcis.net; web: www.metropolischamber.com

Taos Poetry Circus, Taos, NM. Contact World Poetry Bout Association, 232 Paseo del Pueblo Sur, 5275 NDCBU, Taos, NM 87571; ℄ 505 758 1800; email: spha@laplaza.org; web: www.poetrycircus.org

Trek Fest, Riverside, IA. Located on Hwy 218, 20 miles south of I-80/Iowa City; web: www.trekfest.com

Watermelon Thump, Luling, TX. Contact Luling Watermelon Thump, 421 E Davis St, PO Box 710, Luling, TX 78648; ℄ 830 875 3214; fax: 830 875 2082; email: lunlingcc@bsc.net.net; web: www.bscnet.net/lulingcc/thump.htm

World's Longest Breakfast Table, Battle Creek, MI. Contact Battle Creek/Calhoun County Visitor and Convention Bureau; ℄ 616 962 2240 or 800 397 2240

World's Richest Tombstone Race, Fort Sumner, NM. Contact Fort Sumner Chamber of Commerce, De Bacca County Chamber of Commerce, 707 N 4th St, Fort Sumner, NM 88119; ℄ 505 355 7705

JULY

Absolut Chalk Street Painting Festival, Los Angeles, CA. Contact the Light-Bringer Project; ℄ 626 440 7379; fax: 626 440 5152

Ancient and Horribles Parade, July Fourth in the village of Chepachet, Glocester, RI. Contact Glocester Town Hall; ℄ 401 568 6206; web: www.glocesterri.org

Boom Box Parade, Willimantic, CT. Contact wili 14 AM, The Nutmeg Broadcasting Company, 720 Main St, Willimantic, CT 06226; ℄ 860 456 1111; fax: 860 456 9501; web: www.wili.com

Central Maine Egg Festival, Pittsfield, ME. Contact Central Maine Egg Festival Committee, PO Box 82, Pittsfield, ME 04967; web: www.pittsfield.org/eggfes.htm

Cherry Pit Spit (during Sugarbush, VT July Fourth parade). Contact Sugarbush Chamber of Commerce, Rt 100, Box 173, Waitsfield, VT 05673; ℄ 800 517 4247

Cowboy Poet's Gathering, Wyoming Frontier Prison and Old West Museum, 500 Walnut St, Rawlins, WY 82301; ℄ 307 778 7290 or 307 324 4422

da Vinci Days Festival, Corvallis, OR. Contact da Vinci Days Festival, 760 SW Madison, Suite 200, Corvallis, OR 97333; ℄ 541 757 6363 or 800 334 8118; email: davinci@davinci-days.org; web: www.davinci-days.org

Hemingway Days Festival, Key West, FL; ℄ 800 527 8539; web: www.hemingwaydays.com

Horton Bay Parade, Horton Bay, MI. Contact John Rohe, Horton Bay Parade, Box 284, Boyne City, MI 49712; ℄ 231 347 7327; email: rohe@freeway.net

Iron Horse Rodeo, Red Lodge, MT. Contact Red Lodge Area Chamber of Commerce; ℄ 877 733 5634

Kenwood World Pillow Fighting Championship, Sonoma County between Santa Rosa and Sonoma, CA; ℄ 707 833 2440; email: lesley@kenwoodpillowfights.com; web: www.kenwoodpillowfights.com

Mashed Potato Wrestling (during Potato Days), Clark, SD. Contact Clark Area Chamber of Commerce, PO Box 163, Clark, SD 57225; email: clarksd@itctel.com; web: www.clarksd.com/potato/potatowrestling.htm

Oatman Egg Fry, Oatman, AZ. Contact Oatman-Gold Road Chamber of Commerce, PO Box 423, Oatman, AZ 86433; ✆ 520 768 6222; fax: 520 768 4274; email: oatmanaz@ctax.com; web: www.route66azlastingimpressions.com

Oregon Country Fair, Veneta, OR. Contact Oregon Country Fair, PO Box 2972, Eugene, OR 97402; ✆ 541 343 4298 or 800 992 8499; email: ocf@teleport.com; web: www.oregoncountryfair.org

Pageant of Masters, Laguna Beach, CA. Contact Pageant of the Masters, 650 Laguna Canyon Road, Laguna Beach, CA; ✆ 949 497 6582 or 800 487 3378; web: www.foapom.org

Redneck Games, Dublin, GA. Contact: WQZY; ✆ 912 272 4422 or 800 688 0096; web: www.wqzy.com/redneck.htm.

Rolling River Raft Race, Pueblo, CO. Contact Pueblo Chamber of Commerce, 302 N Santa Fe, Pueblo, CO 81003; web: www.pueblo.org

Telluride Nothing Festival, Telluride, CO. Contact Telluride Visitor Services, 700 West Colorado Ave, Telluride, CO 81435; ✆ 888 605 2578; fax 970 728 6475; email: info.tmvs@visit-telluride.org; web: www.visit-telluride.org

Tom Sawyer Days, Hannibal, MO. Contact Hannibal Convention and Visitors Bureau, 505 N Third St, Hannibal, MO 63401; ✆ 573 221 2477; fax: 573 221 6999; web: www.hanmo.com

SPAM™ Town USA Festival and SPAM™ Jam, Austin, MN. Contact Austin Convention and Visitors Bureau; ✆ 800 444 5713; email: visitor@austincvb.com; web: www.austincvb.com

The 'Tory Story in Lower Manhattan' tour, July Fourth with Joyce Gold History Tours New York, NY 10011; ✆ 212 242 5762; fax: 212 242 6374; email: NYCtours@aol.com; web: www.nyctours.com

World Championship Cardboard Boat Festival, Heber Springs, AR; ✆ 501 362 2444

World Lumberjack Championship, Hayward Lakes, WI; ✆ 715 634 2484; web: www.lumberjackworldchampionships.com. Contact Hayward Area Chamber of Commerce, PO Box 726, Hayward, WI 54843; web: www.haywardlakes.com

AUGUST

Domestic Resurrection Circus, Bread and Puppet Theater, Glover, VT. Contact Bread and Puppet Theater and Art Museum, Box 153, Glover, VT 05839; ✆ 802 525 3031

Fools Rules Regatta, Jamestown, RI. Contact Jamestown Yacht Club, PO Box 562, Jamestown, RI 02835; email: jwc@dotcomnow.com; web: www.jyc.org

Grape Stomp and Harvest Festival, Llano County, TX. Contact Fall Creek Vineyards; ✆ 512 467 4477; web: www.fcv.com

Hamburger Festival, Seymour, WI; ✆ 920 833 9522

Largest Roach of the Year Contest, Plano, TX. Cockroach Hall of Fame, The Pest Shop, 2231-B West 15th St, Plano, TX 75075; ✆ 972 519 0355

Love Israel Ranch Annual Garlic Festival (at Israel Family Ranch), 13724 184th St NE, Arlington, WA; ✆ 360 435 8577

Mutt Strut, Stowe, VT. Contact Go Stowe, Main St, Box 1320, Stowe, VT 05672; ↘ 877 GOSTOWE; email: askus@gostowe.com; web: www.gostowe.com

The National Hobo Convention, Britt, IA. Contact Hobo Foundation, PO Box 413, Britt, IA 50423; ↘ 641 843 9104 or 641 843 3840; web: www.hobo.com

National Mustard Day, Mt Horeb, WI. Contact Mt Horeb Mustard Museum, 109 E Main St, Mt Horeb, WI 53572; ↘ 800 438 6678; email: curator@mustardweb.com; web: www.mustardweb.com. Located about 20 miles west of Madison.

Office Olympics, Shreveport, LA. Contact Melinda Coyer; ↘ 318 865 5173; web: www.shreveport-bossier.org

The Orange Show Foundation, Art Car Weekend, Houston, TX. The Orange Show 2402 Munger St, Houston, TX 77023; ↘ 713 926 6368; fax: 713 926 1506; email: orange@insync.net; web: www.orangeshow.org

Pageant of Masters, Laguna Beach, CA. Contact Pageant of the Masters, 650 Laguna Canyon Road, Laguna Beach, CA; ↘ 949 497 6582 or 800 487 3378; web: www.foapom.org

Potato Days, Barnesville, MN. Contact Barnesville Potato Days, PO Box 345, Barnesville, MN 56514; ↘ 800 525 4901 or 218 354 2145; email: spudlady@potatodays.com; web: www.potatodays.com

Potato Feast Days, Houlton, ME. Contact Greater Houlton Chamber of Commerce; ↘ 207 523 4216; email: chamber@houlton.com

Sturgis Motorcycle Rally, Sturgis, SD. Contact Premier Rally Services, Inc, PO Box 189, Sturgis, SD 57785; ↘ 605 347 6570; email: premier@sturgisrallynews.com; web: www.sturgisrallynews.com

Tug Fest, LeClaire, IA and Port Byron, IL. Contact LeClaire Chamber of Commerce; web: www.leclaireiowa.org

Ugly Face Contest and **Me and My Pet Costume Contest** (part of the Grand River Renaissance and Fantasy Festival), Grand Junction, CO. Contact Grand Junction Jaycees; ↘ 970 523 7841 or 970 241 8706; web: www.faires.com/GrandRiver

Weird Contest Week, Ocean City, NJ. Contact Public Relations Office; ↘ 609 525 9300

World Freefall Convention, Quincy, IL. Contact World Free Fall Convention Headquarters, Rt 1, Box 123, Quincy, IL 62031; ↘ 217 222 5867; fax: 217 885 3141; email: wffc@freefall.com; web: www.freefall.com

Zucchini Fest, Ludlow, VT. Contact Ludlow Area Chamber of Commerce, PO Box 333, Okemo Marketplace Clocktower, Ludlow, VT 05149; ↘ 802 228 5830; web: www.vacationinvermont.com/zfest

SEPTEMBER

Bald is Beautiful Convention, Morehead, NC. Contact Bald-Headed Men of America, 102 Bald Drive, Morehead City, NC 28557; ↘ 919 726 1855

Beef-A-Rama, Minocqua, WI. Contact Minocqua Chamber of Commerce; ↘ 715 356 5266; web: www.minocqua.org

Berkeley Doo Dah Parade, Berkeley, CA. Contact John at Café Venezia; ↘ 510 849 4688 or the Berkeley Convention and Visitors Bureau; ↘ 800 847 4823; web: www.howberkeleycanyoube

British Invasion, Stowe, VT. Contact Ye Olde England Inne, 433 The Mountain

Rd, Stowe, VT 05672; ↘ 800 253 2106; fax: 802 253 8944; web:
www.britishinvasion.com

Buckwheat Festival, Kingwood, WV; ↘ 304 329 1780 or 304 329 2501; email:
buckwheatfest@abac.com; web: www.buckwheatfest.com

Burning Man Festival, Black Rock Desert, NV. Contact Burning Man, PO Box
884688, San Francisco, CA 94188; ↘ 415 TO FLAME; web: www.burningman.org

Burning of Zozobra (Fiestas de Santa Fe), Santa Fe, NM. Santa Fe Convention and
Visitors Bureau, email: scenter@ci.santa-fe.nm.us; web: www.santafe.org

Chippiannock Cemetery Tour, Rock Island, IL. Contact Quad Cities Convention
and Visitors Bureau; ↘ 800 747 7800.

Clinton Testicle Festival, Clinton, MT. Contact Rock Creek Lodge, Clinton, MT,
59825; ↘ 406 825 4868; web: www.testyfesty.com

Garlic and Herb Festival, Wilmington, VT. Contact Jay Powell or Steve Wrathall,
932 Fowler Rd, Whitingham, VT 05361; ↘ 802 368 7147

Gone But Not Forgotten Tour, Moline, IL. Contact Quad Cities Convention and
Visitors Bureau; ↘ 800 747 7800.

Great San Pedro Lobster Festival, San Pedro, CA; ↘ 310 366 6472; email:
lobstermaster@lobsterfest.com; web: www.lobsterfest.com

Hands on a Hard Body, Longview, TX. Contact Joe Mallard Nissan, 1201 McCann
Rd, Longview, TX; ↘ 903 758 4135 or 800 256 2514; email:
mail@joemallardnissan.com; web: www.joemallardnissan.com

Inkslingers Ball, Redondo Beach, CA. Contact Tattoo Mania's Inkslingers Ball, PO
Box 2208, Redondo Beach, CA 90278; ↘ 800 824 8046; email: saunderosa@aol.com;
web: www.tattoos.com/inkslingers

The Mud Bowl Championships, North Conway, NH. Contact New Hampshire
Division of Travel and Tourism Development; ↘ 800 FUN IN NH; web:
www.visitnh.gov

Oatmeal Festival, Bertram, TX; ↘ 512 335 2197

Polkamotion, Ocean City, MD. Contact Fred and Marsha Bulinski; ↘ 410 787 8675
or Ocean City Visitor Bureau; ↘ 800 626 2326

Roadkill Cookoff, Marlington, WV. Contact West Virginia Division of Tourism,
2101 Washington St E, Charleston, WV 25305; ↘ 304 558 2220 or 800 225 5982; web:
www.callwva.com

Running of the Sheep, Reedpoint, MT; ↘ 406 326 2288

San Francisco Fringe Festival, San Francisco, CA 94102; ↘ 415 931 1094; fax: 415
931 2699; email: mail@sffringe.org; web: www.sffringe.org

State Prison Outlaw Rodeo, McAlester, OK; ↘ 918 423 2550; fax: 918 423 1345;
web: www.doc.state.ok.us/docs/osp/htm

Wigstock, New York City, NY; ↘ 212 439 5139; web: www.wigstock.nu

Wizard of Oz Fest, Chesterton, IN. Contact Duneland Chamber of Commerce,
303 Broadway, Chesterton, IN 46304; ↘ 219 926 5513; fax: 219 926 7593

World Chicken Festival, London, KY; ↘ 800 348 0095; web: www.chickenfestival.com

OCTOBER

Annual Yo-Yo Championships, Chico, CA 95928; ↘ 530 893 0545; fax: 530 893
0797; web: www.nationalyoyo.org

Beatty Burro and Flapjack Races, Beatty, NV. Contact Beatty Chamber of Commerce, 119 Main St, PO Box 956, Beatty, NV 89003; ℩ 702 553 2424

Clam Linguini Eating Contest, Redondo Beach, CA. Takes place during the Lobster Festival. Contact Redondo Beach Visitors Bureau, 200 N Pacific Coast Hwy, Redondo Beach, CA; ℩ 319 364 2161 or 800 282 0333; web: www.lobsterfestival.com

Corn Dog Festival, Dallas, TX; email: cdogefest@aol.com; web: www.corndogfestival.com

The Cowboy Trade Day, Claremore, OK. Located north of the city on Historic Route 66, watch for the Git 'N Go Store, then turn east onto Blue Starr Drive and go 1 mile to Round Up Club. Contact Cowboy Trader; ℩ 918 341 6985; web: www.cowboytrader.com

Emma Crawford Coffin Races, Manitou Springs, CO. Contact Manitou Springs Chamber of Commerce; ℩ 719 685 5089 or 800 642 2567; web: www.manitousprings.org

Exotic Erotic Halloween Ball, San Francisco, CA; contact Perry Mann Presents the Exotic Erotic Ball, 2443 Filmore St, Suite 286, San Francisco, CA 94115; ℩ 415 567 BALL; web: www.exoticeroticball.com

Fantasia Fair, Provincetown, MA; web: www.fantasiafair.org

Fantasy Fest, Key West, FL. Fantasy Fest, PO Box 230, Key West, FL 33041; ℩ 305 296 1817; fax: 305 294 3335; web: fantasyfest.net

Festival of Scarecrows, Rockland, ME; ℩ 207 596 6457. Contact Rockland-Thomaston Chamber of Commerce; ℩ 207 596 0376

Fryeburg Fair, Fryeburg, ME. Contact West Oxford Agricultural Society, Fryeburg Fair Association, PO Box 78, Fryeburg, ME 04037; ℩ 207 935 3268 or 207 935 3662; email: info@fryeburgfair.com; webwww.fryeburgfair.com

Ghost Walk, Carson City, NV. Contact Carson City Convention and Visitors Bureau; ℩ 775 687 7410; web: www.carson-city.org

Halloween Night Tours, Wyoming Frontier Prison and Old West Museum, 500 Walnut St, Rawlins, WY 82301; ℩ 307 778 7290 or 307 324 4422

Hogeye Festival, Elgin, TX. Contact City of Elgin, Texas 78621; ℩ 512 281 5724; web: www.elgintx.com

Lobster Festival, Redondo Beach, CA. Contact Redondo Beach Visitors Bureau, 200 N Pacific Coast Hwy, Redondo Beach, CA; ℩ 319 364 2161 or 800 282 0333; web: www.lobsterfestival.com

Lobster Pet Parade, Redondo Beach, CA. Takes place during the Lobster Festival. Contact Redondo Beach Visitors Bureau, 200 N Pacific Coast Hwy, Redondo Beach, CA; ℩ 319 364 2161 or 800 282 0333; web: www.lobsterfestival.com

Mountain View Bean Festival, Mountain View, AR. Contact Mountain View Area Chamber of Commerce; ℩ 870 269 8068 or 888 679 2859; email: mychamber@mvtel.net; web: www.mountainviewcc.org

New River Gorge Bridge Day, Festival Fayetteville, WV; web: www.nps.gov/neri/bridgeday.htm. Contact New River Convention and Visitors Bureau; ℩ 800 927 0263; email: newriver@newrivercvb.com

Outsider Art Show, Indianapolis, IN. Contact Midland Arts and Antique Market, 907 E Michigan St, Indianapolis, IN 46202; ℩ 317 267 9005

Penn's Store's Great Outhouse Blowout and Race, Gravel Switch, KY. Contact Penn's Store, 257 Penn's Store Rd, Gravel Switch, KY 40328; ↘ 859 332 7715 or 859 332 7706; web: www.pennsstore.com

Sea Witch Halloween and Fiddlers Festival, Rehoboth Beach and Dewey Beach, DE. Contact Rehoboth-Dewey Chamber of Commerce; ↘ 800 441 1329 or 302 227 2233

Spooky Goofy Golf Tournament, Antlers, OK. Contact Antlers Springs Golf Course, Antlers, OK 74523; ↘ 580 298 9900.

Yellville Turkey Trot, Yellville, AR. Contact Yellville Area Chamber of Commerce, PO Box 369, Yellville, AR 72687; ↘ 870 449 4676 or 800 832 1414; email: chamber@yellville.com; web: www.yellville.com

NOVEMBER

Doo Dah Parade, Pasadena, CA. Contact Pasadena Convention and Visitors Bureau, 171 South Los Robles Ave, Pasadena, CA 91101; ↘ 626 795 9311; web: www.pasadenavisitor.org

Historic Pursuit Limo Rally, Miami, FL. Contact Historical Museum of Southern Florida, 101 W Flagler St, Miami, FL 33130; ↘ 305 375 1492; web: www.historical-museum.org

Giant Omelette Celebration, Abbeville, LA. Contact Wendy Atchetee, PO Box 1272, Abbeville, LA 70511

Punkin' Chunkin', Georgetown, DE. Contact Pumpkin Chunk Association, c/o B&B Mechanical RD #4, Box 192-D, Georgetown, DE 19947; ↘ 302 856 1444; web: www.punkinchunkin.com

DECEMBER

Christmas in the Big House, Wyoming Frontier Prison and Old West Museum, Rawlins, WY 82301; ↘ 307 778 7290 or 307 324 4422

King Mango Strut, Coconut Grove, FL. Contact Coconut Grove Chamber of Commerce, 2820 McFarlane Rd, Coconut Grove, FL 33133; ↘ 305 444 7270; fax: 305 444 2489; email: info@coconutgrove.com; web: www.coconutgrove.com

Part Two

Eccentric States

WISCONSIN, MINNESOTA, IOWA & ILLINOIS

CANADA

Lake of the Woods

Rainy Lake

Ice Box Days, International Falls

Red Lake

Lake Superior

Copper Harbor

Grand Forks

Crookston

Greyhound Bus Origin Center, Hibbing

Virginia

Sandpaper Museum, Two Harbors

MICHIGAN

Bermidji

Leech Lake

Duluth

Marquette

Moorhead

Fargo

Potato Days, Barnesville

Fish House Parade, Aitkin

Mille Lake

Great American Think-off, New York Mills

Ironwood

Escanaba

Natl Freshwater Fishing Hall of Fame, Hayward

World Lumberjack Championship, Hayward Lakes

Beef-A-Rama, Minocqua

Iron Mountain

Ugly Truck Contest, Pelican Rapids

MINNESOTA

Wisconsin Concrete Park, Phillips

Rhinelander

Menominee

St Cloud

Rice Lake

WISCONSIN

Wausau

Green Bay

Ortonville

Willmar

Eau Claire

Hamburger Festival, Seymour

Green Bay

Minneapolis

ST PAUL

Houdini Historical Center, Appleton

Two-Story Outhouse, Belle Plaine

Mississippi

World's Largest Trivia Contest, Stevens Point

Manitowoc

Mankato

Rock in the House, Fountain City

LaReau's World of Miniature Buildings, Pardeeville

West Bend Inn, West Bend

Sod House B&B, Sanborn

Rochester

Ed's Museum, Wykoff

La Crosse

Baraboo

House on the Rock, Spring Green

Mary Nohl's House, Fox Point

Sioux Falls

Luverne

Albert Lea

SPAM Events, Austin

Jailhouse Historic Inn, Preston

Scenic Ridge View Ranch, Harpers Ferry

Milwaukee

Waterloo Workshop, Dorchester

Elm Farm Ollie Day, Mt Horeb

MADISON

Spinning Top Exploratory, Burlington

Britt

Spencer

Grotto of the Redemption, West Bend

Bily Clocks Museum & Dvorak Exhibit, Spillville

Mason City

Don Q Inn, Dodgeville

Grandview, Hollandale

Watson's Wild West Museum, Elkhorn

Adventure Inn Motel, Gurnee

Sioux City

Fort Dodge

Waterloo

Dyer-Botsford House & Museum, Ames

Dickeyville Grotto, Dickeyville

Rockford

Ahlgrim Acres, Palatine

Amazing Maize Maze, Princton

Cermak Shopping Plaza, Berwyn

Elgin

Chicago

Cooking with Worms, Ames

Cedar Rapids

Tug Fest, LeClaire

Tug Fest, Port Byron

African-American Heritage Museum, Aurora

Joliet

DES MOINES

Davenport

Squirrel Cage Jail etc, Council Bluffs

Riverside

Chippiannock Cemetery Tour, Rock Island

Gone But Not Forgotten, Moline

Omaha

Ottumwa

Des Moines

Max Nordeen's Wheels Museum, Alpha

Bishop Hill

Remir

LINCOLN

Peoria

Bloomington

Beatrice

ILLINOIS

Riley

St Joseph

Chillicothe

World Freefall Convention, Quincy

Pearson Museum, SPRINGFIELD

Decatur

Terre Ha

Marysville

Hannibal

Two Story Outhouse, Gays

Vandala

Kansas City

Columbus

World's Tallest Man Exhibit, Alton

Vincen

Junction City

TOPEKA

Kansas City

MISSOURI

St Louis

East St Louis

Newton

KANSAS

JEFFERSON CITY

Evans

Wichita

Lake of the Ozarks

Rolla

Mississippi

N

Ft Scott

0   150km
0   150 miles

Superman Celebration, Metropolis

KY

Springfield

Ohio

Carthage

Cairo

Midwest/North Central Region

WISCONSIN

Wisconsin has the highest proportion of eccentric environments in the USA, more than 10% of the total.

Eccentric environments

The House on the Rock, located in Spring Green, looks like an architectural impossibility, perched as it is on the pinnacle of a rock in a spot so improbable that you won't believe your eyes. You'll immediately notice the most extraordinary feature of the 14-room house: the Infinity Room, a 200-foot structure with 3,000 windows that juts out precariously over the Wyoming Valley far below. What you'll see when you get up to the house is just as amazing: a peculiar, outlandish complex of rooms, streets, buildings and gardens covering 200 acres.

The post World War II house is the work of Alex Jordan, an eccentric wannabe architect who wanted most of all to be left alone to pursue his creative quirks. When he saw the rock in 1946, he knew he'd found the place of his dreams. Working alone, he built the original studio by carrying stones and mortar up to the site in a basket strapped to his back. Eventually, he built a ramp through the treetops to make the site more accessible. The studio fireplace, the largest you'll ever see, has a stairway in its flue and a secret room hidden within it.

As his fantasy grew in size, so did the curiosity surrounding it. Irritated by nosy neighbors, he thought he'd discourage gawkers by charging admission. Not only didn't this ploy work, it attracted even more attention. So Jordan used his ever-increasing income to indulge further his bizarre and fertile imagination with incomprehensible thoroughness.

Over the next four decades he expanded his attraction to include dozens of strange exhibits. There are structures built just to house his collections and displays: doll houses and dolls; suits of armor, mechanical banks, paperweights, a one million piece miniature circus; a pyramid of life size elephants, model ships, giant organs, weaponry and oriental artifacts. He assembled the greatest collection of automated music machines in the world. The Blue Room contains the world's only mechanically operated symphony orchestra. A $4.5-million carousel boasts 240 animals, not one of them a horse. Twenty thousand lights illuminate it and hundreds of topless angels cavort

overhead. In the Streets of Yesterday, he recreated the 19th century complete with a sheriff's office, carriage house, wood-carver's shop, homes and gas lamps.

Shortly before he died in 1989, he sold the House on the Rock to a long-time friend and collector who added a Heritage of the Sea building housing a 200 foot sea creature engaged in a titanic struggle with an octopus. Also new is the Transportation building which offers a terrific view of the house itself. At Christmas, they trot out thousands of Santas, including life-sized replicas from around the world.

You'll be grateful for the on-site café. You'll need sustenance to see and absorb this most eccentric of American attractions.

The House on the Rock, 5754 Hwy 23, Spring Green, WI 53588; ✆ 608 935 3639; email: information@thehouseontherock.com; web: www.thehouseontherock.com. Directions: from Madison: Hwy 18/151 W to Dodgeville, then Hwy 23 N. *Open regular season: Mar 15–Oct 29; daily 9.00am–7.00pm; winter season: Jan 8–Mar 12; Sat–Sun 9.00am–6.00pm; Christmas season: Nov 4–Jan 7; 9.00am–6.00pm.*

Nick Engelbert was a dairy farmer who immigrated to America early in the last century. He led a relatively normal life – if you don't count the 40 concrete, glass, shell and stone sculptures he made in between milking the cows and making cheese. Or that he covered every inch of his farmhouse with concrete inlaid with china, glass, buttons, beads, and shells.

At his home in Hollandale, which he called **Grandview**, he crafted sculptures like Snow White with five of her seven dwarfs, a lion, an eagle and an organ grinder. There's also Neptune's fountain, a lighthouse, an elephant, and a stork carrying a baby. Some of Nick's sculptures were built to pay tribute to his friends while three Swiss patriots honor his wife, a Swiss immigrant.

He used the same technique for all his sculptures: arranging wooden boxes for structure, wrapping them with nets made of metal, then covering them with cement and adding the decorative touches. When he got too old to make any more sculptures, he turned to painting, producing 200 oils before his death in 1962. The environment is visible from the road during the winter months when the facility is closed, but you can call for an appointment off-season if you want to see the house.

Grandview located on Wisconsin State Hwy 39, west of Hollandale, 30 miles southwest of Madison and 11 miles east of Mineral Point, Wisconsin. For more info or an appt during off-season, contact Bob Negronida, PEC Foundation President, ⟍ 608 967 2140 or email Ricky Rolfsmeyer, foundation vice-president, ricky-r@mhtc.net; web: www.members.tripod.com/PEC-Grandview/index.html

Fred Smith was an extremely prolific concrete and glass sculptor, creating 200 figures of mythical, as well as real, characters and animals at his **Wisconsin Concrete Park** in Phillips. A former logger, farmer, tavern owner and musician, he began his obsession when he retired in the late 1940s. His sculptures, made over a 14-year period as a gift 'for all the American people', all have a joyous, flamboyant quality.

Some of his figures are so large they had to be made in pieces and assembled on their footings. Glass for decoration was readily available from the tavern next door as well as from supportive neighbors who brought colorful bit of glass each time they visited. Fred's characters were taken from regional lore and legendary heroes. The three and a half acre park has tributes to Ben Hur, Abe Lincoln, the Indian princess Sacajawea, and Paul Bunyan.

Wisconsin Concrete Park, Hwy 13, Phillips, WI. Contact Friends of Fred Smith, Price County Forestry Dept, 104 S Eyder St, Phillips, WI 54555; ⟍ 715 339 6371

Kids called **Mary Nohl's** bizarre property tucked away in the woodsy, affluent suburb of Fox Point the 'witch's house'. Human figures made of concrete march along the perimeter of the property while others gather in groups on mounds. Dinosaurs, mythical beasts, fish, massive heads, and twig sculptures join the fray. Homemade windmills and wood silhouettes dangle from tree branches. Her wood fencing is partially made of slats in the shape of human profiles; the house itself is trimmed with wooden fish reliefs.

Inside, the walls and floors have been used as canvases, supportive backgrounds for the hundreds of oil paintings and sculptures within. The neighbors, however, aren't at all appreciative of her art. Rumors that she had killed her family and buried them in the sculptures led to taunts and vandalism. The property is now surrounded with chain link fencing and barbed wire.

Mary Nohl's House, North Beach Drive, Fox Point, WI

Politics and religion mix well at **Dickeyville Grotto**, an environment created in the 1920s and 1930s by Father Wernerus, a German born, Catholic priest with a fondness for concrete and all things that glitter. His sculptures and shrines, located in the grounds of the Holy Ghost Parish in Dickeyville, are a madcap mixture of glass, gems, pottery, shells, starfish, fossils, corals, quartz, iron and copper ore, crystals, coal, petrified wood and moss.

Visitors have been flocking to this eccentric environment for 75 years, probably because its theme is as much about patriotism as it is about religion. Father Wernerus was motivated by two ideals: love of God and love of country, and the Grotto reflects a deep devotion to both. The Grotto of the Blessed Virgin, the main structure, is covered with symbols important in Catholic ritual. A Vatican flag flies at the left, an American flag at the right.

Dickeyville Grotto located at US Rt 151 and West Main St, one block west of the 151/61 intersection.

Looking like something you'd see in a Homer Simpson meets Back to the Future movie, **The Forevertron** is the fantasy – and the alter-ego – of Tom Every who refers to himself as Dr Evermore. Inventive in vision, and astounding in scope, the Forevertron is a gargantuan contraption designed to shoot Dr Evermore, 60, into space using some kind of 1890s magnetic lightning beam propulsion that only he understands. The 320-ton complex is the largest metal scrap sculpture in the world and a monument to the machine age that took the doctor 20 years to construct. The fantastical device, six stories high, is assembled from generators, thrusters, massive machine components and factory scrap collected by this former industrial salvage dealer.

The Forevertron is well thought out, not at all random, and has such well-defined components as the Gravitron, the place where he'll de-water himself to get his weight down, before lift off. (Since humans are made up of about 90% water, this would indeed save a lot of weight.) The Teahouse, which began life as a wrought iron gazebo, is reserved for visiting royalty who will come to watch the event. Celestial Listening Ears, theater speakers in a former incarnation, keep an ear on the universe. Skeptics can follow the Doctor's airborne progress through an enormous telescope, just about the only thing with a recognizable function.

In the Overlord control center (Houston, are you listening?) is a decontamination chamber supposedly from one of the Apollo moon missions. The good doctor himself will take off, electro-magnetically speaking, from a glass ball nestled inside a copper egg. Gathering to watch the festivities is the Big Bird Band, a playful, expectant crowd of several dozen figures made from musical instruments, old tools, gasoline nozzles, bed posts and the like. A huge scrap spider stands poised in anticipation of the event.

For all its madcap madness, The Forevetron is meant to carry the message that we're scrapping a large part of our energy and that staying connected to the stuff of our past is important. If the medium is the message, you may have to stay awhile if you're to understand it.

The Forevertron located at the Art Park on Hwy 12, just south of Baraboo, across the street from the Badger Ammunitions Plant, Baraboo, WI. *Open Mon–Sat 9.00–5.00pm; Sun 12.00noon–5.00pm.*

Just plain weird

You'll witness a strange tale of history repeating itself at the **Rock in the House** in Fountain City, the unlucky site where giant boulders came crashing down onto the same house not once, but twice, in the same century. The first time, in 1901, a huge, 5-ton rock crashed through the roof of the house and killed a woman sleeping in her bed. In 1995 another killer rock, this time two stories tall and weighing an estimated 55 tons, crashed right down into the same spot again. Fortunately, the owners weren't in the bedroom at the time and, recognizing a bad omen when they saw one, packed up and left, selling the house to the present owners who obviously recognized a tourism opportunity right under their noses.

The house is un-staffed and run on the honor system. Park in the driveway, walk to the front door, then follow the handwritten notes. You wouldn't want to tempt fate by failing to leave your dollar donation, would you? T-shirts and photos are also for sale on the honor system.

> **Rock in the House**, 440 N Shore Drive, Fountain City, WI 54629;
> ↘ 608 687 6106

Attractions

You can take in the world in a single afternoon at **LaReau's World of Miniature Buildings** in Pardeeville. Located in a park like setting, the collection includes nearly a hundred Styrofoam scale models of attractions such as the Pyramids, the Great Wall of China, the Vietnam War Memorial, Stonehenge, the United Nations, and a Bavarian castle.

Paul LeReau and his wife Clarice are retired school teachers who have been building these models – in a variety of scales – for 30 years. They've been inviting visitors for the last 15. Paul places little signs by each model describing how many hours it took them to make it. The US Capitol building, one of the most elaborate structures in the collection, took almost 1,500 hours to construct.

> **LaReau's World of Miniature Buildings**, Pardeeville, WI; ↘ 608
> 429 2848. *Open daily May 26–Oct 1.*

Most everyone has fantasized at one time or another about riding a motorcycle, free as bird with the wind in your hair and the bugs in your teeth. The 'Hog' culture (slang for Harleys) and lifestyle will be opening in

Milwaukee at the **Harley Davidson Experience Center** in mid-2002, a $30-million, interactive attraction paying tribute to freedom, leather and the American way.

> **Harley Davidson Experience Center.** Scheduled to be completed in the summer of 2002 in downtown Milwaukee, WI; web: www.harley-davidson.com

Festivals and events

The World's Largest Trivia Contest in Steven's Point brings geeks and nerds from far and wide for a 54-hour marathon of mostly useless knowledge. Five hundred teams – about 12,000 players – from all over the world hang out in the University of Wisconsin's dorms, listening to questions on the campus radio station, then calling in their answers. Eight questions are asked each hour, with each question being worth 2,000 points. Every team getting the correct answer shares in the 2,000 point pot. A movie shown at the start of the weekend is the source for some of the questions during the event. The nerds also strut their stuff float-wise at a parade honoring their geekness.

> **World's Largest Trivia Contest** held annually in April in Stevens Point, WI. Contact University of Wisconsin-Stevens Point Student Radio Station; ↘ 715 346 3755; web: www.momfamilies.com/trivia

You, along with other amateurs, can try your hand at logrolling, chopping, and sawing at the **World Lumberjack Championship** in Hayward. But you'll probably want to leave the pole shimmying to the professional male and female lumberjacks who compete in speed sawing, speed chopping, an 80-foot pole speed climb, and logrolling events. It's amazing how competitors can remain upright, in spiked shoes no less, on a slippery log while trying to knock their opponent into the water.

> **World Lumberjack Championship** held annually in July in Hayward Lakes, WI; ↘ 715 634 2484; web: www.lumberjackworldchampionships.com. Contact Hayward Area Chamber of Commerce, PO Box 726, Hayward, WI 54843; web: www.haywardlakes.com

The Minocque Chamber of Commerce hosts an annual **Beef-A-Rama**, an event involving a parade of beef, a beef roast cook off, and costumed chefs. Lakeland area businesses do the grilling in front of their shops; the roasts compete for best taste, presentation, and appearance. The beef parade is led by a fire truck and followed by folks proudly displaying their cooked roasts. The roasts are than carved, sliced, put on buns, and served to around several thousand visitors. They cook enough roasts to serve 3,000 beef sandwiches which sell out within the first hour.

Beef-A-Rama held annually in September in Minocqua, WI. Contact Minocqua Chamber of Commerce; ☎ 800 44-NORTH; web: www.minocqua.org

The town of Seymour stakes its claim to fame on the accomplishments of one Charlie Nagreen. In 1885, at the age of 15, Charlie was selling meatballs from an ox-drawn wagon at the Outagamie County Fair. But his meatballs proved to be difficult to eat while standing up. So he flattened the beef, placed it between two slices of bread, and called it a hamburger. He went down in history as Hamburger Charlie. Seymour holds a yearly **Hamburger Festival** in August celebrating his stroke of genius. In 1989 they grilled the world's biggest hamburger, 5,520 pounds, a record verified by the Guinness folks.

Hamburger Festival held annually in August in Seymour, WI; ☎ 920 833 9522.

Museums and collections

Barry Levenson was depressed. It was October 27, 1986 and the Boston Red Socks had just lost the baseball World Series. While standing in the supermarket, he told himself it was ridiculous for a grown man to be depressed about a game. He decided right then and there he needed a hobby – and that's when he heard the mustards say 'Buy me, and they will come'.

So he bought, and they have come, to the **Mt Horeb Mustard Museum**, where Barry has 3,400 different kinds of mustard from all over the world, including chocolate fudge mustard. People from all over bring him mustards and send them to him. His newsletter, the *Proper Mustard*, prints 7,000 copies twice a year, and he's the official sponsor of National Mustard Day, the first Saturday in August. The whole town turns out for this festival which features painting with mustard and a mustard wheel of fortune, He holds a Mustard Family Reunion each June – anyone named 'Mustard' can attend.

Barry is also the man behind **Elm Farm Ollie Day**, a tribute to the first cow to fly in an airplane. This happened way back in 1930, when flying was new and daring. The St Louis International Air Exposition was looking for a gimmick to bring folks to the fair. Someone came up with the idea of taking a milk cow up in the plane, milking her, and then parachuting the milk down to the crowds below. To mark the occasion, a bovine cantata is performed every February 18 at his Mustard Museum. He'd like to see three

cows go into orbit in a rocket so he could call them the 'herd shot round the world'.

Mt Horeb Mustard Museum, 109 E Main St, Mt Horeb, WI 53572; ↘ 800 438 6678; email: curator@mustardweb.com; web: www.mustardweb.com. Directions: about 20 miles west of Madison. *Open daily 10.00–17.00.*

Elm Farm Ollie Day held annually in February.

Ever wanted to run away and join the circus? Indulge your fantasy at the **Circus World Museum** in Baraboo, the world's leading repository of circus memorabilia. It's a lively place, recreating the wonder and awe inspired by the Ringling Brothers in the late 1800s. Besides allowing you to get up close and personal to 200 circus wagons, the museum has demonstrations on how those wagons were loaded and how the circus train made the transition from one locale to another. Each year three-quarters of a million people turn out to watch an old-fashioned circus parade leave Baraboo to make its way to Milwaukee, cheering on the 2,000 participants, 700 horses and 55 antique wagons, as well as clowns, musicians, and exotic animals. The museum is also home to the one million-piece Howard Brothers' Miniature Circus.

The Circus World Museum, 426 Water St, Hwy 113, Baraboo, WI 53913; ↘ 24-hr info 608 356 0800; office 608 356 8341; web: www.circusworldmuseum.com. Directions: 15 minutes from Interstate 90/94 and 18 minutes from Interstate 39. *Open daily except holidays Mon–Sat 10.00am–4.00pm; Sun 11.00am–4.00pm.*

Harry Houdini was a brilliant escape artist who many thought to be a few beers short of a six pack for taking the risks he did. The **Houdini Historical Center** in Appleton honors the magician and his bag of tricks, including his locks, picks, handcuffs, and straitjackets. Demonstrations and hands-on exhibits offer more opportunities to learn about his escapades and escapes.

Houdini Historical Center located in the Outagamie Museum, 330 E College Ave, Appleton, WI 54911; ↘ 920 733 8445. *Open Tue–Sat 10.00am–5.00pm; Sun 12.00–5.00pm. Open Mon 10.00am–5.00pm Jun, Jul, Aug. Admission charge.*

The world's largest fiberglass structure will 'lure' you in at the **National Freshwater Fishing Hall of Fame** in Hayward. You can stand in a giant fiberglass musky – that's a fish – that's half a block long and four stories tall. The observation deck is in its wide-open mouth. It's also the world's largest fiberglass structure and you know you're there when it looms up in front of you from the road. This place is like one huge tackle box, with 5,000 lures, whole rooms of rods and reels, outboard motors, examples of really bad taxidermy, and a couple of thousand hooks, removed by doctors, that snagged the unfortunate human holding the rod. If you're a fisherman, 400 trophies should make you tremble with excitement. The World Records Gallery is crammed with statistics of where, how, and with what, so you leave nurturing the fantasy that you could someday duplicate the feat. Outside, they've thoughtfully provided you with a number of photo ops, so you can bag a print that makes it look as if you're reeling in a big one.

National Freshwater Fishing Hall of Fame, 10360 Hall of Fame Dr, Hayward, WI 54843; ↘ 715 634 4440; fax: 715 634 4440; email: fishhall@cheq.net; web: www.freshwater-fishing.org. Directions: Jct State Hwy 27 and County Hwy B. *Open daily Apr 15–Nov 1 10.00am–5.00pm.*

Everyone who walks into **Watson's Wild West Museum** in Elkhorn gets a personal tour from Doug Watson, a cowboy character who captures your imagination with tall tales, cowboy poetry and humor. This replica of an 1880s general store has thousands of artifacts and memorabilia from the cowboy era, including 2,000 branding irons, 115 saddles and a bathroom papered in wanted posters.

Watson's Wild West Museum, W4865 Potter Rd, Elkhorn, WI 53121; ↘ 262 723 7505; web: www.watsonswildwestmuseum.com. Directions: 10 minutes north of Lake Geneva, WI up Hwy 12, 1 mile north of highway's 12/67 merger, east of Hwy 12/67 on Potter Rd. *Open Tue–Sat 10.00am–5.00pm; Sun 11.00am–5.00pm Jun, Jul, Aug. Open Sat 10.00am–5.00pm; Sun 11.00am–5.00pm; weekdays by appt; May, Sept, Oct. Admission charge.*

American culture is tied to advertising like no other culture on earth and a visit to the new **Eisner Museum of Advertising** in Milawaukee will show you how and why. Taking you through the past, present and future of American advertising and design, the museum presents a complete history of the slogans, campaigns, and logos that made America the consumer capitol of the world. An interactive radio booth lets you record and play back your own advertising spot. You'll learn about 'profiling', experiencing first hand how advertisers target their market. Other exhibits include the shopping bag as portable art and using album cover art to sell records. It's a world of pop culture in there, filled with messages and memories.

Eisner Museum of Advertising, Milwaukee Institute of Art and Design, 208 N Water St, Milwaukee, WI 53202; ↘ 414 203 0371; web: www.eisnermuseum.org. *Open Tue–Sat 11.00am–5.00pm. Admission charge.*

The **Spinning Top Exploratory Museum** in Burlington has 2,000 tops, yo-yos, and gyroscopes. A 75-minute presentation includes videos, demonstrations and tricks with 35 spinning tops. Advance reservations are necessary.

Spinning Top Exploratory Museum, 533 Milwaukee Ave (Hwy 36), Burlington, WI; ✎ 414 763 3946. *Open year-round; reservations required.*

Quirky cuisine

If you don't know the password, you might not be allowed in – unless you're willing to make a fool of yourself by doing silly things that will appear on the big screen inside. You've arrived at the *Safe House*, a restaurant and bar with a theme so weird you just have to experience it for yourself.

The term 'safe house' is of course used by international spies to describe a secure meeting place, which usually operates in premises disguised as a respectable business. International Exports Ltd is your safe house when mystery and intrigue bring you to Milwaukee. Make sure you're not being followed, then slip inside, whisper the password and enter through the bookcase. The place is filled with spy-like contraptions, secret escape routes,

A WISCONSIN TURKEY

It's a shame the Gobbler Supper Club and Motel no longer exists. It was one of America's finest examples of loony, over-the-top marketing: the stretching of a theme to the outer boundaries of sanity. Billed as a 'new and exciting experience in good living', the place took itself seriously, promoting a world of romance and intimacy. Describing its features, the proprietors proudly referred to the natural lava stone exterior of the building that simulated ruffled turkey feathers.

The lobby of the futuristic, vaguely turkey-shaped building was carpeted in a custom turkey pattern, while the walls, railings, and doors were covered with pink and purple shag carpet. It must have been done by demented designers or, perhaps more likely, the owner's wife. In the Royal Roost Cocktail Lounge, the platform holding your plastic, button-tufted, barrel chair rotated completely around so you could fully absorb the fine collection of turkey art, animal oils, and a rare John Wayne on velvet. The only taste this place ever exhibited was turkey: almost every item on the menu in the lavender dining room, which sat 350 people, featured turkey in one form or another.

No bad idea was ever rejected, nor any good idea proposed, in the motel's romantic suites. The Passion Pit had a television imbedded in the clamshell headboard of the bed, but this was way before VCRs so the purpose was murky indeed unless watching band leader Lawrence Welk on 'live' TV rang your chimes. Stereo turntable and eight-track tape players were provided, but it was strictly bring your own sounds.

Their brochure claimed a mission to 'enhance the role of Tom Turkey as the all-American delicacy'.

bullet proof windows, and a CIA cover phone guaranteed to hide your whereabouts from the enemy.

The Safe House, 779 North Front St, Milwaukee, WI 53202; ↘ 414 271 2007; web: www.safe-house.com

Quirky quarters

Fifteen FantaSuites are featured at the **Don Q Inn** in Dodgeville. Each suite has its own theme such as the Blue Room's 300-gallon copper cheese-vat tub, the Float's Viking ship waterbed and heart-shaped hydro-therapy tub and the Swinger's suspended swinging bed.

Meanwhile, 25 FantaSuites are featured at the **West Bend Inn** with themes like Arabian Nights – a suite complete with a sheik's tent and overhead starlight mirror. The Continental suite has a 1964 Lincoln Continental bed, the Medieval Castle Dungeon sports wall shackles and oversized whirlpool, while the Teepee has a waterbed in a forest setting with a mirrored ceiling. Well, no one ever said Americans have taste. Tours are held at both properties on Saturdays or Sundays at 3pm, or you can buy a video in the lobby if you're so enamored.

Don Q Inn, 3656 State Hwy 23 North, Dodgeville, WI 53533; ↘ 608 935 2320 or 800 666 7848; web: www.fantasuite.com

West Bend Inn, 2520 West Washington Street, West Bend, WI 53095; ↘ 262 338 0636 or 800 727 9727

Loy Bowlin was a real-life rhinestone cowboy. Inspired by the famous Glen Campbell song, he set out to transform himself from a lonely retiree into someone who could make people laugh. Starting with his apparel, he covered his clothes with rhinestones, glitter and pictures of himself. Then he covered his car and then his false teeth. Happy with the results of his transformation, he turned to his house, covering every inch with polka dots, glitter, sparkling collages and Christmas ornaments. Each day he'd go into town, dressed in a different outfit, and sing and dance his way into people's hearts. His house, originally located in Mississippi, has been preserved by the John Michael Kohler Arts Center in Sheboygan. It should be on display by 2002.

MINNESOTA

It's been said that you know you're in Minnesota when all the festivals across the state are named after something you eat, something you hunt, or something you endure and that Minnesotans think driving in the winter is easier because the potholes are filled with snow. Minnesota has proportionately more wacky festivals than Wisconsin and only a single eccentric environment. Go figure. Their governor, Jesse Ventura, is an ex-wrestler with a penchant for flamboyant histrionics.

Festivals and events

It's tough for folks who live in the 'Ice Box of the Nation' to find a reason to get out of bed in January. To make it easier they've created four days of organized insanity in January called **Ice Box Days** during which they go frozen-turkey bowling, play golf on the ice and run in the snow in a Freeze yer Gizzard Blizzard Run. They hold an Ode to the Cold poetry contest, a pre-school olympics, a townwide scavenger hunt and some Mutt Races so the dogs don't feel left out. If you can drive a tricycle and balance a pizza in one hand, you can join in the Cold Pizza Delivery race. If that doesn't appeal, there's always the Beach Party (dress appropriately), a snow sculpture contest and the Barrel Sauna and Polar Bear Dip.

> **Ice Box Days** held annually the third weekend in January at Voyageurs National Park located in north central Minnesota on the northern border of Minnesota, about 15 miles east of International Falls, MN and 300 miles north of Minneapolis–Saint Paul, MN. Contact International Falls Area Chamber of Commerce; ⟍ 800 325 5766 or 218 283 9400; web: www.internationalfallsmn.com

For three months out of the year, thousands of wooden fish houses are constructed on a huge, frozen lake in Aitkin. Residents play cards, watch TV, work on their computers, cook and have parties while their automatic lines go fishing for them. Some folks live on the ice for weeks. The temporary city includes plowed streets, stores, sanitation facilities and, obviously, electricity. The houses are transported to the lake at a wacky **Fish House Parade** the day after Thanksgiving.

> **Fish House Parade** held annually the day after Thanksgiving in downtown Aitkin, MN. Contact Aitkin Area Chamber of Commerce, PO Box 127, Aitkin, MN 56431; ⟍ 218 927 2316; email: upnorth@aitkin.com; web: www.aitkin.com

Replenish the energy you expended getting in and out of your snow wear by downing a nice plate of SPAM!, that pink blob of gelatinous spiced ham product famous the world over. Minnesota is home to the Hormel Corporation, inventor of the miracle meat of which it has sold more than 5 billion cans. That's enough to feed three meals a day to a family of four for four-and-a-half million years. Oh, yum.

Hormel is so proud of its creation that it honors the blob with a **SPAM™ Jamboree** and with its very own **SPAM™ Museum**. Past recipes using SPAM™ include SPAM™ strudel with mustard sauce, SPAM™ mousse, and SPAM™ cheescake"! Yum, yum. The new museum, scheduled, to open in the summer of 2001, will feature displays pertaining not just to SPAM™, but to Hormel's other processed food products as well. The diner will serve SPAM™ burgers, and SPAM™ dogs. Yum, yum, yum.

SPAM™ events: SPAM™ Town USA Festival and SPAM™ Jam held annually in July in Austin, MN. Contact Austin Convention and Visitors Bureau; ↘ 8004445713; email: visitor austincvb.com;web: www.austincvb.com

People from time immemorial have grappled with such questions as whether life has meaning, whether humans are inherently good or evil, and whether God exists. In more modern times man has debated whether honesty is always the best policy or if the death penalty is ethical in a civilized society. **The Great American Think-off**, held at the Regional Cultural Center in New York Mills, ponders such weighty questions at an annual sports-like event that pits armchair philosophers against one another in a debate to win the title of America's Greatest Thinker. Each year, the contest asks the nation to provide a written answer to a provocative question, in 750 words or less, based on personal experience.

Real philosophers need not apply: the event is meant to encourage normal, everyday folks to have their say. The best essayists are brought to the town for the battle of the brains, with the audience deciding the ultimate winner.

The Great American Think-off held annually in June at the New York Mills Regional Cultural Center, 24 North Main Ave, New York Mills, MN 56567; web: www.think-off.org

At long as it's licensed and running, that truck your friends are always making fun of could win you one-upmanship prizes at the **Ugly Truck Contest** in Pelican Rapids each July. Entrants are judged according to the worst body condition, the worst interior, the most obnoxious exhaust, the most rust and who has the most air where windows used to be.

Ugly Truck Contest held annually in July in Pelican Rapids, MN, located at the intersection of Hwy 59 and Hwy 108. Contact Jeff Johnson, PO Box 1540, Pelican Rapids, MN 56572; ↘ 218 863 6693

Virtually everything you can think to do to a potato is done at the **Potato Days Festival** every August in Barnsville. The spuds are picked, peeled, tossed, fried, raced, baked and even worn. Activities include loony mashed potato wrestling, a potato-sack fashion show, potato-car races, speed peeling contests, potato billiards, potato golf, a potato hunt, a potato scramble and a Mr Potato Head competition.

Potato Days held annually in August in Barnesville, MN. Contact Barnesville Potato Days, PO Box 345, Barnesville, MN 56514; ↘ 800 525 4901 or 218 354 2145; email: spudlady@potatodays.com; web: www.potatodays.com

Just plain weird

When the city of St Paul needed room to expand its government buildings, it had to figure out a way to build on land deeded as permanent parkland. A bright, enterprising government employee suggested that the park simply be raised – to the top of the parking structure. And so it was.

Park on Top of Parking Garage, downtown Minneapolis, MN. Contact Greater Minneapolis Convention and Visitors Association; �‍ 612 661 4700; web: www.minneapolis.org

In Belle Plaine you can see a **two-story outhouse**, constructed by a man with too many children and too few outhouse places for them all. All told, the outhouse is a 'five-holer'.

Two-Story Outhouse, Belle Plaine, MN. Contact Belle Plaine Chamber of Commerce; ↘ 952 873 4295; web: www.belleplainemn.com

Attractions

You can take lessons in juggling, yo-yoing, and ping-pong at the country's only juggling academy in Burnsville. **The Air Traffic Juggling Academy** offers instruction almost every day and you're welcome to take just a single class if you wish. Anyone can learn regardless of age. Call for their daily schedule of classes.

The Air Traffic Juggling Academy, 1172 E Cliff Rd, Burnsville, MN 55337; ↘ 952 895 5540; web: www.artraffic.com

Museums and collections

Americans are nothing if not inventive, and nowhere is this more obvious than at the **Museum of Questionable Medical Devices**, the country's very own Quackery Hall of Fame. Robert McCoy, a pediatrician, and his wife Margaret started the collection. Phrenology machines were his specialty, these being devices resembling a spiked helmet that analyze your personality by reading the bumps on your head. 'People fall for things,' he said, 'that are really preposterous, especially about sex.' Why anyone would buy a prostate gland warmer, which was plugged in and then inserted where it would do the most good, is beyond comprehension.

It's impossible not to burst out laughing at most of these utterly absurd contraptions. The sharp metal device that was to be clamped you-know-where to prevent you-know-what is a prime example, as is the MacGregor Rejuvenator, a machine which blasted you with magnetic waves to reverse the aging process. They remind you just how gullible we humans can be. Didn't anyone look around and say, 'Hey, if this thing works, how come there aren't more 120-year-olds walking about?' Someday, future generations will be having a good laugh at the thought of our copper bracelets, adhesive magnets, and Viagra. Today's products may be different, but the intent is still the same and things really haven't changed all that much.

Museum of Questionable Medical Devices located in Historic St
Anthony Main, 201 Main St SE, Minneapolis, MN; ☏ 612 379 4046
(museum); 952 545 1113 (office); fax: 952 540-9999; web:
www.mtn.org/~quack. *Open Tue–Thur 5.00–9.00pm; Fri–Sat
12.00–9pm; Sun 12.00–5.00pm. Admission free.*

Almost everyone knows a pack rat, a person who compulsively saves
everything, no matter how useless. You may even be married to one. But no
one can be as bad as Ed Kruger, who never threw anything away for 50 years
after his wife died, not even junk mail, TV guides, check registers, or his long
dead cat.

Ed ran the Jack Sprat Food store in Wykoff from 1933 until this death in
1989. His will left the store and its contents to the city, providing it was turned
into a museum. The ladies of the Wykoff Progress Club took up the challenge,
hauling away truckfull after truckfull of trash to make enough space to
organize the mess so it could been gawked at. You can see the before and after
pictures at **Ed's Museum**, along with his string collection, every toy Ed ever
had, and every magazine he ever subscribed to. This place is the hen-pecked
husband's ultimate revenge.

Ed's Museum in downtown Wykoff, MN, located in southeastern
Minnesota about 35 miles southeast of Rochester between Spring
Valley and Preston. *Open Sat–Sun 1.00–4.00pm or by appt, Jun–Sept.
Admission free, donations accepted.*

You can play 'Leave the driving to us' by getting behind the wheel of a
Greyhound at the **Greyhound Bus Origin Center** in Hibbing. The town
was the first place to be linked to another by 'bus': a seven passenger
Hupmobile that was stretched to seat ten. From these humble beginnings, the
bus industry was born, and you can see the whole story, complete with
memorabilia and buses, at the center that honors the largest bus company in
the world.

Greyhound Bus Origin Center located in Old North Hibbing at
1201 Greyhound Blvd, Hibbing, MN 55746; ☏ 218 263 5814; fax: 425
699 0717; web: greyhoundbusmuseum.com. *Open Mon–Sat
9.00am–5.00pm; Sun 1.00–5.00pm; mid-May–Sept. Admission charge.*

Sandpaper just isn't glamorous, nor is the **Sandpaper Museum** in Two
Harbors. It marks the spot where the 3M Company got its start, but if you're
a Tim Allen sort, you'll probably appreciate it.

Sandpaper Museum officially known as the 3M/Dwan Museum, 2nd
Ave and Waterfront Dr, Two Harbors, MN; ☏ 218 834 4898. *Tours of
the museum depart from the historical society depot at 10.00am,
1.30pm, and 3.00pm; Memorial Day–Labor Day. Admission charge.*

Tours

Your gangster guide tells it all – the corrupt politicians, the crooked police force, and the underworld leaders who actually ran the city of St Paul in the 1920s and 1930s. The **St Paul Gangster Tour** takes you to the sites of the famous clubs, kidnappings and gun battles.

> **St Paul Gangster Tours** from the Wabasha Street Caves, 215 Wabasha Street South, St Paul, MN; ➘ 612 292 1220. *Offers bus outings that operate Saturdays in the warm-weather months, less frequently in the winter.*

Shopping

What kind of store would need parking for 800 cars plus spaces for boats, caravans and semi-trucks? Try **Cabelas**, a 150,000-square-foot showroom for hunting, fishing and outdoor gear that's so big it takes 4,200 employees to run it. Inside stands a mountain, covered with a hundred North American game mounts. Walk through museum-quality dioramas depicting the circle of life, practice target shooting and archery in the virtual reality range and dine on game delicacies in the restaurant. The grounds are so extensive that they lead tours, while their annual sidewalk sale is so famous that many folks fly in for it.

> **Cabela's Outfitters**, 3900 Cabela Dr, Oatonna, MN 55060; ➘ 507 451 4545; web: www.cabelas.com. *Open Mon–Sat 8.00am–9.00pm; Sun 10.00am–6.00pm.*

Normally, you wouldn't think of a mall as being eccentric, but the **Mall of America** qualifies because it panders to all of America's addictions at once. Not only can you shop, you can send your kid to day camp, get married, visit theme parks, make a teddy bear at a factory, work out, play golf, attend college and, of course, eat – at a different restaurant every day for 40 days before you'd have to duplicate cuisine. The place is so big it could hold 32 Boeing 747 jumbo jets, nine Eiffel Towers, or all four President's heads from Mt Rushmore.

> **Mall of America**, 60 East Broadway, Bloomington, MN 55425; ➘ 952 883 8800; web: www.mallofamerica.com. *Open Mon–Fri 10.00am–9.30pm; Sat 9.30am–9.30pm; Sun 11.00am–7.00pm.*

Quirky quarters

The **Sod House Bed and Breakfast** in Sanborn, open year around, encourages you to dress in prairie clothes, read by oil lamps and play old-fashioned games while sleeping in a real settler's sod house.

> **Sod House Bed and Breakfast**, 12598 Magnolia Ave, Sanborn MN 56083; ➘ 507 723 5138

Thirty fantasy suites are featured at **Quality Inns and Suites** in Burnsville. Each suite has its own theme; there's a sheik's tent with a waterbed and overhead mirror, a thatched jungle hut with mosquito netting over the waterbed and a queen-sized whaling dinghy waterbed with a whirlpool behind the mouth of a whale. Waterbeds went out in the 1970s but today's 20-somethings probably don't know that. Tours are held any Saturday or Sunday at 3pm or you can buy a video in the lobby.

> **Quality Inns and Suites**, 250 N River Ridge Circle, Burnsville, MN 55337; ↘ 952 890 9550 or 800 666 STAY; web: www.fantasuite.com

Travelers with conviction stay at the **Jailhouse Inn** in Preston, an 1869 jail house converted into a bed and breakfast. In the 'cell block' you can sleep behind bars. Or, choose the 'master bedroom' that was the sheriff's personal quarters.

> **Jailhouse Historic Inn** 109 Houston St NW, Preston, MN 55965; ↘ 507 765 2181; fax: 507 765 2558; web: www.jailhouseinn.com

IOWA
Festivals and events

The **National Hobo Convention** is the nation's largest gathering of hobos, ie: vagabonds who ride the rail system on freight trains. Drawing both real hobos and hobos-for-a-week, the event draws around 30,000 people. Spectators are invited to vote for their favorite hobo and hobo-ess; those elected king and queen are rewarded with flowing robes and tin can crowns. The hobos get together to sing, trade, and act out the drama of their lives in the Hobo Theater. The Hobo Museum will be moving to nicer digs by 2003.

> **National Hobo Convention** held annually in August in Britt, IA. Contact Hobo Foundation, PO Box 413, Britt, IA 50423; ↘ 641 843 9104 or 641 843 3840; web: www.hobo.com

> The **Hobo Museum** opening August 2003 in Britt, IA. Contact Hobo Foundation, PO Box 413, Britt, IA 50423; ↘ 515 843 9104; web: www.hobo.com

From mid-July through mid October, the **Amazing Maize Maze** at Carter Farm is four acres of challenge. You're given a game card and sent to wander through two miles of pathways, collecting puzzle pieces to complete your card. Maze masters will help you out if you ask and there's a look-out tower, as well as flags and clues to lead you out.

Amazing Maize Maze, Carter Farm, Princeton, IA; ☏ 319 289 9999. Located 20 miles from Davenport, 2 miles north of Princeton on Hwy 67. Open 10.00am–6.00pm Wed–Sat; 1.00–6.00pm Sun Jul 10–Labor Day; 10.00am–6.00pm Fri–Sat; 1.00–6.00pm Sun Labor Day–mid Oct. Admission charge.

Eccentric environments

Father Paul Dobberstein made a vow to the Virgin Mary that he'd build her a shrine if she'd cure him of pneumonia. She delivered, and so did he. Over 42 years, winter and summer, he built the **Grotto of the Redemption** near Fort Dodge. Setting ornamental rocks and gems into concrete, he created an entire city block portraying scenes from the life of Christ. Eventually nine towering structures were built, making the grotto the largest of its kind in the world. It has a geological value of over $5 million and the largest concentration of minerals in any one spot on earth. After the Father died, his assistant picked up the trowel and carried on for another eight years. For the last six years, Father Gerald Streit has been continuing construction and maintenance.

Grotto of the Redemption, West Bend, IA. Located northwest of Fort Dodge, between State Hwys 18 and 20. Contact West Bend Chamber of Commerce, 121 S Broadway, West Bend, IA 50597; ☏ 515 887 4721

Jill and Michael Stephenson lead a very unusual life. They live, by choice, without modern conveniences at their **Waterloo Workshop** in Dorchester. Ten years ago, following a stint of subsistence farming, they bought an old log home that had never been equipped with electricity. Having limited funds to set up their farm, they decided to forgo electricity along with a few other modern trappings of life in America.

Jill says, 'It's just a matter of learning to do things more directly. If we need water, we walk 100 feet to the pump and fill the pail.'

They have nine grown children who today live in conventional houses. The Stephensons earn a living doing what they love: Michael is a woodcarver and Jill weaves baskets and makes jam. They like the idea that they're living with minimal negative impact on the earth and hope to be an inspiration to others looking for a way to simplify their life. They're almost always home, so you can drop in any time. But if you want to be absolutely sure they'll be there, you'll have to send a note, by snail mail, no less.

Waterloo Workshop, 369 Waterloo Creek Dr, Dorchester, IA 52140

COOKING WITH WORMS

Before you snack on a slice of banana worm bread, you'd better read the disclaimer: 'The Department of Entomology at Iowa State University is not responsible for gastric distress, allergic reactions, feelings of repulsion, or other problems resulting from the ingestion of foods represented on these pages.' The school has a website featuring food made with insects.

Insect Zoo at the Department of Entomology at Iowa State University, Insectary Building, Ames, IA 50011; ↘ 515 294 7400; web: www.ent.iastate.edu

Just plain weird

It's amazing what a determined 'trekkie' can accomplish. Steve Miller, of Riverside City, convinced the city council to declare Riverside the **'Future Birthplace of Captain Kirk'**. Of course it helped that he was a council member himself at the time. Remembering that Kirk supposedly hailed from a small town in Iowa, he impulsively proposed the theme during discussion of an upcoming celebration. The result is **Trek Fest**, Riverside's annual tribute to the future.

The town's motto used to be 'Where the best begins'. With Kirk's impending conception just 228 years off, the motto was revised to read 'Where the Trek begins'. While it's not clear just who will bring the future Kirk into the world, it is clear where it will happen – behind the barbershop.

> **Future Birthplace of Captain Kirk**, Riverside, IA. Located on Hwy 218, 20 miles south of I-80/Iowa City.

> **Trek Fest** held annually in June; web: www.trekfest.com

It's been called the Lazy Susan Jail, the **Squirrel Cage**, and the Human Rotary Jail. This bizarre experiment in jail architecture was invented in 1881 to create a jail that wouldn't require contact between prisoners and guards. With just one deputy, a jailer could provide maximum security and control of the facility. The three-story jail rotated to allow the jailer a view of all the cells without getting up from his chair.

> **Squirrel Cage Jail (Lazy Susan Jail, Human Rotary Jail)**, 226 Pearl St, Council Bluffs, IA; ↘ 712 323 2509. *Open 12.00noon–4.00pm; Sat–Sun, Apr, May, Sept or by appointment.*

Museums and collections

Winters are long and cold in Iowa and having a hobby helps pass the time. In the early 1900s farm boys Frank and Joseph Bily decided that carving clocks would become theirs. It took them two years to build the Apostle Clock, and four years to create the American Pioneer History Clock. Church clocks followed, and the brothers carved until the late 1950s, leaving behind 40 clocks ranging in size from ten inches to over ten feet tall. Each clock chimes, plays music and has moving figures dancing about. Oddly enough, the museum in Spillville is called the **Bily Clocks Museum and Dvorak Exhibit**, partly in honour of the Bily boys' collection and partly reflecting the composer's visit to the town in 1893.

> **Bily Clocks Museum and Dvorak Exhibit**, South Main St, PO Box 258, Spillville, IA 52168; ↘ 319 562 3589; web: www.spillville.ia.us/about.html. *Open May–Oct daily 8.30am–5.00pm; Apr daily 10.00am–4.00pm; Mar and Nov Sat–Sun 10.00am–4.00pm.*

Almost a thousand dolls reside upstairs at the **Dyer-Botsford House and Doll Museum** in Dyersfield. The collection was the passion of Esther Schemmel who prowled farm sales and auctions for 40 years. The collection includes a Charlie Chaplin doll made of wax and collector dolls such as those representing John Wayne, Marilyn Monroe, Shirley Temple, as well as Barbies.

> **Dyer-Botsford House and Doll Museum**, 331 First Ave East, Dyersville, IA 52040; ↘ 319 875 2414. *Open Mon–Fri 10.00am–4.00pm; Sat–Sun 1.00–4.00pm; Fall 1.00–4.00pm; Winter by appointment only. Admission charge.*

Quirky quarters

Scenic Ridge View Exotic Animal Ranch offers teepees for camping, a one-room country schoolhouse with primitive facilities for sleeping, a petting zoo where you can get close to baby animals, and tours through their buffalo and longhorn pastures.

> **Scenic Ridge View Exotic Animal Ranch**, 416 Hwy 76, Harpers Ferry, IA 52146; ↘ 319 586 2721

ILLINOIS

Festivals and events

It's America's biggest tug-of-war. The Mississippi River separates the towns of LeClaire, Iowa and Port Byron, Illinois. At the annual **Tug Fest**, ten teams of 20 pull against one another with a 2,400-foot, 680-pound rope.

The winning town gets to keep the prize statue of a bald eagle in flight for the next year.

> **Tug Fest** held annually in August in LeClaire, IA and Port Byron, IL. Contact LeClaire Chamber of Commerce; web: www.leclaireiowa.org

Illinois is home to two cemeteries that resurrect the dead. Each year in **Moline** and **Rock Island**, costumed actors portray the life of the people buried there. Speaking in lyrical vignettes, and dressed in the era of the times, they tell the stories in entertaining detail. Both cemeteries are known for their unique landscaping and funerary architecture.

Gone but not Forgotten Tour held annually in September in Moline, IL. Contact Quad Cities Convention and Visitors Bureau; ↘ 800 747 7800.

Chippiannock Cemetery Tour, 2901 12th St, Rock Island, IL. Contact Quad Cities Convention and Visitors' Bureau; ↘ 800 747 7800

At an isolated Quincy airfield, around 5,000 adrenaline junkies every year attend the **World Freefall Convention**, a display of kamikaze, freestyle sky diving in which participants compete in sky surfing and accelerated, freefall speed dives. Each day of the event includes several religious services, which is understandable considering how extremely dangerous the sport is.

World Freefall Convention held annually in August in Quincy, IL. Contact World Free Fall Convention Headquarters, Rt 1, Box 123, Quincy, IL 62031; ↘ 217 222 5867; fax: 217 885 3141; email: wffc@freefall.com; web: www.freefall.com

Eccentric environments
'Twenty-four/seven' (24/7) is American shorthand for 24 hours around the clock, seven days a week. Those are the hours you can visit Charles Smith at his **African-American Heritage Museum and Black Veterans Archives** in Aurora. If you ask, he'll tell you how tirelessly he works at sculpting the history of African America out of wood. Charles is fulfilling a vision that came to him from God, who told him, 'Use art. I give you a weapon.' Rising to the occasion, he's filled the large yard surrounding his house with memorials to African American heroes, slaves, soldiers, and martyrs. Each figure is uniquely expressive and communicative.

'People say, when they come by here, "It looks like a cemetery only every body's standin' up, holdin' their own obituary."'

African-American Heritage Museum and Black Veterans Archives, 126 S Kendall, Aurora, IL; ↘ 630 375 0657. *Open daily 24 hours, but visitors should call to arrange a tour.*

Just plain weird
It's an eight car pile up – on a stick, that is. In a Berwyn parking lot at the **Cermak Plaza Shopping Center** stands an odd piece of art called the 'Spindle'. The cars are skewered on a 50-foot spike, with a red Volkswagen 'Beetle' topping it off like a cherry. The object of much controversy, some think

it's delightfully refreshing, while others view it more like garbage on a stick. The center is also home to other bizarre art such as the 'Pinto Pelt' on the wall near Walgreen's. The good citizens of Berwyn have soundly criticized the center's owner, David Bermant, for his artistic taste – or lack of it – and voted in a non-binding referendum to tear down a previous sculpture that was on the site. The cars on a spike, created by artist Dustin Shuler, cost $75,000 in 1989.

Cermak Shopping Plaza, Cermak Road and Harlem Ave, Berwyn, IL.

It's not all grim at Ahlgrim's funeral home, Palatine. In the basement of this mortuary is a macabre miniature golf course called **Ahlgrim Acres**. Started 35 years ago as a pastime for family and employees, word of mouth brought service clubs, scouts and other organizations to play the unique course. Hole #1 is a sand trap with a red-light-blinking skull. Hole #2 is an old casket shipping box with twisting troughs for the ball inside. Other challenges include a guillotine, a haunted house, a pinball-like gravestone bounce and the crematorium. If your ball falls into a grave, you lose. There's no charge to play but you do need to call for a reservation. In the event of a funeral you'll have to reschedule.

Ahlgrim Acres located at Ahlgrim's Funeral Home, 201 N Northwest Hwy, Hwy 14, Palatine, IL 60067; ↘ 847 358 7411

Images of **Robert Wadlow**, the world's tallest man, can be seen in museums and attractions all across the USA. But it was here, in Alton, that Wadlow was born, educated and buried. In kindergarten he was five-and-a-half-feet tall. At the age of 20 he earned a living by touring the states for a shoe company that promoted him and supplied his size 37 shoes. When he died from an infected blister in 1940 at the tender age of 22, he weighed 490 pounds. Today there are drugs to control this freakish physical condition. On the grounds of SIU Dental School, a life size, 8-foot, 11-inch statue of him makes a terrific photo op. Remember to hold your camera vertically.

Alton Museum of History and Art, 2809 College Ave, Alton, IL 62002; email: altomuseum@yahoo.com; web: www.altonweb.com and www. altonhistoryandart.museum.com. *Open 10.00am–4.00pm Mon–Fri; 1.00–4.00pm Sat–Sun. Admission charge.*

A two-story outhouse is the pride of the town of Gays, home to the double-decker privy since its construction in 1869. You'll have to see for yourself how two people could use it at the same time!

Two-Story Outhouse, Gays, IL. Located above the SF Gammill General Store.

Museums and collections

You'll be glad you live in modern times after a visit to the **Pearson Museum** at the SIU School of Medicine in Springfield. Medical practices that seem barbaric today are on display for students to study and for the public to grimace at in horror.

A jar of leeches gets curator Barbara Mason chatting enthusiastically about the insect's value in the healing process of wounds. It seems they attach themselves to dead skin, releasing a natural anesthetic which keeps wounds from getting infected. She also explains how some doctors got rid of headaches in the old days – by punching a hole in the brain to let the pain out.

The founder of the museum, the late Dr Emmet Pearson, was a dedicated collector of medical oddities. He was especially fond of disinfected mail. The mail was fumigated to halt the spread of disease by punching holes in it and exposing it to sulfur fumes.

Pearson Museum Department of Medical Humanities, Southern Illinois University School of Medicine, PO Box 19635, Springfield, IL 62794; email: bmason@siumed.edu; web: www.siumed.edu

Superman comes to the aid of Metropolis tourism in the form of an obsessed collector who's amassed more than 100,000 pieces of the man of steel's memorabilia. Curator of the Super Museum and Gift Shop, Jim Hembrick has been instrumental in seeing that the small town lives up to its potential. At the annual **Superman Celebration**, the town of Metropolis puts on a mock bank robbery that gives Superman the opportunity, once again, to triumph over evil even if he has to do so on the ground instead of in the air.

Superman slogans abound, with practically every business in town finding some way to align itself with the cartoon, television and movie legend that has endured for more than 60 years. After all, isn't tourism an important component of truth, justice and the American way?

Superman Celebration held annually in June in Metropolis, IL. Contact Metropolis Chamber of Commerce, 607 Market St, Metropolis, IL 62960; ☎ 800 949 5740 or 618 524 2714; email: info@hcis.net; web: www.metropolischamber.com

You can take a seat in a real electric chair at the **American Police Center and Museum** in Chicago. They've graciously provided you an opportunity to sit and reflect on the thoughts that must have been going through a condemned man's mind during his last moments. Just ignore the buzzer they've gleefully installed to scare the dickens out of you. It's quite a Kodak moment. Other exhibits include a cop and hippie confrontation, riot displays, gangster goodies and a melodramatic drug coffin.

American Police Center and Museum, 1717 S State St, Chicago, IL; ↘ 312 431 0005. *Open 9.30am–4.30pm Mon–Fri. Admission charge.*

Statues of the doctors who actually used the implements displayed in the **International Museum of Surgical Science** stand silent and imposing in the Hall of Immortals. Gruesome paintings of surgeries long past join devices dating from ancient and not so ancient times. The X-ray room has an X-ray shoe fitter that was routinely used in the 1950s – before the dangers of X-rays were known – to see exactly how your foot fit in your shoe.

International Museum of Surgical Science, 1524 N Lake Shore Dr, Chicago, IL; ↘ 312 642 6502; web: www.imss.org. *Located along 151 bus route, few blocks north of Clark/Division elevated train stop. Open 10.00am–4.00pm Tue–Sat, Closed Sun–Mon. Admission charge.*

Max Nordeen's Wheels Museum, so-called because he loves anything pertaining to wheels, is a bit off the beaten track, so he doesn't get a lot of visitors. When he does, Max loves to talk about his collections, a strange mixture of just about anything and everything that's appealed to him during a lifetime of collecting. He's got a story behind each piece, all 3,700 of them, so plan to stay awhile. You'll see a chunk of coal and a steward's badge from the doomed *Titanic*, a petrified leech, a chunk of glass rubble from the Chicago Fire of 1871, and a prostitute mannequin holding a $100 bill and a key to a hotel room. One of his wheels is more than 12 feet in diameter and weighs 18 tons. From war trinkets to naughty key chains, from spark plugs to gear shift knobs, Max has it.

Max Nordeen's Wheels Museum, 6400 N 400 Ave, Alpha, IL 61413; ↘ 309 334 2589

Grandiose schemes

Several dreamers and schemers have attempted to build meccas to their religions in America. With the exception of the Mormons in Utah, all have failed, leaving behind the architectural skeletons of dashed hopes and dreams.

Eric Jason of Sweden was one of those visionaries. He and his band of Jasonists settled in Bishop Hill in 1846. Life was harsh, and made even harsher by Jason, who insisted on three-to-four-hour services twice daily and three times on Sundays. When a cholera epidemic invaded the colony, Jason refused to allow doctors in, telling his flock they were dying because they lacked faith. A disgruntled colonist finally murdered him. His believers, expecting him to arise from the dead, didn't bury him until the smell convinced them he wasn't coming back.

The colony disbanded several years later. All that's left of Eric Jason's tyranny is the little town called Bishop Hill where you can visit the **Bishop Hill Museum**.

> **Bishop Hill Museum**, PO Box D, Bishop Hill, IL 61419; ↘ 309 927 3345

Tours

Chicago was once home to notorious felons like Al Capone and James Dillinger. On the **Untouchables Tour**, you'll go back to the time of the 1920s and 1930s. Shifty and South Side are your guides, acting out the gangster's parts. This two-hour theater-on-wheels brings to life the bizarre and frightening legends of hoodlums, brothels, gambling dens and gangland shootouts.

> **Untouchables Tour**, PO Box 43185, Chicago, IL 60643; ↘ 773 881 1195; web: www.gangstertour.com

A founding member of the Society for the Investigation of the Unexplained certainly qualifies as an eccentric. And if he's also a member of the Merry Gangsters Literary Society, as well as the only full-time, professional ghost hunter in the Midwest, you're in for a spooky experience. Richard Crowe's **supernatural tours** include True Ghost Stories of Chicagoland, Weird, Weird Chicago, and Ghosts I have Met. His paranormal pursuits take him all over the country, investigating the impossible and believing the unbelievable.

> **Supernatural Tour**, PO Box 43185, Chicago, IL 60643; ↘ 773 881 1195; web: www.gangstertour.com

Quirky quarters

The **Adventure Inn Motel** in Gurnee claims the world's largest selection of 'FantaSuites'. In the Hollywood Motel section you'll find two dozen way-off-the-wall suites, including the Igloo, an ice and penguin fantasy, and Area 51 (referring to Nevada's famed UFO sites), which simply have to be seen to be believed. Other over-the-top themes are the Roman Empire, Under the Sea, Gotham City, Signs of the Zodiac, Jewel of the Nile, and Knight Moves. Tours are offered at 2pm weekdays for the over-21 set.

> **Adventure Inn Motel**, 3740 Grand Ave, Gurnee, IL 60031; ↘ 800 373 5245 or 847 623 7777; fax: 847 623 3606; web: www.adventureinninc.com

The Party-like-a-Rock-Star Suite at **Hotel Monaco** in Chicago has all the amenities you'd expect – along with a few you wouldn't – if you were Mr or

Ms Big Bucks. You'll bed down in a room with a trashed TV, a video jukebox, gold records and an electric guitar. The hotel offers inventive packages such as the insomniac's Movie Marathon; the Ooh Ooh, Baby, complete with massage, chocolate, champagne, hot tub, and gift certificate to Victoria's Secret and the Charge shopping package that can melt your credit card. If you miss your pet, ask for a complementary goldfish to keep you company during your stay.

Hotel Monaco, 225 North Wabash, Chicago, IL 60601; ↘ 800 397 7661; fax: 312 960 8538; web: www.monaco-chicago.com

MICHIGAN
Festivals and events

Entries in the winter **Outhouse Classic** in Trenary are built from wood and/or cardboard, installed with a toilet seat and a roll of toilet paper, mounted on skis, then pushed it 500 feet down Main Street. Some of the entries are built for speed, some for laughs and some are so elaborate you wouldn't mind having them in your backyard. The annual event, just six years old, started out with 20 entries; now it attracts at least 60.

A past humor award went to the costumed 'nuns', who pushed the outhouse while praying and slapping people with their rulers. Their list of ten commandments included, 'thou shalt not leave the seat up, thou shalt spray, and thou shalt not take thy farts in vain.' Another winner was the White House, pushed by Monica Lewinsky and Linda Tripp (not really), while Bill Clinton sat inside; Monica wore a blue dress with the requisite white stains on the front. Thirty-five hundred spectators show up for this event and the little town boasts the only 'outhouse parking' signs in Michigan.

Last year the entries included the Hawaiian Pu Pu Inna Hola, and a house powered by pitted prunes. The event also features Snow Volleyball.

Outhouse Classic held annually in February in Trenary, MI. Contact Outhouse Classic, PO Box 271, Trenary, MI 49891; ↘ 906 446 3504

Any town named Kalamazoo would have to have a sense of humor, and its **Do-Dah Parade** each June proves that it does. Do-Dah is a salute to silliness, a parade that spoofs parades. It's an annual event that draws 1,300 participants and as many as 50,000 spectators. The Keggers, a local nightclub, has its employees form a Keggers Drill Team, performing with empty kegs, rolling and throwing them in formation.

Do-Dah Parade held annually in June in Kalamazoo, MI. Contact Kalamazoo County Convention and Visitors Bureau, 346 W Michigan Ave, Kalamazoo, MI 49007; ↘ 800 530 9192 or Cumulus Broadcasting WKFR; ↘ 616 344 0111; fax: 616 343 0430; web: kazoofun.com

THE HEIDELBERG PROJECT

It happened on Heidelberg Street. One man, working alone, painted polka dots on his house, his car, the trees and the trashcans. Using his blighted neighborhood as his canvas, and a compelling vision as his tools, Tyree Guyton rebuilt the spirit of his riot-torn community through art. The street has been a living kaleidoscope, bursting with exuberant color and pattern. Polka  dots are everywhere, joined by an abundance of found and broken objects transformed into art.

People came from all over the world to visit the Heidelberg Project and experience for themselves Guyton's message of hope penetrating the blight. Unfortunately, the city of Detroit didn't see the street through artistic eyes: all they saw were condemned buildings, which they've twice torn down since Guyton began with his polka dots in 1986. Still inspired to rebuild and expand, he's usually in his outdoor studio each day, showing children that there is a better way. The non-profit organization that manages the project hopes to develop similar art and education projects for youths in other forgotten neighborhoods across the country.

Battle Creek is known as the cereal capital of the world. Each year the Kellog Company, the famous maker of breakfast cereals, pushes 300 picnic tables together and serves a free breakfast for up to 60,000 people at the **World's Longest Breakfast Table**. The company's Cereal City USA™ is an entertaining attraction about the history of cereal and the part it has played in American culture.

World's Longest Breakfast Table, 171 West Michigan Ave, Battle Creek, MI 49017; ⋎ 616 962 6230; web: www.kelloggscerealcityusa.org

Horton Bay spoofs politics at the annual **Horton Bay July Fourth Parade**. No serious entries are allowed; only those that make fun of the year's political foibles can march under the banner of negative campaigning, mud slinging and whining. In the year 2000, presidential candidate John Q Nobody marched under the slogan 'Nobody's Better – Trust Nobody'; Phil A Tank campaigned for 'two SUVs in every garage' and 'Support Global Warming – Improve our Climate'. Prior years saw a Manure Spreader 'spreading political wisdom the old-fashioned way.' Fifteen thousand folks show up to watch this political extravaganza.

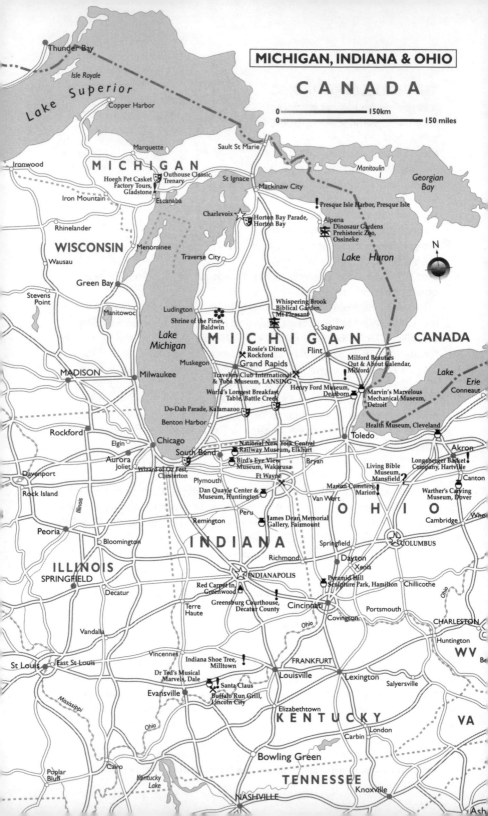

MICHIGAN, INDIANA & OHIO

CANADA

0 _____ 150km
0 _____ 150 miles

Thunder Bay

Isle Royale

Lake Superior

Copper Harbor

Marquette

Sault St Marie

Ironwood

MICHIGAN

St Ignace

Mackinaw City

Manitoulin I

Georgian Bay

Iron Mountain

Hoegh Pet Casket Factory Tours, Gladstone

Outhouse Classic, Trenary

Escanaba

Rhinelander

Charlevoix

Horton Bay Parade, Horton Bay

Presque Isle Harbor, Presque Isle

Alpena

Dinosaur Gardens Prehistoric Zoo, Ossineke

WISCONSIN

Menominee

Traverse City

Lake Huron

CANADA

Wausau

Green Bay

Manitowoc

Stevens Point

Ludington

Shrine of the Pines, Baldwin

Lake Michigan

Whispering Brook Biblical Garden, Mt Pleasant

MICHIGAN

Saginaw

MADISON

Milwaukee

Muskegon

Rosie's Diner, Rockford

Grand Rapids

Flint

Milford Beauties Out & About Calendar, Milford

Lake Erie

Conneaut

Travelers Club International & Tuba Museum, LANSING

World's Longest Breakfast Table, Battle Creek

Henry Ford Museum, Dearborn

Marvin's Marvelous Mechanical Museum, Detroit

Rockford

Do-Dah Parade, Kalamazoo

Benton Harbor

Health Museum, Cleveland

Toledo

Akron

Elgin

Chicago

South Bend

National New York Central Railway Museum, Elkhart

Bird's Eye View Museum, Wakarusa

Bryan

Living Bible Museum, Mansfield

Longaberger Basket Company, Hartville

Aurora

Joliet

Wizard of Oz Fest, Chesterton

Ft Wayne

Canton

Davenport

Plymouth

Dan Quayle Center & Museum, Huntington

Van Wert

Marion Cemetery, Marion

Warther's Carving Museum, Dover

Rock Island

Peru

OHIO

Cambridge

Whe

Peoria

Remington

James Dean Memorial Gallery, Fairmount

Springfield

INDIANA

Richmond

Dayton

COLUMBUS

Bloomington

Xenia

Chillicothe

ILLINOIS

SPRINGFIELD

Decatur

INDIANAPOLIS

Red Carpet In, Greenwood

Pyramid Hill Sculpture Park, Hamilton

Ohio

Terre Haute

Greensburg Courthouse, Decatur County

Cincinnati

Covington

Portsmouth

CHARLESTON

Vandalia

Ohio

Huntington

WV

St Louis

East St Louis

Vincennes

Indiana Shoe Tree, Milltown

FRANKFORT

Be

Dr Ted's Musical Marvels, Dale

Louisville

Lexington

Salyersville

VA

Evansville

Santa Claus

Buffalo Run Grill, Lincoln City

Mississippi

Ohio

Elizabethtown

KENTUCKY

London

Poplar Bluff

Cairo

Kentucky Lake

Carbin

Bowling Green

TENNESSEE

NASHVILLE

Knoxville

Ash

Horton Bay Parade held annually on July 4th in Horton Bay, MI. Contact John Rohe, Horton Bay Parade, Box 284, Boyne City, MI 49712; ↘ 231 347 7327; email: rohe@freeway.net.

Eccentric environments

As a boy, Earl Young liked to collect rocks, much like young boys everywhere. Only for Earl, the rocks became an obsession. Prowling the shores of Lake Michigan and the woods surrounding his hometown of **Charlevoix**, he collected stones that 'spoke' to him, for Earl firmly believed that each stone had a distinctive personality.

The houses he built with these stones and boulders have been called variously, 'gnome', 'mushroom', 'fairy' and 'elf' homes. Earl, with no training as an architect, managed to create a career building these strange, undulating houses which seem to sprout from the earth like mushrooms. No two houses were ever alike, for Earl built to the site, never cutting down trees. Instead, his houses flowed into the setting, undulating and weaving in a mating dance between man and landscape.

He built into the hillsides and into the trees, planning each meticulous detail. A stone's 'personality', and how it would get along with the stone next to it, dictated the placement of each. The results were whimsical and eccentric, both fluid and chunky, with wavy roofs, massive fireplaces and free-form contours that melted into the setting.

Sometimes Earl would find a stone or boulder, then go to great effort to bury it until he found a place for it. He once dropped a nine ton boulder into the lake and, 26 years later, knew exactly where to retrieve it. Twenty-six of his houses can be seen on a self-guided walking tour.

Earl Young Gnome Homes. Information: pick up a brochure and map at the Charlevoix Area Chamber of Commerce, 408 E Bridge St (US31), Charlevoix, MI 49720; ↘ 231 547 2101; fax: 231 547 6633; email: info@charlevoix.org; web: www.charlevoix.org. You can find most of the houses by taking Bridge St to the Pine River Channel. Immediately south of the channel take Park Ave west and south to see a triangular block full of his homes. You can walk, bike, or drive past the houses.

Just plain weird

The folks in Milford, population 5,000, sure know how to have a good time for a good cause. Nine ladies, aged 48–73, have put out a 12-month pin-up calendar in which they appear to be naked. Using liberal amounts of duct tape (otherwise known as Duck tape) to hold strategically placed props, they've posed in the 'nude' in a dozen places around town, leaving just enough to the imagination. November is in the bakery with the 'best buns in town'; January is 'now showing' in the movie theater; while June is being 'busted' by the cops – August has them cooling off at the Cold Butt Euchre event in which the contestants play the card game 'euchre' while sitting on blocks of ice. The **Milford Beauties Out and About** calendar raises funds for building restoration. You can order it through their website or buy it when you're in town.

> **Milford Beauties Out and About**. Contact Huron Valley Chamber of Commerce, 317 Union St, Milford, MI 48381; ↘ 248 685 7129; web: huronvcc@tir.com

Three Depression-era drinking buddies from **Presque Isle Harbor** give the expression 'drop dead' a whole new meaning. It seems that Fred Piepkorn, Charlie Priest, and Bill Green agreed, in honor of their friendship, that as each pal passed away, the others would remember him by pouring a drink into the earth at his gravesite. At the town's cemetery, you can see three cement slabs next to one another, each drilled with a hole – the better for the drop to drip down to the departed chums. Local folks still drink with them.

> **Presque Isle Harbor**. Contact Marquette County Convention and Visitors Bureau; ↘ 800 544 4321 or 906 228 7749; fax: 906 228 3642; email: marinfo@marquettecounty.org; web: marquettecounty.org

You can view the manufacture of pet caskets and tour a model pet cemetery at the **Hoegh Pet Casket Factory Tours** in Gladstone. The casket showroom has velvet paintings of wide-eyed puppies along with caskets from shoe box size on up. The sewing room displays memorial pet plaques after which you'll see the actual manufacturing and quality control process. You end the tour outside in the model pet cemetery.

> **Hoegh Pet Casket Factory Tours**, 311 Delta Ave, Gladstone, MI 49837; ↘ 906 428 2151

Attractions

It may not be the fanciest bible park you'll ever visit, but it certainly reflects the charm and dedication of its creators, Bonnie and Elmer Giese. Bonnie had been fantasizing for 20 years about a building a place for nature and meditation that would appeal to people of all religions. When they retired, she put Elmer to work and the result is the **Whispering Brook Biblical Garden and Nature Trail** located east of Remus.

The Gieses wanted to make sure you could find it, so Elmer built a giant, flat-wood dinosaur to serve as a landmark. In the garden itself, you'll come upon 70 flat-board, painted scenes from both the Old and New Testameᐧts. There's Moses in the rushes, Jesus among the wildflowers, and a Noah's Ark big enough to play in. According to Bonnie, God designed the land the garden sits on; they're just the caretakers.

Whispering Brook Biblical Garden and Nature Trail located 20 minutes west of Mt Pleasant on M-20, Mt. Pleasant, MI. Contact Bonnie and Elmer Giese; ↘ 517 967 3581. *Open daily May–Oct, reservations recommended.*

Another garden, **Dinosaur Gardens Prehistorical Zoo** in Ossineke, features a welcome by Jesus, huge concrete dinosaurs, and a sprinkling of cavemen hunting for their supper. A Mr Domke, who colored his creatures green, gray, and brown, built these strange sculptures in the 1950s. The current owner, Jean Cousineau, has repainted them in bright, cheerful colors. The effect is curious, indeed.

Dinosaur Gardens Prehistoric Zoo, US 23S, Ossineke, MI; ↘ 877 823 5408. *Open daily 9.00am–6.00pm summer.*

Raymond W Overholzer was so enamored of the white pine that he built a cabin, complete with furnishings, as a tribute to the tree. At the **Shrine of the Pines**, the furniture is chiseled from tree stumps and roots that were scraped with broken glass and wire brushes, then finished with sandpaper, resin, and deer hide. You'll see chairs, chandeliers, tables, beds, and candlesticks – more than 200 items in all – in a tranquil setting on the banks of the Pere Marquette River in Baldwin. It's the largest collection of rustic white pine furniture in the world.

Shrine of the Pines located 2 miles south of Baldwin in the Manistee National Forest; ↘ 231 745 7892. *Open May 15–October 15, Mon–Sat 10.00am–6.00pm; Sunday 1.30–6.00pm. Admission charge.*

Museums and collections

The **Henry Ford Museum** in Dearborn has some mighty strange things. Whoever was close to Thomas Edison's mouth when he died took his last breath, which is sealed in a test tube, as well as his false teeth. Assassination-wise, look for the chair in which Lincoln was sitting, as well as the car in which Kennedy was riding, when these presidents were assassinated. A letter from Clyde Barrow, bank robber of Bonnie and Clyde fame, to Henry Ford praised him for the speed of the Ford V8. It seems that vehicle was his car of choice when stealing cars for getaways.

Henry Ford Museum, 20900 Oakwood Blvd, Dearborn, MI 48124; ↘ 313 271 1620; web: www.hfmgv.org. *Open 9.00am–5.00pm; closed Thanksgiving and Christmas. Admission charge.*

Marvin Yagoda has somehow crammed his masses of historical and modern arcade machines, sideshow wonders, and curiosities into every square inch of available floor space at **Marvin's Marvelous Mechanical Museum** in Farmington Hills. Marvin, a 60-year-old pharmacist, admits the museum is a hobby that went way-y-y out of control.

You'll see fascinating old coin operated games, like the gypsy fortuneteller, right alongside modern video games. Here are neon, robots, and animation; signs, dummies, and planes, all clicking and clacking at once in a madhouse filled with his passion gone wild. Somehow, Marvin manages to keep all the games in operating condition. He also has a wicked sense of humor. There's a naked pinup poster of Burt Reynolds with a wooden figleaf covering his privates. Lift up the hinged leaf and a flash bulb goes off in your face.

> **Marvin's Marvelous Mechanical Museum**, 31005 Orchard Lake Rd, Farmington Hills, MI 48334; ↘ 248 626 5020; email: marv@marvin3m.com; web: www.marvin3m.com

Quirky cuisine

Rosie's Diner in Rockford is about two things: food and art. Jerry Berta and his wife, Madeline, bought a decrepit diner for $2,000, moved it to a vacant lot they owned, and restored it for use as an art studio and gallery in which to make and show their work. They did such a good job spiffing up the diner that folks flocked there to eat. So they put up a sign saying, 'No Food, Just Art', but folks still kept coming, buying art and asking for food.

So Jerry found another diner, moved it to his lot, and looked for someone to run the food side of the business since he knew absolutely nothing about it. While he was looking, they hung a sign one morning announcing the opening of the diner. By that evening they had to take down the sign; people were lined up to get in. During the next five years they served more than a million customers. Jerry offers 'Diner Camp' for anyone wanting to learn the business by washing dishes and clearing tables.

The art part is obvious when you see the miniature golf course they've set up. The holes have two themes: food and art. You can play through slabs of ribs, hamburgers, hot dogs, a teapot, tubes of paint, a brush, and a palette. Jerry specializes in outrageous, often bizarre ceramic and neon sculptures such as a domesticated, Godzilla-like figure zapping the kitchen sink with neon rays.

Jerry likes to keep things hopping. He's officially on the local ballot, running for office under the slogan 'I'm not a lawyer'.

> **Rosie's Diner**, 4500 14 Mile Rd, Rockford, MI 49341; ↘ 616 866 2787; web: www.rosiesdiner.com/rosypage.htm

The **Travelers Club International Restaurant and Tuba Museum** in Okemos is an eclectic little place run by Jennifer Boorke and William White. The travel theme is attributed to Jennifer, whose affinity for exotic food is reflected in the restaurant's menu. The tuba part is William's, whose passion for the instrument is evident in the collection.

The Travelers Club International Restaurant and Tuba Museum, 2138 Hamilton Rd, Okemos, MI 48864; ℡ 517 349 1701; web: www.travelerstuba.com

INDIANA
Festivals and events

There are real Munchkins to be seen at Duneland's annual **Wizard of Oz Festival**. Each year around 75,000 people converge on the little town to meet half-a-dozen of the actors who portrayed the original Munchkins in the Wizard of Oz movie and watch them lead the Oz Fantasy Parade in downtown Chesterton. The festival features Oz character look-alike contests, autograph sessions, Town Crier competitions and a collector's swap meet.

Wizard of Oz Fest held annually in September in Chesterton, IN. Contact Duneland Chamber of Commerce, 303 Broadway, Chesterton, IN 46304; ℡ 219 926 5513; fax: 219 926 7593

The Midland Arts and Antiques Market holds an annual **Outsider Art Show** which features pieces done by a dozen or more folks who don't consider themselves artists and who use strange things to create their non-art. Past exhibits have included pictures made out of bubble gum, a dinosaur made from car parts, furniture made from little bits of found objects, aerosol spray paint art and a series of images done by a woman with multiple personalities.

Outsider Art Show held annually in October in Indianapolis, IN. Contact Midland Arts and Antique Market, 907 E Michigan St, Indianapolis, IN 46202; ℡ 317 267 9005

Just plain weird

The town of **Santa Claus** is the only town in the world with a post office bearing the Santa Claus name. The Santa Lodge is a hotel decorated for Christmas year around; the adjoining theme and water park perpetually celebrates Christmas, along with the Fourth of July and Halloween. The place is kept squeaky clean by one of the eccentric owners, Mrs Koch, who, at age 68 can't stand seeing anything dirty. Santa Claus even has a Santa Claus cemetery.

Santa Claus located in Spencer County, IN. Contact Santa Claus Area Chamber of Commerce, PO Box 106, Santa Claus, IN 47579; ℡ 812 937 2848; fax: 812 937 4405

The **Indiana Shoe Tree** has been featured in newspapers, and on television and radio, for most of the 35 years in which it has been collecting thousands of pairs of shoes and other footwear. Originally local folks shoed it just for fun, but now that it's famous, people come from all over to tie their old laces together, then hurl their old shoes up into the white oak tree. Some people put their name and date on the soles before tossing them skyward. In winter you can truly see just how many shoes reside in the tree since there is no foliage to hide its contents.

Indiana Shoe Tree located along County-1, 6 miles south of Milltown, IN. Contact Maxine Archibald, Maxine's Market, Main St, Milltown, IN 47145; ☎ 812 633 4251

In **Greensburg**, the courthouse has trees growing from the roof of its tower. Way back in the 1870s, small sprigs were discovered growing from the tower. Over time, the sprigs blossomed into bushes and then into trees, threatening to collapse the structure. In 1888 all but one tree was removed. However, another tree made its appearance in another corner of the tower and today, both trees continue to thrive, towering over the tower by more than 100 feet.

Greensburg Courthouse located in Decatur County, IN. Contact City of Greensburg, 314 N Michigan, Greensburg, IN 47240; ☎ 812 663 3344; web: www.treecity.com

Museums and collections

The **Dan Quayle Center and Museum** in Huntington is a curious tribute to a former Vice President who made no contribution whatsoever except for his occasional displays of brain-dead aphorisms. He was famous for such Quayl-isms as 'If we don't succeed, we run the risk of failure' and 'A mind is a terrible thing to waste'. Many feel he couldn't pour water out of a boot even if the instructions were printed on the heel. Others think he's been terribly misjudged by an unforgiving press intent on reporting his every tongue-twisted blooper.

The museum, which is also a fascinating look at the Vice Presidency as a whole, is located on the Highway of Vice Presidents, so-called because three of them hailed from this 100-mile section of Indiana 9. One of the displays contains Dan's law diploma, torn to shreds by the family dog.

Dan Quayle Center and Museum, 815 Warren St, PO Box 856, Huntington, IN 46750; ☎ 219 256 6356; fax: 219 356 1455; email: info@quaylemuseum.org; web: www.quaylemuseum.org. *Open Tue–Sat 10.00am–4.00pm; Sun 1.00pm–4.00pm; closed Mon and major holidays. Admission free, donations suggested.*

DeVon Rose's hobby started innocently enough with some props for his son's train layout. Forty years later, he's still building miniatures out of toothpicks, popsicle sticks, wooden grape boxes, cardboard, candy wrappers and whatever other odds and ends strike his creative fancy. He uses steel wool, all fluffed out and spray painted, to make trees. Black pantyhose serves as screening material. His work is so detailed that he's been known to break a toothpick into thirteen pieces and still have a piece left over.

After getting hooked on the hobby, he began a model of his hometown, just as it was in the 1960s, right down to broken windows and construction mistakes. Finished with that, he added buildings surrounding the town, then decided to add landmark buildings from each of the 92 counties in Indiana. Numbering 200 now, his buildings are accurately scaled re-creations of such state landmarks as the Dan Quayle Museum and the courthouse in Greensburg that has the trees growing out of its tower. His most recent accomplishment is the Bag Factory Building; it took 2,438 toothpicks, 588 popsicle sticks, and five months of 40–60-hour weeks to complete it. At this rate he could end up with the entire state of Indiana in miniature.

You can visit his 'town', fully equipped with lights, fences, signs, and streetlights, at his **Bird's Eye View Museum of Miniatures** in Wakarusa. During your tour he'll dim the lights so you can see the intricate lighting he installs in his buildings. His figures of people are all characters with personalities; he delights in telling you their 'stories'.

Bird's Eye View Museum of Miniatures, 325 S Elkhart St, Wakarusa, IN 46573; ↘ 219 862 2367; email: LndRose@cs.com

Also made from toothpicks, 421,000 of them to be exact, is a six foot long, fully detailed steam locomotive. Weighing in at 50 pounds, it took builder Terry Woodling seven years to construct. See it at the **National New York Central Railroad Museum** in Elkhart.

National New York Central Railroad Museum, 721 S Main St, Elkhart, IN 46515; ↘ 219 294 3001; web: nycrrmuseum.railfan.net. *Open Tue–Fri 10.00am–2.00pm; Sat 10.00am–4.00pm; Sun 12.00noon–4.00pm; closed Mon and major holidays.*

Dr Ted's Musical Marvels in Dale is the local doc's personal collection of self-playing musical instruments from around the world. His huge collection includes nickelodeons, music boxes, gramophones, player pianos, street organs and an enormous 24-foot by 12-foot dance organ.

Dr Ted's Musical Marvels located at Exit 57, Hwy 231, (½ mile north of I-64), Dale, IN. Contact RR 2, Box 30A, Dale, IN 47523; ↘ 812 937 4250

You want autopsy tables and brains in jars? Try the **Indiana Medical History Museum** in Indianapolis, housed in the old Pathology Department of the former Central State Hospital.

Indiana Medical History Museum, 3045 W Vermont St, Indianapolis, IN; ↘ 317 635 7329; fax: 317 635 7349; email: edenharter@aol.com; web: www.imhm.org. *Open Thu–Sat 10.00am–4.00pm. Wed by appointment. Admission charge.*

James Dean, popular movie star and culture icon of the 1960s, was born and buried in Grant County. At Fairmount's **James Dean Memorial Gallery**, David Loehr, an all-time Dean guru, has assembled the largest collection of Dean memorabilia in the world. Besides hundreds of novelty items with the actor's likeness, such as lighters, snow domes, and key chains, his address book, his school papers, his motorcycle and his Oscar are all here; and he has a copy of the speeding ticket Dean received just hours before his fatal accident.

> **James Dean Memorial Gallery**, 425 N Main St, PO Box 55, Fairmount, IN 46928; ✎ 765 948 3326; fax: 765 948 3389; web: www.jamesdeangallery.com. *Open 10.00am–6.00pm daily.*

Quirky cuisine

An ostrich egg omelet is the equivalent of a dozen to two dozen eggs, and you can order one at the **Buffalo Run Grill and Gifts** in Lincoln City. You can also dine on ostrich and buffalo steaks, gazing out the window at the sources of your meal. The gift shop sells buffalo chips, buffalo foot lamps and walking sticks made from buffalo penises.

> **Buffalo Run Grill and Gifts**, Hwy 162, Box 28, Lincoln City, IN 47552; ✎ 812 397 2799 or 812 397 2731

How about 'garbage' for breakfast? **Cindy's Diner** in Fort Wayne, whose motto is 'serving the whole world 15 at a time', has only 15 stools at the counter. 'Garbage', a mixture of eggs, green pepper and cheese, is the best selling item on the menu.

> **Cindy's Diner**, 830 S Harrison, F. Wayne, IN; ✎ 219 422 1957

Quirky quarters

FantaSuites in Greenwood at the **Red Carpet Inn** has 24 suites, each decorated with its own theme. The Alien Invasion suite has a flying saucer bed surrounded by rock formations, Cinderella has a queen sized, horse-drawn carriage bed and glass slipper whirlpool, while Cupid's Corner has a heart-shaped bed and mirrored ceiling. Tours are held any Saturday or Sunday at 3pm or you can buy a video in the lobby.

> **Red Carpet Inn and Fantasuites**, 1117 E Main St, Greenwood, IN 46143; ✎ 317 882 2211; fax: 317 885 0657

OHIO
Festivals and events

The **Ohio State Fair** in Des Moines has featured **Butter Sculptures** since the early 1900s. There's always been a butter cow accompanied by other sculptures paying tribute to Ohio themes. Over the years, featured sculptures have included Dave Thomas, the founder of Wendy's hamburger chain, Darth

Vader of *Star Wars* fame, astronauts Neil Armstrong and John Glenn, a tribute to the Columbus Zoo and a tribute to milk delivery.

About 1,000 pounds of butter goes into the annual displays, which take two to four weeks to carve. The butter is applied to welded steel frames and the sculptures typically last about as long as the fair's two weeks. Then the butter turns rancid and is scraped off the frames. Power outages are a butter sculpture's worst nightmare. Without refrigeration, the sculptures turn into giant blobs of melted butter. The fair's top butter-meister recently retired after a 30-year career.

> **Butter Sculpture Display at Ohio State Fair.** ↘ 888 646 3976 or 614 644 3247. *Open 9.00am–9.00pm daily in the Dairy Products Building. Free admission to display.*

Just plain weird

Any basket that can hold 500 people is one B-I-G basket – big as in occupying seven stories and 180,000 square feet, with 84 windows, and weighing in at 9,000 tons. The basket, complete with handles and a 25-foot logo tag, is actually a building housing the home offices of the **Longaberger Basket Company** in Newark; it's undoubtedly the largest – and only – basket building in the world. A short distance away, the company has built the largest basket monument in the world, a replica of their famous apple basket.

The building itself represents the company's most popular market basket. If it seems strange to you that a company would go to such trouble to memorialize a basket, consider this: LBC's basket fans come from all over to worship at the basket shrines and to have their own baskets autographed by the company.

The Longaberger Experience in Dresden involves a tour of the manufacturing campus; a visit to the gift shop; a tour of the Homestead, a mini theme park that pays tribute to the company and their values; and a tour of the basket building. The company even owns and operates its own hotel, The Place off the Square, and its own golf course. This is corporate quirkiness at its finest.

> **Longaberger Basket Company**, 1500 East Main St, Newark, OH 43055; ↘ 740 322 5000; web: www.longaberger.com

In the **Marion Cemetery** is a Ripley's Believe it or Not attraction, a mysteriously revolving, 5,200-pound black granite ball marking the Merchant family plot. Since it was placed there in 1896, the ball has been turning up to two inches per year as measured by the movement of the unpolished area where the ball was placed on its pedestal.

Another grave oddity in Marion County lies in the right of way of a small country road in the county near. When John Grimm was killed by a falling tree in 1833, he was buried where he fell. His grave later ended up being right alongside the roadway, where he remains to this day.

Marion Cemetery, Marion, OH. Contact Marion Area Convention and Visitors Bureau, 1952 Marion-Mt Gilead Rd, Marion, OH 43302; ↘ 800 371 6688; fax: 740 389 9770; web: www.mariononline.com/visitors

What distinguishes the **Field of Corn** in Dublin from thousands of others is that the 109 of the ears are human sized sculptures made of concrete. The field is meant to dramatize the plight of farms being overrun with urban development.

Field of Corn, Sam and Eulalia Frantz Park, Columbus, OH. Contact Greater Columbus Chamber of Commerce, 37 North High St, Columbus, OH 43215; ↘ 614 221 1321; fax: 614 221 9360; web: www.columbus-chamber.org

Attractions

At the **Living Bible Museum** in Mansfield, you take a 'walk of faith' through the bible, encountering along the way 41 dioramas made of wax. Divided into Old Testament and New Testament tour sections, the audio recordings, made by volunteers, bring God's words to life.

The museum was inspired by Pastor Richard Diamond's 1970s vision of such a place. He and his wife Alwilda began searching for figures that could turn their dream into reality. Discouraged that new wax and fiberglass figures were so costly, they prayed they'd find some used ones. Hearing of a defunct outdoor bible walk, they made contact with the owner, who miraculously agreed to donate his 22 weathered figures to the cause. Church members donated their skills, framing the scenes, reconstructing the figures, making the costumes, styling the hair, writing the scripts, and recording the audio. The museum is maintained through the efforts of dozens of dedicated volunteers

There's also has a large collection of Votive Folk Art, ie: bible scenes made from jewelry, hat pins, tie pins, beadwork, cuff links, collar studs and coins.

Living Bible Museum, 500 Tingley Ave, Mansfield, OH; ↘ 419 524 0139; web: www.livingbiblemuseum.org

Museums and collections

There are 64 pieces of carved wood, bone and ivory in Ernest Warther's History of Steam display, part of an extraordinary collection of carved wood locomotives and trains that toured the country in the early 1900s. Henry Ford once offered to buy the collection, but Warther turned him down, opting instead to return home with his hobby. He never sold any of his carvings, and the few he gave away have been returned to complete the **Warther's Carving Museum** in Dover. You can see more than 200 of his carvings there, along with those of his grandson, David, who started carving at the age of six. David's passion is making ships; 33 of his ivory miniatures are on display.

Warther's Carving Museum, 331 Karl Ave, Dover, OH 44622.
Located less than 4 hours from downtown Cincinnati, in northeastern
Ohio, south of Canton on I-77. ➍ 330 343 7513; email:
info@warthers.com; web: www.warthers.com. *Open
9.00am–5.00pm daily. Admission charge.*

One man's efforts to hold greedy developers at bay in Hamilton resulted in a
preserve known as the **Pyramid Hill Sculpture Park and Museum**, created
by Harry Wilkes who bought a 40-acre parcel of prime land in 1984. After
clearing the land, constructing roads, installing ponds and building himself a
7,000 square foot underground house, he dotted the landscape with sculptural
antiquities from Greece, Italy, and Egypt. He was later approached to sell the
land to a developer who was planning to subdivide it and build homes. Wilkes
was so miffed at the developer's lack of appreciation for his efforts that he started
buying up land all around his creation, ultimately ending up with 265 acres.

The park is now an outdoor museum with monumental, contemporary
sculptures added to his antiquities. It's an environment of meadows, forests,
lakes, streams, and gardens, one of only three such parks in the US. Coming
on provocative sculpture in such a setting has a profound and memorable
effect. It's a good thing there are some people who can't be bought; it's clearly
poetic justice that Harry got the last laugh.

Pyramid Hill Sculpture Park and Museum, 222 High St, Suite
201, Hamilton, OH 45011; ➍ 513 868 8336; web:
www.pyramidhill.org

A larger-than-life journey through the human body involves a giant ear, eye,
hand, mouth and nose connected to a giant brain. As you interact with the body
parts, the brain connections light up and signals turn on the part of the brain
used to process each sensation. The **Health Museum of Cleveland** is filled
with such off-the-wall ways of learning. Inside the ear, you ring a bell and
watch the ear drum and ear bones move as sound vibrations are transmitted to
the brain. Stand in front of the eye while someone
else peers into the retina and you'll understand
how the iris works. Try to figure out what kind
of things the hand is touching by looking at the
brain's response. In the mouth, put tasty things
on the tongue to learn where certain flavors are
detected. In the dental area, a giant tooth is 18
feet high and weighs 4,000 pounds. It's so big
you'd need the highway department to do a root
canal. Other exhibits involve 'sperm' marbles,
that have to pass obstacles to fertilize an egg, and
an opportunity to construct a two-year-old
child. There's also a transparent talking woman.

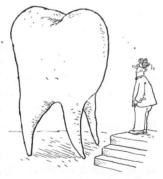

This is one wacky museum. It's enough to make you wonder if anything in the brain would light up if they had a Lazy-Boy, a TV, and a remote control hooked up to it.

Health Museum of Cleveland, 8911 Euclid Ave, Cleveland, OH 44106; ↘ 216 231 5010; fax: 216 231 5129; web: www.healthmuseum.org

NORTH DAKOTA
Just plain weird

A 45-foot tower of tin cans, referred to as the **Casselton Can Pile**, is an accidental example of recycling dating from the 1930s. Made from oil cans discarded by a gas station, the tower grew as the empty cans were tossed into a wire enclosure. Today it's become the state's largest accidental birdhouse. It seems the spout holes are just big enough to attract hundreds of nesting sparrows.

Casselton Can Pile located along the I-94 Frontage Rd, Casselton, ND. Contact City of Casselton, North Dakota; web: www.casselton.com

Along the 30 miles of highway between Regent and Gladstone, you'll see the most unlikely of giant creatures. The world's largest grasshopper is the most recent addition to **The Enchanted Highway**, the brainchild of sculptor Gary Greff. The grasshopper joins a family made of tin, a 75-foot high flock of pheasants and Teddy Roosevelt on a horse. More sculptures are planned with the idea of creating a tourist mecca that would benefit the towns at both ends of the highway.

The Enchanted Highway, located off I-94,10 miles west of Dickinson; take the Gladstone exit, head south 25 miles.

On the wide-open prairie, you need to make things big if you want to get attention. **Og** is a two-and-a-half ton gorilla built out of steel, chicken wire and foam insulation. The **world's largest** – and possibly ugliest – **buffalo**, resides in Jamestown. Built out of concrete, it weighs in at 60 tons; you could hold a family reunion between its legs, if you wanted to. In Dunseith, the **world's largest turtle** is made from more than 2,000 steel wheel rims, painted green. The one-ton head bobs up and down, just like the real thing. And the world's largest dairy cow, dubbed **Salem Sue**, stands 40 feet tall in the town of New Salem. Even in the deepest snowdrifts, you can't miss these roadside giants.

CANADA

N DAKOTA, S DAKOTA & NEBRASKA

World's Largest
Turtle, Bottineau

Northern Lights
Tower, Rugby

Williston

Minot

Devils Lake

Missouri

Lake
Sakakawea

Paul Broste's
Museum, Parshall

Grand Forks

Crookston

N O R T H   D A K O T A

Og, Two and a Half
Ton Gorilla, Harvey

Hobo House,
McHenry

Carrington

Casselton Can Pile,
Cassselton

Little Missouri

Belfield

BISMARCK

Gladstone

Salem Sue,
New Salem

Jamestown

Fargo

Moorhead

dive

MONTANA

Enchanted
Highway

Regent

Lake
Oahe

Bowman

Hunter's Table &
Tavern, Rhame

Petrified Wood Park
& Museum, Lemmon

Mobridge

International Vinegar
Museum, Roslyn

Aberdeen

MINNESOTA

S O U T H   D A K O T A

Shoe House,
Webster

Ortonville

Willmar

Old style saloon #10,
Deadwood

Lake Oahe

Clark

Crazy Horse
Memorial,
Crazy Horse

Sturgis Motorcycle
Rally, Sturgis

Mt Rushmore, Keystone

Cheyenne

PIERRE

Redfield

Bedrock City, Custer

Huron

Black Hills Maze
The Black Hills

Rapid City

Wall Drug Store, Wall

James

Porter Sculpture Park,
Lawrence

Luverne

WYOMING

Winner

Corn Palace,
Mitchell

Souix Falls

Sioux Sundries,
Harrison

Chadron

Outhouse Museum,
Gregory

Spencer

Missouri

Valentine

Bassett

IOWA

Sioux City

Car Henge, Alliance

Scottsbluff

Wayne Chicken Show
& Cluck-Off Contest,
Wayne

N E B R A S K A

Bill's Food Mart, Howells

Fremont

N Platte

North Platte

Merle block's Sod House,
Gothenburg

Grand Island

Umaha

Julesburg

Sterling

S Platte

Fort Kearney Museum,
Kearney

LINCOLN

Avoca Quack-Off,
Avoca

MO

COLORADO

N

Hastings Museum,
Hastings

sburg

Limon

Burlington

McCook

Beatrice

Stockton

Marysville

0 ——————— 150km

0 ——————— 150 miles

Oakley

K A N S A S

Hays

Riley

Junction City

TOPEKA

World's Largest Buffalo located off Hwy 94, at the junction of I-94 and Hwy 281; take exit 258, at the National Buffalo Museum and Frontier Village, Jamestown, ND; ↘ 701 252 8648 or 800 22 BISON; web: www.jamestownnd.com

World's Largest Turtle located in Tommy Turtle Park one block north of Hwy 5, on the east edge of Bottineau, ND. 103 S 11th St E, Bottineau, ND

Salem Sue located off Hwy 94, exit 127, New Salem, ND

Og located US Hwy 52, Harvey, ND. Contact Harvey Chamber of Commerce; ↘ 701 324 2604

Another buffalo, this time a real one, really stands out from the herd. Known as **White Cloud, the sacred white buffalo**, she's an extremely rare albino buffalo. You can see her at the National Buffalo Museum and Frontier Village in Jamestown.

White Cloud located at the National Buffalo Museum and Frontier Village, Jamestown, ND; ↘ 701 252 8648 or 800 22 BISON; web: www.jamestownnd.com

The Northern Lights are nature's way of compensating for the brutal weather endured by people living in the far north. The town of Rugby, the geographic center of North America, celebrates this phenomenon with the 90-foot **Northern Lights Tower**. All lit up at night, it draws your eye to nature's multi-hued light show.

Northern Lights Tower located at junction of Hwy 2 and 3, Rugby, ND; ↘ 701 776 5846

Attractions

During the heyday of the railroads, hobos had a secret 'language', leaving markings around rail yards that only other hobos could understand. Sometimes the markings were warnings, sometimes greetings. When the railroad put up a storage shed in the town of Lamert, it became a hobo version of email. When a tramp wanted to leave a message, he'd carve it in the wood, then move on. Today, the **Hobo House** resides in McHenry, an old-fashioned reminder that communication wasn't always so instantaneous. Each year the town holds an annual Hobo Festival, with everyone dressing like tramps and eating hobo stew.

Hobo House located near the McHenry Loop on Hwy 20 between Devils Lake and Jamestown; ↘ 701 785 2333

Museums and collections

Some of Paul Broste's sculptures at his **Rock Museum** in Parshall look like floor lamps gone bad, while the building itself, which houses his life long obsession with boulders, rocks, and crystals, looks like a psychedelic version of medieval. The farmer turned artist built his museum in the hopes that people would come to appreciate his hundreds of sculptures, painting, poems and, of course, rocks.

All manner of rocks and minerals were his passion, and his collection grew to include some of the finest specimens from all over the world. He cut, ground, and polished them into spheres and slabs, then suspended them, science project style, in space and swirling up the walls. In the hexagonal Infinity Room, he used mirrors to reflect the spheres, so they appear to be forever floating in endless space.

> **Paul Broste's Rock Museum**, ND Hwy 1804 and ND Hwy 37, Parshall, ND; located south of Hwy 23 in central ND; ☎ 701 862 3459

Quirky cuisine

The **Hunter's Table and Tavern** in Rhame is a unique roadhouse constructed of 16-inch thick walls made from masonry that resembles stacks of logs. Light pours in through the wine bottles cemented into the walls. Sawdust provides the insulation. An all-female construction crew built the structure in 1983.

> **Hunter's Table and Tavern** located on Hwy 12 Rhame, ND 58651; ☎ 701 279 6689

SOUTH DAKOTA
Festivals and events

At the annual Potato Days Festival in Clark, the most popular event is **Mashed Potato Wrestling**. The festival also features a potato parade and potato sculptures.

> **Mashed Potato Wrestling** held annually during Potato Days in July in Clark, SD. Contact Clark Area Chamber of Commerce, PO Box 163, Clark, SD 57225; email: clarksd@itctel.com; web: www.clarksd.com/potato/potatowrestling.htm

For the 285,000 motorcycle enthusiasts who invade the town of Sturgis every August, the **Sturgis Motorcycle Rally** is the ultimate experience of the open road. Sixty years old, the annual event started with a small motorcycle race and stunt competition. As the cycling lifestyle gained in popularity, more and more riders flooded to the scenic rally. Today, the festival draws enthusiasts from every walk of life, dispelling the notion that motorcyclists are big, dumb brutes just itching for a brawl. The crowd creates a tidal wave of bikes and people, participating in competitions and cruising to such scenic sites as Mount Rushmore, the Crazy Horse Monument, and the Badlands of the Black Hills region.

Sturgis Motorcycle Rally held annually in August in Sturgis, SD.
Contact Premier Rally Services, Inc., PO Box 189, Sturgis, SD 57785;
↘ 605 347 5670; email: premier@sturgisrallynews.com; web:
www.sturgisrallynews.com

Just plain weird

Most everyone has heard of **Mount Rushmore**, even if they can't name the
presidents carved into the face of the mountain. The mountain is perhaps the
world's largest monument to eccentricity, the result of the relentless pursuit of
a vision by sculptor Gurzon Borglum.

The nearby **Crazy Horse Memorial** isn't nearly as well known, but the
story behind it is no less eccentric. Depicting the Lakota Indian leader,
Crazy Horse, sculptor Korczak Ziolloswki began the project in 1948
because the native tribe wanted to let the white man know 'the red man has
great heroes, too'. The sculptor had just $174 to his name when he started,
living in a tent for seven months while he built a log home. With his wife,
Ruth, he had ten sons and daughters, all of whom became dedicated to the
Herculean task of carving a figure 563 feet high and 641 feet long. The face
alone is nine stories high and took 50 years to achieve. It's so large that all
four faces on Mount Rushmore would fit inside Crazy Horse's head; the
figure's outstretched arm will be almost as long as a football field. Both
monuments are testimony to compulsive tenacity, a common trait among
eccentrics.

Mount Rushmore located in Keystone, SD. Contact Superintendent,
Mount Rushmore National Memorial, PO Box 268, Keystone, SD
57751; ↘ 605 574 2523; web: www.nps.gov/moru

Crazy Horse Memorial, Crazy Horse, SD. Contact Crazy Horse
Memorial Foundation, Avenue of the Chiefs, Crazy Horse, SD 57730;
↘ 605 673 4681; fax: 605 673 2185; email:
memorial@crazyhorse.org; web: www.crazyhorse.org. *Open daily
7.00am–dark summer; 8.00am–5.00pm winter.*

Ken Bell has quite a reputation for strange outdoor sculpture. How about seven,
red Ford sedans marching upright in a parade? He got the idea for that one after
his wife ran their car up on a rock. He couldn't pull it off, so he just added more
to cover up the mishap. Or, how about collection of rusty, bent culverts sprouting
from the ground in a 'tribute' to the troops who fought in the Gulf War?

You never know what you expect when you visit Ken's field of folly west of
Clark. He gets a big kick out of people coming up to him after being told 'You
have to go and talk to Ken Bell, Sr about that stuff out in the pasture'. He'll
usually tell you some crazy guy made it and he has no idea where he might be.
Other times he'll tell you 'Frank Johnson' did it. He calls his stuff
'conversation pieces', designed to provoke lively conversation.

Ken Bell, RR 2, Box 71, Clark, SD 57225; ↘ 605 532 3209

Porter Sculpture Park in St Lawrence features the work of Wayne Porter, a welder who sculpts creatures from scrap metal in his spare time. In the tiny park outside his shop you can see his fantastic creations, including a gigantic fish that spurts water, playful dragons, delicate ballerinas and a host of other colorful characters.

Porter Sculpture Park, PO Box 127, Lawrence, SD 57573; ↘ 605 853 2266

Attractions

It's been said that as many people have heard of **Wall Drug** as have heard of Monica Lewinisky. Now that's a lot of people. But then Wall Drug has had 70 years to build its reputation and it didn't take television to spread the word. Instead, the word was spread with old-fashioned signage, beginning back in the Depression years when cars didn't come with air conditioning.

Ted and Dorothy Wall opened a tiny drugstore in 1931 in the middle of nowhere. Business was slow, so Dorothy suggested tempting people in by putting up a sign advertising free ice water. Ted thought the idea silly, but he listened to her anyway and the rest is history. Folks showed up in droves to cool down. Once Ted saw the value of signs, he went sign-crazy, plastering the landscape with billboards advertising his drug store from coast to coast. The whole point of stopping at Wall Drug became, well … stopping at Wall Drug. By the time they added five-cent coffee, Wall Drug had become a must-see rest stop on the road across the plains. (Isn't there a lesson in here somewhere for husbands?)

But the signage didn't stop with billboards. He printed up souvenir signs, giving them away and imploring folks to post them anywhere and everywhere. They've ended up in some of the most remote places on earth. Servicemen from the state post them all over the globe, as does almost every visitor who's been there in the last 60 years.

The sight itself does America proud as a tourist trap, offering the best in roadside activities: plenty of funky photo ops, giant animals, an arcade, clean rest rooms, plenty of shopping, food, and, of course, free ice water and five-cent coffee. When the freeway was built, bypassing Wall Drug, they erected an 80-foot dinosaur just in case you missed the signs leading to it.

Wall Drug Store, PO Box 401, 510 Main St, Wall, SD 57790; ↘ 605 279 2175; fax: 605 279 2699; email: walldrug@gwtc.net; web: www.walldrug.com

Yabba-dabba-doo! Flintstones – meet the Flintstones – at their **Bedrock City** theme park in Custer. Just like the cartoon, the park has all the familiar rock buildings along with Fred, Barney, Wilma, Betty, Pebbles and Dino. There's a Flintmobile, a drive-in serving Brontoburgers and Dino Dogs, an animated show and Mount Rockmore, a spoof of the big guys down the road.

Bedrock City, Box 649, Custer, SD 57730; ➘ 605 673 4079 or 800 992 9818. Located southwest of Custer, SD near Hwy US 16 and 385.

In Mitchell the world's only **Corn Palace** has been drawing visitors for a hundred years. The palace, shaped like a castle topped with minarets, is 'upholstered' on the exterior with corn, grain, and grass, 3,000 bushels worth. Each year, the designs are redone and colorful new murals go up depicting the current theme. The palace was built in 1892 to prove how rich the soil is in the region.

Corn Palace, 601 N Main, Mitchell, SD 57301; ➘ 605 996 7311 or 800 257 CORN; web: www.cornpalace.com. *Open varied hours year-round; call for information. Admission free.*

The **Black Hills Maze** in Rapid City is a 37,000 square foot, two-story high labyrinth. This is for serious mazeophiles who have to conquer the towers, then try to escape. Real addicts can load up for paint ball games.

Black Hills Maze located 3 miles south of Rapid City on Hwy 16 on the left. ➘ 605 343 5439; web: www.blackhillsmaze.com. *Open May 1–Sept 30, 9.00am–9.00pm.*

It's the only museum in the country in a bar. The **Old Style Saloon #10** in Deadwood was the site where Wild Bill Hickock met his demise. Live re-enactments of the dastardly deed take place daily and the saloon is laden with artifacts from his life. Doeskin figures of Calamity Jane, Wild Bill himself, and Potato Creek Johnny watch over the premises. Maybe they turned outlaw because the other school kids teased them about their names.

The Old Style Saloon, #10, 657 Main St, Deadwood, SD; ➘ 605 578 3346; web: www.saloon10.com.

Museums and collections

There are far more shoes than people in Webster, South Dakota thanks to Mildred O'Neil, a former librarian who moved her 7,000 plus shoe collection to the tiny town in 1994. With a population of just 2,000 souls, Webster welcomed Mildred and her collection to the Wildlife, Industry, and Science Museum by building the **Shoe House**, a two story, shoe-shaped building, to house her collection of soles. Every shoe has its own card, describing its acquisition and its history, in her meticulously kept card catalog. The collection grows monthly as folks from all over send her more shoes.

Mildred's been collecting shoes and shoe-related items since her teens. She's in her mid-70s now which pretty much makes her a world authority on the subject. The shoes, ranging in size from miniature to clown size, are classified into 22 categories, including jewelry, cowboy, sport, straw, children's and baby shoes. Her workshop displays old shoemaking techniques as well as a cobbler's sign, shaped like a boot, that has a bullet hole in it. She once got together with two other major collectors; they only found three duplicate pairs of shoes.

During the season, Mildred can often be found at the museum, dusting the displays and re-arranging the objects of her affection. Occasionally she even dresses up as 'The Old Woman who Lived in a Shoe'. During the winter she'll be happy to meet you at the museum if you call ahead for an appointment.

> **The Shoe House**, Museum of Wildlife, Industry, and Science, W Highway 12, Webster, SD 57274; ➘ 605 345 4751; web: www.webstersd.com/activities/museum

All you'll ever need (or want) to know about vinegar is explained for you at the **International Vinegar Museum** in Roslyn, whose mission is to educate visitors about the 'sour power' of vinegar. You'll learn how vinegar is made in factories, villages and homes all over the world, see vinegar paper, taste vinegars made from all kinds of plants and shop at the most complete vinegar store on the planet.

> **International Vinegar Museum**, Main St, Roslyn, SD; web: www.vinegarman.com. *Open 10.00am–6.00pm Tue–Sat Jun 1–Oct 31.*

Do six items constitute a museum? They do if they're outhouses and six examples probably cover the subject pretty thoroughly. Each of the outdoor toilets (used in the days before indoor plumbing) is named, with a story behind it, at the **South Dakota Outhouse Museum** in Gregory.

> **South Dakota Outhouse Museum**, Napers Emporium, 520 Main St, Gregory, SD 57533; ➘ 605 835 8002

The **Petrified Wood Park and Museum** in Lemmon consists of strange, man-made formations built in the 1930s from petrified wood. The sculptors were unemployed and untrained in art; they worked in exchange for food. There's a castle, a wishing well, a water fountain, and numerous ugly pyramids. The museum itself is petrified wood, too, with displays about as stimulating as bait.

> **Petrified Wood Park and Museum**, 500 Main Ave, Lemmon, SD 57638; ➘ 605 374 5716 or 5760; fax: 605 374 5332; web: www.dakota-web.com/lemmon/about

NEBRASKA
Festival and events
It doesn't get much nuttier than the **Wayne Chicken Show**. At the show's Cluck-Off contest, each contestant imitates either a rooster or a hen. Hopeful

champs have to strut their stuff for at least 15 seconds, trying mightily to sound like a chicken, be heard like a chicken and act like a chicken, all while remembering to stop in under 60 seconds. Hen-picked judges declare the winner. The 1999 champ appeared on Jay Leno's famous late night talk show.

The Chickendale Male Dancers, wearing paper bags over their heads to conceal the identity of the owners of these less-than-physically fit, chicken struttin' bods, are a sight to behold. And the weekend wouldn't be complete without the chicken hat contest; the most beautiful beak and chicken legs competitions; the barehanded egg drop catch – raw eggs dropped from 40 feet up; and a hardboiled egg eating contest. The festival even has a chicken coupe – a 1967, egg-yolk yellow, Cadillac Coupe de Ville with a 12-foot rooster mounted on the trunk.

Wayne Chicken Show and Cluck-Off Contest, Wayne, NE. Contact Wayne Chamber of Commerce, 108 West 3rd St, Wayne, NE 68787; ☎ 402 375 2240; email: chamber@bloomnet.com; web: www.chickenshow.com

Beer and boredom are responsible for the **Avoca Quack-Off**, an annual event involving ducks and an ice covered tennis court. Clipped-wing ducks are prodded across the ice by humans, who may do anything except touch the ducks, to get them across the finish line. Beer clearly helps.

The event began 17 years ago with three ducks, three guys and a substantially higher number of beers. There isn't a lot to do mid-winter in this tiny town of 250 people, and the idea of a duck race became mighty appealing.

Today, the Quack-Off fund-raiser almost triples the town's population as folks come from all over to rent a duck and watch a gang of duck jockeys make fools of themselves on the Webb Foot Raceway. And what becomes of the losing ducks? Lunch, of course.

Avoca Quack-off held annually in Avoca, NE. Contact David Seay ☎ 402 275 3221

The **Nebraska Story Telling Festival** in Omaha, started by four librarians, brings almost 2,000 folks to a weekend of old fashioned entertainment

Story Telling Festival held annually in June in Omaha, NE. Contact Storytelling Festival of Nebraska, 1803 S 58th St, Omaha, NE 68106; ☎ 402 551 4532 or 800 551 4532; email: storygalore@home.com; web: www.storygalore.com

Previous page Mashed potato wrestling at Potato Days in South Dakota (CC)

Above and below Dr Evermore plans to shoot himself into space in his Wisconsin Forevertron. (LH)

Just plain weird

Carhenge, near Alliance, is a replica of Britain's Stonehenge, only this one is made out of cars that are very nearly the same dimensions as those of the famous stones. The cars, 1950s and 1960s models, are planted trunk-down in the ground, with capstone cars perched on top. The number of gray cars welded together in formation, exactly matches the number of stones at the real Stonehenge. The structure is one of the most eccentric in America. Suprisingly, more than half of the visitors to Carhenge don't even know that it's a spoof of one of the world's most mysterious monuments.

Jim Reinders, who originated the idea and lived on the farm on which it sits, dedicated Carhenge on the summer solstice of 1987. Two years later it was in danger of being declared a junk yard and in violation of zoning regulations. When the site was threatened with destruction, thousands of people rallied to its defense. Eventually Carhenge gained government approval and elevated in rank from junk yard to tourist attraction, an approach that could well be applied to a vast number of American roadside stops.

> **Carhenge** located north of Alliance, NE, along Hwy 87. Contact Friends of Carhenge, PO Box 464, Alliance, NE 69301; web: www.carhenge.com

Attractions

Smack dab in the middle of America's conservative heartland lies a new-age mecca called **Prairie Peace Park**. The park's exhibits hope to promote and explain peace, pointing out that war, violence and exploitation are only temporary setbacks that can be eliminated when we're all of one mind.

A visit here includes the World Map of Children's Visions – it's made of film canisters. Farm tool sculptures depict the struggle of farm families while an 80-foot labyrinth of flower-covered mounds help you find inner peace and peace with others You can even play at creating your own peaceful world in a 12-ton sandbox.

In the Turtle Maze you try find your way to all four legs of the turtle, then make a wish for the planet. Artists from all over the world have contributed 1,000 footprints in the 120-foot World Peace Mural. Prairie Peace Park's website provides a forum for futuristic, confrontational and frank discussions of world events.

> **Prairie Peace Park** located at Pleasant Dale/Crete exit (exit 388) next to I 80, seven miles west of Lincoln, NE; �‌ 402 466 6622; web: www.igc.org/PeacePark

Museums and collections

How odd can odds and ends get? Try the **Museum of the Odd** in Lincoln, where Charlie Johnson displays oddities that cover almost every square inch of his house, including floors, walls, and ceilings. What makes this such an astounding place is not that the objects themselves are so odd, but rather that the sheer number of them is so overwhelming.

Charlie's life-long collection of bric-à-brac includes Beta videocassette tapes, severed doll heads, squeaky rubber animals, comic books, bubble bath containers, plastic banks, religious icons, macabre trinkets and so very, very much more, all meticulously organized. Dennis the Menace was Charlie's role model as a child, so its not surprising he'd be up to such mischief himself.

Museum of the Odd, 701 Y Street, Lincoln, NE; ☎ 402 476 6735. *Admission free.*

Samurai warriors, shrunken heads, and dinosaur egg fragments typify the totally unrelated stuff from all over the world displayed at the **Fort Kearney Museum**. Guns, teeth, shoes, whatever – the idiosyncratic collection makes for a nice break from the road.

Fort Kearney Museum located one block north and one block east of the Kearney I-80 interchange. 131 South Central Ave, Kearney, NE; ☎ 308 234 5200. *Open 10.30am–5.30pm Thur–Sat; 1.00–5.00pm Sun, Memorial Day–Labor Day. Admission charge.*

Bill's Food Mart in Howells displays the owner Bill Wisnieski's collection of 900 cookie jars, representing three decades of collecting. Dating from 1930, you can see Disney cookie jars, such as Goofy driving a school bus along with jars depicting cowboys Roy Rogers, Gene Autry, and Hopalong Cassidy. No free cookies to go along with these jars, but you might pick up a donut.

Bill's Food Mart, 112 South Third St, Howells, Colfax County, KS; ☎ 402 986 1141. *Open 7.30am–6.00pm Mon–Sat.*

Merle Block built a sod house on the prairie, cutting, hauling, and stacking 70 tons of sod before he was done. The sod is knitted together with bluestem roots and buffalo grasses; the inside walls are covered with mud, whitewashed with lime and water. If you've ever heard the expression, 'sleep tight', it came from the way a sod house bed is constructed: ropes serve as bedsprings and had to be pulled tight to get a good night's sleep. A full size buffalo made out of four and a half miles of barbed wire sits out front, accompanied by a barbed wire Indian on a horse. The house, in Gothenburg, is now the **Sod House Museum**.

Merle Block's Sod House, Gothenburg, NE. Located at the northwest corner of I-80 interchange at Gothenburg; ☎ 308 537 2076. *Open 9.00am–6.00pm daily May–Sept, 8.00am–8.00pm Jun–Aug. Admission free.*

The **Hastings Museum** has just one eccentric exhibit, but it's a doozy. Find the wooden case with the stuffed rattlesnake on the first floor. Call over the family, then press the secret button. The rattles buzz, rattling the nerves of the unsuspecting.

Hastings Museum, 1330 N Burlington Ave, Hastings NE 68901; ➘ 402 461 2399; web: www.hastingsnet.com/museum. *Open 9.00am–5.00pm Mon–Sat, 11.00am–5.00pm Sun. Admission charge.*

Shopping

The **Fort Cody Trading Post** is one of those places where you can spend hours gazing in amazement at how many truly tacky things are sold in gift shops. While they also carry quality items, it's the tasteless trinkets that will delight. The front of the building has mannequins dressed and posed as cavalry soldiers and Indians. It must be fun to be a buyer for this outfit.

Fort Cody Trading Post located at I-80 and Hwy 83, North Platte, NE; ➘ 308 532 8081. *Open 8.00am–9.00pm daily, 8.00am–6.00pm winter.*

Quirky cuisine

Burger King, eat your heart out. The whopper hamburger served at **Sioux Sundries** in Harrison is 28 ounces of meat, topped with cheese, onions, lettuce, pickles and tomatoes, with chips on the side. The Coffeeburger, as it's called, was named for rancher Bill Coffee who didn't want his ranch hands going hungry.

Sioux Sundries located at the corner of Main and 2nd Sts, Harrison, NE; ➘ 308 668 2577. *Open 7.00am–5.30pm Mon–Fri; 7.00am–5.00pm Sat.*

Elvis and Pancho Villa memorabilia decorates the **La Casita Mexican Café**. The Elvis photo collage was started by Rachael Perez 37 years ago and it just kept growing. Folks from neighboring states drive in for the food.

La Casita Café located 1911 E 4th St on Hwy 30 east out of North Platte, NE 69101; ➘ 308 534 8077

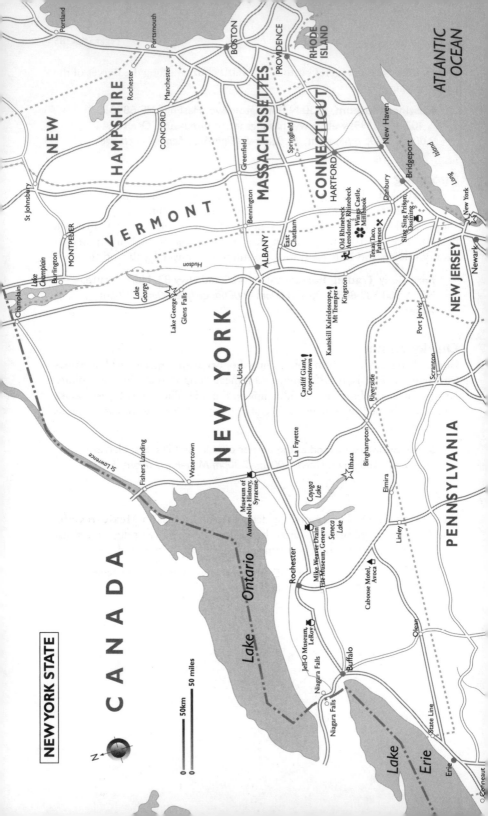

NEW YORK STATE

C A N A D A

ATLANTIC OCEAN

NEW HAMPSHIRE

VERMONT

MASSACHUSSETTES

CONNECTICUT

NEW JERSEY

NEW YORK

PENNSYLVANIA

Portland
Portsmouth
BOSTON
PROVIDENCE
RHODE ISLAND
Rochester
Manchester
CONCORD
New Haven
Bridgeport
St Johnsbury
Bennington
Greenfield
Springfield
HARTFORD
Danbury
New York
Newark
MONTPELIER
Burlington
Lake Champlain
Lake George
Albany
East Chatham
Old Rhinebeck Aerodome, Rhinebeck
Winvar Castle, Millbrook
Texas Taco, Patterson
Sing Sing Prison, Ossining
Hudson
Champlain
Glens Falls
Lake George
Koatskill Kaleidoscope, Mt Tremper
Kingston
Port Jervis
Scranton
Fishers Landing
Waterown
Utica
La Fayette
Cooperstown
Cardiff Giant, Cooperstown
Ithaca
Binghampton
Riverside
Elmira
St Lawrence
Museum of Automobile History, Syracuse
Cayuga Lake
Seneca Lake
Linley
Mike Weaver Drain Tile-Museum, Geneva
Rochester
Caboose Motel, Avoca
Jell-O Museum, LeRoy
Niagara Falls
Buffalo
Olean
Lake Ontario
Niagara Falls
State Line
Lake Erie
Erie
Conneaut

50km
50 miles
0
0

Northeastern Region 5

NEW YORK STATE
Festivals and events

Every year, on the first Saturday after the June 21 summer solstice, thousands of spectators converge on Coney Island to watch the **Mermaid Parade**, a funky spectacle of mermaids, mermen, merbabies, and merpets. Anything goes, costume-wise, as long as it's fish related. In the past, retired mermaids in wheelchairs paraded with Evian water drips and one woman's top consisted only of artfully placed rubber lobsters. There's enough flesh and boisterous behavior to last you quite a while.

> **Mermaid Parade** held the first Saturday following the summer solstice in the Coney Island section of Brooklyn, NY, 11 miles from lower Manhattan; ↘ 718 372 5159; web: whirl-l-gig.com/mermaid.html

Eccentric environments

Over a 25 year period, Peter and Tonni Wing have constructed their very own stone castle out of salvaged materials from ruins and the remains of historic buildings. A gnome would feel right at home in **Wings Castle**, near Millbrook, which sports seven towers, a moat, and a bathroom in the shape of a three leaf clover. Inside is a very eclectic collection of military regalia, carousel horses and other curiosities.

> **Wings Castle**, Bangall Road, Dutchess County, Millbrook, NY 12545. Located 5 miles north of Millbrook on Bengall Rd, 1.2 miles north of Rte 57; ↘ 845 677 9085

Just plain weird

Thanks to Thomas Edison, the folks at Luna Park on Coney Island were able to electrocute an elephant. This was in1903, and Edison had been publicly electrocuting cats and dogs to prove that his direct current electrical system (DC) was safe, while a competing system, alternating current (AC) being touted by Westinghouse, was not. When an elephant named Topsy was sentenced to death for killing three men in three years,

Edison volunteered to fry Topsy as a way to prove his point. With a film crew recording the grisly event, the elephant was led to a special platform and ten seconds later Topsy was toast. You can see the film at the **Coney Island Museum**.

> **Coney Island Museum**, 1208 Surf Ave, Brooklyn, NY 11224-2816;
> ☎ 718 372 5159; fax: 718 372 5101; email: info@coneyislandusa.com;
> web: www.coneyislandusa.com

Issac Abrams is a 1960s artist who never quite outgrew his need to create psychedelic art. The **Kaatskill Kaleidoscope**, which he and his son opened in 1996, is a head – and neck – trip, that's for sure. To see the show, you lean back against padded boards equipped with neck supports, then enjoy 15 minutes of inventive sound and imagery. The whole thing takes place inside the top of a converted grain silo.

> **Kaatskill Kaleidoscope**, Catskill Cors, Mt Tremper, Ulster County, NY; ☎ 914 688 5300

It's nice when you have the money to pull off a really good practical joke. And it's even nicer when the joke earns back hundreds of times what you spent. Often referred to as America's Greatest Hoax, **The Cardiff Giant** in Cooperstown is the 1868 work of George Hull. It seems that Hull was ticked off when a fundamentalist minister stubbornly refused to interpret the Bible, choosing instead to take the scripture literally. So when Hull came upon Genesis 6:4:

> There were giants on the earth in those days, and also afterward,
> when the sons of God had relations with the daughters of men, who
> bore children to them.

he couldn't resist.

He purchased an acre of gypsum-rich land in Iowa and quarried an enormous block of blue-veined stone. Claiming that he was making an

Abraham Lincoln memorial destined for Washington, DC, he hauled the stone, with great difficulty, to the railway station where he sent it on its way to a sculptor in Chicago. Hull himself followed so he could serve as the model for his twelve-foot 'giant', as well as direct the aging process that would render the giant a genuine antiquity. When his 'giant' was suitably aged, he hauled the thing back to New York and buried it behind the barn of William 'Stub' Newell, his relative and fellow co-conspirator.

A year later they professed to need a new well, hiring diggers to commence work. Sure enough, the diggers 'discovered' the buried giant and the trap was sprung. By afternoon, a tent had been erected over the giant's 'grave' and curious visitors were paying 25 cents to view the remains. Word spread far and wide; the price doubled to 50 cents, then doubled again to $1, a huge sum in those days.

Speculation as to the origin of the Cardiff Giant, as it was called, also raged far and wide, with clergy, academics, and politicians postulating all kinds of far-fetched theories. The giant was, depending on your viewpoint, a Jesuit missionary from the 1500s, an ancient Onondaga Iriquois Indian, or a petrified man just as described in the Bible. A letter from a Chicago sculptor claiming to have made the giant was dismissed as the ramblings of a crackpot.

One geologist proclaimed 'It has the mark of ages stamped upon every limb and feature, in a manner and with a distinctness which no man can imitate.'

P T Barnum, America's greatest showman of the time, got wind of the giant and offered Hull $60,000 to rent him for three months. Hull turned him down, so Barnum petulantly made his own giant, claiming to have bought him from Hull, and that Hull's giant was now a copy of his. Hull sued Barnum for copying his fake and for calling him a fraud; in court he gleefully admitted that it was all a hoax. The court ruled that Barnum couldn't be sued for calling Hull's giant a fraud because it was, indeed, a fraud. One of Hull's partners testified, 'there's a sucker born every minute', a remark mistakenly attributed to P T Barnum. You can see the Cardiff Giant at the Cooperstown Farmers' Museum where you'll have to pay a bit more than a quarter.

> **The Cardiff Giant**, located at New York State Historical Society
> Farmers' Museum, State Hwy 80, Cooperstown, NY; ℸ 607 547
> 1400 or 888 547 1450; web: www.nysha.org. Call for hours.
> *Admission charge.*

It's the largest open air graffiti gallery in the world. On the exterior walls of the **Phun Factory**, street kids display their talents – legally– for everyone to admire. Permission to wield their cans of spray paint on one of the 121 spots is given following an 'audition' consisting of photos of previous work. The vivid murals are changed every three months to a year depending upon their location.

> **Phun Factory**, 45–14 Davis St at Jackson Avenue, Long Island City,
> Queens, NY; ℸ 718 482 PHUN

Attractions

Open 24 hours a day, **The Labyrinth** is a walking meditation, a symbolic representation of life's quest. A kind of maze, a labyrinth is said to be a tool for harmonizing the body and mind; walking through one can be calming and energizing. You're supposed to use it at times of uncertainty, when facing an important decision, for healing emotional wounds, during illness and grief and when awestruck by joy.

> **The Labyrinth** Ithaca, NY. Located south of SR 366, Turkey Hill Road exit. Contact Foundation of Light, 391 Turkey Hill Rd, Ithaca, NY 14850

Frankenstein isn't the only monster at the **House of Frankenstein Wax Museum** in Lake George. A gruesome cast of torturers, taking obvious delight in decidedly anti-social behavior, joins the monster in 52 all-too-realistic vignettes. Audio enhanced with screams of terror and pain, some of the exhibits get even weirder with figures that move and talk. The experience is memorable, as is the artistic quality. Sweet dreams.

> **House of Frankenstein Wax Museum**, 213 Canada St, Lake George, NY 12845; ↘ 518 668 3377; email: maddoctor@frankensteinwaxmuseum.com; web: www.frankensteinwaxmuseum.com

The sign at **Magic Forest Amusement Park's Fairy Tale Trail and Safari Ride** claims to have Lake George's only diving horse. You'd think it would also be the world's only horse that dived off a platform into a pool, but it turns out that Atlantic City used to have such a tourist attraction as well. The man responsible for Rex the diving horse is Jimmy Brown, who also puts on a live bird show and a magic act. During the season Brown does three shows a day, every day, for three months straight. Rex doesn't seem to mind, pausing for effect at the top of his platform before plunging in.

> **Magic Forest Fairy Tale Trail and Safari Ride**, PO Box 71, Lake George, NY 12845; ↘ 518 668 2448; email: mgcfrst@aol.com; web: www.magicforestpark.com. *Open 9.30am–6.00pm Jun–Sept. Admission*

Snoopy would be right at home with his Sopwith Camel at the **Old Rhinebeck Aerodrome** in Rhinebeck. The place is a living museum of old- time flying machines, dating from 1900–37, that still take to the air every weekend during the summer. Barnstorming rides in a 1929 open-cockpit biplane are available before and after the shows. The fierce wind, the hair-mussing cap and goggles and the engine's noise will make you appreciate modern aircraft, if only until the peanuts are passed around.

> **Old Rhinebeck Aerodrome**, Stone Church Rd, Rhinebeck, NY 12572; ↘ 845 752 3200; email: info@oldrhinebeck.org; web: www.oldrhinebeck.org

Museums and collections

You would hardly consider drainage tiles worthy of collecting, but Mike Weaver, a drainage and irrigation engineer, collected more than 350 of them. Displayed at the **Mike Weaver Drain Tile Museum** in Geneva, his collection is, not surprisingly, the world's largest. The oldest tile dates from about 500BC. Weaver started collecting the tiles in 1950 and eventually opened the museum in the restored home of John Johnston, the man who brought the idea of drainage tiles from Scotland to the United States.

Mike Weaver Drain Tile Museum, Hwy 5, Geneva, NY; ✆ 315 789 3848. Go to the Rose Hill mansion located on Rte 96A 1 mile south of Rtes 5 and 20 for escorts to the museum. *Open Mon–Sat 10.00am–3.00pm; Sun 1.00–4.00pm.*

Built as a memorial to astronomer Carl Sagan, the **Sagan Planet Walk** in Ithaca visits nine planets along a three-quarter mile route that ends at the Science Center. The layout is a true-to-life model of our solar system; according to the scale, our closest star would be way out in in Hawaii. The Center holds an annual egg drop contest for all ages to see who can build the sturdiest egg holder.

Sagan Planet Walk Science Center, 601 First Street, Ithaca, NY 14850; ✆ 607 272 0600; fax: 607 277 7469; email: info@sciencenter.org; web: www.sciencenter.org

Inside the Ossining/Caputo Visitor Center is a display of prison-made weapons, shanks and shivs confiscated from convicts residing in the notorious **Sing Sing Prison**. The exhibit also has two real-life jail cells, positioned in a mirrored hall, to give you an idea of just how big the 'big house' is. You can take your picture in one of the cells or by 'Sparky', the electric chair, an exact replica of the real sizzler that was made by the prison's vocational class.

Sing Sing Prison, Ossining Visitor Center, 95 Broadway, Ossining NY 10562; ✆ 914 941 3189

Jell-O, America's favorite dessert, sells 1.1 million boxes a day, or 13 boxes every second. But when a young carpenter selling patent medicines invented the wobbly, fruit flavored gelatin in 1897, no one was buying. The dejected inventor sold the trademark to Orator Woodward, the wealthiest man in town, for $450. Woodward, too, had trouble convincing American housewives to try the dessert, so he in turn tried to sell the company to his plant manager (for $35), who also turned him down.

Determined to recoup his investment, Woodward hired a team of stylishly dressed salesmen who showed up in handsome, horse drawn carriages at every fair, picnic, tea, wedding, and church social in the region. Bowls of Jell-O were handed out to immigrants passing through Ellis Island, and he spent $335 for an ad in *Ladies' Home Journal* proclaiming Jell-O 'America's Most Famous Dessert'. He concocted recipes, such as Shredded Wheat Jell-O Apple Sandwich, and convinced doctors to endorse his product. And he took to the streets, selling Jell-O door to door, and printing recipe books in Spanish, Swedish, German, and Yiddish.

Woodward's Jell-O molds became a key element in his brilliant marketing strategy. He gave them away free, emphasizing not just Jell-O's taste, but its aesthetic appeal as well. Today those molds, along with Jell-O boxes, posters, advertisements, and giveaways, are an important part of the **Jell-O Museum** run by the LeRoy Historical Society. Today Jell-O is still designing molds that it sells on its website, including a Super Bowl version, alphabet cutters and a map of the United States. The company even has a Make It Now link: tell them what you have on hand and they'll tell you how to use it in Jell-O. (Can you imagine the crank emails they must get?) The museum is home to the world's only Gelometer, a device that measures the jigglyness of Jell-O.

Jell-O Museum, 23 E Main St, LeRoy, NY 14882; ☎ 716 768 7433 (LeRoy Historical Society; web: www.iinc.com/jellomuseum). *Open Mon–Sat 10.00am–4.00pm; Sun 1.00–4.00pm. Admission charge.*

If it has anything to do with cars, the **Museum of Automobile History** in Syracuse probably has it. You won't find any actual cars here, but you will find everything else auto-related, including billboards, models, gadgets, posters, advertising memorabilia, toys, publications and other accessories. The museum is the realization of a dream for Walter Miller who thinks 'the automobile is the single most important invention of our time'. Miller, a specialist in automobile literature who has been a passionate collector of it for 30 years, has scored such rare artifacts as a complete set of Burma Shave signs, the speeding ticket James Dean received just hours before his death and photos of the accident scene. All in all, there are over 10,000 items relating to over a thousand makes of autos, motorcycles and trucks,

Covering 200 years of auto history, the museum is the first to trace the social effects of America's favorite machine. 'There isn't a person living in America today whose life wasn't influenced or shaped by the automobile', Miller says. 'People under 30 don't know a world without computers. People under 50 don't know one without television. Almost no-one living today remembers the world without automobiles.'

The building's exterior literally stops traffic, covered as it is in 20 full size billboards from the 1940s and 1950s. Inside you'll see original media coverage of the first 'Horseless Carriage Race' held in the US in 1895, and psychedelic posters for the 1970 Plymouth and Dodge muscle cars. The place is a time machine of the auto age; an experience Walter Miller intends you to remember.

Museum of Automobile History, 321 N Clinton St, Syracuse, NY 13202; ☎ 315 478 2277; fax: 315 432 8256; email: info@autolit.com; web: www.autolit.com. *Open Wed–Sun 10.00am–5.00pm. Admission charge.*

Quirky cuisine

At **Texas Taco** in Patterson, the fence is made of tricycles and the entire place is a mosaic, covered with beads and ceramics. Rosemary, the proprietress, is all aglitter with her purple hair, signature overalls, false eyelashes, and spray-painted tennis shoes. Even the parking lot, where you can see her school bus decorated with seashells, radio knobs, and doll heads, is festooned with swirls of color. 'Every day is like being on stage', says Rosemary, who started out in 1970 with a pushcart on Fifth Avenue. The prices haven't changed much since then; there's nothing over $2.50.

> **The Texas Taco**, Rural Route 22, Patterson, NY 12563; ↘ 914 878 9665

Quirky quarters

All five cabooses at the **Caboose Motel** in Avoca have a shower, cable TV, and authentic upper and lower berths for sleeping. Recorded train sounds will lull you to sleep. Open April to October, the motel also has conventional rooms.

> **Caboose Motel**, State Route 415, Avoca, NY 14809; ↘ 607 566 2216; web: www.caboosemotel.net

NEW YORK CITY: MANHATTAN

You'd need a lot more than this chapter to even scratch the surface of Manhattan's eccentrics and eccentricities. The city is a mosaic of creative madness, with weird people and strange businesses in virtually all neighborhoods. They come and go, often quickly, taking their quirkiness to a new street corner or to the newest, cutting edge locations. To fully appreciate the vast cornucopia of curious characters, bizarre businesses, peculiar pastimes and loony lifestyles the city has to offer, get your eyes off the pages of the guidebooks and on to the street where life is being lived by delightfully daft folks quite unlike you and me.

In a city as physically dense and culturally diverse as Manhattan, walking is the best way to explore its neighborhoods. There are hundreds of guides offering walking tours of areas they know and love. The following tours explore some of the more offbeat aspects of life in the Big Apple, with tour guides who are known for their knowledge, showmanship and ability to make you feel comfortable in some mighty strange surroundings. Most of these guides will do a custom tour for you (for a price, of course), based on your interests. The Friday *New York Times* lists dozens of tours for the upcoming weekend, as does the magazine *Time Out New York* which comes out on Thursdays.

Tours

Arthur Marks is in a class by himself, the kind of character you'd love to have for a neighbor if you lived in Manhattan. Often referred to as a living

PECULIAR PRANKS

When Joey Skaggs of New York City goes people fishing, he uses a press release for bait.

'A Cat House for Dogs' promised sexual gratification for your dog without fear of unwanted pregnancy.

'The Fat Squad' promised to send a real person to follow you around and physically restrain you from going off your diet. 'You can hire us, but not fire us' was their motto.

The 'Porto-fess' was a life size, wheeled confessional, complete with a 'priest', that peddled the streets of New York looking for willing penitents.

Joey has sent out dozens of outlandish press releases like these, getting bites from all the major print and broadcast media. For 30 years he's been dreaming up elaborate hoaxes in New York City to prove the media's gullibility and the public's willingness to believe almost anything, no matter how absurd.

Reporters and film crews still show up annually for his April Fool's Day Parade in Manhattan, even though he's been sending out bitingly satirical press releases on this event for 15 years. You'd think a release describing a 'baseball tribute to racism' float, a $10 billion 'Where's Mars?' NASA float, and a 'special auction for custody of Elian Gonnzalez' float would tip folks off to a put on.

You can read his funny parade releases on his website as well as get details of his other pranks. Meanwhile, think through what you're hearing on the TV and radio, and what you're reading in the papers. It may be Joey going fishing.

Alan Able is another master prankster, perpetrating such hoaxes as a Citizens Against Breast Feeding group that demonstrated at the Democratic National Convention. The members were campaigning for expanding smoking privileges, claiming that breast-feeding made them obsessed with oral gratification. Hailing from the east coast, Able has founded such fictitious projects as the World Sex Olympics, a campaign to Clothe Naked Animals ('a nude horse is a rude horse'), and a School for Panhandlers.

landmark, Arthur has been giving tours for 30 years. He doesn't just tell you stuff, he sings it, breaking into song as the mood strikes. He offers an astounding variety of decidedly off-beat tours, dispensing fascinating anecdotes along with his own unique perspective on history.

With Arthur, you can explore east side, west side, and all around the town, giving yourself to Broadway and peeking into the lives of past and present New Yorkers. He knows history and legend, fact and fantasy, whether boring or interesting, and the difference between them. Seeing Manhattan through his eyes is like peering into an urban kaleidoscope, always in motion, always changing.

Arthur Marks Tours for All Seasons, 24 Fifth Ave, New York, NY 10011; ✆ 212 673 0477; fax: 212 673 9142

Michael Kaback has carved out a curious niche for himself in the tour business. Building on a life-long familiarity with the garment trade, his walking tour takes you through the bustling streets of the garment district, dodging 'sidewalk locomotives' laden with clothes, patterns and rolls of fabric. Kaback is full of juicy stories about store buyers, truckers, 'knock-off' artists (who copy designer clothes and sell them for substantially less), and the characters and criminals behind the scenes of this cut-throat trade.

On this lively and offbeat tour, you'll learn quirky trade jargon and hear stories about salaries, commissions, profits, and losses. You also get to shop for bargains among the cancelled orders, overproduction, unsold inventory and one-of-a-kind salesman samples. Cold cash, along with Kaback's advice on bargaining, can net you some outstanding deals on high end fashion.

Kaback also offers the **Bizarre and Eccentric Tour of the East Village**, a voyeuristic evening of tattoo parlors, body piercing, sex shops and vampire haunts. Not for the faint of heart, you get up close and personal to the kind of folks who have hair color usually associated with polyester along with jewelry on body parts usually reserved for that special someone.

Bizarre and Eccentric Tour of the East Village, Michael Kaback Walking Tours, 305 East 40th St, Apt 9F, New York, NY; ✆ 212 370 4214

The **Charles Simon Center for Adult Life and Learning** provides an intriguing series of summer excursions. Join an archeological excavation in Brooklyn, an all night July Fourth walking tour, a pre-Rosh Hashanah Lower East Side tour, Chinatown's herb markets, or a social history of baseball in New York. The walking and riding tour of historic subway routes takes you to Brooklyn and Coney Island.

Charles Simon Center for Adult Life and Learning, New York, NY; ✆ 212 445 5500

Author and political activist Bruce Kayton puts a left-wing spin on his **Radical Walking Tours of New York City**. You can buy his book of 13 self-led tours or go along with him on several tours, including a radical lovers tour of Greenwich Village, a 1960s political/protest tour of the Village, a radical Jews tour of the lower east side, or a tour of Harlem with a left-wing twist. Other tours cover money and other evils; riots, prohibition, and 'trees, grass, and the working class' in Central Park.

Radical Walking Tours of New York, Bruce Kayton, ✆ 718 492 0069; web: www.he.net/~radtours. *No reservations required.*

The dead of centuries past lie below today's bustling downtown neighborhoods. **Joyce Gold** takes you to four graveyards of lower Manhattan on a 'Where they came to rest' tour. In Little Italy she presents a walking tour of crime, describing how the Mafia began, how Prohibition changed the picture, who the main families were, which mobsters owned which restaurants, where the bullets are and why rivals were rubbed out in front of their families. The 'Tory Story in Lower Manhattan' celebrates Independence Day (July Fourth) by looking at the revolution through British eyes. She also offers a 'Macabre Greenwich Village' tour, exploring graveyards, the hangman's house and tree, famous murders, ghosts and hauntings; the 'New Meat Market' tour featuring butchers, bakers, and art scene makers; and a 'Hell Ain't Hot' tour – this here's Hell's kitchen.

Joyce Gold History Tours of New York, 141 W 17th St, New York, NY 10011; ✆ 212 242 5762; fax: 212 242 6374; email: NYCtours@aol.com; web: www.nyctours.com

The real life **Kenny Kramer** (upon whom the quirky character of the TV comedy *Seinfeld* was based) gives a hugely entertaining, slick and professional tour of the people and places that populated the television show about nothing. He unabashedly admits to being a celebrity without accomplishment and to making money for being indirectly famous, not for his own talent, but because he lived across the hall from someone who became famous. (His neighbor was Larry David, co-creator of the show and the personality behind the character of George Costanza.) He does this in such a good natured way that you fall in love with the real Kramer the same way you fell in love with his character on the show.

Following a funny stand up routine, you hop on his bus, where he'll show you the real life places where so many of the show's story lines took place, and tell you all about the real life characters depicted in *Seinfeld*. At Tom's restaurant (called Monk's on the show) he patiently spends as many Kodak moments as it takes to satisfy his guests. The bus portion is funny, non-stop commentary and he'll answer any question you ask. The tour ends with a slice of pizza and a chance to buy the dozen or so Kramer products that he also hawks on his website.

Kenny Kramer Reality Tour starts at the Pulse Theater, 432 W 42nd St (between 9th and 10th Aves), New York, NY; ✆ 800 KRAMERS; 212 268 5525; email: Kramer@kennykramer.com; web: www.kennykramer.com

Paul Zukowski lives and breathes gangsters. He knows where they got their start, how they rose to power and fame, their infamous accomplishments and where they met their ends. As a kid he pretended to be Al Capone, read every book he could get his hands on about the bad boys, and watched every movie and television show that had gangsters. He's a walking encyclopedia of gangsterdom, a dapper young man who conducts his **Gangland Tour** around New York City in a limousine that would do Capone proud.

What makes Paul's passion so extraordinary is that he grew up in Poland, exposed by propaganda only to the bad, evil side of America. Leaving his homeland just a few years ago, he's managed to chase and catch the American dream by turning his hobby into a business. Explaining that it was a lack of opportunity – a tight job market – that had young men turning to crime, he takes you past the Irish, English, German, Jewish, and Italian sites where so much of gangland activity took place. He can barely contain his enthusiasm for his subject and you'll leave his tour reeling from the stories he tells.

> **Gangland Tours**, New York, NY; ✆ 800 968 4264; email: ganglandtors@aol.com; web: www.ganglandtours.com

The Diamond District, with its 24,000 workers, is like a small town with more than 600 merchants. Eighty-five percent of all diamonds entering the US pass through this district, a microcosm of America's free enterprise system. Elaine Wong leads a tour called **Fun in the Diamond District**.

> **Fun in the Diamond District**. Contact Elaine Wong; ✆ 203 894 8043

Off-beat field trips, walking tours, and workshops are offered by several other tour companies, including the **American Museum of Natural History**, that offers tours of such locations as Central Park West, the new Times Square, and urban forest walking tours. **Art Tours of Manhattan** visits the eclectic, eccentric village art scene, while **Doorway to Design** visits village houses and creative firms. Reality meets fiction on the **On Location** bus tour, while **Big Apple Greeter** matches you with a volunteer escort to show you around. **Big Onion Walking Tours** goes where mainstream tours don't, with a Gay and Lesbian History walk, a multi-ethnic eating tour, and a Riot and Rebellion tour.

> **American Museum of Natural History**, Central Park West at 79th St, New York, NY 10024; ✆ 212 769 5200; web: www.amnh.org

> **Art Tours of Manhattan**, 63 E 82nd St, New York, NY 10028; ✆ 609 921 2647.

Big Apple Greeter, I Centre St, New York, NY 10007;
↘ 212 669 8159; web: www.bigapplegreeter.org

Big Onion Walking Tours, 104 S Central Ave, Suite 5, Valley
Stream, NY 11580; ↘ 516 872 3642; fax: 516 872 3642; email:
beertstour@aol.com; web: www.bigonion.com

Doorway to Design, 1441 Broadway, New York, NY 10018; ↘ 212
221 1111; fax: 718 376 7120

On Location Tours depart from Times Square Visitor Center,
located at 1560 Broadway, between 46th and 47th Sts, New York,
NY; ↘ 212 410 9830; email: tvtour@aol.com. *Tours depart 9.00am,
12noon and 3.00pm Mon–Fri; 10.00am, 12noon, 2.00pm and 4.00pm
Sat–Sun. Admission charge.*

Museums and collections

Seven thousand people from 20 different countries lived in the tenement
building that now belongs to the **Lower East Side Tenement Museum**.
For most European immigrants, overcrowded tenements (multi-family
apartment buildings) were the first stop in their quest for the American
dream. The museum offers three tours that trace the lives of immigrant
families through layers of wallpaper and household furnishings. The regular
weekday tour explores the lives of the many families who lived there. On
weekends, the Confino Family tour is led by a costumed interpreter who
welcomes you as if you were newly arrived in this country in 1916, giving
you a unique opportunity to experience immigrant life. You can even reserve
the tenement after hours for an offbeat dinner party in the tenement kitchen
that comes complete with enamel-topped tables and antique décor.

Lower East Side Tenement Museum, 90 Orchard St at Broome
St, New York, NY 10002; ↘ 212 431 0233; fax: 212 431 0402; web:
www.tenement.org. *Open Tue–Fri 12.00noon–5.00pm; Sat–Sun
11.00am–5.00pm. Admission charge.*

It must be nice to have so much money that you can indulge your every
passion. The **Forbes Magazine Galleries** are proof that Malcom Forbes
spared no expense while assembling and displaying his eclectic collections.
The History of the Toy Soldier is a series of dioramas populated with 10,000
soldiers battling for truth, honor, and the American way. The Mortality of
Immortality Gallery features 175 trophies commemorating everything from
the best leghorn chickens at an egg-laying event to the proverbial loving cup.
Papers emphasizing the personalities of past presidents and of the issues they
faced illuminate the Presidential Papers Gallery, while historical versions of
the Monopoly game show all the stages of its evolution. You'll also see
hundreds of ships and toy boats, 12 real Faberge eggs, an autograph gallery and
four historical miniature rooms.

INTERIOR DECOR WITH A DIFFERENCE

Joseph Furey, 75, an ex-prizefighter and retired ironworker, spent the seven years following his wife's death in 1981 transforming his gloomy five-room Brooklyn apartment into a more cheerful place. He covered every surface (except the floors) with multi-colored polka dots, mussel shells spread like butterflies, cardboard hearts and bow-ties, plaster birds on tiny pedestals, colored tiles, chips of mirror, glass beads, and lima beans. His handiwork was discovered by his very surprised landlord shortly before he died. It has since been removed.

Forbes Magazine Galleries, 62 Fifth Ave at 12th St, New York, NY 10011; ℩ 212 206 5549. *Open Tue–Wed; Fri–Sat 10.00am–4.00pm. Admission free.*

Attractions

Times Square is the location for the new, state-of-the-art, **Madame Tussaud Wax Museum**. Unlike most wax museums, here you can touch – even kiss - the characters in the Opening Night Party room. Fifty eerily real celebrities are just waiting for you to join them in the festivities and don't object at all to camera flashes. Besides the party, there's a gallery of world leaders and a multi-decade tribute to pop culture. The art of wax figure-making has it's own display, as does the French Revolution. All told, there are 175 figures of the famous and infamous and you come upon them in weirdly realistic settings. In the gift shop you'll find authentic memorabilia for sale such as Ray Bolger's tap shoes and a hat belonging to Greta Garbo. The museum is named after the woman who made death masks of freshly decapitated aristrocrats guillotined in 1840s France.

Madame Tussaud's Wax Museum, 234 West 42nd St; ℩ 1 800 246 8872; web: madame-tussauds.com. *Open Sun–Thu 10.00am–6.00pm, Fri–Sat 10.00am–8.00pm. Admission charge.*

Shopping

Bats, cats, and rats are favorites at **Evolution**, a very strange store where you can buy freeze dried mice, replicas of velociraptor claws, skull casts of extinct species, lollipops with bugs inside, a mounted bat in a frame and stuffed snakes. Folks who cook bugs and eat them, keep them as pets, or steam and mount them, buy their supplies here.

Evolution, 120 Spring St, New York, NY 10012; ℩ 212 343 1114; fax: 212 343 1815; web: www.evolutionnyc.com

If you can dream it up, **Abracadabra** will rent it to you. This store/museum/freak show/costume shop has every bizarre object in it that anyone has ever requested, along with everything and anything that appeals to owner

Bob Blum who walks around his domain with a parrot named Nairobi on his shoulder. Blum claims to have the largest selection of props in the world, a very believable claim considering the thousands and thousands of things crammed into his two-level shop.

From feather boas to body parts, from lighting to special effects, from magic to the macabre, Abracadabra has it all. The place is a zoo, with people and animals of every description made of materials ranging from rubber to stone. There's a 12-foot-tall wizard and a menacing gargoyle that blows smoke, flaps its wings, and moves its head. Realistic, life-size figures such as the Blues Brothers and cops with guns will liven up any party. Around Halloween, the place is even wilder as hundreds of costume hunters descend on a selection of costume rentals extensive enough to outfit a small city. Speaking modestly, Blum says, it's 'the coolest place on the planet.'

Abracadabra, 19 W 21st St, New York, NY 10010; ↘ 212 627 5194; web: www.abracadabra-superstore.com

At **The Fan Club Celebrity Consignment Shop** you can buy cast-off Broadway show wardrobes as well as clothing worn by your favorite soap opera and movie stars. It's the ultimate in retro shopping, with the source's name on the label and on the price tag. Styles from the 1920s through the 1960s are most popular, but current celeb fashions are also featured. Anything from Grandma's attic is hot, as are original polyesters and beaded gowns from the hippie days. The place is too, too cool as retro shoppers are fond of saying.

The Fan Club Celebrity Consignment Shop, 22 West 19th St, New York, NY 10011; ↘ 212 939 3349

Just plain weird

The shop windows at **Ricky's Drug Store** in the village are known for their bizarre and funky styling. Recently they displayed three mannequins: one male dressed as a doctor, one female as a scantily clad nurse and a third female laying on a table ready for an examination. The other window was filled with antique lunch boxes. You never know what to expect and the displays change frequently.

Ricky's Drug Store, 58 1675 3rd Ave, RM, New York, NY 10128; ↘ 212 974 9603

Festivals and events

It's always a good hair day at **Wigstock** when 25,000 spectators gather to watch New York's preeminent drag queens and transvestites strut their most outrageous stuff. It's eight hours of ribald song and dance, with wigs up to two feet tall taking center stage. The costumes are outlandish, whimsical, and demented like the headdress made of toilet brushes, worn with a coordinating skirt made of pink urinal deodorizer cakes. Wigstock is definitely adult entertainment. Peace, love and hairspray, baby.

Wigstock held annually in September on Pier 54 in New York City, NY; ☎ 212 439 5139; web: www.wigstock.nu

It's a **Rat Race**, all right, and Wall Street brokers really go all out for it. More than a thousand traders, lawyers and accountants race through the financial district wearing rat costumes. Those not dressing as rats wear business attire and run while carrying a briefcase.

Rat Race held annually in May in New York City, NY. Contact Carey International, 575 Lexington Ave, Suite 2840, New York, NY 10022; ☎ 212 980 1490

Quirky cuisine

An intergalactic, virtual reality shuttle speeds you to **Mars 2112** for an extraterrestrial culinary and interactive event. Dubbed 'eatertainment', Mars 2112 in Times Square weaves fantasy and reality through state-of-the-art technology. Kids love the place because of the Red Planet décor, strolling Martians, video games, and kid-friendly food. Adults love it because the kids stay entertained while they enjoy grown-up food that's out-of-this-world yummy.

Mars 2112, 1633 Broadway, New York, NY 10019; ☎ 212 582 2112; fax: 212 489 7955; email: mmars2112@aol.com

Quirky quarters

The **Carlton Arms** in Manhattan is a funky, backpacker-style hotel decorated by artists in exchange for rooms. Everything is painted – the halls, stairways, bathrooms, and guestrooms – with murals and graphics ranging from naughty to nice to the outright bizarre. Their motto, 'We ain't no Holiday Inn', is an understatement.

Carlton Arms, 160 E 25th St, New York, NY 10010; ☎ 212 684 8337; web: www.carltonarms.com

VERMONT
Festivals and events

During Sugarbush's July Fourth Parade, they hold a **Cherry Pit Spit** contest. Men, women, and kids compete in separate categories to see who can chew up the cherry, then spit the pit the farthest. The record is over 58 feet.

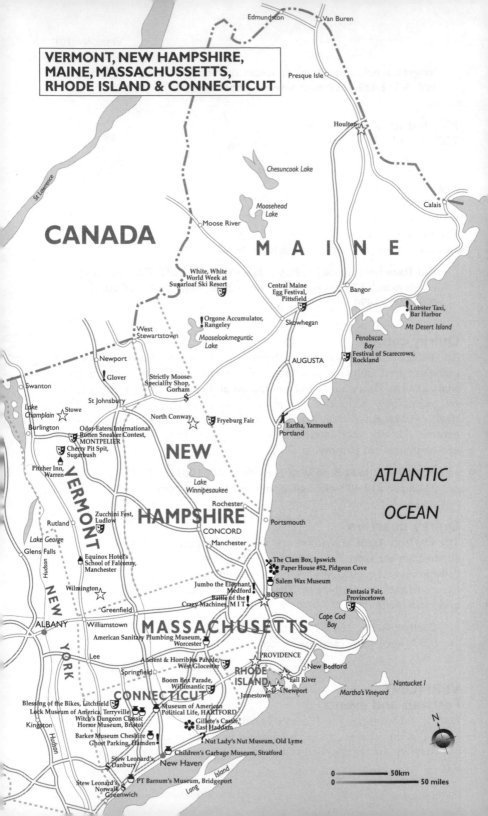

VERMONT, NEW HAMPSHIRE, MAINE, MASSACHUSSETTS, RHODE ISLAND & CONNECTICUT

Edmundston
Van Buren
Presque Isle
Houlton
Calais
Chesuncook Lake
Moosehead Lake
Moose River
St Lawrence

CANADA

M A I N E

White, White World Week at Sugarloaf Ski Resort
Central Maine Egg Festival, Pittsfield
Bangor
Lobster Taxi, Bar Harbor
Mt Desert Island
Orgone Accumulator, Rangeley
Skowhegan
West Stewartstown
Mooselookmeguntic Lake
Penobscot Bay
Festival of Scarecrows, Rockland
AUGUSTA
Newport
Glover
Strictly Moose Speciality Shop, Gorham
St Johnsbury
Swanton
Lake Champlain
Stowe
Burlington
North Conway
Fryeburg Fair
Eartha, Yarmouth
Portland
Odor-Eaters International Rotten Sneaker Contest, MONTPELIER
Cherry Pit Spit, Sugarbush

NEW

Pitcher Inn, Warren
Lake Winnipesaukee

HAMPSHIRE

Rochester
Portsmouth
Rutland
Zucchini Fest, Ludlow
CONCORD
Manchester

VERMONT

ATLANTIC

OCEAN

Lake George
Glens Falls
Equinox Hotel's School of Falconry, Manchester
The Clam Box, Ipswich
Paper House #52, Pidgeon Cove
Salem Wax Museum
Wilmington
Jumbo the Elephant, Medford
Battle of the Crazy Machines, M I T
BOSTON
Fantasia Fair, Provincetown

NEW

Greenfield
Williamstown
ALBANY

MASSACHUSETTS

Cape Cod Bay

YORK

Hudson
American Sanitary Plumbing Museum, Worcester
Lee
Ancient & Horribles Parade, West Glocester
PROVIDENCE
New Bedford
Springfield
Boom Box Parade, Willimantic

RHODE ISLAND

Fall River
Nantucket I
Blessing of the Bikes, Litchfield
Lock Museum of America, Terryville
Witch's Dungeon Classic Horror Museum, Bristol

CONNECTICUT

Museum of American Political Life, HARTFORD
Jamestown
Newport
Martha's Vineyard
Kingston
Barker Museum Cheshire
Ghost Parking, Hamden
Gillette's Castle, East Haddam
Nut Lady's Nut Museum, Old Lyme
Stew Leonard's Danbury
Children's Garbage Museum, Stratford
New Haven
Stew Leonard's Norwalk
PT Barnum's Museum, Bridgeport
Greenwich
Long Island

N

0   50km
0   50 miles

Cherry Pit Spit held annually during Sugarbush, VT, July Fourth parade. Contact Sugarbush Chamber of Commerce, Rt 100, Box 173, Waitsfield, VT 05673; ☎ 802 496 3409

At the **Odor-Eaters International Rotten Sneaker Contest**, kids from all over the country – along with a few from overseas – show off their grungiest, grossest, stinkiest, foulest sneakers, hoping to win a $500 savings bond and prove to their parents that cleanliness isn't always a virtue. The winner also gets a year's supply of Odor-Eater products that probably remain unused.

Odor-Eaters International Rotten Sneaker Contest held annually in March in Montpelier, VT. Contact Montpelier Recreation Department; ☎ 802 223 5141; web: www.mps.k12.vt.us/rec/rec.htm

For four days each year the folks around Ludlow make fun of the lowly zucchini at the **Zucchini Fest**, carving it into weird shapes, racing it, flying it, making creative dishes with it and making up limericks about it. Zucchini chunk ice cream? Oh, yum!

Zucchini Fest held annually in August in Ludlow, VT. Contact Ludlow Area Chamber of Commerce, PO Box 333, Okemo Marketplace Clocktower, Ludlow, VT 05149; ☎ 802 228 5830; web: www.vacationinvermont.com/zfest

Eight hundred classic British motorcars show up for the annual **British Invasion** in Stowe, an event that features a 4WD Land Rover polo match. There's also a tailgate picnic competition, a tug of war between car clubs and guided driving tours through the heart of Vermont's fall foliage display.

British Invasion held annually in September, in Stowe, VT. Contact Ye Olde England Inne, 433 The Mountain Rd, Stowe, VT 05672; ☎ 800 253 2106; fax: 802 253 8944; web: www.britishinvasion.com

Wilmington is a funky, artsy kind of place, with black-and-white spotted busses called Moo-vers that actually moo instead of honk. The town is the site of the **Garlic and Herb Festival**, where you can partake of everything from garlic ice cream to garlic jelly, pickled garlic, roasted garlic, garlic braids, and just plain garlic bulbs of every variety. There are weed walks where you can learn valuable uses for every day weeds and you can also play garlic golf.

Garlic and Herb Festival held annually in September in Wilmington, VT. Located at the junction of Route 9 and Route 100 South in Wilmington, VT. Contact Jay Powell or Steve Wrathall, 932 Fowler Rd, Whitingham, VT 05361; ☎ 802 368 7147

Stowe holds a summer **Mutt Strut**, a festival for animals. You'll see dogs in costume, pet beauty contests, and human/pet look-alike competitions.

Mutt Strut held annually in August in Stowe, VT. Contact Go Stowe, Main St, Box 1320, Stowe, VT 05672; ☎ 877 GOSTOWE; email: askus@gostowe.com; web: www.gostowe.com

Just plain weird

The **Bread and Puppet Theater and Art Museum** in Glover isn't just about the world's largest collection of gigantic puppets. It's about politics, satire, and outrageous performances that do the country proud, eccentrically speaking. In operation since the early 1960s, the theater uses large puppets, masked and unmasked characters, marching bands and music to confront the political and social issues of the day. At their annual **Domestic Resurrection Circus**, up to 30,000 people come to watch the performances in the amphitheater and the sideshows in the pine forests.

Why does it have such a funny name? The theater's originator, Peter Shumann, thought that art was as essential as bread, and should be cheap and available to everyone. At the end of each performance, free, freshly baked bread is given to the audience.

In keeping with the theater's philosophy, grass roots participation is encouraged. Local volunteers perform alongside the professionals as puppeteers, musicians, and masked dancers, lending a sense of community to the event. As one of the oldest nonprofit, self-supporting theatrical companies in the country, it can allow its performers to do and say things that might otherwise be politically incorrect. Some shows are lighthearted, making fun of political pundits and pontificating blowhards; others tackle more serious issues. In the early days they were common fixtures on the streets of America, protesting the Vietnam War. The museum itself displays hundreds of puppets and political artwork used in past performances.

Domestic Resurrection Circus held annually in August at Bread and Puppet Theater in Glover, VT. Contact Bread and Puppet Theater and Art Museum, Box 153, Glover, VT 05839; ☎ 802 525 3031

Quirky quarters

In the winter of 1970, Patty and Bill Pusey bought a rundown piece of property near Wilmington, planning for a quaint bed and breakfast. When they came back to inspect the property in the spring, they discovered they'd bought a full-fledged junkyard containing 3,000 cars. Over time, they've managed to turn their non-working junkyard into a working farm, offering bed and breakfast at their **Shearer Hill Farm Bed and Breakfast**.

> **Shearer Hill Farm Bed and Breakfast**, PO Box 1453, Wilmington, VT 05363; ☏ 800 437 3104; email: puseyshf@sover.net

The **Equinox Hotel's School of Falconry** is one of the only certified places in the country where you can learn the art of handling large birds of prey. Washington, DC must be the other.

> **Equinox Hotel's School of Falconry** located in Manchester Village, Manchester, VT; ☏ 800 362 4747

The elegant **Pitcher Inn** has a whimsical, unexpected ambience. Décor in the 11 rooms emphasizes a different adventure in each one, all part of a history of Vermont theme. Among them is a Masonic lodge, a 19th century schoolroom, a mountain cabin, a hayloft, and the most luxurious duck blind ever imagined. The Trout Room is octagonal with a bed made of tree trunks, a headboard carved with ferns and tree roots that spread out on the floor. A flying trout hangs from a ceiling that is ribbed like the sides of a boat. Add a fireplace, a collection of oars, a fly-tying desk and a porch over a rushing stream and you have a delightfully eccentric experience.

> **Pitcher Inn**, 275 Main St, Warren, VT 05674; ☏ 802 496 6350 or 888 867 4824; web: www.pitcherinn.com

NEW HAMPSHIRE

There's not a lot going on wacky-wise in New Hampshire. It's a very tiny state with a population to match and eccentricity just isn't its strong suit. Here's the best they have to offer.

Festivals and events

Here's a football tournament that would put any detergent to the test: the **Mud Bowl Championships**. Played in North Conway in the only mud football stadium in the eastern US, this touch football tournament requires big, beefy guys to wallow in the knee-deep muck while playing a game they hope resembles the real thing. On the first two days of the event, eight barefoot teams slosh it out in the elimination rounds; the winning two teams go whole hog during the Sunday championship.

Each year, this charity event has a different

theme such as 'Mud Bowl Goes Hollywood'. You can watch competing teams perform skits based on the year's theme, and see the famous lawn-chair precision drill team do its thing at the theme parade.

> **Mud Bowl Championships** held annually in September in North Conway, NH. Contact New Hampshire Division of Travel and Tourism Development; ✆ 800 FUN IN NH; web: www.visitnh.gov

Just plain weird

It's one thing to swoosh down the slopes on skis, sleds, or snow scooters, but it's another thing entirely to be rolled down the slopes at 35mph in a human-sized beach ball. This loony device, called a **Zorb**, hails from New Zealand, where they must be a few clowns short of a circus to come up with something like this. It's a big, fat, bouncy ball that a presumably sane person straps himself into, then hurtles down any hill that has at least a 20% grade. Two feet of air cushioning inside the ten-foot diameter ball keeps the rider safe. Experienced 'Zorbonauts' don't even bother with the straps, preferring to let centrifugal force pin them flat against the inside. You can try it at the Cranmore Ski Resort.

> **Zorb**, Cranmore Mountain Resort, North Conway, NH; ✆ 800 SUN N SKI; email: info@cranmore.com

Shopping

Shish Ka Poop, dehydrated moose dung on a skewer, and Moosletoe, a festive cluster of droppings, are among the thousand moose-related items sold at **Strictly Moose** in Gorham. These ungainly creatures, often described as proof that God has a sense of humor, grace everything from mugs to candles. Try the Moosturd jar – the poopun of choice – or the moose-butt mug. For connoisseurs of moose poop, it's important to collect only winter droppings; their summer diet isn't conducive to the manufacture of moose poop earrings.

> **Strictly Moose**, 129 Main St, Gorham, NH; ✆ 877 250 6713 or 603 466 9417; fax: 603 466 5385; email: kad@strictlymoose.com; web: www.strictlymoose.com

MAINE
Festivals and events

The folks in Pittsfield like to cook up quite an egg fry at their **Central Maine Egg Festival**, using one of the world's largest frying pans: five feet in diameter and weighing 300 pounds. The Alcoa Company made the Teflon coated pan back in 1973; it's heated by gas on its own specially designed burners. The festival also features the Egglympics, with all kinds of run-with-an-egg-on-a-spoon type games, and a parking lot chalk-art contest.

Central Maine Egg Festival held annually in July in Pittsfield, ME. Contact Central Maine Egg Festival Committee, PO Box 82, Pittsfield, ME 04967; web: www.pittsfield.org/eggfes.htm

Lumberjacks do for fun what most of us wouldn't, or couldn't, do for a million dollars. During the Woodsmen Field Day at the **Fryeburg Fair**, they compete in a sort of lumberjack rodeo, trying to out do each other in buck sawing, ax throwing, tree-felling, chain-sawing, and log-rolling competitions. The springboard chop event sends competitors hacking their way to the top of a tall pole. There's also a skillet throwing contest.

Fryeburg Fair held annually in October in Fryeburg, ME. Contact West Oxford Agricultural Society, Fryeburg Fair Association, PO Box 78, Fryeburg, ME 04037; ✎ 207 935 3268 or 207 935 3662; email: info@fryeburgfair.com; web: www.fryeburgfair.com

Rockland is home to the Farnsworth Art Museum, a facility that specializes in innovative community-based art. Each year they, and the local chamber of commerce, co-sponsor the **Festival of Scarecrows**, resulting in dozens of scarecrows popping up all over town. Anyone can enter: businesses, groups, families, and individuals. A parade, barn dance, pumpkin hunt and street bazaar add to the festivities.

Festival of Scarecrows held annually in October at Farnsworth Art Museum, Rockland, ME; ✎ 207 596 6457.Contact Rockland-Thomaston Chamber of Commerce; ✎ 207 596 0376

Three days of potato worship take place each August in Houlton at the **Potato Feast Days**. There's a potato-picking contest, potato relay races, potato peeling contests and a potato-barrel rolling competition in addition to potato carving and tasting. You'll learn a lot of interesting potato trivia, such as that inferior potatoes used to feed farm animals are called hog, or pig, potatoes.

Potato Feast Days held annually in August in Houlton, ME. Contact Greater Houlton Chamber of Commerce; ✎ 207 523 4216; email: chamber@houlton.com

The winter **Moose Stompers Weekend** in Houlton will have you watching human dog sled races (two pull, one rides), human curling, a wiffle snowball tournament and a half dollar scramble which has kids diving in the snow for coins. A giant bonfire and fireworks display tops off the event.

Moose Stompers Weekend held annually in February in Houlton, ME. Contact Greater Houlton Chamber of Commerce; ☎ 207 523 4216; email: chamber@houlton.com

Paul Schipper isn't the first person to dream of buying a ski lodge and skiing every day, but he's probably the most determined. Now 76 years old, the former World War II fighter pilot has skied every day for 3,238 consecutive ski days since 1981. If **Sugarloaf Ski Resort** is open, Paul's there. Nothing stops him, not even pneumonia, liver cancer, or the triple by-pass surgery he postponed one year. When he broke his thumb, the doctor fashioned a special cast to fit around his ski-pole grip. Weather doesn't stop him either. When high winds closed the lifts, he just hiked up the ski hills and dodged moose on the way down. Once he had to ski at midnight by the light of a snow blower to maintain his streak. He's been profiled in *People* magazine and featured on television's *Good Morning America*.

Sugarloaf holds **White, White World Week** in January with a snow sculpture contest and a toga party. The Dummy Dump is the highlight of the week, with an award given for the best stuffed dummy which flies through the air with the most creativity and style, with all pieces intact. A downhill body slide, a waiter and waitress race, and the crowning of Miss Sugarloaf and King of the Mountain conclude the event.

White, White World Week at Sugarloaf Ski Resort, RR1 Box 5000, Carrabassett Valley, ME 04947; ☎ 800 THE LOAF or 207 237 2000; fax: 207 237 3768; email: infosugarloaf.com; web: www.sugarloaf.com

Just plain weird

How can a triathlete stay fit and make money at the same time? Ask Jeffrey Miller of Bar Harbor, who peddles up to three people at a time around town on his **lobster taxi**, a large tricycle chassis outfitted with bright red lobster claws, a lobster tail fender, and cushy seat up front. The lobster measures seven feet long and four feet wide, requiring quite a bit of effort to peddle around by the time you add two people to its 120-pound weight. The town council was reduced to tears of laughter when he came before them to get his taxi permit.

He's accustomed to giggles and stares, can spot finger pointing in the rear-side mirrors and tells doubtful, potential customers, 'Of course I want to peddle you around. Why else would I be sitting here with a giant sofa-of-a-lobster bike?' To catch a ride, just hail the crustacean when you see it or call Jeffrey on his lobster bike hotline.

Lobster Taxi, Bar Harbor, ME. Contact Jeffrey Miller; ☎ 207 288 3028 or 207 266 RIDE

The **Orgone Energy Accumulator** in Rangaley Lakes was the bizarre, 'scientific' invention of a Dr Wilhelm Reich. In 1948, the doctor became fascinated by Freud's concepts and set out to find the physical basis for his theory of neurosis. It was Reich's belief that our species' energy, which he named 'orgone', becomes trapped in the body following traumatic human events. By sitting in his device, a six-sided box of organic materials and metals, you could regain lost orgone.

Not everyone agreed with Reich's theories, however. In fact, the government charged him with all sorts of violations and ordered the accumulator destroyed. He was jailed for contempt of court after an associate refused to obey the order to destroy the accumulator, and Reich died in his jail cell of heart failure. In his will he asked that his work be sealed for 50 years, at which time, he hoped, the world would see the error of its ways and embrace the 'technology' he'd developed. That was in 1957; we've got six more years to see the light.

Orgone Energy Accumulator, Orgonon-Dodge Pond Rd, PO Box 687, Rangeley, ME 04970; ↘ 207 864 5156 or 207 864 3443; email: wreich@rangeley.org; web: www.rangeley.org/~wreich. *Open 1.00–5.00pm Wed–Sun, Jul–Aug; 1.00–5.00pm, Sun, Sep. Admission charge.*

Attractions

This globe is so big that California is almost three-and-a-half feet tall. Dubbed **Eartha™**, this is officially the world's largest revolving globe. Over 41 feet in diameter, it rotates just like the real thing and wears the largest image of earth ever created. It revolves in a three-story glass atrium and was built by a map publisher using a database that took two years to map.

Eartha™ located at DeLorme Headquarters, Two DeLorme Dr, PO Box 298, Yarmouth, ME 04096; ↘ 207 846 7000; web: www.delorme.com

MASSACHUSETTS
Festivals and events

Also known as Transgender Week, the annual **Fantasia Fair** in Provincetown is the Super Bowl of make-up and dress-up for cross-dressers, transsexuals, and gays. Educational and social programs fill the week, but the highlights are the Follies entertainment and the Fashion Show at which the Queen and King of Fantasia are chosen. Unlike most beauty pageants in politically correct America, talent and brains don't really count, only costuming, and the crown goes to those with the greatest skill and creativity in hair, make up, and walking in heels.

Fantasia Fair held annually in October in Provincetown, MA; web: www.fantasiafair.org

Eccentric environments

Today it could be accepted as a novel way to recycle newspapers, but back in the 1920s, building a house out of newspapers was, well, odd to say the least. Elis Stenman, an engineer who designed the machinery that makes paper clips, started experimenting with paper as a building material for his summer home. At his **Paper House** in Rockport, the framework and the floors are wood, but the walls are made of pressed paper about an inch thick. Stedman used an estimated 100,000 newspapers in the two room cabin, pressing layers and layers together with glue and varnish. A normal roof protects the house from weather.

Once the walls were up and he was living there, he couldn't ignore the little voice that told him to keep pasting. So he made the furniture, all of it, out of smaller paper logs around a half inch thick. When he couldn't figure out a way to make a paper piano, he simply covered a real one in newsprint instead. He also made a grandfather clock, using a paper from each of the nation's 48 state capitals.

The house was built with the regular electricity and plumbing of the day, which didn't include indoor toilets. And, no, the outhouse wasn't made of paper.

> **Paper House**, #52, Pigeon Hill St, Pigeon Cove, MA. Directions: On entering Rockport follow 127 to Pigeon Cove, after Yankee Clipper Inn take second left on to Curtis St, then left onto Pigeon Hill St.

Just plain weird

Celebrities often meet strange deaths and **Jumbo the Elephant** was no exception. The 'largest elephant on earth' gained fame and for his owner, fortune, in the late 1800s. Unfortunately, he was run over and killed by a freight train. His owner, circus magnate P T Barnum, had the huge beast stuffed and put on display at Tufts University in Medford, where he became the school mascot. When a fire destroyed him yet again, an enterprising administrator scooped the 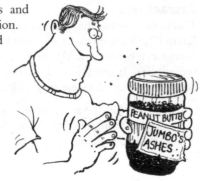 ashes into a peanut butter jar, and there he remains, for Tufts athletes to rub the jar for good luck before their sporting events.

> **Jumbo the Elephant's remains** located at Tufts University in Medford, MA 02155; ℡ 617 628 5000; web: www.tufts.edu. (An empty peanut butter jar holding ashes currently rests in the office of Athletic Director Bill Gehling.)

The **Battle of the Crazy Machines** is a class project designed to challenge the minds of engineering students at the Massachusetts Institute of Technology. Each year the students are given identical kits of unrelated, assorted materials, such as a cardboard tube, a spring, an O-ring, a giant paper clip and half a plastic robot's head. Their challenge is to build a device that will accomplish a specific task, and to do it better than their classmates. One year, the task was to build a machine that would deposit ping pong balls in a trough, all the while fending off opponents. The scoring system is incredibly complex, almost as complex as the theories behind the machines themselves.

Battle of the Crazy Machines held annually at Massachusetts Institute of Technology. Contact MIT; web: pergatory.mit.edu/2.007/

Museums and collections

You may take toilets for granted, but it's a good thing for us that someone takes them seriously. Charles Manoog, a successful plumbing wholesaler, wanted to pay tribute to his trade when he retired, so he began collecting all manner of plumbing parts and pieces, resulting in the **American Sanitary Plumbing Museum** in Worcester. Today, his son carries on the family tradition of attending to all things washable and flushable.

Plumbing industry people are enthralled by the hundreds of tools, pipes, sinks, showerheads, tubs, and toilets scattered about the museum. Older folks are inspired to tell stories from the pre-potty and early-potty days. By the time youngsters realize what the moat that surrounded the castle was for, they stop smirking and begin to realize how good they have it nowadays. Their library can tell you everything you'd ever want to know about the business end of the pipes. Now if they could just do something about plumber's crack...

American Sanitary Plumbing Museum, 39 Piedmont St, Worcester, MA 01610; ↘ 508 754 9453. *Open 10.00am–2.00pm, Tue–Thur or by appointment.*

Science museums aren't dull, academic places any more. In fact, they're become downright inventive, creating playful exhibits that teach without being obvious about it.

Take the Virtual Fish Tank at the **Museum of Science** in Boston. You're 'immersed' in a 1,700 square foot virtual undersea world where you create and interact with your very own virtual fish. Huge projection screens form windows into a central tank that is populated with all kinds of bright, cartoon- like fish.

At the build your own fish stations, you design your own fishies, telling them how to behave, how to react to other fish, how to deal with humans, what to eat and at what depth to swim. Then you let 'em loose and see how much havoc they wreak in the virtual ocean. In spite of yourself, you'll learn how complex behavior patterns can stem from seemingly simple interactions and rules and why simulations provide such valuable scientific information

In the museum's interactive Natural Mysteries exhibit, you move through life-size, life-like dioramas of different environments such as a sandy beach, a rural schoolhouse and a desert cave. Every locale harbors secrets – and only you, using scientific methods, can solve the puzzle. At the beach you'll figure out if you're in Maine or Miami; in the desert you'll identify animals and critters by their footprints; in the schoolhouse, you'll figure out when and how it was built, and by whom. You'll also learn to tell whether a mammal skull belongs to a meat eater or a grazer.

> **Museum of Science**, Science Park, Boston, MA 02114; ↘ 617 723
> 2500; email: information@mos.org; web: www.mos.org. *Open daily,*
> *hours vary by season. Admission charge.*

Glenn Johanson collects dirt, as in the stuff beneath your feet. He has jars and jars of it at his **Museum of Dirt**, collected from places as far flung as Mt Fuji and the Amazon. He's got the dirt from Martha Stewart's house, the grit from Times Square following New Year's Eve, and the grime from O J Simpson's former estate.

Johanson is picky about his dirt: not just any old dirt will do. It needs to be distinctive color-wise, contain bits of something interesting, come from an exotic place, or have some deeper meaning that only the donator can provide. For example, he has the whitest sand, the reddest dirt and the bluest dirt, as well as the pinkest. Celebrities dish out their dirt. Chef Julia Child and entertainers Bob Hope, Mick Jagger, and Dick Clark have all contributed. So have Picasso, Belushi, Versace, and Liberace, although they don't know it. Dave Barry sent lint.

You can see the collection in person if you happen to be in Boston. Or you can enjoy Johanson's strange hobby at his award-winning website. You can also submit your own idea for dirt by filling out the on-line form and explaining why your dirt is so special.

> **Museum of Dirt**, 36 Drydock Ave, Boston, MA 02210; email:
> dirt@planet.com; web: www.planet.com/dirtweb

Some things are just so bad that they become good and you can see why for yourself at the **Museum of Bad Art**. Here, art that's too bad to be ignored is collected from artists who've had a bad brush day, or are just so incompetent that they deserve recognition. You can visit the gallery or attend special events held in the Boston area. Some past exhibitions include 'Know what you like/ Paint what you feel', and 'Gallery in the woods', an art-goes-out-the-window theme that hung from trees in the woods. Only one piece in ten submitted to them actually meets their extremely low standards.

> **Museum of Bad Art**, 10 Vogel St, Boston, MA 02132; ↘ 617 325
> 8224; email: moba@wolrd.std.com; web: www.nvo.com/moba. *Open*
> *6.00–8.00pm Mon–Fri, 1.00–8.00pm Sat–Sun or school holidays.*

The **Salem Wax Museum** explores the hysteria and terror of the famous 1692 witch trials, while Witch Village presents the facts and fantasies surrounding witchcraft. Today, witchcraft is a contemporary, spiritual religion, but back then 'witches' were blamed for society's ills. The witch trials that summer were arbitrary and brutal, representing a lunatic episode in a justice system that doesn't normally succumb to hysteria.

Salem Wax Museum, 288 Derby St, Salem, MA 01970; ➘ 978 740 2WAX or 800 298 2WAX; web: www.salemwaxmuseum.com

Tours

Several companies give Boston tours by land and by sea – all in the same kind of vehicle: World War II amphibious landing craft. **Boston Duck Tours** adds costumed conDUCKtors to show you the sights.

Boston Duck Tours, 790 Boylston St, Plaza Level, Boston, MA 02199; ➘ 617 723 DUCK; web: www.bostonducktours.com

Quirky cuisine

The food isn't quirky, but the building sure is. **The Clam Box** is shaped just like its namesake – a take-out clam box with its flaps open. Built in 1938, when a hurricane plowed through the area, people thought the flaps were sure to take flight. They didn't, and the building has survived subsequent hurricanes just fine.

The Clam Box, 206 High St, Ipswich, MA 01938; ➘ 978 356 9707; web: www.ipswichma.com/clambox

Like the old popular song says, 'everybody plays a fool', but nobody plays it with more outrageous delight than the fool at **Medieval Manor** in Boston, just one of the zanies who run amok in this spoof of the Dark Ages. The manor houses an assortment of oafs, wenches, minstrels and its very own king, who remains benevolent as long as you play by his rules. Songs, stories and assorted antics fill the evening while you consume a six-course meal medieval-style – with your hands. You have your elbows on the table, crumbs fly, and your fingers are in everything. It's fun to act like a toddler again. Dress to mess.

Medieval Manor, 246 E Berkeley Street, Boston, MA 02118; ➘ 617 423 4900; web: www.medievalmanor.com

Quirky quarters

Youth groups can sleep in genuine navy bunks in the crew quarters of the **Battleship** *Massachusetts* docked in Fall River. Chow is served navy style and classes in morse code keep the spirit of the fighting ship alive.

Battleship *Massachusetts*, Battleship Cove, Fall River, MA 02721; ➘ 508 678 1100; email: overnightcoordinator@battleshipcove.com; web: www.battleshipcove.com

'Lizzie Borden took an axe and gave her mother 40 whacks; and when she saw what she had done, she gave her father 41.'

Almost every child in America learns this little ditty which describes the 1892 murder of Lizzie's parents, presumably by Lizzie, although this was never proven conclusively. At the **Lizzie Borden Bed and Breakfast and Museum** in Fall River, you can stand where Lizzie stood and, if you're brave enough, sleep where Mom and Dad did. Overnight guests are treated to a special after-hours tour and served the same breakfast that the victims probably ate. The museum is open for tours during the day.

> **Lizzie Borden Bed and Breakfast and Museum**, 92 Second St,
> Fall River, MA; ✆ 508 675 7333; email: lizziebnb@earthlink.net; web:
> www.lizzie-borden.com

RHODE ISLAND

Rhode Island is known as the vampire capital of America. Researchers have documented at least five deaths attributed to the vampire myth in the early settlement days. By the late 1800s, when embalming practices finally reached rural areas, the idea of digging up bodies to suck their blood clearly lost appeal and the 'vampires' died of starvation.

Festivals and events

The **Fools Rules Regatta** in Jamestown is a zany race of 'anything that floats'. Entrants get two hours at the beach to build their boats from non-marine items such as an old doghouse, car parts, hay bales, and packing crates. The crafts are assigned classes depending upon the number of 'fools' intending to board them. Then the crews prod their reluctant vessels downwind for 500 yards.

> **Fools Rules Regatta** held annually in August in Jamestown, RI.
> Contact Jamestown Yacht Club, PO Box 562, Jamestown, RI 02835;
> email: jwc@dotcomnow.com; web: www.jyc.org

The **Ancient and Horrible's Parade** on Independence Day (July 4th) dates back to 1926 and features several hundred participants dressed in zany, horrible or patriotic costumes. The ancient aspect refers to the past when youth dressed up as historical figures; the horrible part gives folks today an excuse to be as wacky as possible. Many of the entries spoof current events or reflect 'Rhode Island humor', defined as something 'you just have to live here to understand'. Twenty-five thousand folks turn out for the event.

The Beer Can House in Texas is covered entirely with pieces of beer cans. (LH)

Above Only in San Francisco can you find a building demonstrating defenestration, the act of throwing a thing out of a window. (GM)

Below left North Carolina is home to the world's largest chest of drawers. (HP)

Below right Headquarters of the Longaberger Basket Company in Ohio (OH)

THE DANCING COP
Providence's Dancing Cop was the only full time, public eccentric in the state. Tony Lepore, now retired, entertained drivers and pedestrians for years with his 'traffic dance'. Choreographed to his shrill whistling, his leaps, twists, and spins while directing traffic brought him worldwide media attention.

The Dancing Cop, Tony Lepore; web: www.providencedancingcop.com

Ancient and Horribles Parade held annually on July 4 at 4.30pm in the village of Chepachet in Glocester, RI. Contact Glocester Town Hall; ↘ 401 568 6206; web: www.glocesterri.org

The **Penguin Plunge** involves 300 tuxedo-clad swimmers brave enough to take a frigid plunge each New Year's Day.

Penguin Plunge held annually on New Year's Day in Mackerel Cove, Jamestown, RI; ↘ 401 823 7411

Just plain weird
The **Big Blue Bug** that sits atop the New England Pest Control Building has become a Providence landmark. The 58-foot long, 9-foot high subterranean termite – named Nibbles Woodaway – is almost 1,000 times the actual size of a termite. The bug is dressed up with hats and props to celebrate holidays and events.

Big Blue Bug, New England Pest Control Building, 161 O'Connell Street, Providence, RI

Shopping
Oop! is a whimsical and zany gift store with two locations: one in the heart of Providence's historic College Hill district and one in the Providence Place Mall next to Nordstrom. It bottles its own drink called OOP!Juice, offering customized holiday flavors like Ghoulade at Halloween and Turkey Slurpee at Thanksgiving. The stores carry one-of-a-kind knickknacks, home furnishings, jewelry, toys, and trinkets such as naked people candles, nose-shaped pencil sharpeners and fly swatter clocks.

Their motto, 'Shopping for Good, Clean Fun', refers to their inventive in-store games, contests, and special events. They celebrate 'days' like National Sarcasm and Kiss and Make Up Day, star's birthdays, and competitions like National Grouch Day where the grumpiest scowl wins a prize. The stores personify wackiness; their employees are given personas like 'Diva' and 'manager of the Inner Child'.

Oop!, 297 Thayer Street and Providence Place Mall, Provdence, RI 02906; ↘ 800 281 4147; fax: 401 751 9055; web: www.oopstuff.com

Quirky quarters

At the **Rose Island Lighthouse**, the two keeper's bedrooms are available for overnight guests after the museum closes at 4.00pm each day. Restored right down to the pitcher pump at the sink, the lighthouse is furnished with everything you need to play keeper – a gas hot plate, a barbecue, a water pump, solar shower and pollution free, wind-powered electricity. You have to change the bed and clean the place up by the time the museum opens at 10am. They also offer week-long programs where you perform real keeper duties like flag raising, data recording, and maintenance and repairs.

Rose Island Lighthouse, PO Box 1419, Newport, RI 02840; ↘ 401 847 4242; web: www.roseislandlighthouse.org

The **Jailhouse Inn** in Newport is a restored colonial jail with some of the jail accouterments still remaining.

Jailhouse Inn, 13 Marlborough St, Newport, RI 02840; ↘ 401 847 4638 or 800 427 9444; fax: 401 849 0605; email: vacation@historicinnsofnewport.com

CONNECTICUT
Festivals and events

July Fourth, Independence Day, means parades and noise, lots of it. In Willimantic they celebrate with the **Boom Box Parade**, an all-ages procession requiring only a red, white and blue outfit and a cranked-up boom box to enter. No other kind of music is allowed – just these powerful radios which are tuned to station WILI. The event, which began in 1986 when no marching band could be found for the parade, is known for its wacky costumes and floats. The parade's Grand Marshall has worn boom boxes as shoes and towed a bus-sized boom box while skating on roller blades. The precision drill team wields power drills.

Boom Box Parade held annually on July 4th in Willimantic, CT. Contact wili 14 AM, The Nutmeg Broadcasting Company, 720 Main St, Willimantic, CT 06226; ↘ 860 456 1111; fax: 860 456 9501; web: www.wili.com

The annual **Blessing of the Motorcycles** at the Lourdes in Litchfield Shrine is meant to safeguard riders and their bikes from harm, as well as to improve the image of bikers everywhere. A black-robed priest sprinkles holy water on bikers' windshields while offering a prayer to the 50 or so motorcyclists who line their bikes up around the church, single file.

The Blessing of the Bikes annually 3rd Sunday in May in Litchfield, CT. Lourdes in Litchfield Shrine, Rte 118, Litchfield, CT; ☎ 860 867 1041

Eccentric environments

William Gillette was an early 1900s theater actor and playwright who took his role as Sherlock Holmes very personally, so personally, in fact, that he built a replica of 221B Baker Street in the eccentric **Gillette Castle** he built in Hadlyme. With 24 rooms, this rock and cement eccentrocity includes twisting passageways, 47 intricately carved doors equipped with special locking mechanisms, and mirrors strategically placed so he could time his grand entrances for maximum impact. A miniature railway, which once carried visitor Albert Einstein, used to surround the property.

Gillette's Castle, River Road, East Haddam, CT; ☎ 860 526 2336. *Open daily 10.00am–5.00pm May–Oct.*

Just plain weird

The **ghost parking lot** in Hamden causes many a jaw to drop in disbelief. Here, the carcasses of cars past have been mummified in asphalt as a public art project. The sight of these ghostly silhouettes emerging from the deep is quite unsettling.

Ghost Parking Lot, Route 10, Dixwell Ave, Exit 60, Wilbur Cross Parkway, Hamden, CT

Attractions

The nut lady is, as they say in England, one of life's full-on nutters. Elizabeth Tashijian has been elevating nuts to a God-like status for 30 years, turning her estate into an ode to the nut. She sings about nuts, writes about nuts, paints nuts and plugs the power of nuts on radio and television. Of the opinion that nuts are of primeval existence, and that nutcrackers are the nut's worst enemy, her **Nut Museum** in Old Lyme is a sanctuary for abused nuts and a shrine to the virtues of her favorite seed.

The Nut Lady's Nut Museum, 303 Ferry Rd, Old Lyme, CT; ☎ 860 434 7636; web: www.roadsideamerica.com/nut/index.html. *Open Wed, Sat–Sun 2.00–5.00pm or by appointment.*

Museums and collections

The **Children's Garbage Museum** in Stratford makes its point in a big way - big as in a 24-foot long, 12-foot high dinosaur made entirely of trash. The Trash-o-saurus very graphically illustrates how the solid waste monster can grow to overwhelm us. Here, children and adults learn how to reduce, reuse, recycle and rethink our throw-away lifestyles through 15 most unusual, hands-on exhibits.

> **Children's Garbage Museum**, 1410 Honeyspot Rd Extension, Stratford, CT 06615; ➤ 203 381 9571 or 800 455 9571. *Open Wed 1.00–3.00pm Jul–Aug. Admission charge.*

The heroes of horror are honored in style at the **Witch's Dungeon Classic Movie Museum** in Bristol. This one of a kind horrorium features life-size recreations of monster stars in their most famous roles. Cortland Hull, the creator of these creepy dioramas, began molding his characters in 1966 when he was just 13 years old. Frankenstein, Dracula, the Mummy, and the Phantom of the Opera, are among those depicted in movie settings which use actual props from their films. Special voice tracks recorded by the famous voices of horror bring the sets eerily to life. Cortland uses real life casts of the actors and works endlessly on each and every detail. You might say his 30-year pursuit of vampires and other monsters was in his blood.

> **Witch's Dungeon Classic Horror Museum**, 90 Battle St, Bristol, CT 06010; ➤ 860 583 8306; web: www.witchsdungeon.org

Long before television and the internet evolved to entertain and educate, **P T Barnum's Museum** served as a kind of learning center for the masses. Twenty-five cents would buy you hours of outlandish diversion mixed in with fact and history, all disguised as entertainment. Barnum, creator of the 'Greatest Show on Earth' (now Ringling Brothers' Barnum and Baily Circus) was famous for exhibiting freaks of nature, both human and animal. From the smallest man on earth to the bearded fat lady, from Jumbo the Elephant to a two-headed calf, his extraordinary characters astounded 19th-century America.

This Bridgeport museum displays his life as an entrepreneur, politician, journalist, impresario, museum owner, and founder of the famous circus. It's an intriguing reminder of what the world was like before today's political correctness prevented such exploitation.

> **P T Barnum's Museum**, 820 Main St, Bridgeport, CT 06604; ➤ 203 331 1104; fax: 203 339 4341; web: www.barnum-museum.org. *Open Tue–Sat 10.00am–4.30pm; Sun 12.00noon–4.30pm. Admission charge.*

Those of you who think some of our politicians are a few peas short of a casserole will find lots of oddball memorabilia to support your contentions at the **Museum of American Political Life** in West Hartford. Life-sized marching figures lead you into the museum; then a short film introduces you to the history of political campaigns. The Log Cabin to White House display examines how early public relations managers managed to get their candidates to shine in the most favorable spotlight, while the Reform and Protest display features the often quirky characters and groups who brought controversial themes and issues out of the closet. More than 60,000 political objects underscore our colorful past, with new ones added each year. Can Monica Lewinski memorabilia be far behind?

Museum of American Political Life, University of Hartford, 200 Bloomfield Ave, Hartford, CT 06117; ✆ 860 768 4090; fax: 860 768 5159. *Open 11.00am–4.00pm Tue–Fri; 12.00noon–4.00pm Sat–Sun Sept–May; 12.00noon–4.00pm Sat. Donations.*

Back in the 1800s, the Eagle Lock Company was the biggest employer in the area, so locks have a special place in the history of Connecticut. Paying homage to this legacy is the **Lock Museum of America** in Terryville, with more than 23,000 locks, keys and other hardware designed to safeguard man and his material possessions. Eight rooms display locks and safes ancient and modern, including a cannon-ball safe and a chastity belt.

Lock Museum of America, 230 Main St, Route 6, Terryville, CT 06786; ✆ 860 589 6359; web: www.lockmuseum.com. *Open Tue–Sun 1.30–4.30pm May 1–Oct 31.*

The **Barker Character, Comic, and Cartoon Museum** is a nostalgic trip back in time. With its staggering 65,000 items, this Cheshire museum is the lifetime dream of Herb and Gloria Barker, passionate animation collectors for three decades. Their strange hobby has resulted in the most complete tribute to American animation and pop culture existing in the USA today. Besides showcasing movie, television, and cartoon characters, along with their memorabilia, they've acquired advertising characters such as the Pillsbury Doughboy, the Hershey Kisses, Gumby, and the California Raisins.

They'll go anywhere, anytime in search of their piece of Americana, and especially to Florida, the mother-lode of kitsch. Where else would you find a Lone Ranger cereal box ring, a Bing Crosby ice cream box, or a Beatles bobbin' head doll? Nothing in the museum is for sale, but everything is marked with its current market value to collectors. A cartoon theater on the grounds shows old-time cartoons on a big screen. This is a place for sharing childhood memories and gratitude for this couple's obsession.

Barker Character, Comic, and Cartoon Museum, 1188 Highland Ave, Rte 10, Cheshire, CT 06410; ✆ 203 272 2357 or 800 955 2357 or 800 224 2357; web: www.barkeranimation.com/museum. *Open Tue–Sat 11.00am–5.00pm. Admission free.*

Shopping

Now here's something really weird – a supermarket grocery store that goes out of its way to make shopping fun. That's fun, as in a little farmyard zoo out front, staff dressed as cows and chickens, displays that go 'moo' when you push a

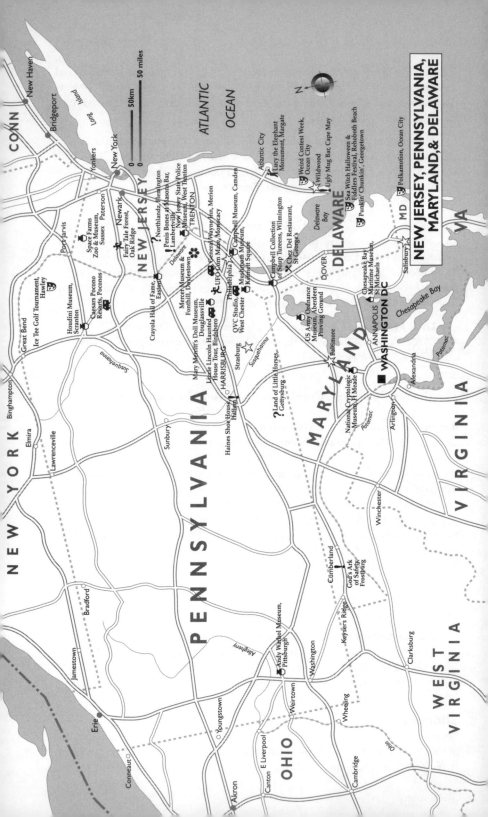

NEW JERSEY, PENNSYLVANIA, MARYLAND, & DELAWARE

button, a free ice cream cone if your bill totals more than $100 and televisions above the check out stations to keep you pacified if you have to wait.

With locations in both Norwalk and Danbury, the staff at **Stew Leonard's** are fond of saying, 'profit is the applause of happy customers'. They must be getting standing ovations because the *Guinness Book of World Records* cites them as having the highest per-square-foot retail sales in the world: an astounding $2,000.

> **Stew Leonard's**, 100 Westport Ave, Norwalk, CT 06851; �‚ 203 847 7214; and 99 Federal Rd, Danbury, CT 06880; �‚ 203 790 8030; web: www.stew-leonards.com. Also located at 1 Stew Leonard Dr, Yonkers, NY 10710; ➚ 914 375 4700

NEW JERSEY
Festivals and events
Ocean City devotes an entire week to weirdness during its **Weird Contest Week**. Even tots are invited to participate. Kids from three to five years old get to demonstrate their abilities to bang on pots and pans, hammer wooden pegs, jingle and jangle bells and generally create a racket. The noisiest kids are crowned Little Miss and Little Mister Chaos.

At the Saltwater Taffy Sculpting event, contestants attempt to create works of art from the sticky, but pliable candy; past entries have featured Ferris wheels, unicorns, computers, and a pair of wearable eye glasses. Participants can also try their hands at french fry and pie sculpting. The wet T-shirt competition doesn't include wearing one; rather, it involves throwing one the farthest.

> **Weird Contest Week** held annually the third week in August in Ocean City, NJ. Contact Public Relations Office; ➚ 609 525 9300

Just plain weird
The ceiling at the **Ugly Mug Bar** in Cape May is covered with mugs emblazoned with the names and numbers of drinking club members. If a mug

---

THE PALACE OF DEPRESSION
The Palace of Depression, an 'eccentrosity' of scrap metal and junk, was built by George Daynor in the early 1930s to show the world that the country's economic Depression wasn't going to get the best of him. A former gold miner, who lost his fortune in the 1929 crash, Daynor heeded an 'angel's' voice that told him where and when to start building. He made a living by giving tours of his palace, the highlight of which was the Knockout Room where he offered to get rid of your bad memories by dropping a bowling ball on your head. (It's unknown if anyone ever took him up on his offer.) The palace was destroyed after his death.

is hanging with its opening facing west, its owner is alive and well, and drinking from his mug whenever he fancies a beer. If its opening faces east, it means the former member is deceased.

Ugly Mug Bar, 426 Washington St, Washington St Mall and Decatur St, Cape May, NJ 08204; ❧ 609 884 3459

Some people collect dinosaur bones. Jack Mason preferred **penis bones**. His collection of animal shafts hangs from the ceiling of Mason's Bar in Lambertville. Bulls, bears, boars, sheep and frogs have given their all to satisfy your curiosity.

Penis Bones, Mason's Bar, 54 N Franklin St, Lambertville, NJ 08530; ❧ 609 397 9874

Museums and collections

Back in the days before soup came in cans, it was actually made in a pot on the stove, a concept difficult for today's youth to grasp. Not only was it homemade, it often simmered for days before being served in a tureen, a deep, covered dish designed for soups and stews. These elaborate utensils, called tureens, are the subject of the exhibits at the **Campbell Museum**.

An impressive tureen was a status symbol for the rich: a communal pot with an attitude. Made from pewter, porcelain and earthenware, tureens most often had animal and food shapes, ranging from cute bunnies to aggressive bulls, and from birds nibbling fruit to swirling grapes and leaves. There are more than 300 of them, ranging from the downright bizarre to the impossibly cute. Soup-o-philes will also be interested in the Campbell Collection of Soup Tureens at Winterthur, DE (see page 140).

Campbell Museum, Campbell Place, Camden, NJ 08103; ❧ 609 342 4800; fax: 609 342 3878; web: www.campbellsoups.com

Space Farms Zoo and Museum in Sussex, named after the Space family, is an odd place filled with old stuff: a miniature circus here, old cars over there, toy collections, Indian skulls, dinosaur bone displays, and an antique merry-go-round. Dead animals in jars and the mounted remains of Goliath, supposedly the world's largest bear, join the live animals in the petting zoo. With more than 100 species, the zoo claims to be the largest private collection of North American wild animals.

Space Farms Zoo and Museum, 218 Route 519, Beemerville, Sussex, NJ 07461; ❧ 973 875 5800; web: www.spacefarms.com

You get to play detective at a crime scene at the **New Jersey State Police Museum** in West Trenton. In the kitchen set up, complete with blood, a chalk outline and yellow crime scene tape, you're supposed to look for clues that will lead to the murderer. Luckily, a video helps you spot what would be obvious to a real detective and you can examine the fingerprints under a microscope. Other displays exhibit an array of confiscated weapons, details on how tough State Trooper training is, the chillingly real Lindberg kidnapping ransom note and an explanation of why America's government was hard at work during the 1930s tattooing chickens to curb the theft of the birds by the hungry unemployed.

New Jersey State Police Museum, PO Box 7068, River Rd,
W Trenton, NJ 08628; ↘ 609 882 2000 x 6400; web:
www.nisp.org/about/museum.html

Attractions

She's six stories tall and weighs 90 tons. Her name is **Lucy**, and she's an elephant monument built in 1881 to draw tourists to the Jersey Shore. A million pieces of wood went into her construction, wood which began showing its age in the 1960s. A 'Save Lucy' committee has raised half a million dollars to get Lucy the plastic surgery she needs. (We should all be so lucky.) She's now open for tours.

Lucy the Elephant Monument, 9200 Atlantic Ave, Margate, NJ;
↘ 609 823 6473

Fairy Tale Forest is a kiddie attraction frozen in time. Dating back to 1957, this delightfully quirky park has winding pathways leading past two dozen child-size buildings. Depicting nursery rhymes and fairy tales, as well as with a few other odd tableaux, the village includes Peter and his pumpkin, the old lady and her shoe, Robin Hood and his merry gang, Goldilocks and the three bears, and the big, bad wolf of Little Riding Hood fame. Children's tunes play throughout the park and storytellers read while sitting in Mother Goose's nest. Santa has his workshop, with elves making presents and playing Christmas carols even in the summer. The place is a real throwback to kinder, gentler days.

Fairy Tale Forest, 140 Oak Ridge Rd. Located south of Route 23,
Oak Ridge, NJ 07834; ↘ 973 697 5656; web:
www.fairytaleforest.com. *Call for hours: they depend on the weather
and season. Admission charge.*

Bruce Zaccagnino has a compulsion to build little bridges, bridges which need to span something if they're to make sense. So Zaccagnino builds little gorges, mountain passes, and rivers. Now his little trains, 135 of them, have something to cross as they run around his not-at-all little **Northlandz** in Flemington, home of his Great American Railway, Doll Museum, and Art Gallery.

Northlandz trains run along eight miles of miniature track while you walk a mile through his world of 35-foot mountains, 40-foot bridges, thousands of buildings and 10,000 freight cars. While the attraction advertises a tour through some of the ' finest scenery in America', you won't see scenery like this anywhere on the planet. His world of cliffs and canyons couldn't possibly be home to cities and towns, so it's best just to appreciate his 25-year effort and leave feeling grateful that you're compulsion-deprived.

> **Northlandz**, 495 Hwy 202 South, Flemington, NJ 08822; ↘ 908 782 4022; web: www.northlandz.com. *Open Mon–Fri 10.30am–4.00pm; Fri–Sat 10.00am–6.00pm. Admission charge.*

Tours
Relive the felt poodle skirt and duck-tail era of the 1950s on the **Doo Wop Trolley Tours of the Wildwoods**. You'll see chrome-plating, pastel neon, and plastic palm trees reminiscent of Elvis-era architecture; buildings with pointy parts, boomerang rooflines, thatched roofs, Kon-Tiki heads, glass walls, and Jetson fins. You'll also experience the social glitter of the entertainment district, playground of such stars as Liberace, Connie Francis and Johnny Mathis.

> **Doo Wop Trolley Tours**, Wildwood, NJ. Contact Doo Wop Preservation League, 3201 Pacific Ave, Wildwood, NJ 08260; ↘ 609 523 2400; web: www.doowopusa.org

Quirky quarters
The Memory Motel is dedicated to music and movies. The roof is bordered with a wavy filmstrip connected to a flashy guitar, the walls are painted – inside and out – with musical and movie theme murals and the water slide is a tongue emerging from a giant pair of lips. The pool is painted with a Yellow Submarine mural in honor of their Beatles' Beach Convention. Screaming neon makes the place hard to miss. The motel's name was taken from a Rolling Stones' song.

Every night they show a feature film, ranging from Disney to classic to contemporary, which you watch while sitting around the pool. Weekly theme weekends include a Jimmy Buffet buffet, Mother's Day with Elvis, and a Parrothead weekend. For seniors, they turn down the rock 'n roll mid-week and crank up the Rat Pack era, playing Sinatra, Martin, Sammy Davis Jr and the rest of the legends. The motel is official headquarters for *Stones People* magazine, the official Rolling Stones' mag.

> **The Memory Motel**, 7601 Atlantic Ave, Wildwood Crest, NJ 08260. ↘ 877 MEMORY 7 (reservations) and ↘ 609 522 3026 (information); ↘ 800 447 7918 (off season); web: www.memorymotel.com. *Open April through September during the season, closed in winter*

PENNSYLVANIA
Festivals and events
It can last ten hours, be two miles in length, and involve 10,000 marchers who spend the better part of each year planning for this most eccentric of parades.

Every New Year's Day, Philadelphia's **Mummers' Parade** takes to the streets with elaborate costumes, comedy, music, and revelry.

Continuing a tradition dating back to colonial times, the parade has its roots in the noisy welcoming of the New Year with firearms and masked processionals. Rowdy revelers would go house to house, chanting, 'Here we stand by your door, as we stood the year before. Give us whiskey, give us gin, open the door and let us in.' It got so out of hand that a law was passed in 1808 declaring such parades to be public nuisances. The celebrations were quieted, but never stopped; today they've evolved into a massive event unifying the various neighborhood groups of yesteryear.

The parade consists of four divisions: the Comics, the Fancies, the String Bands, and the Fancy Brigades. The Comic clubs exist to make people laugh. Experts at satire, they dance their wacky way along the route, making fun of anyone and everything. Nothing escapes their mockery: politics, pop culture, and current events are all fair game. They're judged on originality and how well they play out their chosen theme.

The Fancy division, named for their mission, brings dazzling displays of color, form and texture to life. Magnificent in size, extraordinary in execution, their beauty is stunning. They're judged on color, grandeur and theme; the captain of each club competes in a best-dressed competition.

Fancy Brigades are groups, rather than individuals, presenting choreographed shows in elaborate costumes depicting a theme. Broadway-like stage scenery is carried along on flat bed trucks and assembled each time the brigade stops to perform. How effectively and spectacularly they portray their theme is the criteria for judging.

The String Bands compete for prizes based on their music, their presentation and their costumes. Unusual or unique combinations of instruments may be used, including adding accordions, drums, bells, and saxophones to the stringed instruments. While the core band moves in unison, breakaway groups do specialty acts. Rivalry among bands is quite intense.

You can see and hear all about mummery at the **Mummer's Museum**, open year around. A mummer is defined as any man, woman, or child who participates in the parade, which they do by joining any of the mummer's clubs. Varying tremendously, each club has its own unique style. A truck driver may find himself wearing feathers; while a stodgy judge just might be the clown behind the mask. You'll see some of the past costumes that cost upwards of $20,000 each.

Mummer's Museum, 1100 South 2nd St, Philadelphia, PA 19147; ↘ 215 336 3050; web: www.riverfrontmummers.com/museum/html. *Open Tue–Sat 9.30am–5.00pm; Sun 12.00noon–5.00pm. Admission charge.*

Mummers' Parade held annually on New Year's Day in Philadelphia, PA; web: www.mummers.com. Contact Mummer's Musem (see above).

Just because there's two feet of snow outside doesn't mean you can't play golf. At the **Ice Tee Golf Tournament**, Lake Wallenpaupack is turned into a challenging course complete with tree-lined fairways, greens, water traps, obstacles and roughs. Golfers are limited to two clubs and one putter.

Ice Tee Golf Tournament held annually in Februray in Lake Wallenpaupack, US Hwy 6, Hawley, PA; ➘ 570 226 3191

Eccentric environments

Unlike most self-taught visionary artists who create bizarre surroundings out of misshapen concrete, Henry Mercer used concrete artfully, constructing three architecturally outstanding buildings in the early 1900s to house his twin obsessions: tools and tile. His **Mercer Museum** in Doylestown was built specifically to showcase his extensive collection of tools and work objects, which, he believed, could tell the story of human progress through their evolution and use.

He classified all tools into 12 categories: tools that made other tools, tool used for food, shelter, clothing and transportation; those that aided language, such as books, and the tools used in religion, business, government, art, science, and amusement. Angry that others, especially local historians, didn't share his theory, he designed and built the seven-story structure himself, using just a handful of assistants and a single horse for hauling heavy loads. The tools of 60 trades, including cider-making, black-smithing, printing, and shoemaking, are displayed *en masse*, leaving you to draw your own conclusions as to whether his theory makes sense.

Mercer's obsession with tile led him to build the Moravian Pottery and Tile Works in 1910. Now acknowledged as an artistic leader in the arts and crafts movement of the time, his tiles were used in buildings across America. But it's his home, Fonthill, built in 1908, that gave free reign to his vivid imagination. The 44 room structure was built room by room, stopping only when he'd run out of ideas for more rooms. Fonthill has been called a 'concrete castle for the New World', an amazing tribute to his artistic visions of concrete and tiles. He died in 1930, a lonely and disillusioned eccentric.

Mercer Museum and Fonthill Historical Society, Headquarters, 84 South Pine St, Doylestown, PA 18901; ➘ 215 345 0210. *Open Mon–Sat 10.00am–5.00pm; Sun 12.00noon–5.00pm. Admission charge.*

Just plain weird

The **Haines Shoe House** was the ultimate advertising gimmick – a shoe-shaped building built in 1948 to promote shoes. Designed as a 'promotional' guest house, the shoe motif even appears in the stained glass windows that depict Mahlon Haines, the eccentric millionaire owner, proudly holding a shoe in each hand along with a sign reading 'Haines the Shoe Wizard'. Haines' outlandish promotional antics eventually resulted in a chain of 40 stores throughout Pennsylvania and Maryland. At one time he offered the house free for a weekend to elderly couples so they could 'live like a king and queen'. Another time, he gave the house to honeymooners who had a Haines shoe store in their hometown.

Besides the house, you'll see shoe cutouts in the fence, a shoe doghouse and a shoe-shaped sandbox. When Haines died in 1962, the building was used to sell ice-cream and souvenirs. His granddaughter bought it back 13 years ago and is busy restoring it. There are plans to re-open the shoe house to tourists by the end of 2000.

Haines Shoe House, Hellam, PA; ↘ 717 755 1296. Located on Shoe House Rd, near Hellam exit of US 30. *Scheduled to open 11.00am–6.00pm Wed–Sat.*

Attractions

A giant alien lurks in the **UFO Corn Maze** in Monocacy, waiting to scare the daylights out of anyone making a wrong turn into his domain. The three different mazes, referred to as Area 51, the Crop Circles and the UFO, are inner-connected; your job is to find those connections without being abducted. Correctly answering space trivia questions makes it easier to escape, as does the humiliating waving of a flag, signaling your intention to give up by yelling 'Beam me up, Scotty!'

UFO Corn Maze, Route 724, Monocacy, PA 19542; ↘ 610 404 8366; web: www.ghosttour.com/ufo.html. *Open Sep 15–Oct 31, Fri–Sat 4.00–10.00pm. Admission charge.*

At the **Land of Little Horses** in Philadelphia, miniature Fabellas, only 20 inches high and 70 pounds in weight, daintily strut their stuff at the daily shows in the ranch's arena. The breed ranges in size from poodle to wolfhound, and carry all the familiar equine markings of arabians, clydesdales, and appaloosas.

Land of Little Horses, 125 Glenwood Dr, Gettysburg, PA 17325; ↘ 717 334 7259; email: info@landoflittlehorses.com; web: www.landoflittlehorses.com

Museums and collections

If you weigh as much as 500,000 fireflies, your doctor may want you on a diet. Try cheddar-flavored worm larvae; it's only nine calories a serving and loaded with protein. Barley and bee salad is good, too; just keep away from the chocolate-covered grasshoppers for dessert.

Cooking with bugs is just one of the weird things you can experience at the **Insectarium** in Philadelphia, the country's only interactive, all-bug museum.

You'll get up close and personal to 100,000 insects, 10% of them alive and kicking. The petting corner, where you hold Vinnie the tarantula, and pet a hissing beetle, may be more personal than you'd care to get but, compared to the cockroach kitchen and bath, it may suddenly look mighty inviting.

The kitchen and bath display is the museum's *pièce de resistance*, sitting squarely in the middle of the room surrounded by electrified plexiglass walls and the squeals of the squeamish. Roaches by the hundreds lounge here and there, but flip open the cupboards or sprinkle some water and thousands and thousands more swarm from their dark hiding places. There's never been an escape, or even an escape attempt – why bother when you're living in the buggy version of heaven? Still, the cockroaches eventually die, but don't worry – replacements are bred in cans of garbage behind the scenes.

The Insectarium is the brainchild of Steve Kanya, head bugmeister and former cop, who turned to stamping out bugs instead of crime. Always fascinated with insects, he started displaying his 'catch of the day' in the window of his exterminating business. The display attracted so much attention that he moved to a three story building so he could have his pest execution business on the ground floor and put the museum on the upper two floors. Today half-a-dozen school groups visit every day, and it takes a staff of ten just to manage the bugs and lead tours. It's a favorite place for kids' birthday parties: they're booked months in advance.

Once a year they hold a Bug Olympics. Ants have a weight-lifting competition. Other species, such as roaches, beetles and walking sticks (some grow to a foot in length) get their own racing event; an all-species race is the finale. Downstairs in the gift shop, you can buy lunch boxes, ties, aprons, and picnic cloths festooned with various critters, while their website showcases 500 buggy items for sale.

Insectarium, 8046 Frankford Ave, Philadelphia, PA; ↘ 215 338 3000; web: www.insectarium.com. *Open Mon–Sat 10.00am–4.00pm. Admission charge.*

The **Andy Warhol Museum** in Pittsburg lives up to its eccentric namesake's reputation. Along with displaying the Campbell Soup Cans, the cow wallpaper and double exposures of Elvis, the museum also serves as a sort of living pop culture venue, holding events as strange as the art it contains. Transsexuals have given tours, Tibetan monks have practiced dance routines amid the exhibits, and Friday night happy hours bring in an eclectic mix of Pittsburg's avant-garde along with the just plain curious. Performance art is planned for the future, along with off-beat symphonic concerts and operas.

The Andy Warhol Museum, 117 Sandusky St, Pittsburgh, PA, 15212; ↘ 412 237 8300; fax: 412 237 8340; email: information@warhol.org; web: www.warhol.org. *Open Wed–Sun 10.00am–5.00pm; Fri 10.00am–10.00pm. Admission charge (except Fri).*

Philadelphia produces more mushrooms than any other state – 35% of the entire US crop. So it stands to reason there's a **Mushroom Museum** capping off its achievement. It's a one room place in Kennett Square, but that's big enough to tell you everything you could possibly want to know about mushrooms.

Mushroom Museum, 909 E Baltimore Pike, Kennett Sq, PA 19348; ➚ 610 388 6082 or 800 243 8644; web: www.mushroommuseum.com. *Open daily 10.00am–6.00pm.*

Opened in 1829 as part of a controversial movement to change the behavior of inmates through 'confinement in solitude with labor', **Eastern State Penitentiary** in Philadelphia was the most expensive – and most copied – prison building of the era. Willie Sutton, the 'gentleman bandit' and Al Capone were among its involuntary guests. So was the governor's dog, sentenced in 1924 to life in prison for murdering his wife's precious cat.

All contact between prisoners was prohibited, and full face masks were worn in the rare instances a prisoner was taken out of his cell. Each cell was equipped with feed doors, isolated exercise yards, and sky-lit ceilings. Eventually determined to be cruel and unusual punishment, the system was formally abandoned in 1913. The prison was remodeled over the years before being finally closed in 1971.

You can experience a taste of this bizarre, and now lost and crumbling, world on tours of the facility. Accompanied by a guide, you'll be taken through the central rotunda, the solitary confinement yards, the baseball diamond, and death row. Special events are occasionally scheduled such as Willie Sutton's Birthday, when actors portray the convict's doomed tunnel escape. The Bastille Day Party sees French revolutionaries, armed with muskets and cannon, storm the wall of the prison and capture 'Marie Antoinette' who tosses Twinkies from medieval-style towers. Ignoring her cries of 'Let them eat TastyKake', they drag her to a real, functioning guillotine. The watching crowd decides her fate. Some parts of the prison can be explored without a tour.

Eastern State Penitentiary, 22nd St and Fairmount Ave, Philadelphia, PA; ➚ 215 236 3300; web: www.EasternState.org. *Tours on weekends May–Oct; Wed–Fri summer.*

Houdini lives on, thanks to Bravo the Great and the First Lady of Magic, aka curators John Bravo and Dorothy Dietrich. Their **Houdini Museum** in Scranton is the only one in the world dedicated totally to the magician and escape artist. Houdini, whose real name was Eric Weiss, began performing magic at the age of 12, once running away for a time to join the circus. By the time he was in his 20s, his career as a master illusionist and escape artist was well on its way. Later in life he testified before congress, debunking phony spiritualists and fake mediums. For years after his death, his wife held yearly seances, trying to contact him with a secret code they'd worked out earlier. She never did make contact with him.

Houdini Museum, 1433 N Main, Scranton, PA 18508; ☎ 570 342
5555; web: www.houdini.org

With exhibits from ancient Egypt to the 21st century, the dolls in **Mary
Merritt's Doll Museum** in Douglasville reflect an obsession that led to a
most extraordinary collection. Now run by Mary's daughter, Marjorie, the
museum displays over 1,500 antique dolls, including rarities like a Teddy
Roosevelt safari set, Shirley Temples, and the Dionne Quintuplets. The dolls
don't just sit there, either. Some move mechanically, smoking, cycling, and
dancing. Others are surrounded by friends and family, as in the sets of soldiers
and circuses. Some are doing busywork in the museum's 40 miniature rooms
complete with tiny needlework, dishes and clocks. To keep the guys from
rushing their female companions through the museum, the staff has set up a
re-created toyshop housing thousands of vintage toys made of tin, iron, and
wood. If that doesn't keep the guys busy, you could try pointing them toward
the Ken dolls and G I Joes.

Mary Merritt's Doll Museum, 843 Ben Franklin Hwy W,
Douglassville, PA 19518; ☎ 619 385 3809; web:
www.merritts.com/dollmuseum

While crayons aren't all that eccentric in themselves, America's reaction to
the world's most famous crayon company's decision to retire eight colors in
1990 certainly was. Along with other groups, the Raw Umber and Maize
Preservation Society galvanized the people, forcing the company to
reinstate the wayward hues and to induct them in the **Crayola Factory** in
Easton. Giant, five-foot versions of the wax sticks stand behind glass, ready
to take you down memory lane, accompanied by recorded reminisces. A
free box of crayons awaits you at the end of your tour. You can decide for
yourself if the change from 'flesh' to' peach' was politically correct and
necessary.

Crayola Factory, 30 Centre Sq, Easton, PA 18042; ☎ 610 515 8000;
web: www.crayola.com

You need to schedule a visit to Temple University's School of Podiatry in
Philadelphia in advance if you want to see the **Shoe Museum**, part of the
school's History of Foot Care and the Foot Wear Center. Several hundred of
their 800-plus shoe collection is displayed at any given time. You'll be
blessing your Nikes when you see the 200-year-old wooden shoes from
France, called 'sabots', that gave rise to the expression 'sabatoge', as well as
the Chinese foot- binding exhibit. The miniature salesman's samples are
fun, as is the size 18 shoe worn by a circus giant. Sally Struthers has donated
the six-inch platforms she wore in the 1970s sitcom. *All in the Family*.
Platform shoes have surfaced regularly throughout history, reaching absurd
heights of up to two feet in the 16th century. Wearing the things required

two servants to keep madame upright and looking fashionably frail and dependent.

Shoe Museum, Temple University School of Podiatric Medicine, Philadelphia, PA; ✆ 215 625 5243; web: www.pcpm.edu/shoemus.htm

Voted number one as the 'best place to break the ice on a first date', the **Mutter Museum** in Philadelphia is brimming with bodily oddities too incredible to be kept to yourself. Impeccably displayed at the College of Physicians, this collection of medical specimens from the 1800s includes the result of terminal constipation – a grossly distended colon measuring five feet long and almost a foot in diameter.

The 20,000 items, including fluid preserved specimens, obsolete medical instruments, skeletons, bones and wax models of diseases, combines the collections of many individual doctors. One such doctor in the 1920s carefully catalogued 2,000 objects, removed from the human body, that got there either by swallowing or inhaling: buttons, pins, needles, jewelry, coins, toy jacks, nails and even a bullet. Another collection is a series of wax models showing every disease of the human eye known at the time.

These medical specimens weren't saved for their shock value; they were the teaching and research tools of the 19th and early 20th centuries: 3-D models of the real, not virtual, kind. And knowledge of anatomy wasn't limited just to medical students. The social elite attended medical lectures as well; it was an upscale thing to do.

The museum has some famous body parts, including a tumor removed from President Cleveland's jaw, the thorax of John Wilkes Booth (who assassinated President Lincoln), and bladder stones removed from a Supreme Court justice. Among the most riveting exhibits are those relating to con-joined twins, both dead and still alive, who have been the subject of many a documentary. As disquieting as the displays can be, they're still a fascinating look behind our own scenes.

Mutter Museum, College of Physicians of Philadelphia, 19 South 22nd St, Philadelphia, PA 19103; ✆ 215 563 3737; web: www.collphyphil.org/muttpg1.shtml. *Open Tue–Sat 10.00am–4.00pm; Sun 12.00noon–4.00pm. Admission charge.*

Tours

Mainstream Production Company puts on spooky events such as the **Philadelphia Ghost Tour** which explores the old city streets by candlelight, a **Ghost Tour of Lancaster County** and the **Lizzie Lincoln Haunted House Tour**.

Ghost Tour of Lancaster County. Tour begins at Mrs Penn's Shoppe at the light in Strausburg, PA; ✆ 717 687 6687; web: www.ghosttour.com/lancast.html. *Open Apr 1–Nov 1 varying days 8.00pm. Reservations required. Admission charge.*

Ghost Tour of Philadelphia. Tour begins at 5th and Chestnut Sts, Philadelphia, PA; ↘ 215 413 1997; web: www.ghosttour.com/phila.html. *Tours Apr–May Fri–Sat 7.30pm; Jun–Sep Mon–Sat 7.30pm; Oct daily 7.30pm; Nov Fri–Sat 7.30pm; additional times during summer and Oct. Admission charge.*

Lizzie Lincoln Haunted House Tour, Lincoln Rd, Birdsboro, PA; ↘ 610 40 GHOST; web: www.ghosttour.com/lizzie.html. Directions: Take Rt 422 to Rt. 82 South 1 mile, make right on Lincoln Rd, 1 mile *Open during Oct Fri–Sun. Admission charge.*

If you've ever bought something as a result of a glowing description of it on one of television's many shopping channels, you'll probably enjoy the **QVC Studio Tour** in West Chester. The tour gives you a look behind the scenes of the show whose products beam into one out of every five homes watching TV.

QVC Studio Tour, 1200 Wilson Dr, West Chester, PA; ↘ 800 600 9900; web: www.qvctours.com

Quirky cuisine

Chocolate body parts are big sellers at **Chocolate by Mueller** in Philadelphia. The anatomically correct chocolate heart is popular with cardiologists and their patients, and as the Valentine gift you don't quite know how to react to. 'Oops, I thought you said a dozen noses' explains the chocolate bunch of nostrils. An ear with a chunk bitten out of it is the Mike Tyson special. For the person who's sweet on the outside, but nasty on the inside, send a chocolate covered onion. The selection is always evolving and they're working on a mail order website.

Chocolate by Mueller, Reading Terminal Market, 12th and Arch Sts, Philadelphia, PA; ↘ 215 922 6164 or 800 848 5601; web: www.chocolatebymueller.net

Quirky quarters

Four separate paranormal groups confirm that 17 ghosts haunt the **General Wayne Inn** in Valley Forge. The History Channel, A and E, and Unsolved Mysteries have all made documentaries about the inn. Past guests include William Penn, George Washington, Benjamin Franklin and Edgar Allen Poe.

General Wayne Inn, 625 Montgomery Avenue, Merion, PA 19066; ↘ 610 664 5125

A seven-foot champagne glass whirlpool bath for two awaits you at **Caesars Pocono Resorts**. Famous for their honeymoon packages, the three resorts in Cove Haven, Paradise Stream, and Pocono Palace are for couples only. A fourth resort in Brookdale welcomes families.

There are two dozen different themes in the suites, each of which have four levels, fireplaces and in-room pools and whirlpools, heart-shaped and otherwise. Couples go through 60,000 fireplace logs, 40,000 bottles of bubble bath, 30,000 candles, 20,000 bottles of champagne and 13,000 disposable cameras each year. Frequent guests become members of the Forever Lovers Club.

> **Caesars Pocono Resorts**, Poconos, PA; ↘ 800 942 3301; web: www.caesarspoconos.com

Leave the city behind and awake to a rooster instead of a garbage truck on one of **Pennsylvania's Family Farms**. Member farms offer bed, breakfast and a chance to play farmer for a day or two.

> **Pennsylvania's Family Farms**, Pennsylvania Farm Vacation Association, Inc; ↘ 888 856 6622; email: info@pafarmstay.com; web: www.pafarmstay.com

Sleep in one of 49 restored train cabooses at the **Red Caboose Lodge** in Strasburg. The lodge is the result of an absurdly low bid, made on a dare, to buy snow-bound rolling railroad stock following a 1970 blizzard. The place is listed in the *Guinness Book of World Records*.

> **Red Caboose Lodge**, PO Box 175, Strasburg, PA 17579; ↘ 717 687 5000 or 888 687 5005; email: info@redcaboosemotel.com; web: www.redcaboosemotel.com

The **Fulton Steamboat Inn** in Lancaster County recalls the glory days of river boating. On the promenade deck are nautically themed family cabins with queen beds and bunks for the kids, as well as a pool. The observation deck has the Captain's Quarters, while the sun deck offers adult-only staterooms.

> **Fulton Steamboat Inn**, PO Box 333, Strasburg, PA 17579; ↘ 717 299 9999 or reservations 800 922 2229; email: stmbtinn@800padutch.com

MARYLAND
Festivals and events
A kinetic sculpture is an imaginative, often wacky, but always ludicrous, contraption designed to travel on land, through mud, and over water. These machines can be simple crafts piloted by a single person, or they can be quite

complex, well-engineered vehicles powered by a team of pilots. Used bicycles, gears and machine scraps usually play a big role in their construction, as do a lunatic sense of humor and a wildly inventive brain.

The American Visionary Art Museum sponsors the **Baltimore Kinetic Sculpture Race**, the winner of which races in the world championship. The 30-year-old race has been nominated for a Nobel Peace Prize for recognizing unsung genius, promoting non-polluting transport and lifting the spirit of the communities that hold the race.

There are a number of quirky race rules. The personal security rule requires that each sculpture carry a comforting item of psychological luxury, namely a homemade sock creature made from a not-too-recently washed sock. Another stipulates that each vehicle must be totally human powered, with no pulling, pushing or paddling allowed, although the natural power of water, wind, sun and gravity can be used. The sculptures must also fit on public roads and follow the rules of the open road. Mom's high anxiety clause dictates a quick exit strategy.

The honk and pass politeness rule requires yielding the right of way to another sculpture that wants to pass. A one-finger salute is encouraged. Time penalties are incurred for rule infractions, while time bonuses are given for carrying a passenger, called a barnacle, along the entire course.

The Mediocre Award is given for finishing exactly in the middle. The Next to Last Award is highly coveted, making the end of the race particularly exciting. Awards are also given for best costume, the most memorable breakdown and the most interesting water entry. The winner of the Speed Award gets to be addressed as 'Most Visionary Professor'.

Kinetic Sculpture Race held annually in April in Baltimore, MD. Contact American Visionary Art Museum, 800 Key Highway, Baltimore, MD 21230; ℡ 410 244 1900; fax 410 244 5858; web: www.avam.org/kinetic

More than 2,000 entrants compete each year at the **Ward World Championship Wildfowl Carving Competition** in Ocean City. Carvers enter competitions divided into various levels, divisions, categories, and species. Prizes can run to five figures so it's no wonder they take their craft so seriously. The carvings and decoys are eerily realistic and the art form itself was originated by Native Americans. A fish-carving competition was added in 1998.

Ward Museum of Wildfowl Art, 909 S Schumaker Dr, Salisbury, MD 21804; ℡ 410 742 4988; fax: 410 742 3107; email: ward@wardmuseum.org; web: www.wardmuseum.org

Polka dancers need a lot of stamina. They dance for six to eight hours at a stretch at **Polkamotion**, a continuous music and dance event that stretches over four days. Eight to nine thousand folks attend, but you don't have to dance or dress up to enjoy it. Many people just come to watch and listen to the two dozen or so topnotch bands play Polish polkas, line dances, and waltzes. Dance lessons are offered twice daily if you get the urge to join in.

> **Polkamotion** always held mid-September, the first full weekend after Labor Day, at the Roland E Powell Convention Center, 4001 Coastal Highway, Ocean City, MD 21842. Contact Fred and Marsha Bulinski, ↘ 410 787 8675; or Ocean City Visitor Bureau, ↘ 800 626 2326. *Admission charge.*

Just plain weird

Don't be surprised when a total stranger calls you 'hon' in Baltimore. A cultural quirk, the term is short for 'honey', an endearment extended to one and all. And don't be surprised if the person calling you 'hon' is sporting big hair – really big hair. It's another quirk of the city's reputation for wackiness. While you're there, you might as well do the 'Baltibaloo' which is marketing speak for the off beat attractions the city has to offer.

Pastor Greene had a vision: a large ark, located on a hillside, with people the world over flocking to see it. When (and if) it finally gets built, God's Ark of Safety will serve as a church and as a sign from God that Jesus will soon be coming.

The pastor had his vision in 1974. The completion date is dependent on a schedule set by God, who doesn't seem to be in an awfully big hurry to get this thing built. At this point all you can see are the steel beams forming the structure of the ark, which will be 450 feet long, 75 feet wide, and 45 feet high. Funds to build the ark come from folks donating their time, talent, and money. When finished, it will house a Christian school, a Bible College, a 2,000-seat auditorium, conference facilities, a history room, a counseling center and radio and television equipment. As God provides financing, the pastor's flock moves ahead with construction. Snails will probably be the first in line to board.

> **God's Ark of Safety**, PO Box 52, Frostburg, MD 21532; email: godsark@mindspring.com. Located off I-68, MD Rt 36, left on Cherry Lane.

On Valentine's Day, you can get married, or renew your vows, on ice skates at the **Inner Harbor Ice Rink** at Rash Field in Baltimore.

> **The Inner Harbor Ice Rink** located Rash Field, Key Highway next to the Maryland Science Center, Baltimore, MD; ↘ 410 752 8632

Museums and collections

How many people does it take to change 60,000 light bulbs? You'll have to ask 77-year-old Hugh Hicks, a retired dentist, who has been collecting electric light bulbs since he was a child. At his **Mount Vernon Museum of Incandescent Lighting** you'll see a phenomenal collection of bulbs, the largest of which is a 50,000-watt, three-foot diameter giant made for a 1933 fair; it took ten minutes to reach full brilliance. The smallest bulb, made for missile instrumentation, is a tiny, tiny speck visible only under a microscope. The most expensive bulbs ever made were ordered by the government (naturally!) and they cost $28,000 a piece. There's also an exhibit of Christmas lighting from around the world.

Dr Hicks is most proud of the Edison case, an unbroken history of the rapid evolution of lighting from 1879 to 1892. Developments happened every week, much as in our own high-tech revolution. The private museum is located in a townhouse and you need to call first for an appointment. Leave a message if the doctor isn't in and he'll call you back.

Mount Vernon Museum of Incandescent Lighting, 717 Washington Pl, Baltimore, MD 21201; ❱ 410 323 3453 or 410 752 8586

Outsider artists have a home away from home at the **American Visionary Art Museum** in Baltimore. Outsider art is made by people who are driven to create, but may be unaware they're making art. Such artists are obsessive about their creations, use unusual materials and have little or no knowledge of the mainstream art world. The museum's ever-changing collection is understandably eclectic and ranges from the delightfully naive to the decidedly bizarre. They've had a life-size, interactive chess set populated with angels and aliens and an art car, contributed by psychic Uri Geller, that consists of 5,000, psychically bent, spoons and forks, many of which were used or touched by celebrities.

They hold off-the-wall workshops where you can create your own wacky inventions out of trash and special events, like the double wedding of life-size robot families. Throughout this book you'll find many descriptions of the self-made 'eccentric environments' referred to at the museum

The Visionary Art Museum also sponsors a Strut Your Stuff Pet Parade, with prizes for the best pet and owner look-alikes and the animal 'least likely to succeed as a pet'. Any kind of creature is welcome.

American Visionary Art Museum, 800 Key Highway, Baltimore, MD 21230; ❱ 410 244 1900; fax 410 244 5858; web: www.avam.org. *Open 10.00am–6.00pm, Tue–Sun. Admission charge.*

Baltimore, the city that prides itself on lunacy, is the perfect setting for the **American Dime Museum**. James Taylor, an auditor and life long freak-show fanatic, and his partner, Dick Horne, have opened an entire museum devoted solely to the weird. Located in a dusty row house, it's filled with bizarre oddities like two-headed calves, nine-foot mummies, and flesh-eating toads. James, whose friends include such characters as Alligator-skin Man and his wife Monkey Girl, publishes a journal called *Shocked and Amazed* which recalls the tall tales of the strange, secretive world of the carnivals, exposing some of its secrets as well.

From the mid 1800s up to World War II, carnival side-shows and performances provided bizarre entertainment for audiences willing to allow themselves to be shocked and amazed by human misfits, outlandish oddities and mind-boggling stunts. The last turd to pass from Abraham Lincoln's body is a prime example. At the museum you'll see a boy's head with a kazoo wedged through his mouth and up into his nasal cavity, accompanied by a long winded story, displayed on poorly typed yellowing paper, of how the unfortunate victim came to be in such dreadful circumstances. It's Dick's job to create these fakes – he's an artist, a master of fake fakery, as well as one very creative storyteller.

Dick and James can tell you the difference between born freaks, like the Monkey Lady, and made freaks, like those with pierced and tattooed bodies. Blockheads are folks who shove things like spikes up their nose, and talkers are the glib guys responsible for luring you and your dime into the tent. Their descriptions, calculated to create excitement and anticipation, were marvels of superlatives and promises. Talkers would have made great politicians.

James, who sports a handlebar mustache and dresses like an old-time carnival barker, taught himself how to lie on a bed of nails (the secret is in the spacing). Dick can take a dried piece of liver and, with skill and imagination, convince you it's the lip of a lion shot by Teddy Roosevelt or some equally preposterous tale. It's all in the presentation. Their extensive library even has an antique how-to book entitled *Presenting Human Oddities for Amusement and Profit*. James abhors the book's premise, which is understandable in today's culture.

American Dime Museum, 1808 Maryland Ave, Baltimore, MD 21201; ☏ 410 230 0263; email: showmanjames@netscape.net. *Open Wed–Fri 12.00noon–3.00pm; Sat–Sun 12.00noon–4.00pm. Admission charge.*

Children can pretend to be dentists, watch videos sitting on giant molars, and learn all about the tooth fairy at the **National Museum of Dentistry** in Baltimore. This quirky, entertaining little museum explores the world of teeth, a world no one likes to think about until pain gives them a compelling reason to do so. George Washington's famous 'wooden' teeth are here; turns out they aren't wooden at all.

National Museum of Dentistry, 31 S Greene St, Baltimore, MD 21202; ☏ 410 706 0600; web: www.dentalmuseum.org. *Open Wed–Sat 10.00am–4.00pm; Sun 1.00–4.00pm. Admission charge.*

Great Blacks in Wax in Baltimore may not be the glitziest wax museum you'll ever see, but it certainly has the most heart. Owners Elmer and Joanne Martin have been nurturing their museum along since 1980 when it consisted of just four figures in the back of their truck. Determined to instill pride in black culture and history, they took their show on the road, visiting schools and churches to get their message across. Eventually they were able to open an actual museum, with almost two dozen figures, in 1983.

Today they have 130 of them, representing key figures in American black history and culture. The most gripping display is a slave ship documenting the horrid conditions the slaves had to endure as they were imprisoned and sent to America in slave ships. Rosa Parks, who triggered the civil rights movement by refusing to sit in the back of the bus, is shown being arrested by white officers as she stepped off the bus. Former black congresswoman Shirley Chisholf donated two of her outfits, one for winter and one for summer. To make their figures economically, the owners construct only the black heads and hands of their models; the bodies are those of white mannequins.

Great Blacks in Wax Museum, 1601 E North Ave, Baltimore, MD; ℩ 410 563 3404; fax: 410 675 5040; web: www.greatblacksinwax.org

Part museum, part tattoo parlor, the **Baltimore Tattoo Museum** gives you a glimpse into the art of tattooing, an art grossly under-appreciated by most folks. The walls are covered with panels of tattoo designs and photographs of people proudly showing off their decorated bodies. And if someone is being tattooed, you're welcome to watch as long as the tattoo isn't going on a body part best left unexposed to strangers.

Baltimore Tattoo Museum, 1534 Eastern Ave, Baltimore, MD; ℩ 410 522 5800; web: www.baltimoretattoomuseum.com. *Open daily 12.00noon–7.00pm.*

This place just oozes with testosterone. Grown-up GI Joes are transported back to childhood, or war time, as they climb all over the rockets, cannons, and tanks displayed at the **US Army Ordnance Museum** in Aberdeen. The 25 acres of rusted, used equipment give you some idea of how the Pentagon spends our money. Hey, where are those $600 toilet seats?

US Army Ordnance Museum, Bldg 2601, Aberdeen Proving Ground, MD 21005; ℩ 410 278 3602 or 410 278 2396; fax: 410 278 7473; web: www.ordmusfound.org. *Open daily 10.00am–4.45pm; closed national holidays except Armed Forces Day, Memorial Day, July 4, Veterans Day. Admission free, donations appreciated.*

Cryptology is a hidden world, shrouded in secrecy if it succeeds and steeped in despair when it fails. The **National Cryptologic Museum,** which opened its doors in 1993, welcomes the public to look behind the curtain at the people

– and the machines they invented – that were responsible for transmitting and intercepting secure communications. While computers have transformed the field, it would still be difficult today to break a code based on an obscure language that only a few people speak, as was the case with the Navajo Code Talkers of World War II.

National Cryptologic Museum located at the intersection of Maryland Route 32 and Maryland Route 295; ☎ 301 688 5849; web: www.nsa.gov/museum. *Open Mon–Fri 9.00am–4.00pm; Sat 10.00am–2.00pm.*

It takes a duck to bag a duck, and the Ward brothers spent most of their lives making realistic decoys to help hunters get their bird. The **Ward Museum of Wildfowl Art** in Salisbury preserves their legacy and the brothers' carving techniques are still carried on here. A detailed decoy can take up to three days to make and cost upwards of $100.

Ward Museum of Wildfowl Art, 909 S Schumaker Dr, Salisbury, MD 21804; ☎ 410 742 4988; fax: 410 742 3107; email: ward@wardmuseum.org; web: www.wardmuseum.org

Quirky quarters

Youth groups can bring their sleeping bags and stay overnight at the **Chesapeake Bay Maritime Museum** in St Michaels. Addressing each other as 'Keeper so and so', they learn about the lifestyle of lighthouse keepers. Everyone performs all the traditional duties of a keeper, including standing watch. The overnight program is offered weekends in April, May, September and October. During the summer, families can stay, too, during one of the three public lighthouse programs.

Chesapeake Bay Maritime Museum, Mill St, PO Box 636, St Michaels, MD 21663; ☎ 410 745 2916; fax: 410 745 6088; web: www.cbmm.org

DELAWARE
Festivals and events

Delaware's home grown insanity event goes by the name of **Punkin' Chunkin'**, an annual November occasion pitting man against pumpkin. It started back in 1986 when some guys with way too much time on their hands came up with a challenge to see who could design a machine to throw a pumpkin the farthest. Of the three original contraptions, the winning chunker, with a 128-foot throw, was a bunch of garage door springs connected to a car frame. The losers had to pack up their ropes, tubes, pulleys, springs, and poles and slink off into the night.

Today, 48 teams and 30,000 spectators form the world's largest hurling party. There are only four rules: all the pumpkins must weigh between eight and ten pounds, pumpkins must leave their machine intact, no part of the machine can cross the starting line and no explosives are allowed. The chunkers themselves have several categories, including human powered, unlimited, centrifugal, catapult, air cannon and pneumatic. Even the whimpiest of contraptions manages over 250 feet today, while the most sophisticated can hurl a pumpkin almost 3,700 feet. On two earlier occasions the activiity had to be moved to larger quarters when the machines became so effective that the pumpkins started out-distancing the fields in which the event was held.

Punkin' Chunkin' held annually in November in Georgetown, DE. Contact Pumpkin Chunk Association, c/o B&B Mechanical RD #4, Box 192-D, Georgetown, DE 19947; ☎ 302 856 1444; web: www.punkinchunkin.com

The **Sea Witch Halloween and Fiddlers Festival** at Rehoboth Beach features a broom-tossing contest, a huge costume parade, and a best costumed pet contest.

Sea Witch Halloween and Fiddlers Festival held annually on Halloween weekend in October in Rehoboth Beach and Dewey Beach, DE. Contact Rehoboth-Dewey Chamber of Commerce; ☎ 800 441 1329 or 302 227 2233

Museums and collections

The **Campbell Collection of Soup Tureens** at Winterthur is unusual in containing nothing except soup tureens and soup-related items. The collection provides a fascinating look at the history of food from as far back as 500BC. Some of the tureens are quite unusual and bizarre, resembling everything from animals to fruit. Soup-o-philes will also be interested in the Campbell Museum in Camden, NJ (see page 122).

Campbell Collection of Soup Tureens at the Winterthur Museum, Garden and Library, Route 52, 6 miles northeast of Wilmington, DE; ☎ 302 448 3883; web: www.wintherthur.org.

Quirky cuisine

If you've got a hankering for muskrat, two restaurants can oblige: **ChesDel Restaurant** in St Georges and the **Wagon Wheel Restaurant** in Smyrna. Wonder if you can ask for a muskrat bag for leftovers?

Ches Del Restaurant, US 13 North, St. George's, DE; ☎ 302 834 9521

Wagon Wheel Family Restaurant, 110 S Dupont Blvd, Smyma, DE 19977; ☎ 302 653 1457

Southeastern Region

WASHINGTON DC

See the secret side of Washington, DC, through real spy's eyes with retired agents from the FBI (Federal Bureau of Investigation), the CIA (Central Intelligence Agency), and the KGB. The two-and-a-half-hour **Spydrive Tour of Washington, DC**, long considered the spy capital of the world, is still home to clandestine operations. According to our leaders, at any given moment someone is likely spotting potential recruits, photocopying or stealing secret documents, using dead drops, evading surveillance, writing up intelligence reports, sending coded messages or living a double life. The tour covers 30 sites involving major spy cases over the past 50 years. Seeing the places where unnoticed events often meant deadly consequences will give you a whole new perspective on James Bond movies.

> Spydrive Tour of Washington, DC. Optional pick-up in Virginia.
> ℩ 1 866 SPYDRIVE; web: spydrive.com. *Admission charge.*

VIRGINIA
Eccentric environments

Pharmacist John Hope estimated he'd saved about 10,000 bottles back in the 1940s, which he used to build the **Bottle House**, a one-room cottage his children used as a playhouse. The walls are formed using bottles of all kinds – clear, colored, gallon size and pint sized – which are laid so that flat bottle bottoms are on the inside and the uneven bottle tops are on the exterior. The bottles light up when the sun shines through; at night a blue bottle chandelier provides illumination.

> **Bottle House**, 1551 N Main St, Hillsville, VA.

In 1980 John Miller told everyone he was going to build a castle. Being a man of his word, he followed through – with a 7,000-square-foot castle built to withstand attack. **Bull Run Castle** in Aldie is for real, complete with an armory, two portcullis barricades, tunnels and arrow slits. The dungeon is accessed through a trap door. While John, now 71, doesn't expect to have to

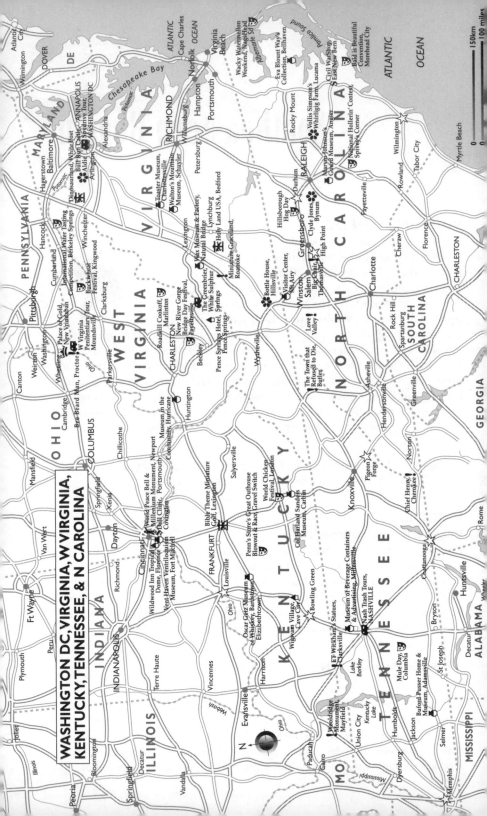

defend his castle, he is a stickler for details. 'Just like I wouldn't build a bike I couldn't ride, I wouldn't build a castle that couldn't be defended,' he said.

Eventually, he'd like to open as a bed and breakfast, but for now the fortress with its 89 windows and 14 closets has served as the meeting site for a vampire group, for a couple of medieval weddings and for a few masquerade parties now and then.

Bull Run Castle located on Route 15, 2 miles south of Hwy 50, Aldie, VA; ↘ 703 327 4113

Just plain weird

It's a little **Miniature Graceland** in Roanoke, a knee high tribute to the King built by Don and Kim Epperly. In the side yard of their home are miniature versions of Graceland, Elvis' Tupelo birthplace, Elvis' car museum, and several performance halls where the King performed. A little revolving Elvis stands on the stage of a miniature auditorium before an audience of Barbie groupies. Tiny groupies also cavort around the bedpan swimming pool behind Graceland. The display is lighted at night and you're invited to visit anytime.

Miniature Graceland, 605 Riverland Dr, Roanoke, VA; ↘ 540 56 ELVIS

Attractions

They may not be anatomically correct, but the 35 quasi-realistic beasts at **Dinosaur Land** in White Post do have a certain quirky appeal. Dating from the early 1970s, when scientists believed dinosaurs were slow, squatty and stupid, the creatures in this prehistoric forest are still worthy of a Kodak moment, if only for the nostalgia of it all. A more up-to-date addition is a scene involving a T-Rex ripping the flesh from a screaming herbivore who bleeds from an invisible tube pumping out a stream of blood through his gaping wounds. It's enough to make you appreciate the oldies, but goodies. And while it may not make a lot of scientific sense that King Kong, a 20-foot cobra, and a giant octopus share forest quarters with dinosaurs, it does make tourism sense.

Dinosaur Land, Rt 1, Box 63A, White Post, VA 22663; ↘ 540 869 2222; fax: 540 869 0951; email: info@dinosaurland.com; web: www.dinosaurland.com

Don't just show up at **Holy Land USA** in Bedford unless you plan to walk three miles through the life and deeds of Jesus Christ. It's best to schedule a journey well in advance and to allow about three-and-a-half hours to complete it. Holy Land itself is a nature sanctuary dedicated to the journeys and deeds of Christ. Two-hundred-and-fifty acres contain replicas – or representations – of the biblical lands in Israel, Syria, and Jordan. The trail winds from Bethlehem to Jericho to Galilee, then to Jerusalem, to Lazarus, and back again to Bethlehem.

You have plenty of choices as to the type of journey you can take: walking with a guide; riding with a guide in an air-conditioned and heated vehicle; riding in a set of farm wagons pulled by a 4WD vehicle; riding in a bus with or without air-conditioning; riding in an air conditioned van; riding in a hay wagon; or (whew!) riding in a truck. A Holy Land guide accompanies your journey.

Holy Land USA, 1060 Jericho Rd, Bedford, VA 24523; ☏ 540 586 2823; web: www.holyland.pleasevisit.com

Museums and collections

One-hundred-and-twenty-five wax figures come together to narrate historical vignettes at the **Wax Museum and Factory** in Natural Bridge. Aided by electronic animation, light, and sound, the figures act out scenes from Virginia history, including the founding fathers, Confederate soldiers and generals, and moon-shiners. You take a seat for the theatrical presentation of 'The Last Supper'. A tour of the wax factory follows.

Wax Museum and Factory, PO Box 57, Natural Bridge, VA 24578; ☏ 800 533 1410; email: natbrg@aol.com

Eric Norcross didn't plan on opening a **Toaster Museum**. The art gallery/café owner was working in his tiny kitchen one day when he realized he could gain space if the toasters were put out on the tables. They were an instant hit with the customers, who could now get their toast exactly the way they liked it. The toasters became conversation pieces and Eric started looking for unusual ones to keep the buzz going.

Five hundred toasters and one museum later, Eric and his wife Kelly are so passionate about toasters that they've formed a non-profit foundation with a mission to teach about history, design trends, and cultural preferences as seen through the slots of a toaster. They have no plans to add blenders or electric fry-pans: that would dilute the purity of the museum. Eventually they'd like to display every toaster ever made, anywhere in the world.

These toaster archeologists figure out a toaster's age by researching old advertisements and catalogs but accurate dating isn't always easy. If you need an old toaster repaired, they can refer you to toaster geeks. Living encyclopedias of toaster talk, they can tell you that the word 'toast' came from the old French '*toste*' meaning to scorch or to burn. They can even explain the dreaded phenomenon of toast sweat to you. At the moment, the museum is homeless, but the proprietors expect to be popping up again for visitors soon.

Toaster Museum scheduled to open in Charlottesville in late 2001.
Call Eric or Kelly for an appointment; ↘ 804 293-3569; web:
www.toaster.org

Even people who never watched *The Waltons*, a show that ran on TV between
1972 and 1981, still know who John-Boy was. The **Waltons' Mountain
Museum** in Schuyler pays tribute to the actor and the series; the museum's
goal is to perpetuate the family values portrayed on the show.

Waltons' Mountain Museum, PO Box 124, Rt 617 Schuyler, VA
22969; ↘ 804 831 2000; web: www.waltonmuseum.org. Located
between Charlottesville and Lynchburg. *Open daily 10.00am–4.00pm
Mar–Nov. Admission charge.*

WEST VIRGINIA
Festivals and events
The spa town of Berkeley Springs came up with a novel way to promote itself.
It holds an annual **International Water Tasting Competition**, part of a
three-month long Winter Festival of the Waters, and it's the largest water-
tasting competition in the world. Municipal waters from several dozen states
compete for the honor of best-tasting tap water; bottled waters, both still and
sparkling, from 18 states and half-a-dozen countries, compete not only for
taste but for best packaging honors as well. The awards presentation itself is a
'black tie or bib-overall' optional event. Taste is rated in three categories –
flavor, aftertaste and mouth-feel – and is judged by journalists from magazines
and newspapers around the country.

International Water Tasting Competition held annually in
February in Berkeley Springs, WV. Contact Travel Berkeley Springs,
↘ 800 447 8797; web: www.berkeleysprings.com/water

One day each year, the world's longest, single-arch-span bridge is closed to
traffic and open to 100,000 people who gather to watch several hundred hardy
souls fling themselves off it into the water 1,000 feet below. Known as BASE
(bridge, antenna, spans and earth-fixed-objects) jumpers they consider the
New River Gorge Bridge Day Festival in Fayetteville to be their annual
convention. Beneath the bridge, rock climbers practice their skills and the
roads leading up the bridge are filled with several hundred vendors ready for
a feeding frenzy of funnel cakes, corn dogs, barbecue, and handmade ice
cream.

New River Gorge Bridge Day Festival held annually in October in
Fayetteville, WV; web: www.nps.gov/neri/bridgeday.htm. Contact
New River Convention and Visitors Bureau, ↘ 800 927 0263; email:
newriver@newrivercvb.com

Several years ago, when the state of West Virginia made it legal to take home – and use – animals killed by cars, the **Roadkill Cookoff** in Marlinton was born. Dishes with names like Thumper Meets Bumper, Asleep at the Wheel Squeal, One Ton Wonton, Rigormortis Bear Stew, Tire Tread Tortillas and Deer on a Stick are judged for their taste – or lack of it. Citizens of the state have been picking up, and cooking, roadkill for a long time now; they just hadn't named a festival in honor of the practice.

> **Roadkill Cookoff** held annually in September in Marlinton, WV. Contact the Pocahontas County Tourism Commission; ↘ 1 800 336 7009; or the West Virginia Division of Tourism, 2101 Washington St, E Charleston, WV 25305; ↘ 304 558 2220 or 800 225 5982; web: www.callwva.com

In Kingwood, the **Buckwheat Festival** serves up 20,000 buckwheat pancake, sausage and apple-sauce meals at the annual festival that also features a lamb-dressing competition, as in bonnets and bows, à la contrary Mary.

> **Buckwheat Festival** held annually in September in Kingwood, WV; ↘ 304 329 1780 or 304 329 2501; email: buckwheatfest@abac.com; web: www.buckwheatfest.com

Just plain weird

Steve Conlon has a mighty peculiar talent. He takes a queen bee, puts her in a tiny box on his chin and then waits for the thousands of bees that follow her to form a huge beard of bees on his chin and neck. Known as the **'Bee Beard Man'**, Steve has been doing this for more than a decade and claims to love every minute of it. He appeared on Jay Leno's famous late-night talk show where he endured an unusually high number of stings – about 50 or 60.

Steve and his wife, Ellie, raise honey bees and produce honey on their farm, Thistledew, in Proctor. He and his bee beard can be seen at the annual Honey Festival in Parkersburg, occasionally at other events around the state and at his Thistledew Farm.

> **Steve Conlon, Bee Beard Man**, ThistleDew Farm, RR 1, Box 122, Proctor, WV 26055; ↘ 800 85 HONEY; fax: 304 455 1740; email: thistle@ovis.net; web: www.thistledewfarm.com

Grandiose schemes

Dubbed 'America's Taj Mahal', the **Palace of Gold** at the Hare Krishna's New Vrindaban complex near Moundsville is an astounding example of faith based architecture. Built by self-taught devotees of Srila Prabhupada, the inventor of the 'religion' best known for its robed, shaved-head airport beggars, this Indian-style palace is an extravagant, ornate, and bizarre structure. Certainly the most unusual, and startling building in the state, it was built specifically to draw tourists to the teachings of Krishna.

The rose, black and gold palace is topped with a 22-karat, gold-leaf dome, and furnished with ornate carved panels, gold bath fixtures, crystal murals and chandeliers, stained glass windows and four dozen varieties of marble, onyx, and other stones. The palace contains rooms supposedly used by the guru, but in fact he died before its completion. A life-size idol of his guru-ness sits on a platform above a figure of Christ, who is portrayed sitting in the lotus position. Devotees, who have renounced all their worldly possessions, worship at the idol's feet.

At the peak of the Hare Krishna movement in the 1980s, hundreds of followers lived at the complex, dominated by a man who called himself Bhaktipada. Until he (and his cohorts) received long prison sentences for murder and racketeering in 1996, he ruled his kingdom with an iron fist, establishing rigid rules and regulations and meting out punishments, such as days of silence, for transgressions. Every act of coitus had to be authorized by Bhaktipada. Today just a few dozen believers remain at the compound, keeping the tourist fires burning and trying to rebuild the sect's tattered image.

> **Palace of Gold**, New Vrindaban, WV. Directions: from I-70 exit to Wheeling I-470, take exit 2 (Bethlehem) south to Rt 88, right on Rt 88 to end and stop sign, turn left, look for signs for Palace of Gold, approximately 4 miles to left at fork in road. Rd 1, NBU#24, Moundsville, WV; ✆ 304 843 1812; web: www.palace of gold.com

Museums and collections

An entire building exposes itself at Hurricane's **Museum in the Community**. Built to demystify architecture, most everything is exposed to view. Painted pipes can be followed all through the structure, as can its exposed ductwork and plexiglass-covered wiring and switches. The structure is like a three-dimensional textbook, built on a marked, eight foot grid.

> **Museum in the Community**, 3 Valley Park Dr, PO Box 423, Hurricane, WV 25526; ✆ 304 562 0484; email: info@museuminthecommunity.org; web: www.museuminthecommunity.org

Tours

The **Greenbrier** is an ultra-posh hotel with a secret: it has an underground cold war facility designed to house congressional members in the event of a nuclear strike on Washington, DC. Called the Government Relocation Center, the bunker was equipped to house 1,100 congressmen, staff, government officials and their families. Payroll, social security and health documents were stored there so citizens could still get their monthly checks.

A stay in the bunker would have been very strange indeed, especially considering what would be going on topside. Everyone in the contamination-free facility would have been dressed in green jumpsuits, slept in bunk beds and shared meals of freeze-dried foods in the cafeteria. An electronic media production room would have allowed this elite group to stay in touch with survivors, if there were any. The bunker was maintained at top readiness for 34 years. The mechanical systems were tested each week and food supplies rotated. Even the magazines were kept current. They give guided tours daily March through December. Information about the Greenbrier was the basis for a $1 million question on *Do you want to be a millionaire?*

> **Greenbrier Hotel**, 300 West Main St, White Sulphur Springs, WV 24986; ↘ 800 453 4858; fax: 304 536 7834; web: www.greenbrier.com

Staff on the **West Virginia Penitentiary Tour** treat you like inmates, loading you on the prison bus, fingerprinting and photographing you on arrival, then leading you into your impossibly tiny cell and slamming the door shut (you get to leave if you want to). Later, you'll see prison art, the gallows and an electric chair. The Gothic-style fortress, built with convict labor, was closed in the mid 1990s, when these very experiential, very memorable, tours were instituted. The prison gift shop sells tin cups, prison garb, and handcuffs.

> **West Virginia Penitentiary Tour**, 818 Jefferson Ave, Moundsville, WV 26041; ↘ 304 845 6200; email: info@wvpentours.com; web: www.wvpentours.com

Quirky quarters

The **Historic Pence Springs Hotel** began life as a resort in the 1920s, then became the State Prison for Women from the mid 1940s until 1983. Once again a hotel, the building still has some features from its former days, including graffiti, peep holes and steel bar doors.

> **The Historic Pence Springs Hotel**, PO Box 90, Pence Springs, WV 24962; ↘ 304 445 2606 or 800 826 1829; fax: 304 445 2204; email: pencehotel@newwave.net; web: www.wvweb.com/www/Pence-Springs-Hotel

KENTUCKY
Festivals and events

Penn's Store, the oldest country store in America, holds the **Great Outhouse Blowout and Race** in Gravel Switch each fall. The event was started when the store, previously potty deprived, celebrated the installation of an outhouse for customer use in 1992. The store still doesn't have indoor plumbing.

> **Great Outhouse Blowout and Race** held annually in October in Gravel Switch, KY. Contact Penn's Store, 257 Penn's Store Rd, Gravel Switch, KY 40328; ↘ 859 332 7715 or 859 332 7706; web: www.pennsstore.com

What weighs 950 pounds and measures 29 feet by 12 feet? The world's biggest, fresh-baked brownie. Every year the folks at the **Duncan Hines Festival** in Bowling Green try to better their prior year's record size. On Friday evening they assemble the ingredients: 615 packages of brownie mix (Duncan Hines, of course), nine-and-a-half gallons of water, 1,845 eggs, 19 gallons of oil, and 615 pounds of frosting. Saturday is bake day. The giant batch of brownies takes 325 hours of baking at 350 degrees, the equivalent of 13 full days of baking. More than 250 volunteers assemble, bake and decorate the brownie. Serves about 12,000 people. Don't try this at home.

Duncan Hines Festival held annually in June in Bowling Green, KY. Contact Bowling Green Convention and Visitors Bureau; ☎ 270 782 0800; web: www.duncanhinesfestival.com

Rats race for bits of Fruit Loops cereal at **Spalding University's Running of the Rodents**. The bizarre event began in 1971 when a science teacher heard a student complain that 'Life is like a rat race.' The event uses lab rats trained to run farther and faster around a track by dangling the cereal in front of them. The contestants are given names based on the theme. In 1999 it was 'Hooray for Hollywood', with contenders sporting names like Humpfry Bograt and The Talented Mr Ratley. The students themselves compete in a Fruit Loop eating Contest and a Rodent Parade. Betting is limited to a 25 cents maximum. Winning rats wear Fruit Loop garlands, at least until they've finished eating them.

Spalding University's Running of the Rodents held annually in April in Louisville, KY; ☎ 800 896 8941 extension 2422; web: www.spalding.edu/events/ratrace.htm

The annual **World Chicken Festival** is a 'finger-lickin' good' tribute to Colonel Sanders, founder of Kentucky Fried Chicken. A quarter of a million folks attend the four day event, held in the town of London. Thirty thousand chickens get fried in the world's largest skillet, which measures ten-and-a-half feet in diameter, weighs 700 pounds and boasts a handle eight feet long. Contests abound, including competitions in the Survival Egg Drop, Chicken Wing Eating, Best Chicken Costume, Chick-O-Lympics, Rooster Crowing, Strutting, and Clucking and Colonel Sanders Look-a-Like events.

World Chicken Festival held annually in September in London, KY; ☎ 800 348 0095; web: www.chickenfestival.com

Just plain weird

It's a group of very stoned people, all marching in line but going nowhere. Called the 'strange procession that never moves', the 18, life-sized stone statues mark the gravesite of Colonel Henry Wooldridge. The good colonel commissioned the statues of his parents, sisters, brothers, nieces and of his childhood sweetheart, who died tragically young, before they could marry.

The **Wooldridge Monuments** at Maplewood Cemetery in Mayfield are all carved of granite; only the colonel himself is carved out of marble. His statue shows him mounted on his faithful horse 'Fop'.

> **Wooldridge Monuments** located US 45 North, Mayfield, Graves County, Mayfield, KY. Contact Mayfield-Graves County Chamber of Commerce, 201 East College St, Mayfield, KY 42066; ➦ 270 247 6101; fax: 270 247 6110; web: www.ldd.net/commerce/mayfield

Attractions

Ecumenically speaking, the **Lexington Ice and Recreation Center's Bible Theme Miniature Golf** has something for everyone: 18 Old Testament holes, 18 New Testament holes and 18 biblical miracle holes.

When Sally and Tom Christopher first broached the idea of building a faith-based golf course, people just laughed. Such in-your-face faith seemed a bit too much. But Sally and Tom persevered, holding prayer meetings and praying for guidance as to the subject of each and every hole. According to Tom, combining a business and a ministry is quite difficult, yet the center has been making money ever since it opened.

Speaking of which, it almost didn't. Building the first 18 holes drained all the Christophers' capital and they didn't have any money left to advertise their attraction. Then a tornado came to the rescue, tearing the roof off their adjoining ice center. The publicity from the storm damage was enough to jump start the golf enterprise. Maybe they should add a tornado hole to the miracle section.

> **Lexington Ice and Recreation Center's Bible Theme Miniature Golf**, 560 Eureka Springs Dr, Lexington, KY 40517; ➦ 606 269 5686

This is one BIG bell: it's 12 feet high, 12 feet wide and it weighs in at 66,000 pounds. Named the **World Peace Bell**, the world's largest bell resides at the world's largest monument, the **Millennium Monument** in Newport. Ascend to the top and you can have the very freaky experience of stepping out on to a glass floor and looking through it to the ground a thousand feet below. In case that isn't scary enough for you, try the 200-foot, vertical SpaceShot ride.

> **World Peace Bell and the Millennium Monument**, 403 York St, Newport, KY 41071; ➦ 606 655 9500; fax: 859 655 9577; web: www.millenniummonument.com

Museums and collections

Whether you like yours extra crispy or original, you're sure to crave Kentucky Fried Chicken by the time you finish touring **Colonel Harland Sanders Museum** in Louisville. The Colonel was 65 years old and flat broke when he parlayed his fried chicken recipe into a worldwide phenomenon. He became so famous that his body lay in state at the capitol when he died. A yellow line leads the way to his gravesite at the Cave Hill Cemetery.

Colonel Harland Sanders Museum, 1441 Gardiner Lane, Corbin, KY; located off US-25E (I-75, exit 29); ↘ 606 528 2163. *Open daily 7.00am–11.00pm.*

Walk into the **Vent Haven Ventriloquism Museum** in Fort Mitchell and 1,000 eyes belonging to 500 dummies will stare back at you. The collection belonged to William Berger, a man who became enamored with the business as a child after his actor father entertained him with hand puppets. Berger mastered throwing his voice as a teenager, but he didn't get serious about collecting until after his retirement.

Dummy heads are supported on a pole, with strings coming down the back. Dummies can spit, salute, move their eyes and eyebrows, cry and wiggle their noses and ears. As a matter of fact, they can do almost anything except speak. (For that you need a teenager.) The ventriloquist doesn't actually 'throw' his voice. The 'vent' is an illusion in which the performer changes his or her tone of voice, playing on the imagination and willingness of the audience to go along with the charade. It's the only museum in the world devoted to ventriloquism.

Vent Haven Ventriloquism Museum, 33 West Maple Ave, Fort Mitchell, KY 41011; ↘ 859 341 0461; web: www.venthaven.com

Corvette enthusiasts will love the **National Corvette Museum** in Bowling Green. Inside are 50 Chevrolet Corvettes, one-of-a-kind concept cars, and related advertising memorabilia spanning the history of the car. The cars are displayed in period settings of full-scale dioramas.

National Corvette Museum, 350 Corvette Dr, Bowling Green, KY 42101; ↘ 270781 7973 or 800 53 VETTE; fax: 270 781 5286; web: www.corvettemuseum.com

Kentucky is famous for its whiskey as well as for its prohibition-era stills. The **Oscar Getz Museum of Whiskey History** takes you through the history of the whiskey industry from pre-colonial days through the 1960s. You'll see a copper still that once belonged to George Washington and an 1854 E C Booze bottle, the brand from which the word 'booze' originated. One of the decanters claims that whiskey is 'the best medicine ever used'.

Oscar Getz Museum of Whiskey History, Spalding Hall, 114 N Fifth St, Bardstown, KY; ↘ 502 348 2999. *Open May–Oct, Mon–Sat 9.00am–5.00pm, Sun 1.00–5.00pm. Hours vary the rest of the year.*

Shopping
Betty Bryant herself isn't weird but her **Doll Clinic** in Covington certainly looks a bit strange. Spare doll parts pile up alongside stuffing supplies as she

goes about her business of repairing dolls and stuffed animals shipped in from around the world. She's repaired thousands of them during her 36-year career, saying, 'They all have a story and a reason why their owners want them repaired.' Sometimes the dolls arrive headless or eyeless which is when the stash of spare body parts comes in handy.

Doll Clinic, 528 Main St, Covington, KY; ↘ 859 291 1174. *Open 11.00am–5.00pm Tue–Sat or by appointment.*

Quirky cuisine

If you get impatient waiting for your food at **Lynn's Paradise Café** in Louisville, she'll probably tell you to be quiet and play with your toys. The Paradise is a place where guests, wearing banana noses, can play with potato guns as they sit under a giant, egg-decorated tree in her zany dining room-cum-playhouse. Visitors are encouraged to play, climbing on the animals in the colorful cement 'zoo' and taking their pictures beside the larger-than-life coffee pot that actually pours 'coffee' into a giant cup.

Each year Lynn sponsors the ugliest lamp contest at the Kansas State Fair. Since both the winners and losers tend to end up at the restaurant, you have an idea of what the place must look like. A huge eight-foot-by-24-foot mural made entirely of colored corn cobs decorates the side of the building; the mural's theme is changed annually. She's been written up in more magazines than she can remember.

Lynn considers children – both the kid and grown-up kind – to be her greatest asset. There's always something going on that's bound to delight as she unleashes her off-the-wall imagination on her restaurant and her guests.

Lynn's Paradise Café, 984 Barret Ave, Louisville, KY 40204; ↘ 502 583 3447; fax: 502 583 0211; web: www.lynnsparadisecafe.com. *Open 7.00am–10.00pm Tue-Sun.*

Quirky quarters

The **Wildwood Inn Tropical Dome and Spa** in Covington takes the theme concept to the extreme. The Cave Suite has stalagmites, stalactites and a waterfall spa. In the Happy Days Suite, you sleep in the back of a 1950 Caddy in a room decorated like a 1950s diner. Other outrageous suites include the Safari, Contemporary, Western, Champagne, Cupid, and Nautical. In the Shi-Awela Safari Village, you can sleep in a hut complete with mosquito net, spa, mini kitchen, and a projection television system with surround sound. The main dome has a lagoon pool, steam room and sauna, along with billiard and ping pong tables.

Wildwood Inn Tropical Dome and Theme Suites, 7809 US 42 Florence, KY 41042; ↘ 859 371 6300 or 800 758 2335; web: www.wildwood-inn.com

Wigwam Village in Cave City is a restored version of the original roadside attraction that had kids clamoring to sleep in its teepees. The 15 concrete wigwams, arranged in a semi-circle, have the original hickory bark and cane furniture. The new owners are in the process of replacing the authentic Indian artifacts that were plundered by the previous owner.

> **Wigwam Village**, 601 North Dixie Hwy, Cave City, KY 42127;
> ↘ 270 773 3381; web: wigwamvillage.com

TENNESSEE
Festivals and events
It's **Mule Day** in Columbia, and mules stretch as far as the eye can see. Back in the 1930s when the parade started, there could be as many mules as there were people. Today, folks celebrate the hardy, if grumpy creatures by throwing a party in their honor, complete with parade, liar's contest, mule-driving show, and mule-pulling competition.

> **Mule Day** held annually in April. Contact Mule Day Office, 1018 Maury Co Park Dr, Columbia, TN 38401; ↘ 931 381 9557; web: www.muleday.com

Just plain weird
Butler, Tennessee was a town that refused to die. In 1948, the powers that be revoked the town's charter, dammed up the nearby river and drowned the whole town. The citizens didn't take kindly to the event, moving many of the town's buildings to higher ground before the flooding took place. Today, a tour boat will ferry you down the old Main Street, pointing out the buildings you're floating above.

> **Butler, Tennessee**. Contact Elizabethton-Carter County Chamber of Commerce, 500 19E Bypass, PO Box 190, Elizabethton, TN 37644; ↘ 423 547 3850; fax: 423 547 3854

The **Peabody Ducks** are award-winning fowl, not because of any pedigree but rather for their marching abilities. The hospitality industry's Lifetime Achievement Award went to the birds for their twice daily red-carpet 'march' from their rooftop quarters to the travertine fountain in the lobby and back again.

> **Peabody Ducks at The Peabody Memphis**, 149 Union Ave, Memphis, TN 38103; ↘ 800 PEABODY; email: lestes@peabodymemphis.com; web: www.peabodymemphis.com

Headless statues lurk eerily by the roadside, erected by a man named **E T Wickham**. They're part of a memorial he made to his family who lie in the nearby cemetery. Depicting assorted people and animals, including a 'gallery' of great Americans, they rest in an overgrown tangle of brush and weeds beside the road near Palmyra.

E T Wickham's statues. Contact Clarksville-Montgomery County Convention and Visitors Bureau, Economic Development Council, PO Box 883, 312 Madison St, Clarksville, TN 37041; ☎ 800 530 2487; web: www.clarksville.tn.us/

Attractions

If there were a list of the top ten group eccentricities worldwide, the adulation of a dead rock and roll singer would have to be on it. Nowhere is this more evident than in Tennessee, where Elvis Presley's birth, death, and every detail of his life, is celebrated, mourned and examined.

Graceland in Memphis is the home, and final resting place, of the phenomenon known as Elvis. 'The image is one thing, and the human being is another,' he said in 1972, 'and it's very hard to live up to an image'. Maybe for him it was, but not for his fans in America, who have long since exceeded living up to his image; they now live way, way beyond it – past legend and into the realm of worship.

Even if you aren't an Elvis fan, a visit to Graceland is worthwhile if only for a glimpse into the psyche of true fans. People gape, they gasp, they tear up, they sob. They gaze lovingly up at the mansion while waiting their turn for a tour, one of which begins every three minutes and lasts for two hours. Elvis lived in this mansion for the last 20 years of his all-too-short life, and every detail of his lifestyle, including what should be none-of-your-business stuff, is exposed for all to venerate. From what he ate, to how he ate it, from where he sat and with whom; to where he slept and with whom; it's all absorbed in hushed awe. The most memorable rooms in the main house are probably his Jungle Room, with its waterfall and green shag carpeting, and his mirrored television room.

After the house, the tour continues in the Trophy Room, where fans can reminisce to their heart's content surrounded by the largest privately owned collection of gold records in the world. Then it's on to the Meditation Garden, the racquetball court where he spent some of his last moments, the pool area, and the nearby grave site. Fans the world over send fresh flowers every day.

They also leave messages, some quite intimate, on the long fieldstone wall. John Lennon once said, 'Before Elvis, there was nothing.' But after Elvis there sure is plenty. Every August they host Elvis Week.

Graceland, 3734 Elvis Presley Blvd, Memphis, TN 38186; �‚ 901 332 3322 or 800 238 2000; web: www.elvis-presley.com. *Open daily; closed on Tue Nov–Feb; closed Thanksgiving Day, Christmas Day and sometimes on New Year's Day. Call for other holiday hours.*

Country singer Dolly Parton tells her rags-to-riches story at her museum in **Dollywood** in Pigeon Forge. The park is every bit as sweet as the singer and the songs she sings; she just wants y'all to have fun. In addition to the thrill rides, you can learn to make barrels, buy pork rinds from a sidewalk vendor, and eat at the Ham 'n Beans restaurant.

Dollywood, 1020 Dollywood Ln, Pigeon Forge, TN 37863-4101; ↘ 865 428 9488; email: guestservices@dollywood.com: web: www.dollywood.com. Located: 35 miles SE of Knoxville in Pigeon Forge, TN.

Rock City, located near Chattanooga, itself isn't at all eccentric. Its signs, however, painted on the sides of barns throughout the south and mid west, are famous, reminding folks who might never get within a hundred miles of the place to 'See Rock City'. Between the 1930s and the 1960s, more than 900 barns were painted with this advertising slogan, with the farmer getting his barn painted for free in exchange for letting the side or roof of it be used as a billboard. Today, there are only a few dozen left to see because billboards are no longer politically correct; the 1960s Highway Beautification Act outlawed most of them. But folks still can see Rock City, a lovely garden park on Lookout Mountain, and you can still see new 'See Rock City' signs, only now they're in cyberspace on Rock City's website.

Rock City located atop Lookout Mountain, approx 6 miles from downtown Chattanooga, 1400 Patten Rd, Lookout Mountain, GA 30750, on the border of Tennessee and Georgia; ↘ 706 820 2531; web: www.seerockcity.com

Rock and roll was born at **Sun Studio** in Memphis, where the early songs of B B King, Ike Turner, and, of course, Elvis, were recorded. The voices from 50 years ago are haunting and the memorabilia stimulating. It's still a working studio by night, but by day you can tour the facility – even pretend you're recording a song.

Sun Studio, 706 Union Ave, Memphis, TN 38103; ↘ 901 521 0664 or 800 441 6249; fax: 901 525 8055; email: info@sunstudio.com; web: www.sunstudio.com. *Open daily 10.00am–6.00pm except Thanksgiving and Christmas.*

Museums and collections

If it has a soda or beer logo, Tom Bates has probably got it at his **Museum of Beverage Containers and Advertising** in Millersville. Certified by the *Guinness Book of World Records* as the largest of its kind, his collection of cans, bottles, and advertising memorabilia numbers in excess of 50,000 items. Among the more unique cans are the camouflage ones soldiers drank from during World War II, K-9 cola cans for dogs and Pussy Pop for cats,

Tom was 13 when, inspired by his aunt and uncle's modest can collection, he took up the sport of 'dumpster diving' himself, digging through garbage cans and scavenging beneath old buildings. Soon his collection outgrew his room, then the den, and then a trailer out back, finally ending up in a 2,500-square-foot building he and his family built in 1986. Today, Tom is a walking encyclopedia of beverage can lore and is often asked by writers and producers to suggest which cans and bottles belong in a particular period in history. It's pretty much a full-time job and the lure of a dumpster is still hard to resist.

Museum of Beverage Containers and Advertising, 1055 Ridgecrest Dr, Millersville, TN 37072; ↘ 615 859 5236 x 218 or 800 826 4929; web: www.gono.com/vir-mus/museum.htm. *Open Mon–Sat 9.00am–5.00pm; Sun 1.00–5.00pm. Admission charge.*

Buford Pusser has two museums memorializing him: the **Carbo Smoky Mountain Police Museum** in Pigeon Forge and the **Buford Pusser Home and Museum** in Adamsville. Buford was a legendary lawman who managed to survive being shot eight times and being knifed seven times before dying behind the wheel of his car at age 37.

Elected sheriff of McNairy County in 1964, the soft-spoken, six-and-a-half-foot, 250-pound man became every bad guy's worst nightmare. With unusual and heroic dedication, Buford took his duties very seriously, one time fighting off six men at once, sending three to jail and three to the hospital. In 1965 alone, he destroyed 87 illegal whiskey stills, acts that didn't exactly endear him to the still's tenders.

He was like a one-man army, going forth where no man had gone before, and with good reason: the mob controlled Buford's territory and no one had ever had the nerve to oppose them before. His zeal would cost him dearly; his wife was murdered before his eyes in 1967. He never got over her death, going on a rampage of revenge until his death in 1974. The subject of several books and movies, Buford was a real life Dirty Harry. Go ahead, make his day…

Carbo Smoky Mountain Police Museum, 3311 Parkway, Pigeon Forge, TN; ↘ 865 453 1358. *Open various days and times; call museum for information. Admission charge.*

Buford Pusser Home and Museum, 342 Pusser St, Adamsville, TN 38310; ↘ 901 632 4080. *Open Mon–Sat 9.00am–5.00pm; Sun 12.00noon–6.00pm; Nov 1–Apr 30 Sun 12.00noon–5.00pm.*

The National Knife Collectors Association has its own museum in Chattanooga. The **National Knife Museum**, supported by its 6,500 members, displays 12,000 knives, swords, razors and cutlery items of all kinds.

> **National Knife Museum**, 7201 Shallowford Rd. Directions: exit 5 off I-75, Chattanooga, TN 37424; ↘ 423 892 5007. *Open Monday through Saturday 10.00am–4.00pm. Admission charge.*

Tours

Billed as the wackiest tour in Nashville, **Nash Trash Tours** puts on a two-act, 90-minute comedy on wheels, with performers singing and dancing their way through Memphis pop culture in a bright pink bus. Brenda Kay Wilkins and Sheri Lynn Nichols are so entertainingly off beat that you don't even mind learning that their Southern accents are phony, or object to being served hors-d'oeuvres consisting of Cheese Whiz (foam-like cheese that squirts out of a can) and stale crackers. It's a country musical-comedy extravaganza as the two sisters who run it, the personification of poor white trash, dish out the dirt on not-so-squeaky-clean stars and fill you in on all the latest gossip. No charge for makeup and styling tips.

> **Nash Trash Tours**, Nashville, TN. Directions: leave from the north end of the Farmers Market, next to the Bicentennial Mall; look for the Big Pink Bus; reservations are required; ↘ 615 226 7300 or 800 342 2132; email: info@nashtrash.com; web: www.nashtrash.com

Quirky quarters

It's inevitable that you'd find a **Heartbreak Hotel** in Memphis. The standard rooms feature the expected 1950s decor and Elvis photos. The suites, however, are appropriately gaudy, inspired by various aspects of Elvis' life, career and personal style. The Graceland suite lets you pretend to be living at Graceland itself; The Hollywood pays homage to his movie star persona; the Gold and Platinum is rock 'n roll retro, and the Burning Love is a red-and-gilt tribute to his image as a romantic idol.

> **Heartbreak Hotel** ↘ 877 777 0606 or 901 332 3322; web: www.elvis-presley.com/epheartbreakhotel

Forty-eight train cars make up the **Chattanooga Choo Choo Holiday Inn** in Chattanooga. Each 'room' is in all or part of a restored passenger car.

> **Chattanooga Choo Choo Holiday Inn**, 1400 Market St, Chattanooga, TN 37402; ↘ 423 266 5000 or (reservations) 800 872 2529; fax: 423 265 4635; web: www.choochoo.com

NORTH CAROLINA
Festivals and events

They're going for a record at the annual **Hillsborough Hog Day**, trying to break Sydney, Australia's Guinness world record for the largest number of attendees at a one-day barbecue. Thirty-six teams cook up 7,500 pounds of barbecue while live, dressed-up porkers compete for the title of Best Dressed Pig. Birds of prey also get in the act.

> **Hillsborough Hog Day** held annually in June in Hillsborough, NC. Contact Hillsborough Chamber of Commerce, 960 Corporate Dr, Suite 101, Hillsborough, NC 27278; ↘ 919 732 8156; web: www.hillsboroughchamber.com

Hollerin' is much more than just yelling; it's a lost art that's been celebrated for 32 years at the **National Hollerin' Contest** in Spivey's Corner. Long before modern communications, folks is rural areas communicated by hollering over long distances to express distress, call in the livestock, or just plain 'chat'. Some hollers rhymed in a sing-song way. Every morning each family would holler to let others nearby know all was well. If someone failed to check in, neighbors would come to investigate.

Today's event gives each contestants four minutes to demonstrate their hollerin' skills. Finding a place to practice is problematic as anyone nearby is easily startled by the ruckus. Last year's winner appeared on David Letterman's talk show. You have to wonder if old time politicians hollered ' Vote for Joe!'

> **National Hollerin' Contest** held annually in June in Spivey's Corner, NC; ↘ 910 567 2600

Bald-headed men of America (BHMA) unite at the **Bald is Beautiful Convention** in Morehead City (get it?) The Bald Pride organization sponsors National Rub a Bald Head Week, publishes *Chrome Dome*, a periodic newsletter, operates a bald hall of fame and generally champions the position that bald men have that extra-special something. Their slogans, which appear on caps, mugs, and T-shirts, include Bald is Beautiful, Bald is Bold, Hairless Hunks and The Few! The Proud! The Bald! Twenty-thousand guys (and a few women) belong to BHMA, adding up to a considerable number of the follically challenged.

> **Bald is Beautiful Convention** held annually in September in Morehead City, NC. Contact Bald-Headed Men of America, 102 Bald Dr, Morehead City, NC 28557; ↘ 919 726 1855

Eccentric environments

Clyde Jones is a lucky man, for he has very few needs. He makes his living mowing lawns, and makes his art because it makes him feel good. An old mill house in Bynom is his home, but it's his yard that will attract you. It's filled with hundreds and hundreds of his 'critters': wood and scrap creatures that he's lovingly crafted using a chain saw. Seeing animals and faces in wood stumps and fallen logs, Jones carves out their personalities, resulting in critters with amazingly lifelike expressions. Balls, film canisters, tin cans; you name it, all are put to use bringing his critters life. Nails become teeth, plastic flowers become eyes. No two of his works are ever alike.

You can't buy one of his pieces, for he rarely sells them. You may, however, be given one, which is the only way he parts with his pets except for the occasional museum exhibition or art show. He's been known to turn down thousands of dollars. One time, world-famous dancer Mikhail Baryshnikov pulled up in a white limo. After touring the yard, he asked, 'How much?' Jones glanced over at the limo and said something like 'it don't look to me like you need one.' Eventually, he sent one, free of charge, after he found out who the visitor was.

> **Clyde Jones** located south of Carroboo/Chapel Hill. Directions: go south on 15-501 heading towards Pittsboro, turn left on Thompson Rec Road. Clyde's is the fourth house on the right, just after the ball field; web: http://carrboro.com/clydejones.html. Contact Chatham County, ℆ 800 468 6242; email: ccucc@emji.net; web: www.co.chatham.nc.us

Vollis Simpson's Whirligig Farm in Lucama is a riot of color and motion. The metal figures, massive contraptions whirling in the wind, are made by the 82-year-old Simpson who creates them to keep busy. Some of the sculptures are five and six stories high, looming over the field where he's planted at least 20 of the fruits of his labor. The cacophony of jangling and clinking metal, pie pans, ice cream scoops, old signs, and bicycle wheels turn the field into a menagerie of laughing giants.

There was nothing in Simpson's past to suggest this eccentric talent would blossom in later life. He was a farmer, a household mover, and a repairman. During World War II, however, he did collect parts from a wrecked plane and built a wind-powered washing machine. Except for those two instances, he waited until 1985 to unleash his creativity. The art world, though, has gotten wind of his creations and his work has been exhibited from coast to coast.

> **Vollis Simpson's Whirligig Farm**, Wiggins Mill Rd, Lucama, NC 27851; ℆ 800 497 7398

Museums and collections

Four out of every five species on earth are insects and the **North Carolina Museum of Life and Science** in Durham doesn't want you to forget it. At the annual **Bug Bowl South**, creepy crawlies get an entire weekend devoted to their kind, although they may not be so enthusiastic about some of the activities. Cricket spitting is an event attempting to break the prior Guinness record of 32½ feet.

Then there's bee dancing, edible insect cooking demonstrations and hissing cockroach races. Besides the 'Ewe, yuk!' stuff, the Bug Bowl features displays on beneficial insects you should be appreciating as well as insects like mosquitoes that will be forever appreciation-deprived.

North Carolina Museum of Life and Science, 433 Murray Ave, Durham, NC 27704; ↘ 919 220 5429; fax: 919 220 5575; email: pr.ncmls@mindspring.com; web: www.herald-sun.com/ncmls/. *Bug Bowl South held annually in June. Open Mon–Sat 10.00am–5.00pm; Sun 12.00noon–5.00pm; open summer until 6.00pm. Admission charge.*

Pack-rat-itis is a common trait of eccentrics, and **Eva Blount Way's Collection** at the Bellhaven Museum is one of the strangest of all. How about 30,000 buttons, arranged into maps of the United States, labeled as 'vitamins', and glued onto geometrically arranged cards? Or a series of glass jars, filled with formaldehyde, containing a pig with one eye, a two-headed pig, an eight-legged pig, a ten-pound tumor, and rattlesnakes, lots of them. Eva, who died in 1962, was proud to have personally killed three to five rattlesnakes each year, using a hoe, for the 40 years she lived on a farm. She made a necktie from snakeskin as well as jewelry from snake bones.

She saved everything that ever came her way: porcelain dolls, typewriters, a dress belonging to a 700-pound woman who had to be taken out her window with a crane when she died, ingrown toenails, cataracts and a jar of her chicken fat. She also wrote rhymes of advice to farmers' wives:

> If the hens don't lay, and the price don't suit,
> Can that hen and have her to boot.
> If the hens don't lay, and the price is bad,
> Can that hen and have her, by gad.
> If the hens don't lay, and the price don't reach her,
> Can that hen and feed her to the preacher.

Eva Blount Way's Collection, PO Box 220, Bellhaven, NC 27810; ↘ 252 943 3055

There are gourds as small as robin's eggs, gourds taller than a man and gourds so strong you can stand on them. At **Marvin Johnson's Gourd Museum** in Angier, you can see more than 200 different kinds of gourd, all grown by Johnson at one time or another. Back in 1964, his wife, Mary, told him to get the gourds out of the house, so he built the museum behind his home. There's a Last Supper made out of gourd seeds, a gourd Popeye and gourd reptiles, elephants, and dinosaurs. He's a world authority on gourds, never selling any, just sharing them with fellow craftspeople.

Marvin Johnson's Gourd Museum located at the intersection of US 401 and Hwy 55 W, Angier, NC; ↘ 919 639 2894

The **Visitor Center** in Mount Airy is home to Emmett Forrest's collection of Andy Griffith memorabilia. Forrest has been collecting all things Andy for three decades, putting his high school friendship with TV star Andy Griffith to good use. Andy himself donated the suit he wore while playing a lawyer on his *Matlock* television series.

Visitor Center, 615 N Main St, Mt Airy, NC; ↘ 800 576 0231; web: www.visitmayberry.com

Just plain weird

If you like big chests and curvy legs, you'll love the area around High Point, North Carolina. The heartland of American furniture manufacturing, this region is home to the world's largest chair, bureau, and highboy. These three nearby sites are part of a friendly, long term rivalry among east coast municipalities, all of whom want to lay claim to having the world's largest piece of furniture.

Starting life in the 1920s as the 'bureau of information', the 18th-century-style dresser at the intersection of Hamilton and Westwood streets in downtown High Point, stands 40 feet tall, twice as high as the house next door. A human can reach up as high as the top of the **world's largest bureau** legs and the socks hanging from the third drawer are six feet long.

Thomasville's Big Chair, Duncan Phyfe style, has hosted the seats of governors, beauty queens, and even President Lyndon Johnson. Once you enter the town, just roll down your window and ask anyone, 'Where's the chair?' Everyone knows and will happily point the way to the downtown square area. Built in 1948 out of steel and concrete to replace the 1920s wood version which had disintegrated, the chair stands 30 feet high from the bottom of the base to the top of the 18-foot chair. The seating area is ten-and-a-half

HERMIT WITH A GUESTBOOK

Robert Harrill was a hermit with a guest book. From 1955 until his death in 1972, he lived in salt marsh near Fort Fisher, setting up housekeeping in an abandoned World War II concrete bunker. An opinionated, crusty old gent, Harrill started a 'guest register' of the folks who came upon him. Eventually, he logged in 17,000 visitors as hundreds of newspapers and magazines ran stories about him, dubbing him the Fort Fisher Hermit. Occasionally he'd hold 'seminars' on hermit philosophy and dreamed about one day starting a 'School of Common Sense' right there on the marsh. He lived off of donations left in his frying pan. When he died, more than $1,000 in change was found in the bunker. Legend has it he buried tens of thousands more in the shifting sands nearby.

feet wide but you won't be able to pose up there unless you can manage to scale the 12-foot high base. A bench is thoughtfully provided in front of the structure so you get the proper perspective in your photo.

Not to be outdone, nearby Jamestown entered the competition in January, 1999 with the world's largest highboy on the facade of the world's largest home furnishings showroom, **Furnitureland South**. An astounding 85 feet tall, the underside of the chest serves as a roof for the outdoor seating area. You can sit on the ball-and-claw foot for your picture and imagine stacking cars three deep, with room left over for a few sofas, underneath the chest. The gold leaf handles alone are three feet wide.

World's largest bureau located at the intersection of Hamilton and Westwood Sts in downtown High Point, 508 North Hamilton St, High Point, NC. Contact High Point Convention and Visitors Bureau, 300 S Main St, High Point, NC 27261; ☏ 336 884 5255 or 800 720 5255; web: www.highpoint.org

Thomasville Furniture's Big Chair, Thomasville, NC. Contact Thomasville Furniture, PO Box 339, 401 E Main St, Thomasville, NC 27361; ☏ 800 927 9202; fax: 336 472 4093; web: www.thomasville.com

Furnitureland South, High Point, NC. Contact Furnitureland South; ☏ 336 841 4328; web: www.furniturelandsouth.com

Chief Henry claims to be the world's most photographed Indian. For 50 years he's been posing for a living on the Cherokee reservation, standing stoically in his feathered finery for camera toting tourists. His picture has appeared on hundreds of posters, place mats, and postcards. Even if you've never seen him in person, you'll probably recognize his image. Today he has lots of competition from feathered poster boys all along the highway.

Chief Henry located at Chief Henry's Tepee Village parking lot along Highway 19 at Chief Saunooke's Trading post, Cherokee, NC. *The Chief charges per photo.*

Andy Barker is the mayor of **Love Valley**, a town where you won't find any cars, fast food, or drive thrus of any kind. What you will find are horses, cowboys, wood sidewalks, hitching posts, a saloon and a dance hall. But this isn't a movie set or a tourist trap; this real, live western town, smack dab in the eastern US Love Valley, was a quirky dream that Barker has turned into reality, complete with a marshall to keep the peace. You can do anything you like in Love Valley – as long as you do it Barker's way.

Love Valley located on Fox's Mountain in northwest Iredell County, NC. Contact Andy Barker, Box 265, Love Valley, NC 28677; ☏ 704 592 7451

Tours

On the nightly **Ghost Walk of Old Wilmington**, costumed guides take you on a chilling tour of the sites haunted by those who have succumbed to piracy, murder, yellow fever and hangings.

> **Ghost Walk of Old Wilmington** tours meet riverfront at Market and Water St, Wilmington, NC; ↘ 910 602 6055; email: ghosts@hirchak.com; web: www.hirchak.com/Ghosts.html

Shopping

The European trolls of legend were always ugly, scary monsters ready to snatch up a misbehaving child. At **US Trolls** in Wilmington, they've been creating cute, friendly trolls, each with a cute story, for 50 years. Kids are welcome to write to the trolls and will be thrilled to receive a response from them. Troll story readings are held daily; on Saturdays, a life-size troll may make a guest appearance.

> **US Trolls**, 2505 Market St, Wilmington, NC 28403; ↘ 910 251 2270; fax: 910 772 9038; web: www.trollforest.com

In Cape Fear there's a shop devoted solely to the Civil War. Catering mainly to re-enactors, the **Civil War Shop** buys, sells, trades and makes custom orders for anything related to the war between the states.

> **Civil War Shop**, 3910 US Hwy 70, East New Bern, NC 28560; ↘ 252 636 3039; fax: 252 637 1862; web: http://civilwarshop.com

MISSISSIPPI
Festivals and events

Why anyone would want to shoot an anvil is anybody's guess, but shoot them they do at the world's only **Anvil Shooting Contest** at the Forestry and Wood Products Expo. The 100-pound anvils are lined up on platforms over explosive black powder, then fired into the air by fuses or remote controls. Some of them shoot up to 400 feet into the air. The competition is judged both for height and for landing accuracy; the closer the anvil lands to the platform, the better.

> **Anvil Shooting Contest** held annually in April in Laurel, MS during the Mississippi Forestry and Wood Products Expo. Contact Economic Development Authority of Jones County, PO Box 527, Laurel, MS 39441; ↘ 601 649 3031

Eccentric Environments

Earl's Art Shop is much more than a store. It's a gallery-cum-disco-cum-museum-cum-workshop-cum-café; it's also his home. Unlike many self-taught artists, Earl Simons didn't just suddenly start painting one day. He's

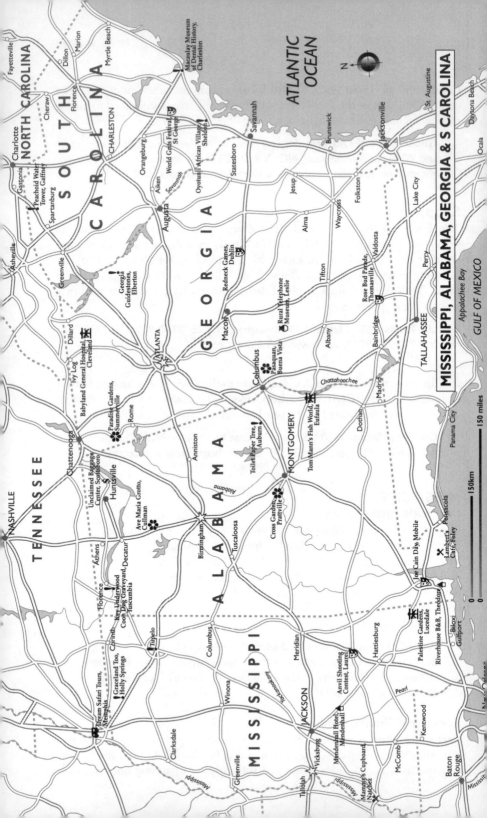

been making things from scrap and salvaged materials since childhood. Now middle age, he's been following his instincts for 20 years, making model trucks, buses, and cars, along with juke boxes that house tape players. Earl's property just ambles along, sort of like Earl. His cluster of 20 odd buildings evolves as the mood strikes, with a room added whenever it pleases him to do so. When he added the café, and started selling snacks and beverages, he made signs advertising what he was doing. People started buying the signs, so now he makes them too.

Earl's Art Shop, Vicksburg, MS; ✆ 601 636 5264. Located: 8 miles east of Vicksburg, MS, on I-20, take the Bovina exit, head south across US 80 and the railroad tracks, veering left at the Y and continuing south.

Widow Margaret Dennis of Vicksburg operated what was once a small, unassuming roadside snack store. Unassuming, that is, until the Reverend Dennis came along 20 years ago and made her a promise she couldn't refuse: 'Marry me, and I'll turn your store into a castle.' She accepted the offer, which was pretty courageous seeing as how she would be the Reverend's fifth wife, and **Margaret's Grocery** was thrust into the realm of the strange and wacky.

Reverend Dennis turned the place into a red-and-white cinder-block version of a castle. Friendly religious messages pop up everywhere; the sign as you enter proclaims his philosophy: 'All is welcome, Jews and Gentiles here at Margaret's Gro. & Mkt. & Bible Class.' While you're no longer able to shop in the grocery, you're still welcome. He preaches out front in a bus that's been converted into a church complete with pulpit and pews. And what a church it is: all metallic paint, tin foil, and duct tape – a true 'reflection' of heaven.

Margaret's Grocery, Route 4, Box 219, Hwy 61, Vicksburg, MS

Just plain weird

Graceland Too in Holly Springs puts even the staunchest Elvisite to shame. Paul MacLeod and his son, Elvis Aaron Presley MacLeod (yup – that's the name his Dad gave him), are building a database of every reference to the King ever made, including print, broadcast, and electronic media. They'll probably record this guidebook entry before long.

They're at work 24 hours a day, 365 days a year, taking turns monitoring a bank of TVs, VCRs and radios, ready to spring into action at the mere mention of the great one's name. Thousands of newspaper and magazine clippings, along with memorabilia of all things Elvis, are crammed into their antebellum home.

Paul has been collecting Elvis memorabilia for 44 years with a determination that gives new meaning to the word 'fanatic'. When his wife demanded, 'It's me or Elvis', you can guess his reply. He's even planning to be buried in a copy of Elvis' gold lamé suit.

Drop in any time; one of the MacLeods is always available, although they do appreciate a phone call first.

Graceland Too, 200 East Gholson Ave, Holly Springs, MS 38634; ❯ 622 252 7954; fax: 601 252 1918; email: ultimate1@gracelandtoo/; web: www.gracelandtoo.com

If you're following the Elvis route, you're bound to end up in **Tupelo**, the town of his birth. Thousands of fans gawk at the hallowed ground containing the small, two-room house where he was born, pray at the Elvis Chapel, and wipe the occasional tear from their eye at the wonders displayed in the Elvis Museum.

Tupelo, ❯ 662 841 6521 or 800 533 0611; web: www.tupelo.net

Today you couldn't even get a drafting student, let alone an architect, to draw up the plans for **Mammy's Cupboard** in Natchez, a restaurant so politically incorrect that it's become a pop culture icon. Picture this – a 30-foot tall, large buxom, black, woman, wearing a full-length skirt, with a pill-box hat on her head. You eat in the skirt part while the upper body is sort of like a huge chimney on the top. This racist stereotype, built in the 1940s, pays homage to the southern vision of the 'Mammy' as the idealized servant; as former slave turned much-loved wet-nurse.

Mammy's Cupboard, 555 Hwy 61 S, Natchez, MS 39120; ❯ 601 445 8957

Attractions

A scale model of the Holy Land awaits you at **Palestine Gardens** near Lucedale, built by the late Reverend Jackson. He and his wife filled their 20-acre plot with their own version of the Promised Land. At a scale of one yard per mile, you can walk where Jesus walked, cross the river Jordan, see the Dead Sea, and stroll past two-dozen other biblical sites.

Palestine Gardens, 201 Palestine Gardens Rd, Lucedale, MS; ❯ 601 947 8422. Located 12 miles north of Lucedale, 5.5 miles off US 98 near West Lucedale exit. *Open Mon–Fri 9.00am–4.00pm; Sat 9.00am–6.00pm; Sun 1.00–5.00pm.*

Tours

American Dream Safari takes you on an eight-hour 'blues and blacktop' tour in a 1955 Cadillac, driving along the Delta regions of Mississippi and Tennessee through the birthplace of the blues.

American Dream Safari, PO Box 3129, Memphis, TN 38173; ❯ 901 527 8870; fax: 901 527 3700; email: tad@americandreamsafari.com; web: www.americandreamsafari.com

Quirky quarters

The **Mendenhall Hotel's** claim to fame is its large circular tables where meals are served boarding-house style. Sixteen diners share a table with a huge Lazy Susan turntable built into the center. Platters of food are plopped on the turntable and you help yourself to whatever you want. It's a terrific way to meet locals and other travelers.

Mendenhall Hotel, Old Hwy 49, Mendenhall, MS; ✆ 601 847 3113

ALABAMA
Festivals and events

The pious, mellow people of Alabama are not generally known for excessive partying, yet a general madness overtakes Mobile for a week when the populace celebrates Mardi Gras in quirky Mobilian style. They temporarily suspend most of the rules governing civilized behavior as raucous revelers, determined to enliven the humdrum existence of every day life, hold balls and parades in honor of a man named **Joe Cain**.

The festivities date back to the Civil War when Alabama was defeated and Mobile was especially happiness-challenged. Joe Cain, a lover of strong drink and good times, dressed himself like an Indian, decorated a coal wagon pulled by a mule, and held himself a one float parade to cheer up the townspeople. Their spirits, renewed by this spectacle, rekindled Mardi Gras in their souls; to this day, they give themselves permission to raise cain. Today's procesional involves decorated jalopies, pick-up trucks, flat beds, wheelbarrows and bicycles. The more ridiculous, the better.

Joe Cain Day held annually during Mardi Gras (day before Ash Wednesday) in downtown Mobile, AL. Contact the Mobile Convention and Visitors Corp, PO Box 204, Mobile, AL 36601; ✆ 800 5 MOBILE; fax: 334 208 2060; web: www.mobile.org

Eccentric environments

It may be the Sex Pit signs that first draw your attention, but you'll soon enough get W C Rice's message: 'WARNING: You Will Die – Hell is Hot, Hot, Hot'. Hundreds of hell-fire and damnation signs, joined by as many crosses, line both sides of the road at a place called **Cross Garden** near Prattville. How this place could be called a garden is a mystery, but that's how Rice likes to think of it.

Rice has a major cross fixation, one that has persisted for 25 years. He says that voices told him to create the garden as a testament to his faith. Crosses cover his truck, his house, the junk in his yard, his car and his clothing. There's a ramshackle chapel covered with religions graffiti and a hole he refers to as the Tomb of Jesus. If he's around when you get there, he'll be happy to tell you all about the place, but be warned: he has a one track mind and you'll certainly be thinking about the effects of Hell when he's through with you.

> **Cross Garden** located northwest of Prattville on Hwy 82 past the
> country club, over the hill and left on County Rd 86. Contact the
> Prattville Area Chamber of Commerce, 1002 E Main St, Prattville, AL
> 36066; ↘ 334 365 7392; fax: 334 361 1314; web: www.prattville.com

Brother Joseph had a real thing for cold-cream jars, glass fragments, shells, tiles, stones, marbles and concrete. At the three-acre **Ave Maria Grotto** in Cullman, he constructed 125 miniature versions of religious and Holy Land buildings, including the Hanging Gardens, the Tower of Babel and Noah's Ark. And he did it all from picture postcards, never having had the chance to travel abroad. Brother Joseph, a Benedictine monk, worked incessantly for almost 30 years on his creation often referred to as 'sermons in stone'. Next to his model of Bethlehem you'll see the Tower of Thanks, built to show his gratefulness to all the folks worldwide who sent him bits of glass, shells and fisherman's glass balls. He died in 1961 and is buried on the property.

> **Ave Maria Grotto** located at St Bernard Abbey, 1600 St Bernard Dr
> SE, Cullman, AL 35055; ↘ 256 734 4110; web:
> www.avemariagrotto.com. Snacks available, free picnic grounds
> adjacent. *Open daily 7.00am–dusk; closed Christmas. Admission charge.*

Joe Mintner's Yard in Birmingham is filled with visionary sculptures depicting his African heritage. Directed by You-Know-Who to create this striking tribute, Joe's Garden of Memory is ablaze with monuments, huts, placards and sculptures adorned with historical, biblical and political messages that Mintner says he receives from God.

African warriors, their heads fashioned from the hoods of old hair dryers, stand tall amid sculpture made from thrift shop cast-offs, scraps of wood and bits of metal. A moving memorial to four children killed in the 1963 bombing of a church consists of signs with each child's name and four empty folding chairs. A jail cell surrounds an old toilet, representing Dr Martin Luther King Jr's famous incarceration during the civil rights era. The names of folks who died in race related violence are posted on a tree.

Downplaying the creativity that characterizes the garden, Mintner, 58, simply says, 'All of this is really just the hand of God.'

> **Joe Mintner's Yard**, Birmingham, AL. Directions: I-65 south from
> downtown Birmingham, turn right at Green Springs Ave exit, left on
> Martin Luther King Blvd, right on Nassau. Contact Greater
> Birmingham Convention and Visitors Bureau, 2200 Ninth Ave, North
> Birmingham, AL 35203; ↘ 205 458 8000 or 800 458 8085; fax 205
> 458 8086; web: www.birminghamal.org

Just plain weird

At the **Key Underwood Coon Dog Graveyard** in Tuscumbia, grieving owners honor their pets by erecting headstones resembling dogs treeing their prey. Every year on Labor Day coon hunters and their dogs pay tribute to their fallen brethren and mourn the demise of the good old raccoon hunting days.

> **Key Underwood Coon Dog Graveyard** located 7 miles west of Tuscumbia on Hwy 72, left on Alabama Hwy 247, then approximately 12 miles, turn right and follow signs; ℸ 256 383 0783. Park is equipped with picnic area, restrooms and a pavilion. *Admission free.*

Auburn University's sports fans certainly aren't wishy-washy about their team. Every time they win, fans rush to the **Toilet Paper Tree** in the city center and unfurl toilet paper rolls up into the tree. As many as 50,000 people have been seen celebrating at the tree. Auburn is the only city in the country to have a line item in its budget for cleaning up toilet paper.

> **Toilet Paper Tree** located downtown Auburn, AL, following an athletic win by an Auburn University sports team.

Attractions

Tom Mann's Fish World near Lake Eufaula, is home to the fruit-flavored, plastic jelly worms invented by Tom Mann, the Martha Stewart of the fishing world. It's also the home of a memorial to a dead fish.

Tom was fishing one day, trying out one of his jelly worms, when he tangled with a particularly spunky, large-mouth bass. After winning the tug of war, Tom didn't have the heart to eat the fish so he named him Leroy Brown, put him in a tank and spent the next eight years bonding with him.

When the fish finally croaked, a big funeral was held complete with pallbearers, mourners and a high-school band. Since it was raining that day, Leroy wasn't actually buried, but stored in Tom's freezer until the weather cleared up. That night Leroy's casket, with the frozen body inside, was stolen. By the time an unfortunate baggage handler came upon the casket, the decayed fish was in no shape to be buried. The rotting corpse was disposed of, but the casket was returned to Tom. You'll see the memorial inside the museum.

> **Tom Mann's Fish World**, Route 2, Box 84C, Eufaula, AL 36027; ℸ 334 687 3655

Shopping

Recycled vacuums become lamps and toasters turn into vases at an artists' co-op in a funky, downtown Birmingham building. Dubbed **Naked Art** by owner Veronique Vanblaere, who wants you to see with an unbiased, naked eye, the gallery is unpretentious and homey. Orange walls, couches and way wacky art makes you feel right at home – or, at least the way you'd feel if your home was on another planet. The art is mainly functional, meaning it has to do something besides just sit there and provoke conversation.

Naked Art, 2318 1st Ave North, Birmingham, AL 35203; ↘ 205 326 3994; web: www.nakedartusa.com. Directions: Exit 1-20/59 at 22nd Street exit downtown, turn left, left on First Ave North. *Open Tue–Sat 11.00am–5.00pm.*

Lost luggage doesn't go to some mysterious carousel in the sky: it ends up very much alive, if not especially well, at the **Unclaimed Baggage Center** in Scottsboro. If the store is half as much fun as their website, you'll be well entertained. Every lost piece has a story; your job is to imagine what it might say if it could talk, where its owner was going, what some strange object actually is, or how on earth its owner ever managed to get along without it. New stuff is brought out dozens of times a day and priced 50–80% off retail.

The place is huge, covering an entire city block and many locals shop for bargains there at least once a week. Look for the tiny museum that displays, among other things, a Stetson cowboy hat signed by Muhammad Ali and a puppet from a Jim Henson Muppets movie.

Unclaimed Baggage Center, 509 West Willow St, Scottsboro, AL 35768; ↘ 256 259 1515; web: www.unclaimedbaggage.com. *Open Mon–Fri 9.00am–6.00pm; Sat 8.00am–6.00pm.*

Quirky cuisine

The hot rolls flying through the air astound people eating for the first time at **Lambert's Café** in Foley. It all started back in 1976 when the owner got tired of holding a basket and saying, over and over again, 'Would you care for a hot roll?' One day a customer called out to her, 'Just throw the damn thing'. She did, and everyone else joined in. They've been throwin' 'em, at an average of more than two million a year, ever since. The Home of the Throwed Rolls is also famous for its hubcap cinnamon rolls.

Lambert's Café, 2981 S McKenzie, Foley, Al 36535; ↘ 334 943 7655; fax: 334 943 1422; web: www.throwedrolls.com. Also located in Sikeston, MO and Ozark, MO. *Open daily 10.30am–9.00pm or so.*

Quirky quarters

You'll sleep in a sewer pipe at the **Riverhouse Bed and Breakfast** in Mobile. Owner Mike Sullivan made all the furniture – beds, tables, night stands, and fountains – from plastic PVC pipe. Oprah loved it.

Riverhouse Bed and Breakfast, Box 614, Theodore, AL 36590; ↘ 334 973 2233 or 800 552 9791; fax: 334 973 2588; email: riverhsbb@aol.com

GEORGIA
Festivals and events

Children get their own parade in Thomasville during the annual **Rose Bud Parade**. Babies and toddlers come in costume on decorated strollers, carriages, wagons or tricycles. School and other groups dress and perform according to the parade theme; in the past it's been movies and TV, cartoon characters, the circus, sports, the Olympics, and 'when I grow up'. Kiddie bands play a variety of wacky instruments and costumed pets come along for the ride.

> **Rose Bud Parade** held annually in April in Thomasville, GA. Contact Rosebud Parade Committee, Thomasville Main St, PO Box 1540, Thomasville, GA 31799; ↘ 912 227 7020

Georgia is the heart of America's redneck territory, so it's no surprise that the **Redneck Games** are held here in East Dublin. This is beer, barbeque and arm fart country, where bent coat-hangers with aluminum foil serve as antennas and good ol' country boys keep both dogs and wallets on chains. According to Jeff Foxworthy, grand guru of redneck jokes, you might be a redneck if your wife's hairdo has been destroyed by a ceiling fan, or if your front porch collapses and kills more than three dogs.

The games are down-and-dirty events like bobbing for pig's feet, seed spitting, dumpster diving, hubcap hurling, bug zapping by spitball, an armpit serenade, a big-hair contest, and a mud pit belly flop contest best entered by those with beer bellies and peek-a-boo butt cracks. The trophy is a crushed and mounted Bud Light can, disappointingly empty. L-Bow, the grand guru of the event, claims it's all in good fun, involving 'just plain good ol' boys and gals who'd give you the shirt off their back, although it's doubtful you'd want it'.

Originally dubbed the Bubba-Olympics, the event spoofs the real Olympics held in Georgia in 1996. Country radio station WQZY started the games as a promotional stunt, garnering so much publicity that newspapers and television stations all over the country started covering them.

> **Redneck Games** held annually in summer in Dublin, GA. Contact WQZY; ↘ 912 272 4422 or 800 688 0096; web: www.wqzy.com/redneck.htm

Eccentric environments

Howard Finster of Summerville set out to build his vision of the Garden of Eden. For the foundation he filled in a swamp that had been used as a dump. That took seven years. Since then he's spent 33 more years building **Paradise Garden**, a chaotic masterpiece of junk sculptures, rambling buildings and glittery mosaics, cemented not only by sand, ash and water, but by his abiding faith that his sacred grounds can make a heavenly difference.

Discovered by the media and the art world in the early 1980s, it's clear that he has made a difference, at least to the tourism industry in Georgia. He's the honoree at the Howard Finster Fest and the main man at the Finster Folk Art Gallery. For the thousands who visit the garden each year, his work is both entertainment and inspiration. A combination of biblical text and visual cacophany, the garden is playfully evangelical. An eight foot concrete shoe bears the verse, 'And your feet shod with the preparation of the gospel of peace'. Waste cans implore you to keep the world as clean as your house, which may or may not be a good idea depending upon your housekeeping skills.

As you wander the three acre garden, you'll marvel at structures like the sculpted bicycle tower and museum, which leads to the Tomb of the Unknown Body. There's a meditation building, a renowned people mural, and a cement bed of roses and plants. Walkways are lined with mirrors and bits of jewelry. Howard's never met a person he didn't love, a common characteristic of cement visionaries, so if you're there on a Sunday afternoon you may get him to share some of that love with you.

Paradise Garden, 84 Knox St, Summerville, GA 30747; ⟩ 800 FINSTER or 706 857 2926; web: www.finster.com/paradisegardens.htm. *Open daily 12.00noon–6.00pm. Howard is there Sun 2.00–4.00pm. Admission charge.*

One of the south's most eccentric figures, Edward Martin was also known as St EOM, the Wizard of Pasaquan. The self-described 'Bodacious Mystic Badass of Buena Vista' left behind a legacy of behavior so bizarre that he was often ostracized and shunned during his lifetime.

The son of a poor sharecropper, his eclectic youth was spent wandering the country, and eventually the globe, as a merchant seaman. When he had seen enough of a world he considered deprived, he paid heed to the voice in his head that told him to come home and build a compound to house a visionary religion called **Pasaquan**. St EOM told fortunes to finance the totems, tires, pagodas and paintings that make up his curious compound. The walls are studded with huge guardian figures while concrete pipes painted with the mythical occupants of Pasaquan kept him company.

Rumors of trained rattlesnakes and devil worship swirled about the turbaned man who decorated himself with tattoos and dressed in jeweled robes and feathered head-dresses. Cats, dozens of them, came when he called. Dogs stayed by his side. His beard, stiffened by rice syrup, was shaped upward as an antenna to the universe; his hair remained uncut for more than 40 years. Eventually, misunderstood and alone, he took his own life at the age of 77.

Pasaquan, County Road 78, Buena Vista, GA; web: www.shockoestudios.com/steom.htm. Directions: From the Town Square in Buena Vista, GA, drive north on Hwy 137, take fork in the road to the left, take second paved road to the right, County Rd 78. Pasaquan appears brightly on your right. *Open Wed–Sat 10.00am–5.00pm; Sun 12.00noon–5.00pm.*

Just plain weird

The handful of people who know who's responsible for the **Georgia Guidestones** aren't telling. The enormous cluster of stones, inscribed in eight languages with advice for the preservation of mankind, sits on a hilltop in eastern Georgia. Attracting mystics, spiritualists and UFO buffs, the stones, erected in 1979, are a gift to humanity by an unknown benefactor (or benefactors).

Nineteen feet high, they espouse such advice as 'Maintain humanity under 500,000,000 in perpetual balance with nature'. Oops ... guess India wasn't paying attention. Another instructs us to 'Unite humanity with a living new language'.

They go on to offer constructive ways to preserve our species: 'Protect people and nations with fair laws and just courts', 'Let all nations rule internally, resolving external disputes in a world court', and 'Avoid petty laws and useless officials'. Oops, again ... there goes our vice presidency.

Georgia Guidestones, Hwy 77, Elberton, GA. Contact The Elbert County Chamber of Commerce, 148 College Ave, Elberton, GA 30635; ↘ 706 283 5651; email: chamber@elbertga.com; web: www.elbertga.com

Attractions

Coca-Cola™ bills itself as the 'most successful product in the history of commerce'. Bill Gates may be gaining on them, but you can't argue with the influence of Coke world-wide. The **World Of Coca-Cola Pavilion** proves their contention with mind boggling exhibits and statistics extolling the virtues of Coke.

Interactive videos, astounding trivia and cheerfully obsequious 'hosts' accompany you through the Coke experience. The Every Day of Your Life Theater shows Coke being drunk in every corner of the world. At the Real Thing Gallery, you're treated to all the advertising jingles that made this the most popular drink on the planet – and off it, as evidenced by the Space Can that became the first to rocket into orbit. The soda fountain is like a virtual reality experience without the virtual part and Tastes of the World leaves you merrily entertained by the expressions of those brave enough to sample the concoctions masquerading as soft drinks in other lands. Are you brave enough to walk in carrying a Pepsi?

World Of Coca-Cola Pavilion, 55 Martin Luther King Jr Dr, Atlanta GA 30303; ↘ 404 676 5151

Twenty years ago, anxious parents stood in line for hours, sometimes days, waiting to 'adopt' a Cabbage Patch Doll. Employees dressed as doctors and nurses made an elaborate display of presenting the unique doll and its adoption certificate to wide-eyed tykes who cherished, at least temporarily, their kiddie version of the American dream. You can visit the 'hospital' and the cabbage patch from which this merchandising genius was born at **Babyland General Hospital**.

Babyland General Hospital, 19 Underwood St, Cleveland, GA; ↘ 706 865 2171. *Open Sun 10.00am–5.00pm; Mon–Sat 9.00am–5.00pm. Admission free.*

Museums and collections
The mission of Georgia's **Rural Telephone Museum** near Leslie is to leave you with a greater appreciation of the wonders of telecommunications. You certainly wouldn't have to convince any teenager, or, for that matter, any cell-phone addicted workaholic, of the value of being accessible 24 hours a day. But you'll leave with a greater appreciation of how far we've come, in a relatively short time from the days of party lines and operators. Anyone under the age of 40 probably doesn't even know what those terms mean, let alone realize the significance of being able to buy, rather than lease, your telephone.

You can thank Tommy C Smith, an ex-telephone company CEO, for amassing the world's largest collection of telephones and memorabilia such as switchboards and phone booths. The collection numbers around 1,500 phones ranging from early Alexander Graham Bell versions to novelty fashion phones and modern wireless phones.

Rural Telephone Museum, 135 N Bailey Ave, Leslie, GA 31764; ↘ 912 874 4786; web: www.sowega.net/~museum. *Directions: exit 33 from I-75 in Cordele on to US Hwy 280 west. Open Mon–Sat 10.00am–3.00pm.*

Quirky cuisine
The landmark **Varsity Restaurant** in Atlanta is where you go for a 'lube job', ie: to fill up on their greasy chili dogs, onion rings and fried fruit pies. 'Have your money in your hand and your order in your mind' when you approach

the 150-foot-long counter – the Varsity staff put on quite a show as they implore you with chants of 'What'll you have? What'll you have?' and 'Next, next ... next'. Every day they serve two miles of hot dogs, 2500 pounds of potatoes, and 5,000 fried pies. The maze of dining rooms are named after television broadcasters so you can eat with the media personality of your choice. In the gift shop you can buy their famous pin honoring the Olympics: a formation of five sacred onion rings. The Varsity still has a drive-in (the world's largest) with car-hop service and the highest Coca-Cola consumption in the world: three million servings annually.

> **Varsity Restaurant**, 61 North Ave NW, across the Interstate from Georgia Tech, Atlanta, GA 30308; ↘ 404 881 1706; web: thevarsity.com. *Open 9.00am–11.30pm Sun–Thu; 9.00am–12.30am Fri–Sat.*

SOUTH CAROLINA
Festivals and events
They're literally rolling in grits at the **World Grits Festival** in St George. A local supermarket discovered that people in the low coastal plains of the state consume unusually high portions of the cooked cereal, a fact confirmed by the country's main supplier, Quaker Oats Company. Every April, 50,000 people attend an event that includes contests for corn-shucking, grits-eating and the crowning of Miss Grits. The Rolling-in-the-Grits competition involves a vat of grits and a 15-second timer. Contestants are weighed, then attempt to collect as many pounds of grits on their body as possible in the time allotted.

> **World Grits Festival** held annually in April in St George, SC. Contact Granny Grits; ↘ 843 563 4366; or the tourist bureau; ↘ 800 788 5646

Just plain weird
Three-dozen followers of a religion started in the 1970s by a used car dealer live in their own 'country' known as **Oyotunji African Village** in Sheldon. The village, filled with dirt streets, crumbling buildings and tumble-down shacks, is populated by believers in a religion called 'New World Yoruba' a term which cynics might think equates to 'I can get away with tax evasion.'

> **Oyotunji African Village** located near the intersection of US 17 and 21, Highway 17, PO Box 51, Sheldon, SC 29941; ↘ 843 846 6859; web: http://oyotunjivillage.net

When the town of Gafney needed a new elevated water-storage tank, they built it in the shape of a giant peach. The 'stem' is 12 feet long, while a huge leaf, 60 feet long and six feet wide, hangs on the side. The 'peach' itself, complete with a nipple, holds half-a-million gallons of water.

Peachoid Water Tower located in Gaffney, SC, on I-85 near the exit for Hwy 11 in the Cherokee Foothills Scenic Hwy; web: www.gaffney-sc.com/waterpeach.htm

Neill Macaulay was a dentist fond of collecting the memorabilia of his trade. The **Macaulay Museum of Dental History** displays his collection of dental chairs, early X-rays, molds for making teeth, dental instruments, dental books and a nostalgic fee bill.

Macaulay Museum of Dental History, 175 Ashley Ave, Medical University of South Carolina, Charleston, SC 29425; ➘ 843 792 2288. *Open 8.30am–5.00pm Mon–Fri. Admission free.*

FLORIDA
One of the strangest – and coolest –things you can do in Florida waters is swim with dolphins. The experience doesn't come cheap, but it will stay with you for a lifetime. Just search the web for 'swim with dolphins, Florida' and almost a dozen possibilities will pop up.

Festivals and events
At **Fantasy Fest** in Key West, a new dress code stipulates that body paint no longer constitutes a costume. This regulation, though, is largely ignored in favor of the old standard that decreed the minimum 'legal' female costume to be any kind of bottom covering and at least a painted top. These are issues of great importance to the tens of thousands of revelers who attend this ten-day, adults-only costume event.

Key West is an extremely tolerant town, the kind of place where the unusual is the norm. During Fantasy Fest, however, they leap way, way over the top as far as outrageous behavior goes. During the ten days of the festival, there are several dozen events, including numerous parades, costume contests and street fairs.

The costumes and floats are the main attractions, becoming ever more creative and bizarre from year to year. The first parade 22 years ago saw a float with a human hood ornament wearing only bikini bottom and silver paint. Today's floats can be incredibly complex and high tech, with themes such as the landing of an alien spacecraft, a fire-breathing dragon and an entire tropical jungle village with huts, trees, a volcano, a waterfall, and prehistoric creatures. The whole spectacle is like Vegas on wheels – and on ecstasy.

The costumes range from the comic, such as giant M&Ms (she was plain, he was with nuts); to the risqué, such as the extension cord (she was the socket, he the plug); to the flamboyant, such as a living coral reef, to the outrageously expensive, such as the leviathan, a fiberglass and mylar costume with armed warriors fighting dragons and snakes.

The events include a Ripley's Believe It or Not Sideshow and Circus, a mask-as-art exhibition, a building façade competition, a headdress ball, a pet masquerade, a celebrity look-a-like contest, and umpteen costume and parade

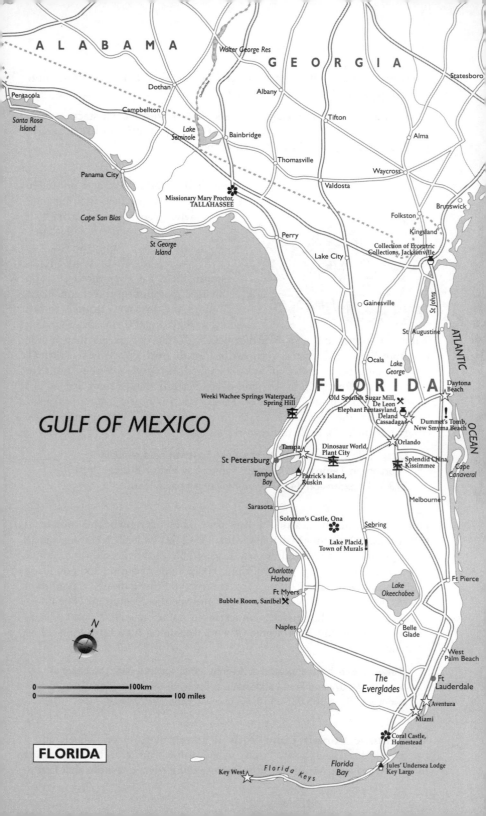

ALABAMA

GEORGIA

Walter George Res

Statesboro

Dothan

Albany

Pensacola

Campbellton

Tifton

Alma

Santa Rosa
Island

Lake
Seminole

Bainbridge

Panama City

Thomasville

Waycross

Missionary Mary Proctor,
TALLAHASSEE

Valdosta

Brunswick

Cape San Blas

Perry

Folkston

Kingsland

St George
Island

Lake City

Collection of Eccentric
Collections, Jacksonville

GULF OF MEXICO

Weeki Wachee Springs Waterpark,
Spring Hill

Gainesville

Ocala

St Johns

St Augustine

ATLANTIC

Lake
George

FLORIDA

Daytona
Beach

Old Spanish Sugar Mill,
De Leon
Elephant Fantasyland,
Deland
Cassadaga

Tampa

Dinosaur World,
Plant City

Dummett's Tomb,
New Smyrna Beach

OCEAN

St Petersburg

Orlando

Splendid China,
Kissimmee

Cape
Canaveral

Tampa
Bay

Patrick's Island,
Ruskin

Melbourne

Sarasota

Solomon's Castle, Ona

Sebring

Lake Placid,
Town of Murals

Charlotte
Harbor

Lake
Okeechobee

Ft Pierce

Ft Myers

Bubble Room, Sanibel

Naples

Belle
Glade

West
Palm Beach

N

The
Everglades

Ft
Lauderdale

0   100km

Aventura

0   100 miles

Miami

Coral Castle,
Homestead

FLORIDA

Key West

Florida Keys

Florida
Bay

Jules' Undersea Lodge
Key Largo

extravaganzas. If this all sounds too weird for words, you can buy a 90-minute video (R to X rated) from their website.

Fantasy Fest held annually in October in Key West, FL. Contact Fantasy Fest, PO Box 230, Key West, FL 33041; ↘ 305 296 1817; fax: 305 294 3335; web: http://fantasyfest.net

Picture this: a thousand grown men, dressed in knickers and eye patches, wearing their wives' gold hoop earrings. It may not be a pretty sight, but it surely is a funny one as you watch these pretend pirates swarm their way over the decks of a pirate ship, sail it up the channel, and capture the Invasion Brunch bunch waiting at the Tampa Convention Center. With their crepes and eggs benedict held high, the buccaneers then invade Bayshore Boulevard for the **Gasparilla Parade and Pirate Fest Festival**. After flinging beads and doubloons to the cheering crowd, they hunt for treasure at the Pirate Chest Arts and Crafts Festival along Ashley Street. The rowdy event has been a fixture of Tampa Bay for nearly a hundred years. Named after the legendary pirate Jose Gaspar, the event also has live entertainment and a brilliant fireworks display.

Gasparilla Parade and Pirate Fest Festival held annually in February in Tampa, FL. Contact Tampa Bay Visitor Bureau; ↘ 813 223 1111 extension 44; web: www.visittampabay.com

During the holiday season, a life size, edible **gingerbread house** is constructed at Aventura Mall in Aventura. At 12 feet wide, 22 feet long, and 18 feet high, it comes with edible windows, edible chandeliers, and an edible fireplace. It takes 1,000 pounds of flour, 800 pounds of butter, 300 pounds of sugar, a ton of icing and 2,000 eggs to construct it. Fifteen thousand pounds of M&Ms, Mars bars and Nestlé chocolates provide the decorations. The house is constructed by the students and staff of Johnson and Wales Culinary University in around 3,000 hours of work, including nonstop baking for an entire week.

Gingerbread house located at Aventura Mall located near the beaches between Miami and Fort Lauderdale at Biscayne Blvd and 196th St, Aventura, FL; ↘ 305 935 1110; web: www.shopaventuramall.com

The **Historic Pursuit Limo Rally** is a cocktail party on wheels and a fundraising scavenger hunt. Teams of ten cruise from clue to clue, testing their knowledge of Miami's history by answering trivia questions that lead to the next clue. Sometimes they have to do something silly, like sing or dance, but it's all for a good cause: the Historical Museum of Southern Florida.

Historic Pursuit Limo Rally held annually in November in Miami, FL. Contact Historical Museum of Southern Florida, 101 W Flagler St, Miami, FL 33130; ↘ 305 375 1492; web: www.historical-museum.org

The **King Mango Strut** is one weird parade. It's completely home grown and free of such pesky irritants as commercial sponsors. Anything goes, the funkier the better, as this parody of the Orange Bowl parade struts its stuff down the streets of CocoNUT Grove. The strut has been making fun of the big parade for 20 years, ever since its application to march in the Orange Bowl parade was rejected as 'unsuitable'. Around 5,000 people turn out to watch the parade, famous for its biting political satire. Anyone and anything that happened during the last year is fair game for the two-to-three dozen marching units who express their political sentiments in irreverent, often tasteless, but always funny ways.

The Grand Marshall for 2000 was Wayne Brehm, an ardent parade participant who had died two weeks earlier. His last wish was to be in the strut 'one way or another', so his urn led the parade and he was allowed to make an ash of himself one last time. True to their political mission, the 2000 parade also included a 'Million Chad March' and a butterfly ballot flyover in which presidental candidate 'Gore' tries to catch votes with a butterfly net.

For the millennium parade they featured the Y2Kmart – hoard now, pay later – led by 'Martha Stewart' demonstrating how to make unique campaign contribution baskets and kick-back arrangements. Presidential candidate Dave Barry, a renowned humor columnist, 'ran' under the slogan 'We'll get those damn stickers off your fruit'. During the Clinton scandal, 'Ken Starr' passed out subpoenas; the Monica look-alike winner won knee pads and a cigar while her infamous blue dress had its own float guarded by the not-so-secret service.

In a previous year an oil slick was depicted, a huge black plastic sheet representing the oil, with dead fish hanging off it and people bobbing and weaving down the street, their heads barely above the water line. The event is always held the weekend preceding New Years. Their mission: to keep the NUT in CocoNUT Grove.

King Mango Strut held annually in December in Coconut Grove, FL. Contact Coconut Grove Chamber of Commerce, 2820 McFarlane Rd, Coconut Grove, FL 33133; ↘ 305 444 7270; fax: 305 444 2489; email: info@coconutgrove.com; web: www.coconutgrove.com

Ernest 'Papa' Hemingway was famous for carousing in Key West during the 1930s, and the town remembers him fondly in the **Hemingway Days Festival**. Everywhere you look you'll see bearded men looking vaguely familiar, as well they should. They're all hoping to win the Hemingway Look-Alike contest. Then, for inexplicable reasons, there's a re-enactment of the running of the bulls in Spain, only this one has people in two-person bull suits running around and falling down. A bull on wheels, along with a real live one, adds to the confusion. The Cayo Heuso Arm Wrestling Competition follows, as does the Papas on Parade. The activities are spread out over ten days, leaving lots of time for literary competitions too.

Hemingway Days Festival held annually in July in Key West, FL; ➥ 800 527 8539; web: www.hemingwaydays.com

With the typically bizarre manner in which Florida reacts to current events, you won't be surprised to learn that the Florida Keys seceded from the United States in 1982 in response to a US Border Patrol road blockade. The blockade resulted in a massive traffic jam, choking off tourism and effectively cutting off the Keys from the rest of the country.

A hastily formed 'Conch Republic' seceded from the Union, declared war, immediately surrendered and demanded foreign aid. Since the government never acted on the demand, the Keys have been 'operating' since then under some obscure legal notion that governs 'adverse possession between sovereign nations', whatever that means. The main effect of this status is an annaul **Conch Republic Independence Celebration** during which the royal subjects behave in a particularly notorious manner for ten days. Long live the Conch Republic.

Conch Republic Independence Celebration held annually in April. Contact the Office of the Secretary General of the Conch Republic; ➥ 305 296 0213; fax: 305 296 8803; web: www.conchrepublic.com

Eccentric environments

Unrequited love was a powerful motivator for Ed Leedskalnin. Jilted by his fiancée on the eve of their wedding, Ed, just 26 years old, wandered aimlessly for several years before settling in Homestead in south Florida, determined to build a monument to his lost love. Single-handedly, the five-foot tall, 100- pound man labored for 20 years cutting and carving 1,100 tons of coral into a **Coral Castle**.

At one point, when a housing development threatened his privacy, he moved 16 years' worth of carvings ten miles away to their present site, using only a truck and tractor. When the carvings were all in place, he erected the castle walls, leveraging the 13,000 pound blocks into place by himself. The really weird thing is that he never let anyone see him working, and his feat baffles scientists and engineers even to this day. He wrote several pamphlets, including 'Mineral, Vegetable and Animal Life' which explain his beliefs on the cycle of life. He died at the age of 64, leaving behind a memorial to a broken heart.

Coral Castle, 28655 S Dixie Hwy, Homestead, FL 33033; ➥ 305 248 6345; web: www.coralcastle.com

A GRANDIOSE SCHEME

If you're set on re-creating the Garden of Eden, Florida's a good place to try, possessing all the requisite foliage and serpents you could ask for. In 1869, a 30-year-old Chicago physician, believing himself to be the Messiah, changed his name from Teed to Koresh and founded Koreshanity, a religion he hoped would supersede Christianity. In 1894 he convinced his small band of believers to follow him to Florida to build New Jerusalem, a city that was supposed to house ten million Koreshantites.

With his 200 or so helpers, Teed built an economically independent community in Estero which supplied all their needs and then some. Women had equal rights, a concept almost unheard of at the time. Arts and crafts flourished, a print shop put out a weekly newspaper, and evenings saw classical and Shakespearean performances in the Art Hall. Teed supplied scientific enlightenment with his theory that the earth was a hollow orb with the continents and oceans on the inside. The sun, moon, and stars were just reflections in the ball of gas that constituted the orb's core.

Teed also thought that celibacy created immortality, so men and women lived separately and children were raised communally. Obviously, celibacy wasn't strictly observed, nor was immortality. When Teed died, his followers propped him up on the Art Hall stage, assuming he'd resurrect himself after the customary three-day waiting period. Then they waited, and waited ... and waited. Eventually the health inspector insisted they dispose of the body, so they put him in a mausoleum by the beach. Thinking he was just being stubborn, or perhaps delayed by some kind of heavenly construction project, they kept up a 24-hour vigil for 13 years until his body was washed to sea by a hurricane. The last remaining Koreshan died in 1982.

Mary Proctor of Tallahassee has spent most of her life around junk. Following a tragic fire that killed three family members, Mary heeded a voice telling her to paint one of the doors in her junkyard. Before long, she was painting everything in the yard with scenes from her life and messages she was driven to share with others.

Calling her former junkyard her **Folk Art Museum**, Missionary Mary Proctor, as she is now called, uses just about any small scrap that comes along to decorate the larger scraps she paints. Stuff is glued on her paintings to give them dimension; sentiments and sayings surround her subjects. Her Hall of Presidents is quite extraordinary: here are life-size replicas of every single US President made out of cut-up Coke cans, complete with a history and a quote about each one. Lately she's been working on garage doors. Mary loves showing visitors around her domain and she's busy making a dozen new things each day.

Folk Art Museum, 3919 Woodville Highway, Tallahassee, FL 32311; ↘ 850 656 2879; web: www.marysart.com. If you call first she'll be sure to meet you. Her environment is very visible from the road.

Solomon's Castle in Ona is big and shiny, which is no wonder considering the exterior is completely covered with reflective aluminum printing plates. Complete with towers, stained glass windows, and a moat with a restaurant boat in it, the castle was built entirely by one man, Howard S Solomon, who has been building it since 1972. The 8,000-square-foot castle houses his family and pieces of his sculpture that are for sale.

Solomon's Castle, 4533 Solomon Rd, Ona, FL 33865; ↘ 863 494 6077; fax: 863 993 0755; email: castle@cyberstreet.com; web: www.solomonscastle.com. *Open 11.00am–4.00pm daily except Mon; Oct–Jun. Admission charge.*

Just plain weird

The little town of Lake Placid has big designs on tourism, several dozen of them, in fact. Known as the **Town of Murals**, its scenes are painted around town on the sides of buildings and on concrete abutments. Even trashcans are painted to match the mural's themes which usually tell the story of some historical event in the region's past. Some of the murals have motion-activated sound effects. The town even has a moving billboard: murals promoting the murals are painted on the sides of a long haul truck trailer that carries the town's message throughout the south and mid west.

The mural project is the passion of Harriet Porter, who founded the Lake Placid Mural Society. Inspired by a similar project she'd seen in Canada, she's the spark behind the murals; the lady with the vision that pulled the town out of its economic slump. The Chamber of Commerce displays renderings of all the murals and the story behind each one.

Town of Murals, Lake Placid, FL. Contact Lake Placid Mural Society, PO Box 336, Lake Placid, FL 33862; ↘ 863 465 4331 or 800 557 5224; web: www.lpfla.com

If the village of Cassadaga seems unusually tranquil, it's because half of the hundred or so people living there are practicing psychics or mediums who can 'read' your present situation by channeling their spirit guides or using some other form of divination such as palmistry or tarot card reading.

The area, known as the **Cassadaga Spiritualist Camp**, was established a century ago by George Colby, whose Indian spirit guide informed him during a seance that he was meant to establish a haven for spiritualists in the South. Colby searched the wilds of Florida until he found a spot that looked exactly like the vision he'd had during the seance, and he set up the camp as a winter haven for visiting spiritualists. Today it's their year-round home where they offer private readings, seminars, workshops and educational programs for believers and skeptic alike. At Cassadaga you can delve into astrology, numerology, palmistry, runes, tarot cards, dream analysis, spiritual contact and past life regression.

> **Cassadaga Spiritualist Camp** located between Orlando and Daytona Beach, FL. Directions: From I-4 use exit 54 (SR 472) travel west to CR 4101 (Dr Martin Luther King Beltway), turn right to CR 4139, right again into town.Contact Cassadega Spiritualist Camp; ↘ 904 228 2880

Around 1860, Charles Dummet was accidently shot and killed while hunting with a friend. His father built a tomb for his son's body on the spot where he died. A hundred years later, Cordova Drive in New Smyrna Beach was built around Dummet's tomb, and the three-foot monument today stands right in the middle of a residential neighborhood.

> **Dummet's tomb** located on Canova Drive in the middle of a residential neighborhood, New Smyrna Beach, FL. From the North Causeway, take S Peninsula, right onto Columbus which turns into Canova Drive. Contact Gary Luthers Publishing, 1009 N Dixie Frwy, New Smyrna Beach, FL; ↘ 386 423 1600; web: www.newsmyrnabeachonline.com

Gibsonton is known as the circus freak wintering camp, once home to off-duty circus performers like Percilla the Monkey Girl, the Anatomical Wonder and the Lobster Boy. During its heyday, it had the only post office with a special counter for midgets (called 'little people' in today's politically correct terminology) and offered special zoning laws that allowed residents to keep elephants in their yard and circus trailers in their driveways. Al, an eight-foot four-inch giant and his wife Jeanie, a two-foot six-inch girl, built the camp from a swamp. Their daughter has a monument business at the camp that displays hundreds of photos of celebrities and circus greats.

> **Gibsonton** located 10 miles south of Tampa, FL.

Attractions

As the story goes, scientists were working on a top secret experiment to harness the power of a man-made tornado. Something goes terribly wrong, and the building is deposited, upside down, on top of an old brick warehouse in Orlando. The upside down building, while certainly extraordinary from an architectural standpoint, is just another good reason to visit this famed city of make believe, home of over-the-top marketing hype.

LIFE'S UPS AND DOWNS

Steve Brown is determined to become the most tattooed yo-yo demonstrator on earth. His mission in life is to 'teach the world about the power of a spin-top' and you can often find him behind the cash register at Lofty Pursuits in Tallahassee. He's a complete yo-yo freak, well versed in the quirkier aspects of yo-yo history such as demonstrator brawls and nasty sales tactics. web: tattoedfreak.com

The nine-story-high structure, a relatively standard building wrapped in a decidedly non-standard facade, houses the **WonderWorks**, an interactive theme attraction that explains the unexplainable in nature. The entrance, through what appears to be a large crack in the roof, leads to the 'laboratory' and the experiential exhibits inside. You can experience what it looks and feels like when a quarter of a million watts of electricity makes your hair stand on end, as well as play in hurricanes and earthquakes. A vertical wall in the Challenge Arena tests your agility.

> **WonderWorks**, 9067 International Dr, Pointe Orlando, Orlando, FL 32819; ↘ 407 351 8800; web: www.wonderworksonline.com. *Open daily 9.00am–12.00midnight. Admission charge.*

The world's largest dinosaur attraction, **Dinosaur World** in Plant City, lets you get up close and personal with around a hundred of the accurately modeled beasts whose construction reflects current theories about dinosaur colors and behavior. Arranged chronologically in a variety of settings, the atmosphere is so spookily realistic that you can practically see them moving through the trees and swamps.

> **Dinosaur World**, 5145 Harvey Tew Rd, Plant City, FL 33565; ↘ 813 717 9865; fax: 813 707 9776; email: info@dinoworld.net; web: www.dinoworld.net. *Open daily 9.00am–dusk. Admission charge. Children under three and dogs on leashes are free.*

You can't miss the entrance to **Gatorland** in Orlando, a kitschy, open-jaw welcome that could hold a dozen people at once in its gaping mouth. Famous for its gator-wrestling and dead chicken snatching show, the 50-year-old park is also the site of the annual **Gator Cook-off** that brings cooks from all over the country to compete for the best gator sausage, gator linguini, gator gumbo and gator pizza. The attraction is a little slice of 1950s life; a reminder of what touristic Florida was like before Mickey Mouse and his corporate competitors arrived.

> **Gatorland**, 14501 S Orange Blossom Trail, Orlando, FL 32837; ↘ 407 855 5496 or 800 393 JAWS; email: customerservice@gatorland.com; web: www.gatorland.com. *Open daily 9.00am–6.00pm, rain or shine. Admission charge.*

Depending who you believe, **Splendid China** is either a cultural theme park or a propaganda ploy run by the communist Chinese government. This curious attraction, which takes itself quite seriously, sits subdued in the land of make believe, out of sync with its flashier theme park neighbors. Protesters have picketed the place since its opening, doing their best to turn away potential tourists. The Citizens Against Communist Chinese Propaganda maintain that the park ignores China's oppression of Tibet and Mongolia, exhibiting the region as the contented state of Eastern Turkestan. Meanwhile Splendid China continues to promote their 60 replicas of Chinese historical sites and landmarks, all hand-crafted by artisans from China, as a journey through 5,000 years of Chinese culture. Attendance is a paltry few hundred per day, so the attraction may not survive. Besides, they keep losing their entertainers, who keep requesting political asylum here in the States.

Splendid China, 3000 Splendid China Blvd, Kissimmee, FL 34747; ↘ 800 244 6226 or 407 396 7111; e-mail: schina@earthlink.net; web: www.floridasplendidchina.com. *Open daily, hours vary by season. Admission charge.*

Wannabe race-car drivers can do a few laps around the track at the **Richard Petty Driving Experience** in Lake Buena Vista. The ticket, which includes admission to **Daytona USA**, takes you three times around the two-and-a-half mile track, screeching around 31° banks at speeds up to 150mph. Helmets and seatbelts are provided; courage isn't.

Richard Petty Driving Experience, Walt Disney World Speedway, Lake Buena Vista, FL; ↘ 800 BE PETTY; web: www.1800bepetty.com

It's not easy becoming a mermaid. First you have to pass an interview, then a formal audition. After that, there's a year of on-the-job, underwater, tail-wiggling and smiling training. Finally, there's a tank test: you have to hold your breath for two-and-a-half minutes while changing costumes in a 72° spring. Fewer than half make the final cut and become genuine mermaids at **Weeki Wachee Springs Water Park** in Tampa.

With the country's only underwater lagoon theater, the park has been operating since the 1940s when Newton Perry had the idea for hose breathing, a technique which lets you stay underwater by breathing through an air hose. The Mermaid Museum next door tells the story, with photos, costumes and props from the past, as well as videos of the park's history.

You can get your picture taken with a mermaid and watch the mermaids-in-training. The attraction includes a waterslide park and a wilderness river cruise.

Weeki Wachee Springs Water Park located 45 minutes north of Tampa, FL at intersection of Hwy 19 and State Road 50; ℩ 877 GO WEEKI; web: www.weekiwachee.com. *Open daily at 10.00am. Admission charge.*

A brand new, interactive **Guinness World Records Experience** in Orlando completely immerses you in bizarre goings-on that have made the famous *Guinness Book of World Records* so fascinating. You can shrink yourself in the Shrinkenator, take a tiny version of yourself on an exploration of the insides of a computer, then let the Molecular Expander restore you to your original size (no, you can't program a different restored size). An inverted pyramid puts you in a visual kaleidoscope of images depicting some of the most extreme human accomplishments. The Monster Monitor challenges you to answer trivia questions with your feet while Guinness Town, a multi-media streetscape, is lined with record holding tenants such as Bill Gates, Elvis, and the Telephone Pole Sitter.

The place is ripe with Kodak moments, especially the one where you appear so tiny compared to the world's fattest man. A motion simulator ride has you experiencing world record feats as they're projected onto the world's largest movie screen.

Guinness World Records Experience, at the Mercado 8437 International Dr, Orlando, FL 32819; ℩ 407 345 9255

The **Peabody Ducks** became world-famous back in the 1930s when the manager of the Peabody Hotel in Memphis, along with his hunting buddies, had a bit too much whiskey and decided it would be funny to put their live duck decoys in the hotel's lobby fountain. Today at the Peabody Hotel in Orlando, the ducks are world renowned for their twice-daily duck march from their roof-top quarters down to the fountain and back again.

Ducks at the Peabody, Orlando, Peabody Hotel, 9801 International Dr, Orlando, FL 32819; ℩ 407 352 4000 or 800 PEABODY; fax: 407 354 1424; web: www.peabody-orlando.com

Museums and collections

Harry Sperl has a hamburger waterbed and a hamburger motorcycle, both of which are sensible things to own if you also have the world's only **Hamburger Museum**. He collects hamburger items because they're American icons and because he loves Americana. He's working with an architect to design a fitting building in which to house his collection of 500 different hamburgers, but for now the museum is in his home. He's got hamburger banks, jars, clocks, magnets, and music boxes; hamburgers made from tin, ceramic, glass, cloth, clay, and plastic; and hamburger signs, posters, T-shirts, towels and calendars.

The International Hamburger Hall of Fame, 'Hamburger' Harry Sperl, Hamburger Collector, 1000 N Beach St, Daytona Beach, FL 32117; ☎ 386 254 8753; fax: 386 255 2460; email: harry@burgerweb.com; web: www.burgerweb.com

The **Springfield Heritage Museum** has a collection of eccentric collections. Hoping to explain the difference between a pack rat and a collector, they define a collection as three or more of anything, emphasizing the 'anything' part since someone is bound to be collecting it if more than three of anything exists. Not all the collections it features are actually in the museum, but photographs of them are. In fact, you can contribute a photo of your own eccentric collection if you wish.

Some of their eccentric collectors include Raymond Tyre who's been collecting wedding cake toppers, Smurfs, cows, corks and the like all his life. His father collects shot glasses; his mother, flower frogs. Pat Till has a bathtub full of stuffed animals and a house full of bride dolls; her granddaughter collects Barbies. Her kitchen walls are covered with antique cooking implements; her husband, Jim, says his only eccentric collection is his family.

Barbara Breaker collects dolls, especially African-American ones. Her late mother collected spoons; her mother-in-law, thimbles. Son Danny Breaker makes animated Lego trains. Marcy McCann collects fruit juicers; Michael Tautman, mechanical banks; and Barbara Gibbs loves hurricane lamps. If the museum's collection of collections is any evidence, America is a nation of collectors. Just check out E-Bay, the internet auction site; you'll be astounded by what is collected and how much it's worth.

Springfield Heritage Museum, 210 W Seventh St, Historic Springfield, Jacksonville, FL 32206; ☎ 904 355 5012; fax: 904 356 1213; email: springfieldhistoricdistrict@worldnet.att; web: www.historicspringfield.com

The elephant collection of Mrs Hawtense Conrad, nicknamed 'Fuzzy', is displayed at **Elephant Fantasyland** in Deland. For 40 years Fuzzy indulged her passion for pachyderms, resulting in more than 1,000 elephants of every size, shape, color, and material. They're made of glass, crystal, ceramic, wicker, wood, paper, stone, plastic and metal. Alone and in herds, elephants grace everything from bookends to wind chimes; lamps to can openers.

Across the hall from the elephants are the toys Robert Conrad and his sister, Dorothy, played with as children. It's not a collection: someone just saved every toy the kids ever had. It's enough to make your electronically addicted child stop and think for a moment before returning to their Game Boy.

Elephant Fantasyland, 230 N Stone St, Deland, FL; ☎ 904 734 5333. *Open 10.00am–3.00pm Wed–Sat. Admission free.*

Shopping

Build-A-Bear Workshop at the Aventura Mall takes a novel approach to selling teddy bears: you build your own. You choose the style, stitch it and stuff it, fluff it and dress it, give its heart a special touch of love and walk out with your new best friend.

> **Build-A-Bear Workshop**, Aventura Mall. Located near the beaches between Miami and Fort Lauderdale at Biscayne Blvd and 196th St, Aventura, FL; ➘ 305 935 1110; web: www.shopaventuramall.com

Quirky cuisine

The **Tantra Restaurant and Lounge** in Miami Beach is no place to come without a lover. With its aphrodisiac menu, fresh-cut grass on the floor, soothing waterfall, fiber-optic starlight and vanilla-scented candles, the place is designed to awaken all five senses. Tantric (Indian) food is supposed to make men more virile and women more appealing, while the pointedly sensual atmosphere paves the way to a (hopefully) predictable result.

> **Tantra Restaurant and Lounge**, 1445 Pennsylvania Ave, Miami Beach, FL 33139; ➘ 305 672 4765; fax: 305 672 4288; web: www.tantrarestaurant.com

A sign on the wall of the **Desert Inn** in Daytona Beach makes its philosophy perfectly clear: 'Tinkers, pig stye keepers, bankers, hair salesmen, newspaper people, cess pool engineers, card sharks, and interior designers will not be served.' A leering male mannequin hangs out in the ladies room, poised to invite the lowering of his zipper; give in to the impulse and the zipper alarm sounds, resounding throughout the inn. Plastic spiders and bats hang from the ceiling, controlled by a barman who delights in lowering them on unsuspecting guests. A plastic tarantula lurks, hidden, somewhere in the men's room. It's a quirky place, with chickens running loose, a resident mongoose, a bordello museum and jackasses being raised in the back. Turtle, gator, and frog are on the menu, while the bar serves an 'Ass Grinder', a drink packing the kick of a mule.

> **Desert Inn Resort Motel and Suites**, 900 N Atlantic Ave, Daytona Beach, FL 32118; ➘ 800 826 1711; web: www.desertinnresort.com

The **Bubble Room** in Sanibel is unlike anything you've experienced before – or likely will again. A sensory overload of twinkling lights, fairy tales, Christmas and Hollywood, this famously insane restaurant was a happy accident waiting to happen. Twenty years ago, when Jamie and Katie Farkmusen bought this building, they put everything they had into opening a restaurant. Unfortunately – or fortunately, as it turned out – everything they had wasn't quite enough.

As opening day approached, they still hadn't decorated the place and barely had enough money for food. So Katie, who had just inherited some antique bubble type Christmas tree lights, hung them up, along with several hundred old black-and- white movie pictures she'd cut out of magazines while growing up. Jamie set up his Lionel trains to run through the restaurant, then threw in his wind-up Victrola, which played old 78 rpm records, for atmosphere. They told their waitress wear something funky; she showed up in her Girl Scout uniform.

Now you know the background, try to picture this: the roofs and siding of the three-story building are purposely crooked so the place looks like it's in motion; the paint job is five pastel colors, while the awnings are bright circus colors. A yellow brick road leads across yellow bridges; gnomes, elves, mermaids and frogs abound. Santas are everywhere, as are the pulsating lights. Chandeliers spin, festive music from the 1930s and 1940s adds nostalgic ambiance, and antique toys are everywhere, even inset into the glass top dining tables. The servers wear khaki, decorating their uniforms and hats to express their personalities. It can't get more unpredictable than this, especially since customers are always contributing more stuff to add to the décor.

Bubble Room, 15001 Captiva Drive, Sanibel, FL 33957; ➘ 941 472 5558; web: www.bubbleroomrestaurant.com

OK, so its corporate kitsch, but its still counts as weird. The **Monster Café** at Universal Studios beckons you with rotating monsters on top of the building. Frankenstein holds a menu, Wolf Man holds a pizza, and the Creature is frosting a cake with a boat oar. Inside, each dining area has a theme like the Mummy's tomb, Frankenstein's Lab, and Dracula's Mansion. Monster rock fills the air, classic images line the walls, videos play trailers and outtakes, and monster displays are everywhere. What's really strange is that, disconcertingly, everything's in color; the original monster flicks were always in black and white.

Monster Café, 1000 Universal Studios Plaza, Orlando, FL 32819-7610; ➘ 407 363 8000; web: www.usf.com

The **Old Spanish Sugar Mill** in Deleon Springs puts a unique spin on its pancakes: you cook them at your own table griddle. They give you pitchers of

pancake batter, along with all the toppings you could want, and leave the cooking to you. Just watch where you flip. They do offer other food besides pancakes.

> **Old Spanish Sugar Mill**, 601 Ponce Deleon Blvd, Deleon Springs State Recreation Area, Deleon Springs, FL 32130; ✆ 904 985 4212; web: www.dep.state.fl.us/parks. Located 1 hour north of Orlando and ½ hour west of Daytona Beach. *Open 9.00am–4.00pm Mon–Fri; 8.00am–4.00pm Sat–Sun.*

Quirky quarters

Couch potatoes will feel right at home in the **cinema suites** at the Lake Buena Vista Holiday Inn Resort. The dual recliners, 60 inch televisions, and surround sound would delight Homer Simpson.

> **Cinema Suites**, Holiday Inn Family Suites Hotel, 14500 Continental Gateway, Orlando, FL 32821; ✆ 877 387 5437; web: www.hifamilysuites.com

Dubbed the 'rock 'n roll hotel' of Miami's South Beach, the **Marlin Island Outpost**, home to a state-of-the-art recording studio, is also an all-suite hotel with a guest list that includes such notables as Mick Jagger, U2 and Johnny Depp. Featuring Afro-Urban décor, along with a few theme suites, each suite offers cutting edge communications. The **Cavalier Island Outpost** is decorated with an African theme and displays in-room photographs that capture the history of fashion photography.

> **Marlin Island Outpost**, 1200 Collins Ave, Miami Beach, FL 33139; ✆ 305 604 5063; fax: 305 673 9609; web: www.islandoutpost.com/Marlin

> **Cavalier Island Outpost**, 1320 Ocean Dr, Miami Beach, FL 33139; ✆ 305 604 5064; fax: 305 531 5543; web: www.islandoutpost.com/Cavalier

On **Patrick's Island** at Ruskin you'll be the only guests in the only house on the island. You can go fishing, boating, or just lounge around your very own fantasy island.

> **Patrick's Island**. Contact Pat and Rick Spears, Proprietors, 7341 Nebraska Way, Longmont, CO 80501; ✆ 303 684 9626; fax: 303 774 1398; email: Patrick.island@juno.com

The **Pelican Hotel** in Miami is decorated in high Fellini-esque kitsch with 30 witty, one-of-a-kind rooms sporting names like Best Whorehouse, Psychedelic Girl, the Executive Fifties, and Jesus Christ, Megastar. The

Pelican Penthouse, at $2,000 a night, features a canary yellow dining room, a round tropical fish tank, a round bed, his and hers walk-in closets and a nine-screen video wall. The Pelican is a favorite with the fashion, music and publishing set.

Pelican Hotel, 826 Ocean Dr, Miami Beach, FL 33139; ➘ 305 673 3373; fax: 305 673 3255; web: www.pelicanhotel.com

You have to scuba dive to stay at **Jules' Undersea Lodge** in Key Largo. The entire hotel is built in a 30-foot deep lagoon that it shares with an underwater research facility. One of only two such habitats in the world, certified divers enjoy unlimited diving with a continuous air supply from 120-foot lines. You can stay more than one night but don't plan on flying for 24 hours after surfacing. Gourmet food is part of the many dive packages the hotel offers.

Jules' Undersea Lodge, 51 Shoreland Dr, Mile Marker 103.2, Oceanside Key Largo, FL 33037; ➘ 305 451 2353; fax: 305 451 4789; email: info@jul.com; web: www.jul.com

The **Cassadaga Hotel** is the psychic center of a spiritualist camp where you can take advantage of on-site New Age pursuits such as astral projection, reincarnation and other parapsychology offerings.

Cassadaga Hotel Spiritualist Camp, 355 Cassadaga Rd, Cassadaga FL 32706; ➘ 904 228 2323; web: www.cassadagahotel.com

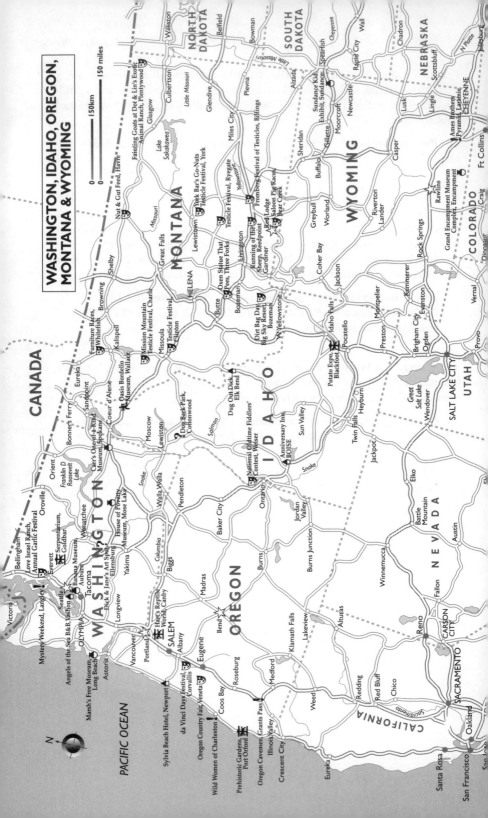

WASHINGTON, IDAHO, OREGON, MONTANA & WYOMING

CANADA

NORTH DAKOTA

SOUTH DAKOTA

NEBRASKA

MONTANA

WYOMING

WASHINGTON

IDAHO

OREGON

NEVADA

UTAH

COLORADO

CALIFORNIA

PACIFIC OCEAN

N

0   150km
0   150 miles

Williston

Belfield

Bowman

Cheyenne

Wall

Chadron

Rapid City

Spearfish

Sundance Kid Exhibit, Sundance

Newcastle

Gillette

Moorcroft

Ames Brothers Pyramid, Laramie

CHEYENNE

Scottsbluff

Lingle

Lusk

N Platte

Ft Collins

Rawlins

Grand Encampment Museum Complex, Encampment

Craig

Dinosaur

Vernal

Provo

Ogden

Evanston

Brigham City

Kemmerer

Rock Springs

Great Salt Lake

SALT LAKE CITY

Wendover

Montpelier

Preston

Pocatello

Idaho Falls

Potato Expo, Blackfoot

Heyburn

Twin Falls

Jackpot

Elko

Battle Mountain

Austin

NEVADA

Winnemucca

Fallon

Reno

CARSON CITY

SACRAMENTO

Oakland

San Francisco

Santa Rosa

Sacramento

Redding

Red Bluff

Chico

Weed

Eureka

Crescent City

Klamath Falls

Lakeview

Alturas

Medford

Illinois Valley

Grants Pass

Oregon Caverns

Prehistoric Gardens, Port Orford

Wild Women of Charleston

Coos Bay

Roseburg

Eugene

Oregon Country Fair, Veneta

da Vinci Days Festival, Corvallis

Albany

SALEM

Bend

Hart's Reptile World, Canby

Portland

Vancouver

Longview

Astoria

Marsh's Free Museum, Long Beach

Angels of the Sea B&B, Langley

Mystery Weekend, Langley

Victoria

Bellingham

Love Israel Ranch, Annual Garlic Festival

Everett

Seattle

Serpentarium, Goldbar

Banana Museum, Auburn

Tacoma

Dick & Jane's Art Spot, Ellensburg

OLYMPIA

Yakima

Wenatchee

Oroville

Orient

Bonner's Ferry

Franklin D Roosevelt Lake

Sandpoint

Eureka

Kalispell

Furniture Races, Whitefish

Whitefish

Shelby

Browning

Great Falls

HELENA

Missoula

Mission Mountain Testicle Festival, Charlo

Testicle Festival, Clinton

Clinton

Carr's One-of-a-Kind Museum, Spokane

Oasis Bordello Museum, Wallace

Coeur d'Alene

Moscow

Lewiston

Dog Bark Park, Cottonwood

Salmon

Dug Out Dick, Elk Bend

National Oldtime Fiddlers' Contest, Weiser

Anniversary Inn

BOISE

Sun Valley

Ontario

Jordan Valley

Burns Junction

Burns

Madras

Biggs

Pendleton

Walla Walla

House of Poverty Museum, Mose Lake

Columbia

Snake

Snake

Butte

Bozeman

Dirt Bag Day, Big Sky Resort, Bozeman

Yellowstone

Three Forks

Oxen Statue That 'Pees, Three Forks

Livingston

Running of the Sheep, Reedpoint

Gardiner

Red Lodge

Bear Creek Saloon Pig Races, Bear Creek

Testicle Festival, Rygate

Fromberg Festival of Testicles, Billings

Billings

Lewistown

York Bar's Go-Nuts Testicle Festival, York

Fainting Goats at Dot & Lin's Exotic Animal Ranch, Plentywood

Nut & Gut Feed, Havre

Havre

Shelby

Missouri

Lake Sakakawea

Little Missouri

Glasgow

Culbertson

Glendive

Miles City

Plevna

Sheridan

Buffalo

Worland

Greybull

Coher Bay

Jackson

Lander

Riverton

Casper

Little Missouri

Wolf Creek

Alzida

Baker City

Salem

Victoria

Missouri

Northwestern Region

7

WASHINGTON

Home to Microsoft and Starbucks Coffee, this previously culturally deprived neck of the woods has emerged as a high-tech, sophisticated – and some say insufferably snooty – state more interested in the pursuit of big money than in the pursuit of the elusive Big Foot.

Festivals and events

Love Israel's his name; commune is his game. Also known as 'Love is Real', he's the head guru of a group of several hundred people who give themselves names like 'Forgiven', 'Patience', 'Charity', 'Serious', and 'Honesty'. These nouns, verbs and adjectives all live together in harmony on the **Love Israel Ranch** northeast of Arlington, where 20,000 people flock each August to their **Garlic Festival**. This event draws just as many breeders as it does aging hippies, all anxious to partake of everything garlic. During the festival, and most Saturdays, they'll let you tour their five-acre garden. They also operate the Bistro Café in downtown Arlington, showing that they understand perfectly what it takes to finance eccentricity. They're also known as the Church of Armageddon. They believe that as long as they follow the Law of Love, they don't need to obey any other laws.

> **Love Israel Ranch**, annual Garlic Festival held in August at Israel Family Ranch, 13724 184th St NE, Arlington, WA; ☎ 360 435 8577

Just plain weird

The **Fremont Neighborhood**'s official motto is 'Freedom to be Peculiar'. Residents take this responsibility very seriously, as evidenced by three signs, the first of which says 'Entering the Republic of Fremont, the Center of the Universe, set your watch back five minutes'. Another repeats the same phrase, except says to set your watch ahead five minutes. The last again repeats, but instead suggests you just throw your watch away.

This Seattle neighborhood is home to an abundance of street art, including the Fremont Troll, who lives under the Aurora Bridge. He lurks in the shadows, a cuddly two tons of concrete holding a real VW bug.

'Waiting for the Interurban' are three stone figures waiting for a trolley which no longer comes. They're usually all dressed up by the residents, but with no way to go. A bronze sculpture of Lenin, brought over by a teacher who found the figure discarded in Slovakia, is infamous – and it's also for sale at just $150,000.

Fremont is known for its Saturday night outdoor cinema. Flocks of people lounge outside on funky furniture, dressed in costume (simply because they can), watching their favorite cult and classic B movies in the only walk-in outdoor theater in the west.

Fremont Neighborhood located in North Seattle, WA. Contact Greater Seattle Chamber of Commerce, 1301 5th Ave, Suite 2400, Seattle, WA 98101; ↘ 206 389 7200; fax: 206 389 7288; web: www.seattlechamber.com

The town of Langley really knows how to plan a party. On the last weekend in February, it involves the entire population, plus guests, in a quirky **Mystery Weekend**. The town, an art colony just three blocks long by two blocks wide, boasts around 1,000 residents.

The Mystery Weekend is a two-day, interactive play which takes place all over town. Written by local authors, it involves local actors, shopkeepers, the mayor, and everyone else who wants to play. The entry packet includes a newspaper that has stories about the mystery, a map with the location of the crime and where to find clues.

Participants go around town collecting clues and interviewing folks who are roaming the streets, and in the shops and cafes. Not everyone is truthful, which adds to the fun. When you think you know who done it, you submit your entry at the visitor center. On Sunday evening the 'detectives' gather the 'suspects' on stage, solving the mystery in a little playlet. Drawings are held for various prizes among those who guessed correctly.

Mystery Weekend held annually in February in Langley, WA. Information: Contact Langley Chamber of Commerce, PO Box 403, Langley, WA 98260; ↘ 360 221 5676

Gary Golightly of Seattle is a one man bubble festival, performing his bubble ballet in nearly 30 countries. Calling himself the **Bubbleman**, he makes extraordinary bubbles from ordinary objects, even putting himself inside a giant bubble. His bubbleosophy is simple: to go where there is misery and bring joy. You can view his performance schedule on his website.

Bubbleman, Garry Golightly, PO Box 31347, Seattle, WA 31347; ↘ 206 781 6749; email: goligthly@bubbleman.com; web: www.bubbleman.com

Attractions

Big Red, a bright pink woman with road reflector breasts, welcomes you to **Dick and Jane's Art Spot** in Ellensburg, a private home with a yard straight out of fantasyland. Dick Elliott and Jane Orleman have filled their home and property with a mad mixture of oddball sculpture that started out as junk and ended up with personality. They've been working at this for 12 years, creating such characters as Eric Etch-a-Sketch, a Polaroid camera man, an 'art lives' fence and a bicycle tire tree.

> **Dick and Jane's Art Spot**, 101 North Pearl St, Ellensburg, WA. Located across from the police station.

With a name like the Reptile Man, folks are sure to take notice. Scott Petersen runs the **Washington Serpentarium** in Goldbar, home to a menagerie of chameleons, scorpions, turtles, spiders, snakes and lizards. He gives live demonstrations, encouraging hands-on familiarity with his pythons and alligators. The kids love it even though some adults act like they'd rather be having root canal treatment.

> **Washington Serpentarium** located on Hwy 2 in Goldbar, WA; ↘ 425 778 4941; email: info@reptileman.com; web: www.thereptileman.com. *Open daily 10.00am–6.00pm. Admission charge.*

Famous for its Frank Gehry architecture, the **Experience Music Project** is a spectacularly eccentric building complex that can best appreciated when seen from the observation tower of the nearby Space Needle. The building, with its swooping lines, metallic roofs, undulating walls, and vibrant colors, is a fitting way to pay tribute to modern music.

In the Sky Church entry hall, the world's largest video screen plays videos produced just for the museum: videos with throbbing motion, pulsating light, and swirling colors. The floor is translucent with glowing time capsules filled with objects donated by various bands. Your museum guide is a hand-held computer that lets you hear narration, interviews, and music. In glass-walled studios you can follow electronic prompts that show you how to play the drums or an electric guitar. The main exhibit hall has tens of thousands of items, including Ray Charles' debut recording, a 1960s FBI file investigating the lyrics of 'Louie, Louie', and Janis Joplin's floral bell-bottoms, circa 1970.

> **Experience Music Project**, Seattle Center Campus, 325 5th Ave N, Seattle, WA 98109; ↘ 877 EMPLIVE or 206 EMPLIVE; fax: 206 770 2727; email: experience@emplive.com; web: www.emplive.com

Museums and collections

Carr's One-of-a-Kind Museum really is just that, a privately owned collection of unusual stuff like celebrity limousines, a Chinese junk made of

RECORDING MARATHON

For 24 years the Reverend Robert Shields recorded every detail of his life in what is now known as the world's longest diary. He rarely left his house so he wouldn't get behind in logging everything he ate, every move he made, all the junk mail he received, every dream he remembered and most all of his body functions. Until suffering a stroke in 1996, he spent four hours a day on his obsession. The 35 million-word diary, consisting of 90 carefully labeled boxes of typewritten, bound, legal-size ledgers, is being preserved by Washington State University which is in the process of putting the diary onto acid-free materials for protection over time.

matchsticks, and a navy destroyer. Marvin Carr, a retired World War II vet, has a penchant for collecting weird things such as a 13-foot snake that electrocuted itself by chewing through a stereo cord, a full case of President George Bush's innagural champagne, a model ship made of 27,500 matchsticks, and a 99-year-old wheelchair. His car collection includes Elvis Presley's Lincoln, Jackie Gleason's limo, and JFK's personal Lincoln which, they say, played a part in the affair he allegedly had with Marilyn Monroe.

Carr's One-of-a-Kind Museum, 5225 North Freya, Spokane, WA 99217; ➘ 509 489 8859 or 800 350 6469; fax: 509 489 8859

Located in the Pike Place market, the **Giant Shoe Museum** offers peep-show glimpses of such super-sized shoes as a four-foot wingtip and a huge clown shoe. The shoes are behind curtains; drop in a quarter and the curtains part.

Giant Shoe Museum, Old Seattle Paperworks, 1501 Pike Pl, Seattle, WA. Located in the lower level of Pike Place Market; ➘ 206 623 2870

Monte Holm is a wealthy man who came from a very dysfunctional family, so dysfunctional that he had to leave at age 13 in the middle of the Great Depression. He rode the rails for six years, begging for food and standing in bread lines; one of his favorites was the soup kitchen run by Al Capone. Life was miserable and Monte vowed that if he ever had money, he'd be good to people. He also vowed that no one would ever kick him off a train again.

Monte arrived in Washington with one thin dime in his pocket. He parlayed that over the next 40 years into a successful junkyard business in Moses Lake. Next door to the junkyard he built a warehouse, stocking it with antique cars, old steam engines, and enough interesting old stuff to keep you entertained for hours. And behind the warehouse, which he called the **House of Poverty Museum**, sits the **Mon-Road Railroad** where you can see a real train, including the 1915 presidential passenger car that once carried presidents

Wilson and Truman. No one pays a dime at the museum; in fact, you leave richer for the experience.

Mon-Road Railroad and House of Poverty Museum, 258 Commerce Way, Moses Lake, WA 98837; ↘ 509 765 6342

The first place you could say 'Fill 'er up' was right in Seattle, home to the world's first gas station. Before it opened in 1907, you had to bring the gas to your car in a can; reversing the process seemed like a modern miracle. At the **General Petroleum Museum**, you'll see a lot of gas pumps, including an all-glass model that wasn't too successful because cars kept running into it. The second floor holds a full-scale replica of an art-deco era gas station as well as exhibits of the freebies offered over the years to entice customers to buy. Folks used to collect entire sets of dinnerware that way, a sort of frequent gas program.

General Petroleum Museum, 1526 Bellevue Ave, Seattle, WA 98122; ↘ 206 323 4789. *Open by appointment.*

You'd never guess that Ann Lovell, the mild-mannered Auburn librarian, is bonkers over bananas. Also known as Anna Banana, she's curator of the **Banana Museum** she's set up in her home. Her collection, amassed over 20 years, numbers an astounding 4,000 banana-related items: magnets, jewelry, cookie jars, cookbooks, cartoons, pillows, inflatables, crates, shipping labels, fabrics, aprons, even boxer shorts. She talks on a banana phone, writes with banana pens, reads by a banana floor lamp, even has a banana Christmas tree.

You never know when an event is going to trigger such a collecting frenzy. For Ann it was a trip to Hawaii and an Anna's Bananas T-shirt. Without being consciously aware of it, she just started buying things with bananas, any size, any material and for any purpose. Today, she's a leading expert on banana crates, labels, and invoices, and hopes the Smithsonian may someday be willing to take her collection. For now she just enjoys sharing her passion, and playing her tape of 40 banana songs while she shows you around. Her most prized banana? A Chiquita fiberglass banana cello.

Banana Museum, Auburn, WA, ↘ 253 833 8043; email: abanana@mail.gr.cc.wa.us; web: www.geocities.com/NapaValley/1799. *Open by appointment only.*

Tours
Windsor Olson is a real private eye who takes visitors to the locations of some of Seattle's most grisly crimes. **Private Eye on Seattle** investigates a mass murder, the Tong wars, a million dollar burglary, bordellos, arsonists, and the soy sauce murder mystery.

Private Eye on Seattle, Seattle, WA; ➘ 206 365 3739; email:
Jake13@foxinternet.com; web: www.privateeyetours.com

A number of companies give amusing tours of Pioneer Square's abandoned
subterranean world, among them Bill Speidel's **Underground Tour**.
Accompanied by a wise-cracking guide, you'll wind through the long
abandoned storefronts under Seattle's streets, hearing about the exploding-
toilet debacle that forced the city to raise the streets fourteen feet up as well as
the scandals that gave rise to the expression 'skid row'.

Underground Tour, 610 1st Ave, Seattle, WA 98104; ➘ 206 682
4646; web: www.undergroundtour.com

Shopping

Joe Standley had a life long passion for nature's curiosities, collecting oddities
like a preserved prospector, the Lord's Prayer engraved on a grain of rice, fleas
in dresses, a three-tusk walrus and the smallest ivory elephants in the world.
He began this Seattle collection during the Civil War, eventually calling it **Ye
Olde Curiosity Shop**. There've been many imitators since, but he was one
of the first to recognize the drawing power of weird.

Ye Olde Curiosity Shop, 1001 Alaskan Way, Pier 54, Seattle, WA
98104; ➘ 206 682 5844; web: www.yeoldecuriosityshop.com

Quirky quarters

What makes the **Angels of the Sea Bed and Breakfast** in Vashon so special
is the proprietress, Marnie Jones, a singer and harpist known for her healing
sessions using sound and music. During breakfast she plays the harp and sings
with her guitar. She'll even serve you breakfast in bed if you request it.

Angels of the Sea Bed and Breakfast, 26431 99th Ave SW,
Vashon, WA 98070; ➘ 800 798 9249 or 206 463 6980; web:
www.angelsofthesea.com

IDAHO
Festivals and events

It takes six days of fiddling around to win the **National Old Time Fiddlers'
Contest** in Weiser, long considered the fiddling capital of the world.

Hundreds of entrants from every state, many of them winners of local and
regional championships, gather for a week of jamming and friendly competition.

Each fiddler has four minutes to play a hoe down, a waltz and one other
tune of their choice to qualify. Going over the time limit by even a second can
cost them the title. If you've never been to a fiddling event, you'll be surprised
at how much musical variety you'll hear. Each state, and even each region
within a state, has its own unique sound and experienced fiddlers can tell

where a person is from just by listening to his or her music. Folks of all ages – even children – participate in the competition.

National Oldtime Fiddlers' Contest held annually in June in Weiser, ID. ➘ 800 437 1280; web: www.fiddlecontest.com

Attractions

The girls left in a hurry, such a hurry that their clothes, makeup, and personal possessions were all left behind. To find out why, take the tour of the **Oasis Bordello Museum** in Wallace.

Oasis Bordello Museum, 605 Cedar St, Wallace, ID 83873; ➘ 208 753 0801

The world's biggest beagle welcomes you to **Dog Bark Park** in Cottonwood, home of chain-saw artists Dennis Sullivan and his wife, Francis Conklin. The park got it's name from Dennis, who claims he can hear hundreds of dogs barking when he puts his ear up to a dead tree. All sizes of dog are carved out of Ponderosa pine using a chain saw. You can't miss the place: the beagle out front is more than three stories tall.

Dog Bark Park located off Route 12, Hwy 95 at the Dog, Cottonwood, ID; ➘ 208 962 DOGS

Blackfoot, known as the potato capital of the world, is home to Idaho's **World Potato Exposition**. Besides learning everything you'd ever want to know about potato farming, you'll see the world's largest potato chip – a two-foot Pringle – and get a chance to buy potato fudge, potato ice-cream and potato hand-cream at the gift shop.

World Potato Exposition, Hwy 91, Blackfoot, ID 83221; ➘ 800 785 2517 or 208 785 2517; email: potatoexpo@idaho.net; web: www.ida.net/users/potatoexpo. *Open 10.00am–7.00pm Mon–Sat May–Sept.*

Quirky quarters

For 40 years **Richard Zimmerman**, aka Dugout Dick, has been digging caves using only a pick, a shovel, and a pry bar. The four-room, warren-like cave he lives in himself has no electricity, heating, or plumbing, at least of the modern kind. An ice cave provides refrigeration, wood-burning stoves provide heat and car windshields set into the rubble walls serve as windows to keep out the weather and let in light.

Zimmerman has dug so many caves that he rents several of them to campers or wannabe hermits for a couple of dollars a day. Some of his tourist caves are heated with homemade stoves vented with a milk can stovepipe. Built in beds hang from the rock walls, and kerosene lamps supply the illumination. Don't expect room service.

Now age 84, Zimmerman emerges from his cave to attend church, an activity he only recently embraced. He likes to write songs about his Salmon River home and entertains himself by simultaneously playing the guitar and harmonica while dancing. He's been profiled in a book called *Idaho Loners* by Cort Conley which is devoted to the state's many hermits, solitaries, and individualists.

Richard Zimmerman, Hwy 93, Elk Bend, ID. Located above the banks of the Salmon River and visible from Hwy 93.

The **Anniversary Inn** in Boise is a theme hotel with rooms like Sleeping Beauty's Suite, a medieval adventure with a drawbridge leading to your room, breakfast in the turret and projection television. The Oregon Trail suite has a bed in a covered wagon; Mammoth Ice Cave, complete with stalactites, boasts a hot tub. The Hay Loft is two stories with a windmill waterfall shower.

Anniversary Inn, 1575 Lusk Ave, Boise, ID 83706; ➘ 208 331 7740; web: www.anniversaryinn.com

OREGON

This feisty state is a leader in environmental protection, population growth controls and medically assisted suicide. They'd also like to see their borders closed to Californians, whom they view with ill-disguised contempt for their materialistic habits.

Festivals and events

It's not quite the spectacle that Burning Man (see page 247) has become, nor is it just a bunch of aging hippies desperately clinging to the past. The **Oregon Country Fair** is a modern, somewhat sanitized, version of a 1960s be-in. Still idealistic, yet realistic at the same time, the fair has evolved in 30-something years into an event drawing mainstream families and corporate types along with the requisite hippies. Somehow the fair has managed to please a very diverse crowd with an eclectic mix of crafts, food, entertainment and environmental guilt.

At the archaeology booth you'll learn that the site itself has been a gathering place for 11,000 years while the Energy Park is all about renewable and alternative energy sources. To make learning more entertaining, the park staff provides thought-provoking performers and creative thinkers to help get its message across.

There are 350 booths in all, peddling everything from portable Yurt homes to log tables, brooms, masks, puppets and herbs. The food ranges from

FOR WALKERS ONLY?

Brian Walker, 44, is planning to be the first private individual to go into space in a home-built rocket. The successful toy inventor plans to power his nine-foot capsule with hydrogen peroxide rockets, the kind used to power superfast cars and motorcycles. Meanwhile, he's training his body to handle gravitational forces in his homemade backyard centrifuge, one of many tips he picked up while attending a cosmonaut training class offered in Russia to wealthy, wannabe cosmonauts. Before he can blast off, however, he's got to convince the government to issue the necessary permits to launch the rocket. Experts who've reviewed his plans find them space-worthy enough to conclude that he just might be able to enter the record books with his scheme.

burritos to blintzes and from deep-fried bananas to organic juices. There's a full spectrum of entertainment, with musicians, magicians, jugglers, puppets, belly dancers and storytellers. Three vaudeville-type stages host acts like the Spoonman, Dr Atomic's Medicine Show and Leapin' Louie Lichtenstein, the Jewish Lithuanian Cowboy. Cozy performance spaces on the fringes offer eco-folk music, a poetry circus and a variety of alternative acts. A bevy of wandering performers do their thing as well. When you get tired, dozens of masseurs and bodywork therapists are there to rejuvenate you.

Of the 150,000 or so people who attend the three-day event, around 7,000 will camp at the site, using solar-heated showers, eating organic food, recycling, composting and joining feel-good 'om-m-m' circles.

At issue for fairgoers past is whether the country's premier 'alternative' festival has sold out to the 'destructive, consumerist death culture' believed to be contrary to 'communitarian thinking'. If you ask the folks at the Community Village, they'll tell you they're working to expand their consciousness beyond the fair and out into the world at large. It doesn't sound like the message – or the medium – has changed all that much since the 1960s.

Oregon Country Fair held annually in July in Eugene, OR. Contact Oregon Country Fair, PO Box 2972, Eugene, OR 97402; ↘ 541 343 4298 or 800 992 8499; email: ocf@teleport.com; web: www.oregoncountryfair.org

The **da Vinci Days Festival** in Corvallis celebrates art, science and technology with kinetic sculpture races, street performers, storytellers and participatory art projects. Teams of people who have designed and built a human-powered, all-terrain sculpture try to ride their vehicle through a 100-foot mud bog, down two miles of river, across 3,000 feet of pasture, and over a 100-foot sand trap. Besides speed and terrain worthiness, teams are also scored on the artistry of their sculpture and on the overall show they put on for the spectators. They make fools of themselves for your viewing pleasure, so cheer them on encouragingly. Besides the kinetics, the festival offers skateboard and roller blade contests, a sidewalk chalk art competition, a canine Frisbee championship, and enough fair food to keep you going a long time.

> **da Vinci Days Festival** held annually in July in Corvallis, OR.
> Contact daVinci Days Festival, 760 SW Madison, Suite 200, Corvallis,
> OR 97333; ↘ 541 757 6363 or 800 334 8118; email: davinci@davinci-days.org; web: www.davinci-days.org

Just plain weird

You can't just walk into Portland's **24-hour Church of Elvis** and browse. You must take a tour, which, according to owner Stephanie G Pierce, is an original work of art. There's no fixed charge because, Stephanie says, she has a 'social contract' with you, trusting that you'll recognize the value of her art form and donate appropriately. In her own words, she, and it, is 'something that cannot be described'.

This place is impossibly, improbably wacky, a manifestation of its owner's fertile and nutty imagination. The personification of eccentric, Stephanie's quite fond of self-described titles. Thus, this celebrity/spokes model/minister is happy to give you a tour of her church/gallery/non-retail experience. Her 'religion' is to worship plastic, styrofoam and Elvis. Her tour includes the Miracle of the Tortilla of Turin, a tortilla chip with the face of Elvis on it,

Her gift shop alone is worth the visit. You can buy a pocket-size Elvis X-ray, supposedly taken by the FBI when Elvis applied to become an undercover drug agent. 'The vocal cords are stunning' points out Stephanie. There's a Guardian Angel Apron, which will protect you from culinary dangers; it's covered with plastic flies. And who can get by without a Church of Elvis Checkbook Cover, with glow-in-the-dark dots and logos galore? She's even made an Elvis Detector, a card you hold between your fingers that will eventually tell you if the King's spirit is nearby. At one point, Stephanie lived in her shop window for three months, converting it to a biosphere/diet center/breast enlarger. Try explaining that one.

Despite its name, it's not open 24 hours, so you should call ahead to be sure Stephanie is in attendance.

> **24-hour Church of Elvis**, 720 SW Ankeny, Portland, OR 97205;
> ↘ 503 226 3671; web: www.churchofelvis.com

They're the **Wild Women of Charleston**, and all it takes to join in their high jinks is knowing the length of your home extension cord. This satirical group sponsors events like clam squirting contests, a fisherman's rubber boot beauty contest and tricycle racing in the mudflats. You don't even have to be a woman to join; just give them 34 cents and you, too, can race with an oyster on your nose or a fish on your head.

Wild Women of Charleston, Charleston Visitor and Information Center, PO Box 5735, Charleston, OR 97240; ☎ 800 824 8486

He's 17 feet tall, dumb as dirt, and stands guard at the corner of 6th and Morgan next to the Chamber of Commerce Visitor Center. The **Oregon Cavemen** Club, an organization dating back to 1922, placed him there. Why the business owners who formed the club chose a caveman to promote their businesses is a mystery, but their antics are the stuff of legend. Dressed in animal skins and carrying clubs, they made surprise visits when someone important or famous came to Grants Pass. Shirley Temple, Thomas Dewey, John F Kennedy, and Robert Kennedy were all ambushed by the cavemen; Ronald Regan was made an honorary member.

Oregon Cavemen located at the corner of 6th and Morgan next to the Chamber of Commerce Visitor Center, Grants Pass, OR.

Attractions
Feeding chickens to the alligators is one of the highlights at **Hart's Reptile World** in Canby. So is snake petting, although the kids seem more enthusiastic than the adults. A tame alligator that had the run of the place was, sadly, poisoned last year. Live mice and rabbits are kept on hand for snake food on weekends; the Easter Bunny Feed is an annual, if macabre, event.

Hart's Reptile World is non-profit. The animals, mostly discarded pets or reptiles confiscated during drug raids, are lovingly cared for by owner Mary Esther Hart. If an alligator or large snake is on the loose somewhere, chances are she'll be called to the rescue. Mary Esther says she prefers reptiles over cats and dogs because they're quiet and because she's genuinely fond of all things reptilian.

Godzilla the Alligator is one of the park's stars; 11 feet long, he's the largest alligator in captivity outside of zoos. Mary Esther rescued him from a field in California.

Hart's Reptile World, 11264 S Macksburg Rd, Canby, OR 97013. Located about 20 miles south of Portland, OR; ☎ 503 266 7236.

Prehistoric Gardens is filled with concrete replicas of dinosaurs and amphibians, peering amusingly above dense foliage. It's the setting of this park, in a landscape similar to our fantasies of dinosaur environments, which make this 'lost world' so much fun. You can't help but be entetained by the two dozen 'authentic' creatures in this forest menagerie.

Prehistoric Gardens, 36848 S Hwy 101, Port Orford, OR 97465. Located between Port Orford and Gold Beach, OR; ☎ 541 332 4463

Most people can think up weird things to do, but rarely get around to acting on their impulses. At the **Funny Farm** in Buffet Flat, Gene Carsey gives himself permission to do whatever pops into his head. For example, a bowling ball garden – the largest of its kind in the world; he even sells packets of bowling ball seeds. The farm's collection of bowling balls, now 300 strong, keeps growing because folks donate their no-longer-used balls.

There's a wall covered with brightly colored washing machine agitators, in front of which he's thoughtfully supplied political picket signs just in case you're gripped by a sudden need to agitate. After all, he says, 'without agitators, nothing in the world would come clean'. A Wizard of Oz theme sort of meanders through the place, sometimes featured, sometimes forgotten. At the heart-shaped Love Pond, he offers a Free Wedding Day each June. Last year three couples were actually married at the pond by Marilyn, an 82-year- old minister, and her assistant, Victoria.

Gene and his partner, Mike, are working on a Wizard of Oz Bed and Breakfast at the 'farm'.

Funny Farm, 64990 Deschutes Market Road, Bend, OR 97701; ↘ 541 389 6391 or 800 247 6391; email: genecarsey@aol.com; web: www.funfarm.com

Museums and collections

It may not be very glamorous, but the lowly vacuum cleaner played a big role in freeing us from drudgery. Spanning a 100-year history, **Stark's Vacuum Cleaner Museum** in Portland displays models ranging from the old hand-pumped versions to today's super suckers. We can thank a night janitor named James Spangler for inventing the future Kirbys, Royals, Hoovers, and Eurekas we all know and love.

Stark's Vacuum Cleaner Museum, 107 NE Grand Ave, Portland, OR; ↘ 800 230 4101; fax: 503 235 9723; web: www.starks.com/museum.html

There are more than a million things in the **World Famous Fantastic Museum** south of Redmond, which is famous, among other things, for having so many things so completely unrelated to so many other things. Celebrity stuff, like Elvis's silver tour bus, mixes it up with a mummy. Collections of matchbooks, marbles, and buttons, of which there are estimated to be almost a million, still await counting. From cars to Hitler stamps, from pots to pans, James Schmidt's 35-year passion for auctions and collecting things makes for an eccentric stop, made even more so by the fact that he can afford to buy just about anything that strikes his fancy.

World Famous Fantastic Museum located south of Redmond on Hwy 97 at Airport Way Road, Bend, OR. *Open daily 10.00am–9.00pm. Admission charge for activities.*

As the world's leading consumer nation, America's had a lot of help from advertisers on how to shop and what to buy. The **American Advertising Museum** in Portland spans almost 300 years of social history, telling the story of America's spending habits from colonial days to modern times. It's a fascinating look at one of the quirkier aspects of American culture, showcasing such groundbreaking events as registered trademarks, celebrity endorsements, and silly slogans as signs of the times. Why is it that folks who swear they never watch TV still seem to know the commercials?

American Advertising Museum, 211 NW 5th Ave and Davis St, Portland, OR 97209; ↘ 503 226 0000; web: www.admuseum.org. *Open Mon–Fri by appointment, Sat 12.00noon–5.00pm.*

Quirky quarters
At the **Sylvia Beach Hotel** in Nye Beach, all the rooms are decorated in a literary theme. The Edgar Allen Poe room has a pendulum over the bed as well as a stuffed raven. Dr Zeuss has a trundle bed, a drafting table, hats, fish, colorful murals and Zeuss memorabilia. The Mark Twain room is full of quotes and woodsy ambiance; The Hemingway has a twig bed set in a fishing and hunting theme. The Inn is designed so guests can easily congregate and converse. Even the dining room follows that premise, serving all meals family-style at a communal table.

Sylvia Beach Hotel, 267 NW Cliff, Newport, OR 97365; ↘ 541 265 5428; web: www.sylviabeachhotel.com

MONTANA
Festivals and events
You only need to know one word to describe Montana's favorite festivals: balls. As in testicles. As in **Testicle Festivals**. Half a dozen communities pay tribute to the business parts of the bull by marinating them in beer, breading them, then frying them in hot oil. The result resembles breaded tenderloin even though technically they're breaded 'tendergroin'. Many places in the world consider testicles a delicacy, so consuming them with copious amounts of beer isn't all that strange. It's only when some partygoers paint their own with fluorescent paints that it gets weird. Festivals are held in Rygate, Clinton, Charlo, Fromberg, York and Havre.

Clinton Testicle Festival held annually in September. Contact Rock Creek Lodge, Clinton, MT, 59825; ↘ 406 825 4868; web: www.testyfesty.com

Fromberg Festival of Testicles located near Billings, MT; ↘ 406 668 7642

Nut and Gut Feed located 90 miles from Havre, MT; ↘ 406 654 2678

Mission Mountain Testicle Festival located 50 miles from Missoula, MT. Contact Branding Iron Bar and Grill, Charlo, MT, 59824; ↘ 406 644 9493

Ryegate Testicle Festival held annually in June in Ryegate, MT; ↘ 406 568 2330

York Bar's Go-Nuts Testicle Festival held annually in May in York, MT; ↘ 406 475 9949

Dirt Bag Day at the Big Sky Resort in Bozeman is all about getting grungy, as grungy as you possibly can. Designer ski togs stay in the closet while folks don the tackiest clothes they can find and hit the slopes. That evening, the sleaziest one wins the title of King or Queen Dirt Bag at the Dirt Bag Ball.

Dirt Bag Day held annually in March in Bozeman, MT. Contact Big Sky Resort, PO Box 160001, 1 Lone Mountain Trail, Big Sky, MT 59716; ↘ 800 548 5000; email: info@bigskyresort.com; web: www.bigskyresort.com

What do you get when you cross alpine skiers and cowboys? **Skijoring**. At Red Lodge, a horse and rider pull a skier through an oval-shaped speed course consisting of jumps and gates. This is serious competition; competitors must be upright, with at least one ski on the ground, when crossing the finish line.

Skijoring held annually in March in Red Lodge, MT. Contact Skijorama; web: www.skijorama.com

Reedpoint's only paved road is the site for the annual **Running of the Sheep**. This don't-blink-or-you'll-miss-it burg is outnumbered ten-to-one when 1,000 or so sheep are herded through the three block town. The event brings in thousands of visitors to watch the parade and 'Smelliest Sheepherder' and 'Miss Sheep Drive' competitions. There's no danger of being gored by a sheep. They don't even run; in fact, if you try to join them, the whole herd will probably stop dead in their tracks.

Running of the Sheep held annually on Labor Day weekend in Reedpoint, MT; 201 North Division, Reedpoint, MT 59069; ↘ 406 326 2288

Several hundred race enthusiasts cheer for their porker to bring home the bacon at the pig races, sponsored by **Bear Creek Saloon**, the only bar left in Bear Creek since the other one closed in 1980.

Bear Creek Saloon Pig Races. Contact Bear Creek Saloon, 108 Main St, Bear Creek, MT; ↘ 406 446 3481

The annual **Iron Horse Rodeo** in Red Lodge brings motorcyclists together for a weekend of competition. In the slow race, contestants have to go as slow as possible and are disqualified if their feet touch the ground; the last one to the finish line wins. Next, the front tire of the cycle has to push a keg as fast as possible to the finish. Finally, riders are tested by throwing a water balloon over a bar ahead of themselves, then catching it, unbroken, on the other side. They also have to gather unbroken eggs while riding the bike; ride over a teeter-totter and return with their feet still on the pegs; and run the course again, this time backwards, replacing the unbroken eggs. Points and time determine the winner.

Iron Horse Rodeo held annually in July in Red Lodge, MT. Contact Red Lodge Area Chamber of Commerce; ↘ 877 733 5634

Sofas, chairs, and bathtubs take to the slopes at Big Mountain Resort's annual **Furniture Races** in Whitefish. All manner of furniture (very loosely defined) is firmly attached to skis, towed to the top of the slope, then raced full-throttle down to the bottom. Competitors are judged on speed, ability to stop reasonably close to the finish line, and on style. Winner gets a new piece of furniture.

Furniture Races held annually in April in Whitefish, MT. Contact Big Mountain Ski and Summer Resort, PO Box 1400, Whitefish, MT 59937; ↘ 800 858 3913 or 406 862 1900; fax: 406 862 2955; email: bigmtn@bignmtn.com; web: www.bignmtn.com

At the Red Lodge Winter Carnival, the highlight of the weekend is the **Cardboard Classic**, when costumed racers slip and slide down the hill in their corrugated craft made only from cardboard, glue and duct tape. The same festival features firemen in full gear racing down the hill with a 50-foot section of fire hose.

Cardboard Classic at the Red Lodge Winter Carnival held annually in March in Red Lodge, MT; ↘ 406 446 2610

If you startle these strange animals, they'll become stiff and fall over just as if they were dead. **Dot and Lin's Exotic Animal Ranch** in Plentywood specializes in fainting goats. These animals, a real breed, suffer from what in medical terms is called myatonia, a condition that causes them to lock up their legs and fall over when startled. There's even an International Fainting Goat Association which ranks the breed in three categories: premium if they readily faint; regular if they stiffen but don't fall; and breeding stock: limber females who neither stiffen nor fall, offspring of the premium kind.

Fainting Goats at Dot and Lin's Exotic Animal Ranch, Plentywood, MT. Located at the Hallard's, 2 miles west of Plentywood on MT 5.

Attractions

If you have to work as a cashier, you might as well do it somewhere fun. At the **statue of the oxen that pee** in Three Forks, cashiers inside wait for unsuspecting tourists to get up close and personal with the two, 12-foot long, ox statues that appear to be pulling the building. They turn a secret handle, and – *voilà!* – the oxen pee.

Statue of the oxen that pee, Prairie Schooner Restaurant, 10770 US Hwy 287, Three Forks, MT 59752; ↘ 406 285 6948

WYOMING
Just plain weird

Standing lonely and forlorn on an 8,000-foot high plateau near Laramie, the **Ames Brothers Pyramid** is a seven-story monument to two men's egos. Built in 1882 on the highest point along the route of the Union Pacific Railroad, the pyramid looked down on the tracks and the town that the Ames brothers had bribed Congress to finance. When the tracks and the town were abandoned, so were the brothers, whose giant-size portraits, carved into the stone, are admired by no one and look out upon nothing.

Ames Brothers Pyramid, Laramie, WY. Located east of Laramie on I-80.

Museums and collections

'There's a place behind bars for you' at the **Wyoming Frontier Prison Old West Museum** in Rawlins, where the guides have a sense of humor. During pitch-black night tours, one guide tells of prison suicides while another tosses a dummy from the second tier into the group. You can also try out the gas chamber, going so far as to be strapped in and having the door shut. This is reality tourism at its best. They also sponsor a Cowboy Poets' Gathering in July, special Halloween Night Tours in October and Christmas in the Big House in December.

Wyoming Frontier Prison Old West Museum, 500 Walnut St, Rawlins, WY 82301; ❧ 307 778 7290 or 307 324 4422

At the **Grand Encampment Museum Complex** in Encampment, you'll come to understand the practicality of having a two-story outhouse; ie: one for summer (below) and one for winter (above). Before the advent of indoor plumbing, folks had to use the 'outhouse', and keeping the path to the potty cleared of snow in the winter was an added aggravation. Two-story outhouses solved the problem. The museum also has a folding bathtub from 1895 and a square grand piano.

Grand Encampment Museum Complex, 7th and Barnett Ave, Encampment, WY 82325; ❧ 307 327 5308 or 307 327 5558; email: GEMuseum@aol.com

The **Carbon County Museum** in Rawlins certainly has one of this country's most grotesque items of memorabilia: a pair of shoes made from the skin of an executed killer. This bizarre artifact was the product of an inept train robber in the 1880s by the name of Big Nose George. George's nose was so big that there wasn't any point in wearing a mask; he was easily identified and subsequently captured, mask or no mask. After several failed attempts at escaping from jail, he was finally hung and pronounced dead by a Dr John Osborn. Inexplicably, the doctor cut off the top of the bandit's skull, made a death mask of his face from plaster of Paris, and removed skin from George's thigh and chest before sealing his remains in a whiskey barrel rather than a coffin. The deceased's nose was too big to allow the lid of a coffin to close.

Osborn then made a pair of shoes from the dead man's skin that he wore quite publicly. The good doctor went on to be elected Governor of Wyoming and served as Secretary of State under President Wilson. It's hard to decide which is freakier: the shoes themselves or the obvious lack of judgement on the part of the voters. You can see the gruesome tale unfold at the museum.

Carbon County Museum, PO Box 52, Rawlins, WY 82301

The museum at Sundance has a fun display of the **Sundance Kid** that centers around the time the famous bandit was held in their jail for horse stealing.

Sundance Kid Exhibit, Crook County Museum and Art Gallery, 309 Cleveland, PO Box 63, Sundance, WY 82729; ❧ 307 283 3666; fax: 307 283 1091; email: crookmuseum@mcn.net

Tip the world over on its side and everything loose will land in Los Angeles

Frank Lloyd Wright

Maryland's Kinetic Sculpture Race features ludicrous contraptions designed to travel on land, through mud, and over water (AV)

Above Salvation Mountain, a tribute to God made entirely of adobe and paint in Southern California (JF)

Right The Extraterrestrial Highway near Area 51 is a well-known, top-secret government installation in Nevada where some sort of alien exchange program is supposedly taking place. (NT)

Below Carhenge in Nebraska spoofs England's famous Stonehenge. (DC)

Western Region

NORTHERN CALIFORNIA
Festivals and events

Humans have cooked up some bird brained schemes in an effort to keep the swallows returning to **Mission San Juan Capistrano**. For centuries the birds have migrated to the area each March after flying 7,500 miles from their winter 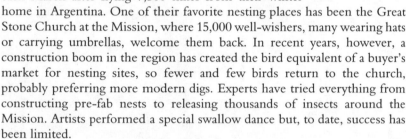 home in Argentina. One of their favorite nesting places has been the Great Stone Church at the Mission, where 15,000 well-wishers, many wearing hats or carrying umbrellas, welcome them back. In recent years, however, a construction boom in the region has created the bird equivalent of a buyer's market for nesting sites, so fewer and few birds return to the church, probably preferring more modern digs. Experts have tried everything from constructing pre-fab nests to releasing thousands of insects around the Mission. Artists performed a special swallow dance but, to date, success has been limited.

> **Mission San Juan Capistrano**, PO Box 697, San Juan Capistrano, CA 92693; ✆ 949 248 2048; email: mission@fea.net; web: missionsj.com. *Open daily 8.30am–5.00pm; closed Thanksgiving, Christmas and Good Friday pm. Admission charge.*

Two thousand frogs get involved in the **Calaveras County Fair and Jumping Frog Jubilee**. There's a lot at stake here as frog jockeys compete for some serious money: $5,000 if the frog breaks a world record; $1,000 if it equals the record and $500 if it just wins without setting any record. The winning jumper in 1928, the first year the Jubilee was held, bounded just three-and-a-half feet. The world record holder today is Rosie the Ribiter who went 21 feet, 5.75 inches. That's the equivalent of a human jumping the length of a football field.

> **Calaveras County Fair and Jumping Frog Jubilee** held annually in May in Calaveras County, CA; web: www.frogtown.org. Contact Calaveras County Chamber of Commerce, 1211 S Main St, PO Box 1145, Angels Camp, CA 95222; ✆ 209 736 2580; fax: 209 736 2576; web: www.calaveras.org

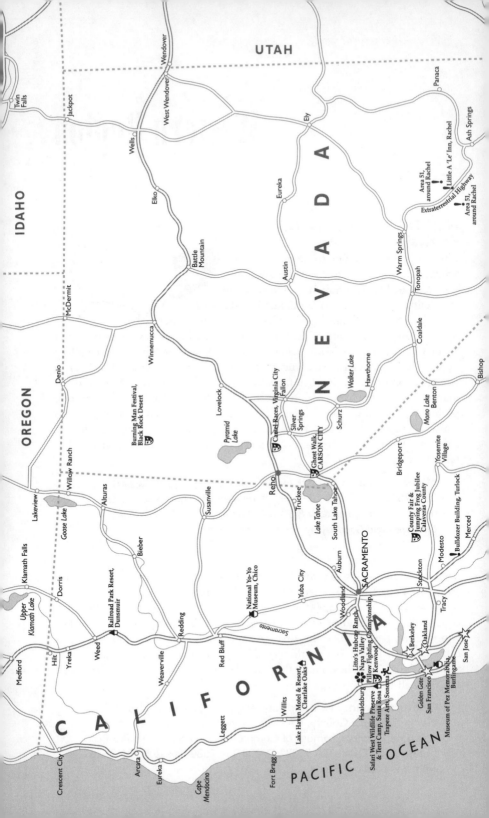

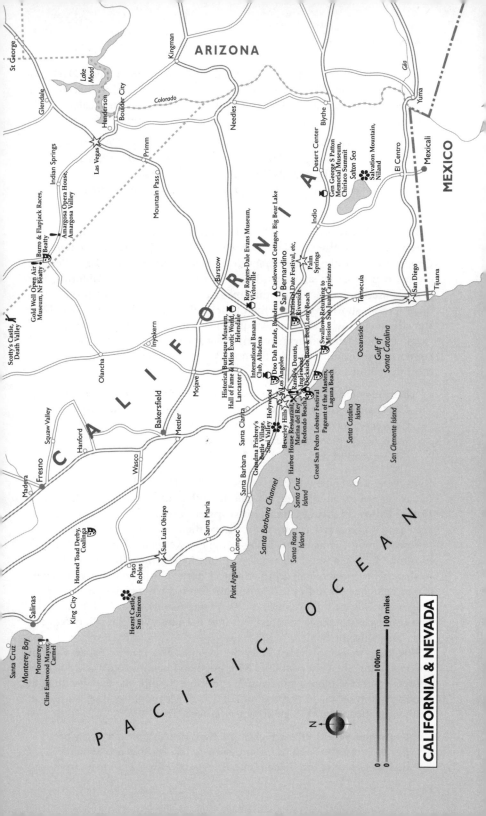

CALIFORNIA & NEVADA

ARIZONA

MEXICO

PACIFIC OCEAN

St George
Glendale
Lake Mead
Kingman
Henderson
Boulder City
Colorado
Gila
Yuma
Needles
Las Vegas
Blythe
Mexicali
Indian Springs
Primm
Desert Center
Gen George S Patton Memorial Museum, Chiriaco Summit
Amargosa Opera House, Amargosa Valley
Salton Sea
Salvation Mountain, Niland
El Centro
Burro & Flapjack Races, Nr Beatty
Beatty
Mountain Pass
Indio
Palm Springs
Gold Well Open Air Museum, Nr Beatty
Tijuana
Scotty's Castle, Death Valley
Barstow
Castlewood Cottages, Big Bear Lake
Roy Rogers-Dale Evans Museum, Victorville
San Bernardino
Riverside
San Diego
Temecula
Oceanside
Inyokern
Helendale
Swallows Returning to Mission San Juan Capistrano
Gulf of Santa Catalina
Olancha
National Date Festival, etc, Indio
Historical Burlesque Museum, Hall of Fame & Miss Exotic World, Helendale
International Banana Club, Altadena
Doo Dah Parade, Pasadena
Santa Catalina Island
Mojave
Lancaster
Los Angeles
Randy's Donuts, Inglewood
Dockside Boat & Bed, Long Beach
San Clemente Island
Bakersfield
Hollywood
Santa Clarita
Beverly Hills
Marina del Rey
Pageant of the Masters, Laguna Beach
Metler
Simi Valley
Harbor House Restaurant
Great San Pedro Lobster Festival
Grandma Prisbrey's Bottle Village, Simi Valley
Redondo Beach
Hanford
Wasco
Santa Barbara
Santa Cruz Island
Fresno
Madera
Santa Maria
Santa Rosa Island
Santa Barbara Channel
Squaw Valley
Lompoc
San Luis Obispo
Point Arguello
Paso Robles
Horned Toad Derby, Coalinga
King City
Hearst Castle, San Simeon
Salinas
Monterey Bay
Monterey
Clint Eastwood Mayor, Carmel
Santa Cruz

C A L I F O R N I A

N

0   100km
0   100 miles

If you couldn't get enough in Calaveras, the annual **Horned Toad Derby** in Coalinga pits 'Toadtanic' and 'Toadquila' against their challengers while firemen compete in human water-fights. The toads are captured in the Coalinga Hills with permits since they're a protected species. Very PC, very California.

Horned Toad Derby held annually in May in Coalinga, CA. Contact Coalinga Chamber, 380 Coalinga Plaza, Coalinga, CA 93210; ☎ 559 935 2948 or 800 854 3885; fax: 559 935 9044; email: exec@coalingachamber.com; web: www.coalingachamber.com

Berkeley, often referred to as Berserkly, holds its own spoof version of the already irreverent Pasadena Doo Dah Parade during the city's 'How Berkeley Can You Be?' Festival. The vibrant diversity of cultural, political, and ethnic groups that make up the town, home to the University of California, is a perfect breeding ground for this most eccentric of events. Seventy-five organizations show up to make fun of themselves in the **Berkeley Doo Dah Parade**, including a café that catapulted giant meatballs on to a huge plate of spaghetti, pregnant mothers from Birthaways marching with synchronized contractions, a group called the Fashion Police and around 80 of the country's most delightfully daft art cars.

Berkeley Doo Dah Parade held annually in September in Berkeley, CA. Contact John at Café Venezia, ☎ 510 849 4668, or Berkeley Convention and Visitors Bureau; ☎ 800 847 4823; web: www.howberkeleycanyoube.com

Remember those pillow fights you had as a kid? Remember how much fun it was to play in the mud? Well, you can do both at the same time at the annual **World Pillow Fighting Championships**, now in its 35th year. Anyone over the age of 14 can enter as long as they leave their maturity outside the arena.

Competition begins by straddling a slippery wet pole suspended over a pit of mud. Holding a wet feather pillow in one hand, you slither along the pole to the starting position, an achievement in itself. During combat your hands can't touch the pole and you can't use your feet to unseat your opponent. Your only weapon is the pillow which can be swung using one or both hands. The first contestant to topple his opponent into the mud wins the fall; two out of three falls wins the bout.

You have to swing at least every 30 seconds. If a minute passes without anyone falling, the bout continues with one hand behind your back. After yet another minute without a fall, fighting continues holding the pillow with both hands. As long as you're prepared to fall down, get muddy and be laughed at, you're qualified to enter. Sign in to play no later than 9am.

Kenwood World Pillow Fighting Championship held annually on July 4. Located in Sonoma County between Santa Rosa and Sonoma, 60 miles north of the Golden Gate Bridge, off Hwy 12, 14 miles from

Santa Rosa. The fair is in Plaza Park on Warm Springs Rd, two blocks from the highway. ↘ 707 833 2440; email: lesely@kenwoodpillowfights.com; web: kenwoodpillowfights.com. *Admission charge.*

Eccentric environments

Sarah Winchester was tormented by the evil spirits of those killed by her husband's famous Winchester rifle, dubbed the 'Gun that Won the West'. When both her baby and her husband met untimely deaths, she consulted a medium who convinced her that continuous building would appease the evil spirits set on revenge. Fortunately she had the money, $20 million dollars worth, to hire carpenters to build 24 hours a day, 365 days a year, until her death 38 years later.

The **Winchester Mystery House** in San Jose is the bizarre result, with 160 rooms, staircases that lead nowhere, chimneys that end below the ceiling, doors that open into walls and a window built into the floor. The house is impeccably detailed with intricately carved wood walls, floors, and ceilings. It has modern heating, sewage systems, gas lights, working elevators, and 47 fireplaces. No expense was spared; she installed Tiffany art glass windows, and gold and silver chandeliers. At the holidays, non-profit groups compete in Christmas decorating contests. Every Friday 13, and at Halloween, you can take a spooky Moonlight Flashlight Tour.

> **Winchester Mystery House**, 525 South Winchester Blvd, San Jose, CA 95128; ↘ 408 247 2000; web: www.winchestermysteryhouse.com

Litto, the Pope Valley Hubcap King, collected more than 2,000 hubcaps over a 30-year period which he arranged, along with bottles and pull tops, into various constructions at **Litto's Hubcap Ranch** in Pope Valley.

> **Litto's Hubcap Ranch**. Contact Napa Valley Visitor's Bureau, ↘ 707 226 7459; email: info@napavalley.org; web: www.napavalley.org

Just plain weird

Carmel is an incredibly picturesque village, famous for its past mayor, Clint Eastwood, and for its ordinance banning high-heeled shoes. The reason is simple: the streets are cobblestone or brick and the many ancient trees have roots protruding in the walkways. Anyone spotted wearing the offending shoes will be reminded of the ordinance, but their credit card will still be accepted in the shops even if they are scofflaws. Clint Eastwood actually ran on the platform that he would allow ice cream to be sold on the streets again.

Carmel, CA. Contact Carmel California Visitor and Information Center, San Carlos between 5th and 6th, Carmel-by-the-Sea, CA 93921; ↘ 831 624 2522 or 800 550 4333; fax: 831 624 1329; email: Brenda@carmelcalifornia.org; web: www.carmelcalifornia.org

Attractions

At **Trapeze Arts** in Oakland you get to fly through the air, if not with the greatest of ease, at least with a modicum of style. The set up is just like you see in the circus, only with plenty of nets and safety harnesses. People of all ages and abilities usually manage to overcome their fears after practicing pulling themselves up and hanging by their knees on a stationary bar. Then it's up the ladder and into the air.

The experience is awesome whether you participate or just watch. Part sport and part art, the secret is in technique and form, not in brute strength. Regulars do it for fun, for physical fitness or because it's cheaper than a therapist. Trapeze Arts also teaches trampolines, aerial arts and wire walking. With just a single class you might progress from 'no way am I doing that' to launching yourself from the platform, swinging by your knees and catching the arms of an instructor in mid-air. Call first: you need to reserve a spot in class.

Trapeze Arts, 1822 9th St, Oakland, CA 94607; ↘ 510 419 0700; 16331 Norrbon Rd, Sonoma, CA 95476 (spring/summer months only); web: www.trapezearts.com

Museums and collections

It's a small museum, but then you don't need a lot of space to display almost every Pez candy dispenser ever made, 500 in all. The **Burlingame Museum of Pez Memorabilia** represents more than a decade of collecting by Gary and Nancy Doss who readily admit their strange fixation has taken over their lives.

Pez, the quirky plastic statues that spit candy from their necks, are beloved by young and old alike. The museum, along with their website, draws collectors from all over the world. A Make a Face model from the 1970s can fetch $4,500 if it's still in the box; a 1960 model with a working slide rule can run $800. An interactive display tells you everything you'd ever want to know about Pez.

Burlingame Museum of Pez Memorabilia, 214 California Dr, Burlingame, CA 94010; ↘ 650 347 2301; web: www.spectrumnet.com/pez. *Open Tue–Fri 10.00am–6.00pm; Sat 10.00am–5.00pm; closed major holidays. Admission free.*

When that craving for a donut kicks in, head to **Lou's Donut Museum** in San Jose. Open 6am until the donuts sell out, you can munch while taking a behind-the-scenes tour of the art of donut-making. Don't forget to ask what happens to the donut holes.

Lou's Living Donut Museum, 387 Delmas, San Jose, CA 95162; ↘ 408 295 5887; email: lousdonuts@yahoo.com; web: www.heartsdelights.com/lous/. *Open Mon–Sat 6.00am–2.30pm.*

Every year the best yo-yo players in the country end up at the **National Yo-Yo Museum** in Chico to compete for two national titles: the yo-yo single and the yo-yo double championships. New tricks are introduced every year to keep players on top of their game. The museum is home to the Duncan family collection as well as to the world's largest wooden yo-yo that was yo-yo-ed half a dozen times by a crane over San Francisco Bay. During the annual championships the first week in October, you'll meet Steve Brown whose claim to fame is being the most tattooed yo-yo spinmeister in the world.

National Yo-Yo Museum, 320 Broadway, Chico, CA 95928; ↘ 530 893 0545; fax: 530 893 0797; web: www.nationalyoyo.org

Tours
The **Black Panther Tour** of West Oakland is a strange, unsettling experience. The radical 1960s group, led by Huey Newton, was a significant force for social change during the revolutionary 1960s. This raw, reality tour explores the Black Panther legacy in an area of the city still plagued with poverty and strife.

Black Panther Tours, 18th and Adeline St, Oakland, CA 94612; ↘ 510 986 0660; fax: 510 986 1169; web: www.blackpanthertours.com

SAN FRANCISCO
Festivals and events
It's the wildest, largest, and one of the oldest footraces in the world. The *San Francisco Examiner* **Bay to Breakers Race** draws 75,000 to 110,000 casual joggers, costumed partygoers, elite runners and centipedes (groups of 13 people tethered together). While the world-class runners compete for cash prizes, world-class party joggers vie for costume recognition. One group, calling themselves the Spawning Salmon, run upstream against the dense waves of humanity.

Live bands entertain the runners and fans along the seven-and-a-half-mile route starting at Howard and Spear streets and ending at the Great Highway at Ocean Beach. The elite runners lead the pack followed by serious, then not-so serious joggers. The Back of the Pack is a special section for walkers. You'll see a lot of political statements among the costumed runners, as well as a few expressing themselves by wearing nothing at all. From there the party moves to the **Footstock Festival** at the Polo Field in Golden Gate Park. Don't even think about driving in the city on Bay to Breakers Sunday. Special public transportation is scheduled to handle the hoards.

> *San Francisco Examiner* **Bay to Breakers Race** held annually in May in San Francisco, CA. Contact Examiner Bay to Breakers, PO Box 429200, San Francisco, CA 94142; ➘ 415 808 5000; email: breakers@examiner.com; web: baytobreakers.com

> **Footstock Festival** held immediately following Bay to Breakers Race at the Polo Field in Golden Gate Park in San Francisco, CA. Contact Examiner Bay to Breakers, PO Box 429200, San Francisco, CA 94142; ➘ 415 808 5000; web: baytobreakers.com

Each September the city lives up to its reputation for the outrageous by hosting the **San Francisco Fringe Festival**, a series of dance and performance art pieces presented by more than 50 theater groups. Often dreadful, sometimes brilliant, but always provocative, the pieces carry names like 'My Penis: In and Out of Trouble' and 'Jack the Ripper Slept Here: an Underground Comedy.'

For ten days, theater companies from around the country present hour-long pieces that cost no more than $8 to view. The playlets vary from comedy to solos; from literary to dance. You can't make reservations, which leads to mad dashes to get in line when word of mouth detects a winner. The festival prides itself on being 'noncensored, noncurated, and nonjuried', so the first 50 entries to pay the entrance fee by the deadline each get a slot. Winning the 'Best of Fringe' award gives new artists a chance for recognition they might otherwise never receive.

> **San Francisco Fringe Festival**, 156 Eddy St, San Francisco, CA 94102; ➘ 415 931 1094; fax: 415 931 2699; email: mail@sffringe.org; web: www.sffringe.org

Chocaholics are in their element at the **Ghirardelli Square Chocolate Festival**. Besides the famous **'Earthquake' Ice Cream Sundae Eating Contest** where the winner gets his or her weight in chocolate, there's a display of famous faces carved in chocolate. The Sweet Talker, a human centerpiece wearing chocolate on her head and skin, is quite a sight to see.

> **Ghirardelli Square Chocolate Festival and 'Earthquake' Ice Cream Sundae Eating Contest**, Ghirardelli Square, 900 North Point St, Suite 100, San Francisco, CA 94109; ➘ 415 775 5500; fax: 415 775 0912; web: www.ghirardellisq.com

Halloween is an especially wild time in San Francisco when the city moves from weird, which is the norm, to the positively insane. People of all persuasions descend on Civic Center and the Castro, dressed in unimaginably creative and outlandish costumes. Almost half the city turns out for this major San Francisco holiday.

Originally, the predominantly gay Castro district was the hub of activities, but the celebration, which today attracts almost 100,000 participants, became too large to fit into the district. With the crowds now spread out between the Castro and Civic Center, it's easier to see and appreciate the artistry that's gone into the costumes. Food booths line the streets, along with face painting and henna body tattooing stations for those who show up sans costume. There are laser shows, live bands and images of partygoers projected onto the outside walls of the Civic Auditorium. The city has come a long way from the time in 1961 when a person could be arrested for impersonating the opposite sex.

Halloween held annually October 31.

It's famous, it's wild and it's wicked. It's the **Exotic Erotic Halloween Ball**, the most uninhibited celebration of erotica on the planet. Originally an underground, bizarre-erotica gathering, the ball has gone more mainstream, if you can call the world's largest and sexiest masquerade party mainstream. Fifteen thousand people attend and many spend all year planning their costumes – or lack of them.

As sexy as burlesque, as loud as a rave, the ball is every bit as carnal as carnival. Celebrities like Nicholas Cage, Joe Montana, Madonna and Dennis Rodman lend their panache, although the event hardly needs celebrities to achieve notoriety. With $10,000 in prizes for the winners of the Mr and Miss Exotic Erotic and other costume contests, there's no shortage of shocking, electrifying creativity.

Exotic Erotic Halloween Ball held annually in October in San Francisco, CA. Contact Perry Mann Presents the Exotic Erotic Ball, 2443 Filmore St, Suite 286, San Francisco, CA 94115; ☏ 415 567 BALL; web: www.exoticeroticball.com

San Francisco's street performers show off their zany acts and comedic talents at **Pier 39's Street Performers' Festival**. The two-day event includes jugglers, magicians and mime artists who perform on unicycles, eat fire and clown around.

Pier 39's Street Performers' Festival held annually in June at Pier 39, San Francisco, CA; ☏ 415 705 5500; fax: 415 981 8808; web: www.pier39.com

One hundred thousand folks descend on Haight Street during the annual **Haight-Ashbury Street Fair**. The fair aims to relive the 1960s heyday with a laid-back, do-your-own-thing kind of feel. To experience the Haight at other times, see the Flower Power tour listing below.

> **Haight-Ashbury Street Fair** held annually in June on Haight St between Stanyan St and Masonic Ave in San Francisco, CA; ↘ 415 661 8025; email: pabloji@earthlink.net; web: www.haightstreetfair.org

Dress in costume, bring noise makers, confetti and socks for the sock exchange and you'll be part of the April Fool's Day **St Stupid's Day Parade** put on by the First Church of the Last Laugh.

> **St Stupid's Day Parade** held annually on April Fool's Day in San Francisco, CA. Contact First Church of the Last Laugh; web: www.saintstupid.com/parade.htm

Just plain weird

You expect to find furniture IN a building, not ON it. But at an abandoned tenement at Sixth and Howard streets, artist Brian Groggin launched a project he called **Defenestration**, defined as the act of throwing a person or thing out of a window. Twenty-three pieces of seemingly animate furniture hang out the windows and run down the sides of the four-story building, looking, perhaps, for freedom or maybe a chance to dance with the appliances for sale across the street. Tables, chairs, lamps, grandfather clocks, a refrigerator and couches hug the walls, their legs seeming to grasp the surface.

The furniture, like the neighborhood, is cast off and appreciation deprived. Brian rescued the pieces, 're-animating' them for their new role. For the installation itself, Brian held an Urban Circus with artists, performers and musicians, many dressed as clowns, putting on freak shows and vaudeville-style acts. Participants included members of the Church of the Subgenius, the Cacophony Society, Circus Redickuless, First Church of the Last laugh and the Sisters of Perpetual Indulgence. The property was donated by the owners who have the building up for sale – with or without the furniture.

> **Defenestration**, 214 Sixth St at Howard, San Francisco, CA; email: briangoggin@yahoo.com; web: www.defenestration.org and www.metaphorm.org

Theater

If you're going to take in just one show while in San Francisco, make sure it's **Beach Blanket Babylon**. This fast-paced, satirical musical review, famous for its ludicrous headdresses and zany characters, has been playing to sold out crowds for 24 years. It's the quintessential San Francisco experience: irreverent, topical, and joyously funny. The review follows Snow White around the world as she looks for love in all the wrong places. Animate and inanimate objects cavort in the most riotous ways and pop culture, religion, sex and politics are all targets for sarcastic songs. The costumes are extraordinary and the foot stomping finale always brings down the house.

Beach Blanket Babylon, Babylon Blvd, Green St, San Francisco, CA; ↘ 415 421 4222

Tours

It would be difficult to find a tour of San Francisco that didn't touch on the weird or wacky.

The corner of Castro and Market Streets is known as the gayest four corners on earth. That's where you meet Trevor Hailey for her **Cruisin' the Castro Tour**, a walking tour of the Castro from a highly entertaining and historical point of view. Trevor radiates with personality as she puts the gay and lesbian experience – and the city itself – in sociological and psychological perspective. By the time your tour is over, you'll have a much better understanding of the chain of events that allowed California, San Francisco and the Castro district to become such meccas of tolerance. The tour includes a lovely lunch so you have plenty of time to ask questions and discuss current issues.

Cruisin' the Castro Tour, 375 Lexington St, San Francisco, CA 94110; ↘ 415 550 8110; email: trvrhailey@aol.com; web: www.webcastro.com/castrotour

Meet the ghosts who call San Francisco home with Jim Fassbinder, a genuine member of the International Ghost Hunter's Society and the Institute for Paranormal Research. Jim leads quite a convincing tour around elegant Pacific Heights on his **San Francisco Ghost Hunt Walking Tour**. Dressed in a black cape and top hat, his passion for his subject is obvious .

'The spirits tell us if they're willing to have visitors today', he says. He does his part by building a profile of each ghost and setting the mood. You do yours by getting into the spirit of the hunt. By the time you've heard the stories, and seen the haunts of half a dozen ghosts, you may become a believer yourself, especially when you see the spot where a key jumps mysteriously in the palm of your hand.

San Francisco Ghost Hunt Walking Tour departs every evening at 8.00pm, year round, rain or starshine from Queen Anne Hotel, 1590 Sutter, San Francisco, CA; ↘ 415 922 5590; web: www.sfghosthunt.com

EMPEROR OF SAN FRANCISCO

San Francisco is fertile breeding ground for eccentrics. One of its most famous was Emperor Norton, a flamboyant businessman who proclaimed himself Emperor of the United States in 1859 after he lost all his money. Immensely popular, people greeted him with a bow or a curtsy and saw to it that the penniless eccentric had a decent place to live and never went hungry. He ate free of charge wherever he pleased and the city made him a new uniform when his became too tattered.

Three seats were reserved for him at public performances: one for the emperor and two for his well-behaved canine companions. Dressed in naval regalia, he attended every public function and made daily rounds of his domain, making sure that order and harmony were maintained. He would anoint do-gooders with titles like 'Queen for a day', resulting in people following him around and hoping for a chance to help an old lady across the street while in his presence. Norton even printed his own currency which was accepted everywhere in the city without question. If he needed money, he'd levy a 'tax' for a dollar or two. When he died in 1880, tens of thousands attended his funeral. He's buried at Woodlawn Cemetery in Colma, San Francisco's adjacent cemetery town.

What make's Jay Gifford's **San Francisco Victorian Home Walk** unique is that you take public transportation and, for a few hours at least, see the city as a San Franciscan does. You get to mix with the locals and get to know the city's famous, eccentric Victorian houses known as the Painted Ladies.

San Francisco Victorian Home Walk departs from the Westin Francis Hotel lobby, Union Sq, corner of Powell and Geary Sts, ☎ 415 252 9485; email: jay@victorianwalk.com; web: www.victorianwalk.com

City Guides Neighborhood Walks offers dozens of free walking tours given by individuals with a specific expertise and a passion to share it with visitors. Cityscapes and Public Places is a good one if you want to understand political correctness. Other offerings include the Earthquake and Fire Walk, Literary North Beach, and Sacred Places, Brothels, Boardinghouse and Bawds, a two block stroll that looks at the 'shady' profession and the contribution it made to the city's growth.

City Guides Neighborhood Walks depart daily from various locations around San Francisco. Contact City Guides, c/o San Francisco Public Library, Main Library, 100 Larkin St, San Francisco, CA 94102; ☎ 415 557 4266; web: www.sfcityguides.org

Sex and politics are part of the commentary when you take a walk in Marin County's famous Muir Woods with **Tom's Scenic Walking Tours**. Tom Martell, an eco-guide with a comedic bent, has a decidedly California (read politically correct) perspective on the birds, the bees and hugging trees. You'll learn how redwood trees and spotted owls reproduce and, if you're lucky, you'll see thousands of ladybugs having a not very ladylike orgy. Be sure Tom tells you all about California's 'green' movement. Tours go through Muir Woods to Point Reyes, or along ocean bluffs. Besides spectacular scenery and the serenity that comes with being one with nature, you'll be entertained by Tom's knowledgeable and humorous commentary.

> **Tom's Scenic Walking Tours**, ☎ 800 909 WALK or 415 381 5106; fax: 415 475 7092; email: muirwalker@aol.com

The club scene in San Francisco is typically varied. With **3 Babes and a Bus**, you can experience several different scenes without worrying about driving and parking. Be prepared for some outrageous behavior because the tour is popular with bachelorette parties who bring along certain inflatable body parts.

> **3 Babes and a Bus**, ☎ 866 552 2582 or 415 552 2582; email: pamela@threebabes.com; web: www.threebabes.com

Walking tours of the Mission District Murals are offered by **Precita Eyes Mural Arts Center**. With urban graffiti a problem in all big cities, this is a unique way to decriminalize it, and at the same time preserve the Mission's culture and people.

> **Precita Eyes Mural Arts Center**, 348 Precita Ave, San Francisco, CA 94110; ☎ 415 285 7311; web: www.precitaeyes.org

Explore the tie-dyed cradle of hippie culture with a guide who was part of it all at the **Flower Power Haight-Ashbury Walking Tour**. The Haight was

heart of the 1960s counter culture movement, the center of the Summer of Love and Be-Ins, and home to music greats like Jimi Hendrix, Janis Joplin and Jerry Garcia. One resident, Manny the Hippie, used to appear regularly on David Letterman's late night talk show, teaching America how to talk hippie. You'll see the Grateful Dead house and the stairs where they posed for the famous poster, the house where kidnapped Patty Hearst was held hostage and learn how a dense mass of confused humanity managed to get along sleeping in vans and sharing way too few bathrooms.

Flower Power Haight-Ashbury Walking Tour, PO Box 170106, San Francisco, CA 94177; ☎ 415 863 1621

It's a big, red, shiny Mack fire engine and you get to ride it, bells clanging, from the waterfront, across the Golden Gate Bridge to Sausalito and back again on a campy tour called **San Francisco Fire Engine Tours and Adventures**. Owners Robert and Marilyn Katzman, dress you in fireman coats, pile on the blankets and charge off to dramatic vista points under the bridge as well as on it. The tour in their 1955, open-air truck is hardly low key as Marilyn quickly has you singing silly ditties while people on the streets gawk in amazement.

She regales you with stories, including little-known fire-fighting facts such as the one that in the old days – before city fire departments – volunteer brigades were paid by the fire and there was lots of competition among them to get to a fire first and claim the rewards. When more than one unit arrived at the scene, there was considerable fighting – not of the fire, but between units. The fire engine also tours North Beach, Chinatown and Pacific Heights.

The Katzmans live in a real, restored firehouse bought from the city when modern fire trucks became too large to fit through the doors. They even have a Dalmatian and a real pole to slide down from the upper floors.

San Francisco Fire Engine Tours and Adventures, 117 Broad St, San Francisco, CA 94112; ☎ 415 333 7077; fax: 415 333 7725; email: engineco@aol.com; web: www.tdfa.com/bigred

It's all about romance and lust, animal style, at the **San Francisco Zoo Valentine's Day Sex Tours**. The train tour, hosted by a zoo guide who explains novel ways to love your lover, takes you from the birds and the bees to animals that may – or may not – co-operate by demonstrating their amorous techniques. The tour ends with truffles and champagne.

San Francisco Zoo Valentine's Day Sex Tours held annually in February in San Francisco, CA. Contact San Francisco Zoo, 1 Zoo Rd, San Francisco, CA 94132; ☎ 415 753 7080; web: www.sfzoo.org

Attractions

The **Wax Museum at Fisherman's Wharf** is a dynamic, state-of-the-art facility with 280 figures in settings so realistic you almost feel like you're intruding. Murals, music and sound effects add to the eerie reality, as do the dramatic settings. Dictators stand together amid rubble; Hitler shares a war room with Mussolini and Tojo; and Eisenhower and MacArthur stand among sand bags with a World War II jeep in front of an elaborate mural. Bill Gates looks suitably nerdy next to distinguished scientists Freud and Newton. The Last Supper scene is fully narrated, while a Van Gogh painting is rendered in a 3D display.

Wax Museum at Fisherman's Wharf, 145 Jefferson St, San Francisco, CA 94133; ↘ 800 439 4305 or 415 202 0400; email: jquite@waxmuseum.com; web: www.waxmuseum.com

Museums and collections

Charles Schultz of Peanuts fame helped found the **Cartoon Art Museum** that explores how comics influence politics and pop culture. Displays going back to the 1730s celebrate the history and art of satirical cartooning.

Cartoon Art Museum, 814 Mission St, San Francisco, CA 94103; ↘ 415 CARTOON; web: www.cartoonart.org

Going through the Tactile Dome at the **Children's Exploratorium** is a very strange experience. You crawl, climb, and slide through a variety of tactile textures in complete darkness, using only your sense of touch to guide you. You enter through a light-locked room into a totally dark maze, the purpose of which is to completely disorient you so that you're forced to rely only on touch. You'll emerge with a whole new appreciation for a sense you don't give much thought to. Advance reservations are required.

Children's Exploratorium, 3601 Lyon St, San Francisco, CA 94123; ↘ 415 EXP LORE; located in the Palace of Fine Arts Building in San Francisco's Marina district, off Hwy 101 near the Golden Gate Bridge; web: www.exploratorium.edu

Shopping

The Haight district was the hub of the 'tune in, turn on, drop out' hippie movement of the 1960s. Today the district still attracts teenage weekend pretenders who descend from the suburbs to shop and 'do the Haight' by practicing being cool and trying on personas like they try on shoes. The shops are as individualistic as their owners; Ben and Jerry's ice cream and a Gap store are the only 'corporate' presence. The movie theater, the Red Vic, is worker owned and operated. When Safeway Foods tried to move in, protesters filled up carts with food and then left the store. Within three months Safeway was gone. At the Haight Goodwill, young hipsters shop right alongside the homeless.

The district is filled with health food stores, retro, costume and head shops, cafés, and body shops. **Far Out Fabrics**, located in the rear of Mendel's Art Supplies, is the source for wild psychedelic furs, lycra spandex, oil cloth, and animal prints. **Costumes on Haight** has an outfit for every occasion from politician masks to *Star Wars* characters. The whole district is *très* funky and always cutting edge.

Far Out Fabrics/Mendel's, 1556 Haight St, San Francisco, CA 94117; ↘ 415 621 1287; fax: 415 621 6587; web: www.mendels.com

Costumes on Haight, 735 Haight St, San Francisco, CA 94117; ↘ 415 621 1356; web: costumeshaight.citysearch.com/l.html

The Mission district is a vibrant, predominantly Hispanic area with an eclectic mix of shops. **Dog Eared Books** captures the interests of its clientele with off-beat books and magazines representing the whole spectrum of popular – and not so popular – opinion. Besides queer, ethnic and feminist titles, you can find alternative how-to books like *How to Clear Your Criminal Record, How to Live Without Electricity – and Like it*, and *How to Use Mail Drops for Profit, Privacy, and Self Protection*. **Good Vibrations** is a safe, socially acceptable place to actually see the kind of sex toys you'd never normally admit being interested in seeing. Shoppers range from well heeled matrons to elderly couples holding hands to people just like you and me. From time to time they set up their display of antique vibrators which were prescribed by turn of the (last) century doctors to cure female 'hysteria'.

There are a number of outrageous cross dresser/drag queen shops, such as the **Piedmont Boutique**, with shoes, lingerie, clothing and gowns fit for a king sized queen. Wander into the **New College** and check out the bulletin board. You'll find flyers for workshops like Men in Quest of the Masculine Soul and a Summer Solstice Ritual for Women. **Therapy** is the place for vintage, post World War II pop culture furniture, much of it in the shape of boomerangs. Pick up a copy of the *New Mission News*. The paper's motto is 'comforting the afflicted and afflicting the comfortable since 1980'.

Paxton Gate is one of the more peculiar stores in the Mission district. It carries oddities such as framed and mounted insects, taxidermy, fossils and scientific supplies; rare and unusual oddities inspired by the garden and the natural sciences. Its insect collection is fascinating. The critters are collected in their native habitats and received at the store in dried and packaged form. The beetles are soaked in hot water and the butterflies are kept in a humid container until they've softened. Then the legs and wings are put in the desired positions, sometimes utilizing over 50 pins. Look for the costumed, stuffed mice made by an artist/taxidermist. Paxton Gate has been described as a 'Smith and Hawken [a gardening catalogue] on LSD'. Where else can you find glass eyes for your bobcat?

Dog Eared Books, 900 Valencia St, San Francisco, CA 94110; ↘ 415 282 1901; email: dogearedbook@earthlink.net; web: www.dogearedbooks.com. *Open 10.00am–10.00pm Mon–Sat; 10.00am–8.00pm Sun.*

Good Vibrations, 1210 Valencia St, San Francisco, CA 94110; ↘ 415 974 8990; fax: 415 550 8495 and 2504 San Pablo Ave, Berkeley, CA 94702; ↘ 510 841 8987; fax: 510 841 0172; email: goodvibe@well.com; web: www.goodvibes.com

Piedmont Boutique, 1452 Haight St, San Francisco, CA 94117; ↘ 415 864 8075. *Open 11.00am–7.00pm daily.*

New College, 777 Valencia St, San Francisco, CA 94110

Therapy, 545 Valencia St, San Francisco, CA 94110; ↘ 415 861 6213

Paxton Gate, 824 Valencia St (between 19th and 20th Sts), San Francisco, CA 94110; ↘ 415 824 1872; fax: 415 824 1871. *Open 12.00noon–8.00pm Sun–Thur; 12.00noon–9.00pm Fri–Sat.*

Quirky quarters

'Peace Through Tourism' is the motto at the **Red Vic Bed and Breakfast**, where you can rent a room and live like a hippie. Originally a 'country resort, San Francisco's Red Victorian Bed, Breakfast and Art still reflects California quirkiness. Located in the heart of the Haight district, famous as the hippie capital of the 1960s, this hotel has seen it all, from the peace movement to the ecology movement to the movement for social justice. True to its heritage, it has a meditation room, motivational videos, meditative art and visual poetry. Its theme rooms have names like Summer of Love and Flower Child; one of the bathrooms has an aquarium in the pull chain toilet tank.

Red Vic Bed and Breakfast, 1665 Haight St, San Francisco, CA 94117; ↘ 415 864 1978; fax: 415 863 3293; email: redvic@linex.com; web: www.redvic.com

Three hundred exotic, endangered, and extinct-in-the-wild African mammals and birds are among the guests at **Safari West Wildlife Preserve and Tent Camp** near Santa Rosa. The tents are charming, African style canvas with hardwood floors and en-suite bath located close – but not too close – to the animals. You can play Dr Livingstone by learning how to track animals, taking a wildlife tour in a safari vehicle, or visiting the walk-through aviary. The preserve is open to day visitors with a reservation as well as to overnight guests.

Safari West Wildlife Preserve and Tent Camp, 3115 Porter Creek Rd, Santa Rosa, CA; ↘ 707 579 2551; web: www.safariwest.com

The **Hotel Triton** in San Francisco, with its cutting-edge jewel-tone décor, describes itself as 'an Atlantean kingdom of sophistication and irrepressible charm'. On their politically correct eco floor, the air is purified, the water free of chemical conspiracies and the bed linens are made from naturally grown cotton. The Zen Den is perfect for one – or for two becoming one. Special suites have been created by 1960s musical figureheads Jerry Garcia, Carlos Santana and Graham Nash. The Triton is known for its wacky publicity stunts such as putting stunt men on the roof and drag queens in the lobby. A hot pursuit package includes massage oil and edible undies.

Hotel Triton, 342 Grant Ave, San Francisco, CA 94108; ☎ 800 800 1299; fax: 415 394 0555; web: www.hotel-tritonsf.com

In San Francisco, Oakland and Long Beach, **Dockside Boat and Bed** offers a fleet of yachts for overnight stays. The boats offer terrific views right in the heart of these bustling harbors.

Dockside Boat and Bed, *San Francisco:* Pier 39, C Dock, San Francisco, CA 94133; ☎ 415 392 5526; *Oakland:* Jack London Sq, 57 Clay St, Oakland, CA 94607; ☎ 510 444 5858; fax: 510 444 0420; email: boatandbed@aol.com; *Long Beach:* Dock 5 Rainbow Harbor, 316 E Shoreline Dr, Long Beach, CA 90802; ☎ 562 436 3111; fax: 562 436 1181; email: boatandbed@yahoo.com; web: www.boatandbed.com

The **Railroad Park Resort** 50 miles north of Redding has the Caboose Motel, cabins, an RV Park and a restaurant and lounge built inside antique railroad cars.

Railroad Park Resort, 100 Railroad Park Rd, Dunsmuir, CA 96025; ☎ 800 974 RAIL; web: www.rrpark.com

Castlewood Cottages in Big Bear Lake feature cabins decorated in themes such as King Arthur, Anthony and Cleopatra, *Gone with the Wind*, and Enchanted Forest. The Castle Garden cabin has a waterfall, a moat, a spiral staircase to the tower bedroom and a mural of the English countryside that goes all around the room.

Castlewood Cottages, 547 Main St, PO Box 1746, Big Bear Lake, CA 92315; ☎ 909 866 2720; web: www.bigbear.com/castlewood. *Reservations recommended 3–4 months in advance.*

In Clear Lake, the **Lake Haven Motel and Resort** is a funky fisherman's motel with cabins decorated inside and out, including the roof, with old west theme props and memorabilia.

Lake Haven Motel and Resort, 100 Short St, Clearlake Oaks, CA 95423; ☎ 707 998 3908

Formerly home to a bordello, the **Monte Cristo** in San Francisco is a bed and breakfast with each room decorated in an antique theme, including a Chinese Wedding room, a Gothic room and a Sailing Ship.

Monte Cristo, 600 Presidio Ave, San Francisco, CA 94115; ☎ 415 931 1875; fax: 415 931 6005

SOUTHERN CALIFORNIA
Festivals and events

The ultimate example of life imitating art occurs every summer at the **Pageant of Masters** in Laguna Beach. Part of the Festival of Arts, the pageant is a living re-creation of classical art masterpieces, portrayed by real people posing to look exactly like their counterparts in the original works of art. The audience sits out under the stars in an outdoor amphitheater and watches scene after scene unfold as the giant reproductions of famous works of art are exposed.

Several times during each performance, the lights are turned on as the backdrops and foregrounds are rolled into place and you can see the costumed, made-up actors take their various spots. As the music begins, the actors freeze and the three-dimensional tableau takes form as a masterpiece. Occasionally a pigeon perches on one of the living statues. The evening always closes with a living representation of Leonardo Da Vinci's The Last Supper.

> **Pageant of Masters** held annually in July and August in Laguna Beach, CA. Contact Pageant of the Masters, 650 Laguna Canyon Road, Laguna Beach, CA; ↘ 949 497 6582 or 800 487 3378; web: www.foapom.org

The World's Largest Tattoo and Body Piercing Convention is the **Inkslingers Ball** in Redondo Beach, where tattooed greats compete in categories such as Best Tribal, Best Portrait, Best Back Piece, Overall Male, Overall Female and Best Cover-up. Besides the opportunity to look behind the scenes of a lifestyle unfamiliar to most people, the convention will give you an appreciation for the true artistry involved in tattooing and of the people who express their individuality in this unique way.

> **Inkslingers Ball** held annually in September in Redondo Beach, CA. Contact Tattoo Mania's Inkslingers Ball, PO Box 2208, Redondo Beach, CA 90278; ↘ 800 824 8046; email: saunderosa@aol.com; web: www.tattoos.com/inkslingers

Fifteen hundred madcap marchers make up the outrageously satirical **Doo Dah Parade** held each November in Pasadena. Unlike the structured

Tournament of Roses Parade that it spoofs, anyone with an appreciation of irony can march in the Doo Dah which is organized by the Unorganizers Unofficial Committee. Each year they anoint a Queen; in 1997 it was the deceased Lily Hodge, whose ashes were carried in an urn along the parade route by her husband who claimed Lily had always loved the parade.

The Doo Dah has spawned such legends as the Briefcase Marching Drill Team, the Hibachi Marching Grill Team, and the Invisible Man Marching Band. With marchers like Jerking Man, Confused Dogs in Drag, the Flying Toilet and the Graveyard Farmers, it's no wonder 40,000 people cram the streets to see the spectacle. Want to see the spoof of the spoof? Check out the Berkeley Doo Dah Parade (see page 214).

Doo Dah Parade held annually in November in Pasadena, CA. Contact Pasadena Convention and Visitors Bureau, 171 South Los Robles Ave, Pasadena, CA 91101; ➚ 626 795 9311; web: www.pasadenavisitor.org

How do you call a lobster? Hint: it doesn't involve a cell phone. At the **Great San Pedro Lobster Festival**, you gather at the shore, face the ocean, flail your arms about and shout, chant, rant and rave. This is a lot easier for the 12 and under set, who compete for a prize computer, but there's nothing to stop you from making a fool of yourself if you wish, unless, of course, you consider your pride. In the old days, grown fishermen opened the lobster season by performing this ritual; whether this improved the catch is anyone's guess.

If you'd rather not do the hootin' and hollerin' bit, you can opt to dress up your pet as a lobster – or as any seafood item – and enter the Lobster Dog Pet Parade. If your pet can't, or won't, wear the costume, then build a float with a kid's wagon, put your stubborn pet in it, and drag it along the parade route. If all else fails, dress yourself as a lobster and carry your pet. The parade is based on the legendary exploits of Bob the Lobster Dog who hung out on the docks and supposedly guided in the fleet by barking.

Great San Pedro Lobster Festival held annually in September in Ports O'Call Village, San Pedro, CA. ➚ 310 366 6472; email: lobstermaster@lobsterfest.com; web: www.lobsterfest.com

Redondo Beach has its annual **Lobster Festival**, too, a zany three-day feast and fest with attendees wearing lobster costumes, grass skirts, Hawaiian shirts and bikinis. They're never short of high school athletes to compete in the Clam Linguini Eating Contest.

Lobster Festival held annually in October in Redondo Beach, CA. Contact Redondo Beach Visitors Bureau, 200 N Pacific Coast Hwy, Redondo Beach, CA; ➚ 319 364 2161 or 800 282 0333; web: www.lobsterfestival.com

Using chalk as their medium and the sidewalk as their canvas, artists create out-of-the-ordinary murals at the **Absolut Chalk Street Painting Festival** in Los Angeles. From classical to contemporary, and from whimsical to socially relevant, the festival is the largest of its kind in the world, drawing hundreds of visual artists from all over the region.

> **Absolut Chalk Street Painting Festival** held annually in July in Los Angeles, CA. Contact The Light-Bringer Project; ➤ 626 440 7379; fax: 626 440 5152

San Diego Diver's Supply sponsors an **Underwater Pumpkin Carving Contest** on the Saturday nearest Halloween. Scuba divers bring their own pumpkin and dive knife, then carve underwater. Judging is done later on the beach.

> **Underwater Pumpkin Carving Contest**, Kellog Park/LaJolla Shores, San Diego. ➤ 619 224 3439 fax: 619 224-0596

If you wear a turban or dress like an Arabian knight you get into the **National Date Festival** in Riverside County for free. Otherwise, pay the admission, join 250,000 other folks, and watch jockeys decked out like Ali Baba ride in little chariots hitched to some really big birds during the Ostrich Races. Root for your favorite dromedary during the camel races; cringe during the live alligator wrestling; cheer at the Bull-o-rama Rodeo, and enjoy a Monster Truck making mincemeat out of a car. What does all this have to do with dates? Nothing really, except to celebrate that the region produces 95% of all the dates grown in the United States, and to offer a prayer for date fertility at **The Blessing of the Dates**.

> **National Date Festival and The Blessing of the Dates** held annually in February in Riverside County, CA; ➤ 800 811 FAIR or 760 863 8247; web: www.datefest.org

Eccentric environments

Sixteen years ago, Leonard Knight's hot air balloon, carrying the message 'God is Love', failed him on an impossibly bleak and barren patch of desert near the Salton Sea. It was here, in this inhospitable place, that Leonard had a vision: God wanted him to paint his message on the side of a mountain. There was only one problem. He would have to build the mountain first.

Today, **Salvation Mountain**, and its message of love and redemption, is three stories high and about a hundred feet wide, a brilliant patch of incongruity rising up out of the desolate landscape. Molded entirely by hand, Leonard, now 68, made the mountain out of hay, adobe, old paint, window putty, and truly astounding tenacity. For all these years, he's lived at the foot of his handmade mountain in a ramshackle truck with no electricity, plumbing or water.

To say that Leonard is happy is an understatement. He's a genuinely warm, intelligent, dedicated man, fully aware of his eccentricity. He won't accept any money, asking only for old paint with which he constantly touches up his mountain so it'll stay shiny. He welcomes visitors and delights in telling you about his passion, pressing postcards of his creation into your hands so you can help him spread the word of God's love.

A colossal achievement, Leonard's mountain is a monument devoted to peaceful coexistence. Unfortunately, the government didn't see it quite that way, declaring the place a toxic nightmare a few years back. They were ready to bulldoze it when a legion of Leonard's fans successfully petitioned the legislature to declare it a work of religious art and therefore immune from destruction. He and his mountain are now famous all over the world thanks to bus loads of international tourists and a host of print and broadcast media stories. If you can, bring old paint when you come to visit. But even if you arrive empty handed, you'll come away with postcards and a memory that won't soon depart.

Salvation Mountain, Niland, CA located south of I-10, 5 miles east of Hwy 111 at Niland. Contact Leonard Knight, PO Box 298, Niland, CA 92257. *Visit anytime.*

Love of garbage motivated a 60-year-old woman to spend the last 25 years of her life transforming her third-of-an-acre lot into **Grandma Prisbrey's Bottle Village** in Simi Valley. Using hundreds of thousands of bottles and objects scavenged from the dump, she built 13 structures to house her varied collections along with sculptures, shrines, wishing wells and walkways.

Television tubes form a fence; walkways glisten with broken shards of glass and pottery. A spooky doll-head shrine has discarded heads perched on top of tall poles, while a birdbath is imbedded with car headlights. There's a pencil house to hold her collection of 17,000 pencils, a house made of shells and a shrine made of horseshoes. The Leaning Tower of Bottle Village and an Intravenous Feeding Tube Fire Screen give you some idea of the lengths to which Grandma would go to express her quirky sense of humor.

While she was alive, she delighted in giving you the 25 cent tour, peppering her commentary with anecdotes, then playing the piano and singing risqué songs to you in the meditation room. She died in 1988 after living a tragic life that probably led to her strange obsession. She married her first husband when she was just 15 – and he was 52 – and had seven children by him, six of whom died during her lifetime. She also lost another husband, a fiancée and all but one of her siblings.

Grandma Prisbrey's Bottle Village, PBVC, PO Box 1412, Simi
Valley, CA 93062; ↘ 805 583 1627; fax: 805 527 5002; email:
dpbv@earthlink.net; web: www.bottlevillage.com. *Visits are by
appointment only.*

Hearst Castle is what happens when eccentricity and ego meet big, big
money. Millions of words have been written about this opulent estate of 165
rooms and 127 acres of gardens and no trip to the central California coast
would be complete without experiencing this extraordinary display of wealth.
Tickets for the various tours have to be purchased in advance.

Hearst Castle, 750 Hearst Castle Rd, San Simeon, CA 93452; ↘ 805
927 2020; web: www.hearstcastle.org

Smack dab in the middle of the Watts district, scene of the explosive civil rights
riots of 1965, rises Simon Rodia's **Watts Towers**, a monumental work of folk
art that took this Italian immigrant 33 years to construct. Intended as a tribute
to his adopted country, the enormous structure includes three towers, the
tallest of which is 99 feet high, a gazebo, patios, bird baths, spires and a
structure he called the Ship of Marco Polo. The steel sculptures are covered
with mortar and imbedded with tens of thousands pieces of tile, pottery, sea
shells and glass, and Seven-up and Milk of Magnesia bottles (Rodia especially
liked these green and deep blue colors).

Working from 1921 to 1954, Rodia labored alone, using only simple tile-
setter's tools and a window washer's belt and buckle to scale the heights. The
giant towers dwarfed his tiny house. When he decided he was finished, he sold
the place for a pittance and simply walked away. While his efforts weren't
always appreciated by his neighbors, or by the city, today Watts Towers is
renowned worldwide. The Watts Towers Art Center displays folk art exhibits
and gives occasional tours of Rodia's improbable structures.

Watts Towers, 1765 E 107th St, Los Angeles, CA; ↘ 213 569 8181.
Contact The Center, 10950 S Central Ave, Los Angeles, CA;
↘ 323 563 5639.

Just plain weird

Angelyne is representative of those 'only in LA' stories. Back in 1984, a
woman named Angelyne was promoting her rock band by putting up posters
along the Sunset Strip. On a whim, she put up a billboard of herself that
showed only her buxom, blonde bombshell image along with her first name.
The billboard became the talk of the town and, almost overnight, she became
famous – not for anything she did, but for simply being on billboards.
Hundreds of billboards, bus stop panels, and murals later, she's become a
quirky icon of Hollywood.

The Angelyne phenomena resulted in television and magazine interviews,
radio shows, personal appearances and film cameos all over the world. The

billboards run not just in LA, but in New York, Washington, DC, England, and Europe. Her persona is famous: an aging bombshell, extra big on top, with an extra tiny waist, and driving a pink corvette. Picture Barbie at 50.

Her fan club has 20,000 members, her logo merchandise is sold all over the world, and spotting Angelyne (in person or in her car) is an obsession with many. There's even a website for addicted Angelyne spotters. On Angelyne's own website, she'll 'escort' you around the city, showing you the secrets of Hollywood and some of her own very special, secret places as well. Her fame is quite an achievement considering it started out as a figment of her own imagination.

Angelyne's, web: www.angelyne.com

Urban Mosaic is church with a distinctly Hollywood twist. With a congregation of mostly 20 and 30 something artists, screenwriters and actors, the Southern Baptist church has its own video production equipment, art studios, a 'praise band', a dance team and Bible study by way of painting and play writing. The setting is pure Hollywood. Sunday evening services are held in nightclubs, and have the same pulsating lights and music you'd expect at any hip dance club.

Senior Pastor Erwinn McManus says he's been able to attract Generation Xers by combining creativity and spirituality. The weekly sermons include clay molding, used to parallel God molding humans, and video dramas that explore mortality and life with Christ.

Urban Mosaic, 715 South Brady Ave, Los Angeles, CA 90022; ☎ 323 728 4850; fax: 323 726 1735; email: info@mosaic.org; web: www.mosaic.org

The college town of San Luis Obispo has a truly unique claim to fame: an alleyway whose walls are covered on both sides by tens of thousands of pieces of gum, mostly of the bubble variety. **Bubble Gum Alley** got its first blob sometime in the 1950s and it became a tradition for students to leave a lasting impression on the town by leaving their wads behind. The city tried several times to clean the alley, but finally gave up the effort in the 1960s.

Bubble Gum Alley located in downtown San Luis Obispo, CA. Information: Contact San Luis Obispo Chamber of Commerce, 1039 Chorro St, San Luis Obispo, CA 93401; ☎ 805 781 2777; email: slochamber@slochamber.org; web: www.visitslo.com

Only in LA do you find upscale rooms that rent by the hour. **Splash, the Relaxation Spa** bills itself as a mini vacation, the place where LA goes to relax. Six theme spa suites, each featuring a bubbling hot tub, are rented by the hour for birthdays, anniversaries, and just for a romantic party for two. The entire facility can be rented for larger parties. Among the themes are a cave, a Japanese garden and a jungle.

Splash, the Relaxation Spa, 8054 West Third St (corner 3rd St and Crescent Heights, Los Angeles, CA 90048; ☎ 323 653 4410; reservations ☎ 323 653 4412

For traveling canine owners who have to leave Fido behind, **Hollywood Hounds** will treat their dogs in the style to which they've undoubtedly become accustomed. Pups on vacation get the works: pawdicures, indoor retreats complete with video, exercise and recreation programs and the Dog Day Afternoon spa program. The on-site boutique offers the latest styles in biker jackets, printed  raincoats and baseball caps. To celebrate a special occasion, Hollywood Hounds offers birthday parties, muttramonies and even barkmitvas. Pick up and delivery is available, naturally. They're thinking of adding 'valet barking' to their list of services.

Hollywood Hounds, 8218 Sunset Blvd, Los Angeles, CA 90046; ☎ 323 650 5551; fax: 323 650 5126; email: smarfleet@aol.com; web: www.hollywoodhounds.com

Euphuria is for pets with style. This grooming salon, with its clientele of cats, dogs, bunnies, potbelly pigs and rats, offers a multitude of indulgent treatments from soothing oat baths to invigorating shampoos. If you're attending a theme festival or event, they'll vegetable dye your pet so you can celebrate in style. Euphuria has its own bakery, turning out treats like carob-coated dog biscuits and peanut butter dipped love nuggets and a boutique where your pet can be fashionably outfitted with mood collars, a red feather boa, or a fringed leather jacket.

Euphuria, 10538 Magnolia Blvd, N. Hollywood, CA 91601; ☎ 818 760 2110

A great way to gawk at the beach scenes that define youthful exuberance is to mingle among them, either on bicycle or on roller blades. At **Perry's Beach Café and Rentals**, they'll rent you the requisite equipment to pedal or skate on so you can pretend to fit in, if only for a few hours. You'll see people dressed in bizarre clothing here and characters wearing very little clothing at all.

Look for street performers, like the guy who jumps on to piles of broken glass, psychics, tattoo and henna artists and masseuses. At Muscle Beach you can sit and watch the body builders work out on the equipment. Perry's is located at the Santa Monica, Venice, and Marina del Rey beaches. If only they could rent that perfect, tanned body too.

Perry's Beach Café and Rentals, 2400 Ocean Front Walk, Santa Monica, CA 90405; ☎ 310 372 3138; email: rc3138@aol.com; web: www.perryscafe.com

Attractions

If you're going through Death Valley, a visit to **Scotty's Castle** is a must. Sitting virtually in the middle of nowhere and appearing like a mirage in the desert, the castle was built in the 1920s by a wealthy Chicago couple, the Johnsons, who traveled west to check on an investment they'd made in a gold mine run by a man named Walter Scott. A rowdy, fast-talking con artist, Scott had been bilking investors by claiming that he was building a castle from the profits from a nearby gold mine. When the Johnsons discovered they'd been had, they befriended 'Scotty' and went along with his scam in the hopes they could recover their money. It was the Johnsons who actually built the castle. During the tour, the guides dress as characters from 1939 and bring the castle's heyday back to life.

Scotty's Castle, ☎ 619 786 2392. Directions: I-15 north to US-95, north to SR-267 west (left at Scotty's Junction) to Death Valley National Park and on to Scotty's Castle. *Open 9.00am–5.00pm daily. Admission charge.*

The **Westin Bonaventure Hotel and Suites** in downtown LA is a favorite filming location. If you enter from the lower-level parking garage, you're walking down a poster filled gallery of movies that have been filmed at the hotel, movies like *Rain Man* with Dustin Hoffman and *Strange Days* with Angela Bassett. In the lobby you can relive the famous glass elevator scenes in *Forget Paris* with Billy Crystal, *True Lies* with Arnold Swarzenneger, and *In the Line of Fire* with Clint Eastwood. Plaques have been placed on the elevators used in the filming.

Westin Bonaventure Hotel and Suites, 404 South Figueroa St, Los Angeles, CA 90071; ☎ 213 624 1000 or 800 228 3000; fax: 213 612 4800

If you can't be without your feng shui environment, the **Los Angeles Airport Hilton** is the place to keep your 'chi' flowing. Two agate lions, representing strength and power, welcome you at the front entrance and draw energy and prosperity into the hotel. The lobby corridor is wide enough to promote growth, while a grand staircase resembles the Chinese character 'ji' which stands for luck. A feng shui master visits the hotel once a year to make sure everything stays in proper alignment as this ancient oriental art of placement dictates.

Los Angeles Airport Hilton, 5711 W Century Blvd, Los Angeles, CA 90045; ☎ 310 410 4000; fax: 310 410 6250

Some of the most stunning showgirls in Palm Springs collect Social Security retirement income. The long legged lovelies of the **Fabulous Palm Springs Follies** are all between 55 and 87 years old, performing vaudeville type variety acts during the November through May season. This is no geriatric lounge act. The show is a vibrant extravaganza with Ziegfeld-era production numbers, animal acts, and time-warp comedy schtick. More than a million people have watched these performers shatter stereotypes about old age with their astounding vitality and skill.

> **Fabulous Palm Springs Follies**, 128 South Palm Canyon Dr, Palm Springs, CA 92262; ☎ 760 327 0225; web: www.palmspringsfollies.com/index.html

Museums and collections

You won't know quite what to make of the **Museum of Jurassic Technology** in Culver City, which seems to be precisely what the museum is all about. As you wander through the labyrinth of impeccably displayed exhibits, you won't be alone as you stare quizzically and ponder the sanity of what you're observing. This is a very, very strange place where, according to curator David Wilson, confusion can lead to a very creative state of mind; so creative, in fact, that you could end up believing that eating a mouse on toast can cure bedwetting. It's a place where literature, dreams, and science collide; a place to be fascinated by the inexplicable.

The museum's exhibits aren't necessarily what they seem to be and they ask questions that don't necessarily beg to be answered. The more you see, the less you understand. It's not that you have to suspend belief, just that you have to give up the notion of certainty and just go with the enigma flow. You'll see spore-inhaling ants, incredibly detailed peach pit carvings, inventive theories on the nature of oblivion and bats that can fly through solid objects. You can't quite be sure exactly what is fact and what is fiction, which is the fun of it all.

> **Museum of Jurassic Technology**, 9341 Venice Blvd, Culver City, CA 90232; ☎ 310 836 6131; fax: 310 287 2267; email: museumjt@rhythm.com; web: www.mjt.org. *Open Thu 2.00–8.00pm; Fri–Sun 12.00noon–6.00pm; closed Thanksgiving, Christmas, Easter, 1st Thu in May. Admission free, donation suggested.*

People keep sending Ken Bannister things with bananas on them or things shaped like bananas. This is because Ken, who seems to be a perfectly normal man in other ways, has been collecting all things banana for 30 years. Known as the Banana Man, his collection has been certified by the *Guinness Book of Records* as the 'largest collection of individual fruit items amassed by an individual in the world'. He and his bananas have been on the *Tonite Show* and he even appeared on a revival of *What's My Line*.

His obsession began in 1972 when he started handing out 'smiley' banana stickers at conventions to promote his non-banana business. Banana Man took off from there and now that he's retired, he's grown so accustomed to the attention that he devotes himself full time to his persona.

At his Banana Museum in Altadena, Ken arranges his 17,000-item collection in sections: hard items, food and drug items, clothing, sofa items, and wall items. He's the Top Banana of the **International Banana Club** that has 8,500 members in 17 countries. When you send him a banana item you get a banana merit; collect enough merits and you'll earn a Banana Degree.

Bananas are good for you, he says, with no fat, no cholesterol and lots of potassium, calcium, and vitamins. The record for fast banana eating stands at 12 bananas in two minutes.

International Banana Club, ✆ 626 798 2272; web: www.banana-club.com. *Visits by invitation only.*

The remnant of a World War II Desert Training Center, the **General George S Patton Memorial Museum** makes an especially appealing rest stop for the guys. Here you can play soldier, clamoring all over actual vintage World War II tanks used by General Patton. Inside at the museum, exhibits display memorabilia from his life and career.

General George S Patton Memorial Museum, Chiriaco Summit, CA 92201; ✆ 760 227 3483. *Open daily 9.00am–5.00pm.*

The world of burlesque is still alive at the **Historical Burlesque Museum and Hall of Fame** in Helendale. Lovingly run by Dixie Evans, 74, formerly known as the Marilyn Monroe of Burlesque, the museum is crammed to the gills with gowns, feather boas, panties, lingerie and other memorabilia from the golden age of strippers. Located on an isolated, ramshackle ranch in the desert, roughly halfway between Los Angeles and Phoenix, the retired burlesque queen delights in taking you back into her past, smiling coquetteishly, chattering enthusiastically and happily posing for pictures amid the stuff dreams were made of.

As strippers like Gypsy Rose Lee, Tempest Storm, and Sally Rand passed on, they willed their things to Dixie who somehow makes room for even more breakaway costumes, giant fans, shoes, g-strings, posters and cheesecake photos. She shares these treasured artifacts with today's strippers who compete once a year at the ranch for the **Miss Exotic World** title. Wild and wonderful, gaudy and glamorous, Dixie's museum is a memorial to the gone, but not forgotten, days of burlesque. Be aware: there's no air conditioning, so visit during the cooler months.

Historical Burlesque Museum, Hall of Fame and Miss Exotic World, 29053 Wild Rd, Helendale, CA 92342; ↘ 760 243 5261; web: www.aeve.com/exoticworld

Roy Rogers, the famous King of the Cowboys, liked to save things and his famous horse, Trigger, was one of the things he saved. Displayed at the **Roy Rogers–Dale Evans Museum** in Victorville, Trigger knew more than 100 tricks, including opening gates, dancing the rhumba, and refraining from lifting his tail indoors. When the horse died at 33 years of age, Roy had him mounted in his most famous position: rearing up on his hind legs. You can see him (Trigger, that is) in all his glory at the museum, which houses the memories and treasures of some of America's most beloved icons.

The Roy and Dale husband and wife duo was noted for its clean cut, all-American movies and television shows. Every child of the 1940s and 1950s knew their theme songs, 'Happy Trails' and 'Tumbling Tumbleweeds'. Their images, along with Trigger's, appeared on hundreds of western toys, hobbyhorses and lunchboxes. The museum is filled with memories and mementos of the spirit of the west, including his showy Pontiac Bonneville car with its tooled leather interior, coins imbedded in the upholstery, guns for handles and rifles on the hood.

Roy Rogers–Dale Evans Museum, 15650 Seneca Rd, Victorville, CA 92392; ↘ 760 243 4547; web: www.royrogers.com. *Open daily 9.00am–5.00; closed Easter, Thanksgiving, Christmas. Admission charge.*

Most every baby boomer can remember sneaking illicit peeks into the shop windows of Frederick's lingerie stores. At the **Frederick's of Hollywood Lingerie Museum and Celebrity Lingerie Hall of Fame** you'll see the 'software' that made Mr Frederick famous and the underwear of the famous who wore his sexy creations. His motto was 'Don't dream it … live it', and he not only gave folks plenty to dream about, he made it easy to buy the paraphernalia that fantasies are made of.

Above the retail store is the museum with undies from the rich and famous. See an undershirt autographed by Fabio, a marabou negligée worn by Mae West, Natalie Wood's bra and one of Madonna's infamous bustiers. It isn't difficult to imagine Cher, Loni Anderson, Joan Collins and Robert Redford wearing their unmentionables. Phyllis Diller, though, left instructions; her bra is embroidered with the words 'this side up'. From mementos of Hollywood's golden girls to underwear from every cast

BIZARRE BUILDINGS

California is known for its bizarre buildings. The Los Angeles area is home to two donut-shaped stores – **The Donut Hole** and **Randy's Donut** – along with the Coca-Cola building that looks like an ocean liner. **Tail 'o the Pup** is a 17-foot stucco hot dog which perfectly captures the kitsch that LA is famous for. Venice sports the **Binocular Building**, while Beverly Hills has the **Witch's House**. In central California, there's a building shaped like a **bulldozer**, the office of the United Equipment company in Turlock. It even has dirt and rocks piled in front of the 'blade'. The president of the company sits where the engine should be.

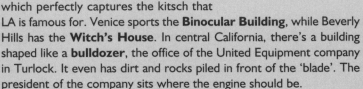

The Donut Hole, 15300 E Amar, La Puente, CA

Randy's Donuts, 805 W Manchester Blvd, Inglewood, CA; ☎ 310 645 4707; web: www.randys-donuts.com

Tail o' the Pup, 329 N San Vicente Blvd, West Hollywood, CA 90048; ☎ 310 652-4517; web: www.tail-o-the-pup.com. *Open 6.00am–5.00pm Mon–Sat; 8.00am–5.00pm Sun.*

Binocular Building located on Main St, Venice Beach, CA. Contact Los Angeles Convention and Visitors Bureau; ☎ 213 624 7300; fax: 213 624 9746; web: www.lacvb.com

The Witch's House, 515 N Walden Dr, Beverly Hills, CA; ☎ 310 271 8174

Bulldozer Building, Visible just off Highway 99, 70 miles north of Fresno in Turlock.

member of Beverly Hills 90210, the museum reinforces the image of Hollywood as a romantic and glamorous place.

Frederick's of Hollywood Lingerie Museum and Celebrity Lingerie Hall of Fame, 6608 Hollywood Blvd, Hollywood, CA; ☎ 323 466 8506

Some eccentrics, infused with the unshakable belief that their way is the right way, manage to attract huge followings. Logically located in the Hollywood land of make believe, the **L Ron Hubbard Life Exhibition** canonizes the guru who started the 'religion' of Scientology.

You can't just browse the 30 or so displays honoring the man who supposedly was proficient in several dozen fields. You have to take a tour of the high-tech exhibition that dramatizes not only his stories and accomplishments, but also the pearls of wisdom he uttered on his way to riches. If you can believe it, Mr Hubbard was – among other things – a master mariner, a police officer, a photographer, an artist, a naval intelligence officer, a daredevil pilot, an explorer, a horticulturist, and a science fiction writer! By the time you finish the not-quite-two-hour tour, you'll be certain of one thing: the guy knew fiction from fact.

L Ron Hubbard Life Exhibition, 6331 Hollywood Blvd, Los Angeles, CA. Located in the Hollywood Guaranty Building at the corner of Ivar and Hollywood Blvd. ✆ 323 960 3511. *Open 10.30am–10.00pm.*

The **African American Firefighter's Museum** harkens back to a time when white firefighters would only show up for fires at white folks' houses; black folks had to have their fires fought by blacks.

African American Firefighter's Museum, 1401 S Central Ave, Los Angeles, CA 90021; ✆ 213 744 1730

Los Angeles is ablaze with neon signs and the best way to experience them is from the top of a double-decker bus at the monthly Neon Cruise tour put on by the **Museum of Neon Art**. Neon at Night takes you past majestic signs and marquees considered to be some of the world's best vintage neon landmarks. At the museum itself, you'll see lots of neon up close, including neon things that move, sparkle and make noise.

Museum of Neon Art, 501 W Olympic Blvd, Los Angeles, CA 90015; ✆ 213 489 9918; web: www.neonmona.org. *Open Wed–Sat 11.00am–5.00pm; Sun 12.00noon–5.00pm; second Thursday of the month 11.00am–8.00pm; closed major holidays. Admission charge.*

The **Ripley's Believe It or Not Museum** in Hollywood features a human-hair bikini, a replica of a half-ton man who weighed 1,069 pounds when he died at the age of 32, art made from dryer lint, a fur covered trout used in a hoax, and hand painted potato chips.

Ripley's Believe It or Not Museum, 6780 Hollywood Blvd, Hollywood, CA 90028; ✆ 323 466 6335; web: www.ripleys.com. *Open 10.00am–10.00pm Sun–Thur; 10.00am–12.00midnight Fri–Sat.*

The **Guinness World Records Museum** tells the story of a man who, in 1900, walked on his hands from Vienna to Paris, a distance of 871 miles. He averaged 1.58mph and completed the journey in 55 ten-hour 'walking' sessions. It also tells of a woman with 20-inch fingernails, a VW Bug with 18 students crammed inside, and a frozen cricket spitting record of 32^1/$_2$ feet.

> **Guinness World Records Museum**, 6764 Hollywood Blvd, Hollywood, CA; ✎ 323 462 5991 or 323 463 6433

Perfectly capturing one of America's greatest obsessions, the **Petersen Automotive Museum** in Los Angeles is dedicated to the influence of the automobile on American life. You'll see hundreds of classic cars, trucks, sportscars and motorcycles displayed in theme settings that showcase Americans' love affair with their cars. The museum has theme shows such as Hollywood Star Cars, a Monster Truck exhibition and an exhibit showcasing the Low Rider Tradition.

> **Petersen Automotive Museum**, 6060 Wilshire (at Fairfax), Los Angeles, CA; ✎ 323 830 CARS; web: www.petersen.org. *Open 10.00am–6.00pm Tue–Sun. Admission charge.*

Tours

Tour guide Anne Block will pick you up in her silver Caddy and show you around the 'real' LA, demystifying a city that many people find alien and intimidating. She takes you beyond the standard tour-bus dreams-come-true rap, concentrating on the eclectic, off-beat and outrageous cultural aspects that real people who live here experience. Specializing in the 'gloriously unusual', she calls her business **'Take My Mother*Please'** since so many of her clients hire her to take their relatives around so they don't have to.

Anne delights in finding the madcap, off-beat soul of a place she truly loves, exploring the ever-changing pop culture that makes Los Angeles so fluid and fascinating. After a day with this vivacious, hip, 50-something woman, you'll see the city in a whole new light and perhaps even understand the quirky essence of one of the most eccentric places on earth.

She began her tour business after escorting the famous comedienne Lily Tomlin to a film festival in Berlin. Anne's tours are totally customized depending upon your interests. Some of her clients' favorites include a beauty day on the Sunset Strip and the Pretty Woman tour, based on the famous movie.

> **Take My Mother*Please Tours (* or any other VIP) Tours**, PO Box 35219, Los Angeles, CA 90034; ✎ 323 737 2200; fax: 323 737 2229; email: takemymom@aol.com; web: www.takemymotherplease.com

See Hollywood's macabre side on a hearse-driven tour of Hollywood's murders, suicides and scandals. From the starlet who plunged to her death from the top of the 50-foot letter 'H' of the Hollywood sign to the bizarre tragedy of Aunt Em from the *Wizard of Oz*, the **Oh, Heavenly Tour** ends

Previous page Houston Art Car Parade (HB)
Above Hamburger Harley by Harry Sperl (HB)
Right Cowasaki by Larry Fuente (HB)
Below The Cameravan art car belonging
to photographer, Harrod Blank (HB)

with a trip to the final resting places of legendary stars. At night the **Grave New World** hearse takes an eerie, two-hour journey through the city's paranormal playground, pausing for the occasional ghost while taking in true tales of hauntings and contacts with the dead.

> **Oh, Heavenly Tours** depart daily 10.00am–1.00pm; **Grave New World Haunted Hearse Tour** departs daily 7.00pm from the lobby of Hollywood's Roosevelt Hotel, CA; ↘ 323 782 9652; email: tourland@aol.com

Shopping

Only in LA could you shop where the witch doctors do – at **Farmacia Million Dollar Botanicas** at the corner of Third and Broadway in downtown LA. This place is, hands down, the most bizarre shopping experience you can have and still be legal. The merchandise is based on various beliefs that herbs, candles, love potions, amulets, spells, powders, saints and rosaries can influence health and happiness

A bewildering array of air fresheners, liquids and oils claim to offer peace and protection, health and wealth, love and luck and spiritual cleansing. Take Dr Buzzard's Court Case Bath and Floor Wash, a liquid to be used when 'justice is in balance and mercy is needed' – when you want the scales of justice to tip in your favor. If you're going to court, pour it in your bath; if it's your business that's being judged, pour it in the water used to wash your firm's floors. The Black Destroyer is a powerful oil that 'destroys curses, hatred, resentments, envies and any evil intention towards you or your home'. . Powdered iguana hand offers protection, while burning candles in the shape of certain male and female body parts will inflame the passions of your intended. A mysterious powder called Tied Up and Nailed pictures an  unfortunate man bound in ropes and nailed to the floor. It's meant to assure that a business deal you really want will, indeed, happen.

They're working on a website so you can see the bizarre inventory for yourself. It's no wonder they do such a booming repeat business. For every purchase there's someone out there who's going to have to shop for an antidote. It's unlikely you'll ever see a sale on spell-breakers.

> **Farmacia Million Dollar Botanicas**, 301 S Broadway (corner of 3rd and Broadway), Los Angeles, CA 90013; ↘ 213 687 3688

All your hot sauce fantasies come true at **Light My Fire**, a stall at the Farmer's Market in Los Angeles. The stall carries nothing but hot sauces rated on a scale from one to ten plus. The sauces have names like Pleasure and Pain, Pain and Suffering, Ass in Hell and Nuclear Waste. Folks either buy the bottles to consume the contents or just to collect them for their conversational value. The latter is less likely to involve paramedics.

Light My Fire at the Farmer's Market, 6333 West 3rd St, #212, Los Angeles, CA 90036; ☎ 323 930 2484; email: pepperlady@hotsaucetogo.com; web: www.hotsaucetogo.com

In North Hollywood, **Eddie Brandt's Film Store** inventories 45,000 movies, including classics, 1950s and 1960s science fiction, westerns, silent films, musicals, vintage television series, music videos, animation, foreign films, documentaries and a special section called 'eyesores', a whimsical assortment of B movies. You'll also find old lobby cards, movie posters and publicity photos.

Eddie Brandt's Film Store, 6310 Colfax Ave, PO Box 3232, North Hollywood, CA 91606; ☎ 818 506 4242 or 818 506 7722

Wacko is an outlandish place selling strange, weird and outrageously fun things like inflatable palm trees, white-trash refrigerator magnets for your front porch refrigerator, head bobbers, lava lamps, a voice changer and books like *101 Uses for Tampon Applicators*. The store is crammed with whimsical cookie jars, lunch boxes, greeting cards and teapots; there's enough kitsch to keep you busy for several hours. Owner Billy Shire just buys anything that appeals to him, commenting that 'bad taste is timeless.'

Wacko, 4633 Hollywood Blvd, Hollywood, CA; ☎ 323 663 0122

When you're flying into terminal one at LA International Airport (LAX) you can avoid that 'How dare you leave me?' look from your pet by picking up a peace offering at **Bow Wow Meow**, the perfect store for neurotic pets and their owners. Items like Pawpcorn, edible cigars, astrological collars, and Timmy HoleDigger Purrfeum mean that you won't have to go home empty handed.

Bow Wow Meow, Terminal One at Los Angeles International Airport (LAX). Contact Trisha Alibudbud; ☎ 310 642 7482; fax: 310 642 7497

'Part of you thinks it's in poor taste, part of you wants an X-large'. That's the slogan at **Skeletons in the Closet**, an improbable gift shop in the Los Angeles Coroner's Office. The shop, squeezed into a second-floor office, sells hats, mugs, clothing, toe tags, beach towels, mouse pads, keychains, magnets and more, all carrying the Coroner's name along with a cute body-outline logo. The 'body bag' garment bag is especially appropriate.

CHANNELING AN ALIEN

'I am Knut. I bring you love' intoned George Van Tassel, addressing one of his interplanetary spacecraft conventions in the 1950s. Knut, it turns out, was an entity supposedly stationed on an alien supply ship not far from the Great Rock Mojave Desert site where the UFO's contactees were gathering. Van Tassel was channeling his alien, as were the many others who believed they had survived physical encounters in spaceships from planets other than earth.

Van Tassel also believed he had received instruction from Knut to build a device that would restore physical youth to humans. Raising money from the sale of his books, *I Rode a Flying Saucer*, and *Into This World and Out Again*, he built a structure in 1959 that he called the Integriton. It didn't restore much youth to Van Tassel; he died despite rocking in a chair inside his fantasy. His eccentrocity has since fallen into ruin.

The idea for the shop came about quite by accident. Employees often had souvenir items made for company events such as picnics and sporting competitions. Friends and relatives clamored for a chance to buy these unique items so a tiny 'shop' was set up in a janitor's closet. The rest is history. The shop is so popular they're getting ready to take over yet another office. The funds raised at the shop support the Youthful Drunk Driver Visitation Program. They're dying for your business.

Skeletons in the Closet, Los Angeles County Coroner's Office, 1104 N Mission Rd, 2nd Floor, Los Angeles, CA 90033; ✆ 323 343 0760; web: www.lacoroner.com. *Open Mon–Fri 8.00am–4.30pm.*

For fake blood, scars and beards, shop where the stars do. Stars like Sharon Stone, Cameron Diaz and Heather Locklear have all purchased products and screen make up from **Naimie's Beauty Center** in North Hollywood.

Naimie's Beauty Center, 12640 Riverside Dr, North Hollywood, CA 91607; ✆ 816 655 9935; fax: 818 655 9932

Quirky cuisine

Hotel Bel Air offers dining with a behind-the-scenes spin. Table One is a private dining room with windows and mirrors that look into the adjoining kitchen so you and seven friends can watch the preparation of your lunch or dinner, with custom menus to satisfy your every whim.

Hotel Bel Air, 701 Stone Canyon Blvd, Los Angeles, CA 90077; ✆ 310 472 1211 or 800 648 4097; fax: 310 476 5890; email: info@hotelbelair.com; web: www.hotelbelair.com

Saturday night dinner takes three hours at the **Harbor House Restaurant** in Marina del Rey. It starts with a cocktail party, then goes on to a four-course meal, all part of an interactive murder mystery. To feel really glamorous, dress in 1940s attire and you'll become part of the show. Music and sing-alongs conclude the evening.

> **Harbor House Restaurant**, 4211 Admiralty Way, Marina del Rey, CA 90292; ↘ 310 577 4555

Quirky quarters

Grandmother of kitsch, the **Madonna Inn** in San Luis Obispo is famous for its décor. The Caveman Room has rock walls, rock ceilings and furniture covered in animal skins. The Madonna Suite is a riot of red, pink, rock and crystal. The men's bathroom in the lobby usually has as many women as men in there, all snapping pictures of the rock waterfall activated by you-know-what. Stop in even if you're not staying there to gawk at the public rooms and watch people walking around with their mouths hanging open.

> **Madonna Inn**, 100 Madonna Rd, San Luis Obispo, CA 93405; ↘ 800 543 9666 or 805 543 3000; fax: 805 543 1800; web: www.madonnainn.com

The **San Diego Yacht and Breakfast Company** is a resort with yachts and floating villas available to overnight guests. You can even untie your room and go for a cruise on the Bay.

> **San Diego Yacht and Breakfast Company**, 1880 Harbor Island Dr, San Diego, CA 92101; ↘ 619 297 9484; fax: 619 298 6625; web: www.yachtdo.com/index.htm

Ballantines Hotel in Palm Springs has 1950s style plastic and chrome theme rooms and suites with furniture by the likes of Eames, Miller and Knoll. The place is upscale, fun, and artsy, and they stock classic and B movies you can watch in rooms dedicated to movie and musical stars. The sun deck is covered with green astroturf, 1950s music is playing, and breakfast is served in your room on Melmac, 1950s style.

> **Ballantines Hotel**, 1420 North Indian Canyon Dr, Palm Springs, CA 92262; ↘ 800 780 3464; fax: 760 320 5308; email: info@ballantineshotels.com; web: www.ballantineshotels.com

At the **Standard Hotel** in Hollywood, the sign is hung upside down and there's a glass enclosure behind the reception desk that serves as a space for human performance art. The on-site barber shop gives you the latest do – or tattoo – so you'll be appropriately styled to join the 20- and 30-something crowd in the bar or on the pool deck. The property used to be a nursing home and has been redone in an over-the-top, retro fifties meets Y2K theme. The lobby ceiling is carpeted and the rooms have silver bean bag chairs.

Standard Hotel, 8300 Sunset Blvd, Hollywood, CA 90069; ↘ 323 650 9090; fax: 323 650 2820

NEVADA

In Nevada, practically everything is 'in the middle of nowhere' but the state goes one step farther, calling US 50 the '**Loneliest Road in America**'. Running east and west across the state from Lake Tahoe to the Utah border, the highway is almost totally empty. The AAA warns its members to stay off the road unless they're sure of their survival skills. The only sights to break the monotony include a pile of windblown sand near Fallon that's popular with off-roaders, a fort near Dayton, the railroad museum in Ely, a Pony Express station at Cold Spring and water at the Lahonton Reservoir. You can pick up a Route 50 Survival Kit in any of the five towns along the route. Stop in all five and you'll get a survival certificate signed by the governor himself. You may find a shoe tree about a hundred miles east of Reno on US 50.

Festivals and events

If any event in America defines 'bizarre', it would have to be **Burning Man**. Thousands of people spend up to a week in the bleakest stretch of nowhere in the whole country, creating the fifth largest city in Nevada for that week. Yet when it's over, there's no sign it ever took place. Its not pagan or hippie; not a concert or a rave. One participant said trying to describe it to someone who has never been there is like describing sex to someone who's never had it.

Try to imagine an outdoor gallery big enough to hold 30,000 performance artists and you get an idea of the scope of this event. Everyone there is a work of art, creating, celebrating, and entertaining in a free spirited, social experience with no boundaries beyond courtesy. A 50-foot Pegasus sculpture rises from the earth. Some guys are giving away 1,500 pounds of tuna and salmon. Hands grope at you through a wall of rubber gloves. Fortune cookies contain dares which are accepted and acted upon.

Forethought is optional, as are inhibitions. Some choose to experience the event sans clothing, perhaps wearing body paint instead of costumes. Most are in costume of some kind. Many arrive with huge performance art installations; others with participatory entertainment. Its an outpouring of lunatic creativity; an eccentric mix of art, music, and wilderness camping.

The Burning Man website is astoundingly complete, giving detailed instructions for collective survival. You're expected to arrive prepared to handle the extreme weather conditions (110 degrees during the day to near-freezing at night) and to be totally self-reliant. Theme camps and villages should be registered in advance so on-site maps can be reasonably accurate. There's an FAC page, a first-timers guide, a volunteer board, a survival guide, and even a Burning Man glossary. The packing list includes common sense, an open mind, and a positive attitude. The site makes it clear the event can stretch your physical, mental, emotional and spiritual boundaries. Death does not entitle you to a refund.

At Burning Man, you give the gift of yourself, unencumbered by cell phones, money, and your rank in the outside world's pecking order. It's a chance to try on new personas, shed the shackles of your preconceptions and burst loose of your own bonds – simply because you give yourself permission to. And when you leave, joining one of the world's biggest traffic jams, you take every trace of the world you built with you and the desert returns to its splendid isolation.

Burning Man Festival held annually on Labor Day weekend in Black Rock Desert, NV; located 120 miles north of Reno, NV. Contact Burning Man, PO Box 884688, San Francisco, CA 94188; ↘ 415 TO FLAME; web: www.burningman.org

Virginia City is an old mining town, sister city to Alice Springs, Australia. Since 1987 these two towns have alternated hosting the annual **Camel Races**. Several dozen jockeys attempt to coerce their stubborn mounts across the finish line in a race with as much control as you'd have over a toddler at a birthday party. The slapstick event also involves ostrich races, so you can imagine the mêlée.

Camel Races held annually in Virginia City, NV. Contact International Camel Races, Virginia City Chamber of Commerce, PO Box 464, Virginia City, NV 89440; ↘ 702 847 0311

The ghosts are waiting for you at Carson City's annual **Ghost Walk**. The self-guided event has you following a blue line through the city's historic district, stopping at historic houses where professional actors portray various ghosts from the past who lived in Carson City.

Ghost Walk held annually in October in Carson City, NV. Contact Carson City Convention and Visitors Bureau; ↘ 775 687 7410; web: www.carson-city.org

If you're wondering what burros and pancakes have to do with each other, take a look at the **Beatty Burro and Flapjack Races**. Following an Old West theme, each contestant has to load up their burro the way prospectors did:

with pick, shovel and other prospecting accruements. Then the race begins, each participant trying valiantly to lead his charge around the track. There's much foot-dragging and ass-sitting (some of it human), but eventually the burros are prodded or carried to the end of the track where the prospector has to unload the gear, build a small fire without using any tinder, cook a pancake and feed it to the burro. The first burro to swallow a cooked flapjack wins. Since burros are quite fond of flapjacks, they often try to eat it before it's cooked and another battle between man and beast ensues, much to the delight of the spectators.

Beatty Burro and Flapjack Races held annually in October in Beatty, NV. Contact Beatty Chamber of Commerce, 119 Main St, PO Box 956, Beatty, NV 89003; ☎ 702 553 2424

Just plain weird

The decayed ghost town of Rhyolite is a particularly appropriate setting for a non-traditional art installation called the **Gold Well Open Air Museum**. Ghostlike figures, looking like humans draped with sheets, appear to float in the vast, empty landscape. One of the figures, the Ghost Rider, stands beside his rusty bicycle, a fitting portrayal of the decaying setting. A soaring nude woman, perched high atop a telephone pole, is worshiping the sky with outstretched arms. Lady of the Desert is a huge, cubistic cinderblock nude. The ghost town itself is unusually interesting because it was built to be permanent. Rhyolites thought they'd have an endless supply of gold, but the town was deserted in 1916 after just 15 years of existence. The Bureau of Land Management provides caretakers for the town – interesting, eccentric characters who hang out as volunteer G-hosts, willing and anxious to share their stories with you.

Gold Well Open Air Museum located near Rhyolite and Beatty, NV, approximately 2.5 miles west of Beatty off State Hwy 374. Beatty is 115 miles north of Las Vegas on Hwy 95. Contact Gold Well Open Air Museum, c/o 1040 N Cordova St, Burbank, CA 91505; ☎ 877 623 5621; email: goldwell@fundraiserx.com; web: www.fundraiserx.com/goldwell.html

Death Valley is a pretty good description of the middle of nowhere. It's the last place you'd expect to find an opera house; the last place you'd expect to find a dancer in her late 70s, performing for royalty and nobility, bullfighters and gypsies, monks, nuns, and cats.

The **Amargosa Opera House** in Death Valley Junction is the unlikely place where Marta Becket, an elderly artist and dancer, has spent a good chunk of her reclusive life. Up until the time she and her husband, Tom, had a flat tire at the Junction en route to a concert tour, her life was fairly normal, at least as normal as life can be for an artist with a tortured soul. While the tire was being repaired, Marta came upon the ruins of the Pacific Coast Borax

Company, an abandoned hotel and outbuildings rotting in the sun. But Marta had eyes for just one thing: a crumbling theater building formerly used for company events.

Marta had found a place for expression, a place for her soul. 'I had to have that theater', she said, believing she would find new life in it and, in doing so, 'perhaps be giving it life. Here', she continued, 'I would commission myself to do work that no one else would ever ask me to do.' Renting, then finally buying, the property, she scheduled performances and danced, regardless of whether she had an audience of a few, one, or none.

Mostly, there were none and after a while she imagined a Renaissance audience completely surrounding her. So, acting on her vision, she spent four years painting her audience on the walls of the theater. The King and Queen have the center box, accompanied by nobility. Two of her cats watch from red velvet cushions. Musicians play, ladies dance. Characters from her imagination spilled out on the walls: revelers, ladies of the night, gypsies, children, courting couples and Indians performing for the entertainment of the King and Queen. Now she would never have to dance alone.

Word of her accomplishment spread and before long, there were real people sitting in real chairs. Today, after more than 40 years in Death Valley, Marta enjoys packed audiences for most of her cool-season performances.

Amargosa Opera House, PO Box 608, Death Valley Junction, NV. Located on Hwy 160 north to Bell Vista, turn left, 30 miles to Death Valley Junction. Contact ☎ 760 852 4441; email: amargosa@kay-net.com; web: www.amargosaoperahouse.org

UFO watchers have been gathering for years at the **Little A 'Le' Inn** south of Rachael in the hope of seeing the same flying saucers that Bob Lazar claimed to have seen in 1988. Back then, there were supposedly nine of the saucers holed up in a hillside hangar; Bob claims he even worked with the aliens to repair one of the craft.

Wednesday nights seemed to be a good time for the aliens to take their saucers out for a spin, so Bob started bringing friends out to the desert to watch. When a Las Vegas TV station broadcast Bob's story, folks began flocking to the site on Wednesday nights. Inn owners Pat and Joe Travis weren't all that convinced that aliens regularly hung out in their neck of the scrub, but what the heck, it was good for business. They changed the name of their bar from the Rachael Bar and Grill to the Little A 'Le' Inn and stocked up on logo hats, shirts, and mugs.

Meanwhile, the highway that runs past the Inn has been designated as the **Extraterrestrial Highway** and the Inn itself sits just ten miles from the entrance to **Area 51**, a well known, top secret government installation where some sort of alien exchange program is supposedly taking place. Rumors of recent spacecraft sightings around Area 51 are always circulating; the Travises are still skeptical but the T-shirts sell real well.

Little A 'Le' Inn, HC 61, Box 45, Rachel, NV 89001; ↘ 775 729 251

The **Extraterrestrial Highway** runs north/south, north of Area 51, Nellis AFB Bombing and Gunnery Range and Tonopah Test Range, from Warm Springs to Ash Springs, NV. Contact Tonopah Convention and Visitors Authority; ↘ 775 482 3558

Area 51 located near Rachel, NV. Contact Tonopah Convention and Visitors Authority; ↘ 775 482 3558

LAS VEGAS

Las Vegas is the world's finest example of corporate eccentricity. It's eccentricity by design and eccentricity for profit; eccentricity on a scale difficult to grasp, even if you've been there. The weirdness is so pervasive, so all-encompassing, that it becomes commonplace, so much so that people living there become immune to it all. One of their state senators is Maggie Carleton. You might meet her while eating at Treasure Island – she's a waitress there.

The mega resorts and casinos along the strip embody American pop culture in their architecture. The buildings are witty, absurd, bizarre, ludicrous, inventive and totally original. Experience the strip at night and you'll be part of something so bright that astronauts could see it from space. Each new resort raises the bar on outrageousness in a place already so over the top that it doesn't seem possible to go any further

Flipping through Yellow Pages gives you a taste of how strange the city really is. There are pages and pages of bail bondsmen, badge-making companies, convention entertainers, wedding chapels, Elvis impersonators, costume rentals, tattoo parlors and 'entertainers'. There are more weird places to explore than you'll have time or energy for. The myriad unique businesses here have unprecedented freedom to flourish in a virtually uninhibited environment. That doesn't explain who belongs to the Personal Injury Multi-Million Dollar Verdicts Club, but in Vegas it's pointless to ask why.

There is normal life outside the tourist areas, but this guide concentrates on the places you're most likely to visit: downtown and the strip. Entries are divided into casino/resort weirdness and weirdness of the non casino, even individual, kind. Keep in mind that eccentricity mid-west style wouldn't even register on the Vegas scale. You've got to be really, really weird, or way, way, way over the top to get noticed in this mecca of madness.

Non casino eccentricities

By any standards, Liberace was strange. The flamboyant pianist, known as 'Mr Showmanship', opened the **Liberace Museum** himself in 1979 to make sure everything shone and glittered to his satisfaction. One building houses his cars, pianos, and awards; the other features his costumes, his jewelry and some furnishings from his Palm Springs estate.

The King of Kitsch had twin beds, one for himself and one for his 26 dogs. He wore the world's largest rhinestone, a 115,000-karat number weighing 50 pounds. It went nicely with his grand piano that was covered in etched mirror-tiles and had a plexi-glass lid. His famous Purple Costume took six months to create by six, sun-glass wearing seamstresses who wore the dark glasses to protect their eyes from the glare of the beads and rhinestones. The volunteer guides enjoy sharing Liberace stories, and the gift shop is high camp.

Liberace Museum, 1775 E Tropicana, Las Vegas, NV 89119; ↘ 702 798 5595; web: www.liberace.org. *Open Mon–Sat 10.00am–5.00pm; Sun 1.00–5.00pm.*

Talk about off the wall – you'll be literally bouncing off padded ones at **Flyaway Indoor Skydiving**. Flapping around like a bird stuck in a silo, you'll 'fly' in a vertical wind tunnel with updraft speeds up to 115mph. But first you need to attend flight school. Here you learn how to position your body for maximum uplift, practice the 'tuck and roll', which is how you exit the updraft safely, and learn the communication hand-signals. Then you'll watch a lawyerly video explaining all the ways you could be hurt or killed (no one ever has); and sign your life away on the liability release form.

After that, it's into your flight suit, knee and elbow pads, helmet, ear plugs and goggles. Then it's into the wind tunnel with up to four of your soon-to-be-best friends. Since your body isn't likely to agree with your decision to leap into a void, your flight suit has handles so your trainer can pull you into and out of the maelstrom.

The tunnel itself is a giant, padded, cylindrical tube with a turbine engine mounted in the floor. The first person to fly flings themselves off the side and on to the air current. Or at least that is the idea; your mind is willing, but somehow your feet stay firmly planted along the outer rim. That's where the handles come in and, before you know it, you really are flying. Exiting the air current isn't quite as scary as entering it and once you get the hang of it, you're ready to go again and again. For an extra charge they'll record a video of your flight.

Flyaway Indoor Skydiving, 200 Convention Center Dr, Las Vegas, NV 89109; ↘ 702 731 4768 or 877 545 8093; web: www.flyawayindoorskydiving.com. *Open seven days a week. Hours are seasonal; phone for current times.*

Elvis is all over the city, eating at restaurants, taking the bus and using the men's room just like everyone else. He's also well represented at the **Elvis-O-Rama Museum**, the number one museum in Vegas. Liberace, who's honored at the other number one museum in Vegas, inspired Elvis at the beginning of his career. A little-known fact is that both were twins at birth. Liberace lent Elvis a jacket for his first appearance in Vegas; and Elvis gave Liberace a ceramic hound dog. Elvis-O-Ramas's owner, Chris Davidson, has been collecting King memorabilia since childhood and has created an impeccable, entertainingly displayed tribute. It's the largest collection of Elvis memorabilia outside of Graceland.

Elvis-o-Rama Museum, 3401 Industrial Rd, Las Vegas, NV; ↘ 702
309 7200. *Open daily 9.00am–7.00pm. Admission charge.*

The **Guinness World of Records Museum** is unusually graphic, with exhibits
that elicit gasps and laughs. The world's largest barf bag collection is there, along
with an 'Eeuuw – gross' display of eating records. Compare yourself to the
world's tallest, smallest, oldest, most tattooed and heaviest humans as well as see
the world's largest collection of refrigerator magnets. Attractive, huh?

Guinness World of Records Museum, 2780 S Las Vegas Blvd, Las
Vegas, NV; ↘ 702 792 0640. *Open daily 9.00am–6.00pm. Admission
charge.*

Even if you're not into gambling, you'll be amazed at what you can buy at the
Gambler's General Store. Besides aisle after aisle of every gambling item
available in the world, there are hundreds of videos and computer games, and
thousands of gambling books, including *Chip Wrecked in Vegas*, *Play Poker, Quit
Work, and Sleep till Noon*, and *How to Become a Casino Cocktail Waitress*. There's
an acrylic toilet seat filled with coins (so you can sit on your assets), and an
astounding array of collectibles from brothels and casinos, including chips,
cards, ashtrays and glasses. Marked cards and loaded dice make fun souvenirs.

Gambler's General Store, 800 South Main St, Las Vegas, NV
89101; ↘ 800 322 2447 or 702 382 9903; fax: 702 366 0329; email:
ggs@fiax.net; web: www.ggss.com. *Open daily 9.00am–5.00pm.*

This store brings a smile of recognition to your face the minute you walk in
the door. 'Hey,' you exclaim, 'I had one of those!' Depending on your age,
you're either looking at your past or shopping for cool retro to impress your
youthful friends. **The Attic** is filled with 1950s, 1960s, and 1970s clothing and

WEDDINGS VEGAS STYLE

Once famous for quickie weddings, Vegas today is also famous for
theme weddings. Settings from the sublime to the ridiculous beckon
the lovestruck who have variously chosen to get hitched in a red, white
and blue helicopter; on the star ship *Enterprise*; in an Egyptian tomb; in
a hot air balloon with 12 witnesses; in a car at a drive-through chapel;
and in the S & M room of a sex-theme chapel. The character doing the
marrying might be a John Travolta character, a gangster, the
Godfather, the grim reaper, or more variations of Elvis than you can
shake your hips at. You can even get married in the buff, wearing just
a veil and a bow tie. Disco, sports, rock, horseback, skydiving – you
name it, and someone in Vegas will do it while getting hitched.

A FUTURE ECCENTROSITY?

A corporate 'eccentrosity' in the making, New Millennium Holy Land is a whopper of a grandiose plan. Jesus will rise over the freeway 33 stories high, welcoming you to a $1.5 billion dollar venture near Mesquite, Nevada. If it ever gets built, the theme park will have computer animation and holography to bring the Bible alive, a pavilion of world religions, and a re-creation of Hell ... (insert your own wisecrack here). Oh, and you'll be able to ascend to the top of Jesus' head.

The Holy Land folks also thought it might be a nifty idea to build a Noah's Ark as long as they're in the neighborhood. If it ever comes to pass, the ark, precisely 465 feet long, 105 feet wide and 48 feet tall, will be built on a high mesa, illuminated at night and made to appear to be floating on water. Let's face it, if Noah had gotten his message from God while living in America, we'd have a Noah's Ark Theme Park and Petting Zoo before you could say 'thunder and lightning'. Want to bet there'll also be a heavenly light show and gift shop?

According to the developers, they chose this desert area because it resembles Israeli terrain. Might they also hope to snag some of the 30 million motorists on their way into or out of nearby Sin City, aka Las Vegas?

furnishings, from boots to saddle shoes, Teen to Vogue, and plastic dinettes to lava lamps; its two floors are crammed, brimming and overflowing with merchandise you won't believe is fetching that much money.

Owner Victor Politis didn't start out envisioning a store as wild and wacky as this. He was in the used textile recycling business; the retro stuff was just the icing on the cake. Eventually he had so much stuff in his yard that the neighbors complained and he was forced to open the Attic. Today he and his wife design outrageous furniture and clothes to add to their displays. They burn incense, serve pastries and drinks, and have a website as off beat as their merchandise.

The Attic, 1018 S Main St, Las Vegas, NV 89101; ☎ 702 388 4088

A good contrast to all the electronics in Vegas is the **Lied Discovery Children's Museum** designed for kids up to ten years old. It doesn't have the latest bells and whistles, but that's part of its charm. Kids learn the quiet, old-fashioned way and you get a break from the hype.

Lied Discovery Children's Museum, 833 N Las Vegas Blvd, Las Vegas, NV; ☎ 702 382 5437; web: www.ldcm.org. *Open Tue–Sun 10.00am–5.00pm. Admission charge.*

At **Bonanza Gifts**, the world's largest gift shop, you'll see virtually every wacky and tacky souvenir available on the planet. If Bonanza doesn't have it, no-one's thought to make it yet. Their collection of Elvis clocks is amazing, as are the Elvis sunglasses with sideburns; a spinning mirrored ball (how romantic!); and the bubble butt boy (how gross!). The place goes on and on, with every trinket, novelty and gag you've ever seen in a catalog. You'd have to have a sense of humor to work at a place like this, listening to 'Honey, you won't believe this but...' all day long. But they get even when you stand before a man-size, stuffed King Kong, sitting on a park bench with his well-stuffed girlfriend. All of a sudden you hear a sound – that sound – and people start looking nervously away, sniffing the air. You'll love that remote-controlled whoopee cushion.

Bonanza Gifts, 2440 Las Vegas Blvd South, Las Vegas, NV 89104; ↘ 702 384 1103; fax: 702 384 0238

Gaming memorabilia fills the **Casino Legends Hall of Fame**, a surprisingly interesting museum with lots of video to supplement the artifacts gathered from casinos now defunct. You can trace the whole history of gambling, see exotic chip collections now worth millions, and experience the cultural implosions Vegas is famous for. Vintage audio and video tapes play constantly in the background. Sections are devoted to showgirls, entertainers, gamblers, builders and visionaries, and to the bad guys (Mafia) who ran da joint until Howard Hughes cleaned up the place in the 1960s.

Casino Legends Hall of Fame located at the Tropicana, 3801 S Las Vegas Blvd, Las Vegas, NV; ↘ 702 739 2222; web: www.tropicanalv.com

Smack dab on the strip, between Sahara and the Stratosphere, sits **Ray's Beaver Bag**. Inside sit Ray and his cronies, looking for all the world like they stepped out of the 18th and 19th centuries. The store sells supplies for mountain men, things like antique muzzle-loading firearms, genuine cooking equipment, jackets sewn with porcupine quill needles and patterns for making authentic clothing and equipment. Mountain Men Rendezvous are big business and participants are sticklers for totally authentic trappings and behavior. Some go so far as to adopt the personality of a specific mountain man, a personality gleaned from reading old letters. Others portray a specific decade or era, such as trappers working for the East India Company. Ray and his buddies couldn't be a greater contrast to the artificial environment raging outside their door.

Ray's Beaver Bag, 727 Las Vegas Blvd South, Las Vegas, NV; ↘ 702 386 8746

As the number of strip mega-resorts grew, traffic at downtown casinos fell and the business owners there knew they had to come up with something spectacular to lure folks off the strip. The **Fremont Street Experience** was their solution – a $70 million canopy covering four blocks of downtown Vegas. Called a 'space frame', it's the world's largest electronic 'sign', filled with 2.1 million light bulbs, strobe lights, and robotic mirrors. Several times nightly the casino lights dim and the canopy explodes with sound and color in a throbbing animated display that leaves the thousands of viewers below gaping in astonishment.

Fremont Street Experience, Las Vegas, NV; ↘ 702 678 5600 or 800 249 3559; web: www.vegasexperience.com

Steven Spielberg is responsible for **Gameworks Showcase**, an industrial-looking, underground environment combining a bar, restaurant, interactive games, and the world's tallest indoor rock-climbing structure. Surge Rock has more than a dozen different routes, varying in difficulty, that end 40 feet in the air or extend all the way to the top, 75 feet up.

One couple even got married on the rock, complete with wedding gown, tuxedo, and minister. The minister and the bride, who was wearing a white helmet with a 35-foot train, rode a hoist to the 40-foot ledge; the groom had to climb. When the vows were complete and the minister said, 'You may now kiss the bride,' she glided to the top in the hoist while the poor groom had to claw his way up another 35 feet to collect his kiss.

Gameworks Showcase, 3785 Las Vegas Blvd, Suite 10, Las Vegas, NV 89109; ↘ 702 432 4263; fax: 702 895 7695

Find out how an M & M candy earns its letter at the **M & M Academy** at M & M World. This tongue-in-cheek, interactive attraction takes you from the coloring, drying and buffing processes, through classroom 'training' and on to graduation. There are three floors of colorful displays, including a store with 3,000 M & M brand products.

M & M Academy located at M & M World, 3769 Las Vegas Blvd South, Las Vegas, NV 89109; ↘ 702 458 8864 or 702 451 8379. *Open Sun–Thur 10.00am–12.00midnight, Fri–Sat 10.00–1.00am. Admission free.*

Clustered in the 2300 block of Las Vegas Boulevard South (the strip) are a number of small businesses catering to the wild side of life in the neon city. **Parisian Wigs** has an impressive collection of head toppers for showgirls and cross dressers. Next door, the **Hemp Store** (that's not their real name but that's what the sign in the window says) has a notice inside saying, 'You will be refused service for saying any of the following words: bong, weed, pot pipe, crack pipe or any other illegal references. All items are intended for use with tobacco only. If you don't know what to say – POINT!' **Diversity Tattoo, Starborn Tattoo** and **Tattoo Heaven** compete for the attention of the body art crowd.

Parisian Wigs, 2305 Las Vegas Blvd S, Las Vegas, NV; ↘ 702 731 3134

Hemp Store located right next door to Parisian Wigs

Diversity Tattoo, 2310 Las Vegas Blvd South, #102, Las Vegas, NV 89104; ↘ 702 382 8820

Starborn Tattoo, 4735 S Maryland Pkwy, Las Vegas, NV 89119; ↘ 702 891 0898

Tattoo Heaven, 2310 Las Vegas Blvd South, #101, Las Vegas, NV 89104; ↘ 702 382 8860

Testosterone-enhanced restaurants

You can't miss the **Nascar Café**. It's the building with the roller coaster that goes inside the restaurant. Carzilla, the world's largest stock car, overlooks the dining area; the roller coaster, named Speed, is the fastest in Vegas. The Nascar theme permeates everywhere, with giant videos, surround sound, driver profiles, stock cars and a realistic, simulated race-car driving experience. You even get a print out of your performance statistics.

Nascar Café located at the Sahara Hotel and Casino, 2535 Las Vegas Blvd South, Las Vegas, NV 89109; ↘ 702 737 2111 or 888 696 2121; fax: 702 791 2027; web: www.nascarcafelasvegas.com

Race Rock is a motor themed restaurant packed with racing memorabilia from all types of motor sport. Video walls, monitors and interactive simulators keep the action going while you eat. There are funny cars, a Bigfoot monster truck, Harleys, dragsters, hydroplanes and a Shrine to Motorsports honoring celebrity owners and driving legends. They focus on the food, too, going beyond hamburger mentality to offer more creative fare.

Race Rock, 495 Fremont St, Las Vegas, NV 89101; ↘ 702 382 7233; web: www.racerock.com

You can see, touch, play, and experience all things Harley at the **Harley-Davidson Café**. Serving all-American road food amid the memorabilia, you're immersed in a 3-D world of past, present, and future Harley culture. A conveyor belt runs throughout the restaurant, showcasing the newest bikes. There's an enormous, chain-link, electric flag covering one whole wall, custom one-of-a-kind and celebrity bikes, and a 28-foot-high, 15,000 pound

Harley replica bursting through the facade to the street. On Valentine's Day they sponsor Harley weddings.

Harley-Davidson Café, 3725 Las Vegas Blvd South, Las Vegas, NV 89109; ⚊ 702 740 4555; fax: 702 740 4222; web: harley-davidsoncafe.com

Steven Spielberg knows a thing or two about set design, so his **Dive!** restaurant is set in a submarine. The exterior is a big, colorful submarine with a wall of water continuously running down the ship. Ping sounds, portholes and fish swimming around an overhead track remind you where you are. A two-story video screen provides the underwater scenery. It's been called a sub shop on steroids.

Dive!, Las Vegas, NV; ⚊ 702 369 3483

Casino eccentricities

Even within the casinos you can find engrossing, off beat diversions that let you escape the clanging madness for an hour to two.

At the Rio you can put on a costume and be part of the **Rio Suite Hotel and Casino's Masquerade in the Sky**. Floating in Mardi Gras style contraptions suspended from a ceiling track, you'll ride along with the showgirls, throwing beads down to the crowd below. While your costume is designed to cover you completely, theirs most certainly is not.

Rio Suite Hotel and Casino's Masquerade in the Sky, 3700 West Flamingo Rd, Las Vegas, NV 89103; ⚊ 702 252 7777; web: www.playrio.com

New York, New York Hotel offers the **Manhattan Express**, a roller coaster that twists, loops, and dives in, out, and around the 12 skyscrapers that make up the resort. Coney Island Emporium has interactive laser tag, virtual reality games, old fashioned bumper cars, and all the latest simulators. At their **America Restaurant**, a 90-foot by 20-foot sculptured map the United States hangs overhead.

Manhattan Express and America Restaurant at the New York, New York Hotel, 3790 Las Vegas Blvd South, Las Vegas, NV 89109; ⚊ 702 740 6969 or 800 693 6783; fax: 702 740 6700; web: www.nynyhotelcasino.com

The **Lion Habitat** at the MGM Grand displays five of their real, live 18 lions at any one time. A glass tunnel lets you circulate beside, around, and under lions being entertained by a trainer tossing big doggie bones. The lions would probably prefer to have a good chew on the swarms of video-camera toting tourists below, all craning their necks and exclaiming 'Wow!' in ten languages.

You can opt to get your picture taken with adorable baby cubs. The **Rain Forest Café** probably has the largest concentration of fake leaves on the planet. Amazon tourist music accompanies the waterfalls, birds, butterflies, monkeys, and simulated tropical rainstorms; all that's missing are the bugs.

> **Lion Habitat and Rain Forest Café**, MGM Grand, 3799 Las Vegas Blvd South, Las Vegas, NV 89109; ➤ 702 891 1111 or 800 929 1111; web: www.mgmgrand.com

Inside **Circus, Circus** is the Adventuredome – the largest indoor theme park in America. The double loop, double corkscrew roller coaster thunders through the park, as does the Rim Runner boat ride which ends with a 60-foot water plunge. The kids can play team laser tag, bounce on the bungee trampoline and take motion simulator rides. It's always 72° in here and it's open every day of the year. It's a great place to leave older kids while you play something more adult.

> **Circus, Circus**, 2880 Las Vegas Blvd South, Las Vegas, NV 89109; ➤ 702 794 3939 or 800 444 2472; web: www.circuscircus-lasvegas.com

The **Las Vegas Hilton's** *Star Trek* **Experience** beams you up to a *Star Trek* action sequence via a motion simulator ride which thrusts you into, and back from, a 20-minute encounter with Captain Kirk and his crew. You're given a briefing on the bridge and taken to the shuttle bay, dodging Klingon warships

along the way. Costumes, make up, weapons, special effects and props from the movies and TV series keep you entertained at the History of the Future Museum while you're waiting in line. At Quarks Bar and Restaurant you can order the Wrap of Kahn, a Romulan Warbird, and Glop on a Stick. The Molecular Imaging Chamber transports you into a *Star Trek* scene to get your picture taken. You can even get married on the bridge of the USS Enterprise.

> **Las Vegas Hilton's** *Star Trek* **Experience**, 3000 Paradise Rd, Las Vegas, NV 89109; ➤ 702 732 5111 or 800 732 7117

A 250-pound head from a decapitated Lenin statue is encased in plexiglass in a vodka freezer at the **Red Square Restaurant** at Mandalay Bay. The surface of the bar is made of ice. Also at Mandalay Bay is the **Aureole**, a restaurant with a four-story wine tower holding 10,000 bottles of wine. The tower is surrounded by catwalks and encased in glass. 'Flying' wine stewards, wearing form-fitting black outfits, ascend to retrieve your selection. The management took great umbrage at the suggestion that this upscale dining experience could be considered the least bit strange or weird.

> **Red Square Restaurant**, Mandalay Bay Resort and Casino, Las Vegas, NV; ↘ 877 632 7800; web: www.mandalaybay.com

> **Aureole Restaurant**, Mandalay Bay Resort and Casino, Las Vegas, NV; ↘ 877 632 7800; web: www.mandalaybay.com

Twenty million dollars buys a lot of reality at **Madame Tussaud's Celebrity Encounter Wax Museum** at the Venetian Resort. Five themed environments showcase a hundred wax figures that are so realistic you'd swear they were real. Each figure takes up to six months to craft and costs $30,000–$45,000. You could easily go through a whole roll of film, snapping Kodak moments sure to liven up your computer screen. The **Warner Brothers Stage 16** restaurant lets you dine in movie settings such as Rick's Café (from the film *Casablanca*), and Gotham City (from the *Batman* movie).

> **Madame Tussaud's Celebrity Encounter Wax Museum**, Venetian Casino Resort, 3355 Las Vegas Blvd South, Las Vegas, NV; ↘ 702 367 1847; web: www.madame-tussauds.com. *Open daily 10.00am–11.00pm. Admission charge.*

> **Warner Brothers Stage 16**, Venetian Casino Resort, 3355 Las Vegas Blvd South, Las Vegas, NV; ↘ 702 367 1847

Treasure Island's trademark event is its outdoor Buccaneer Bay Show which plays late afternoons and evenings. Swashbuckling pirates defend their ships at 90-minute intervals with cannons, munitions and much bravado. Smoke billows, waves crash, seagulls chatter and a ship goes down in flames only to rise again for the next battle. The show has run more than 13,000 times and been seen by 23 million people. The high diver has fallen 70 miles, the captain has swung 125 miles, the ship has sunk 40 miles and the cast has used half a million towels since the casino opened.

> **Treasure Island Buccaneer Bay Sea Battle**, 3300 Las Vegas Blvd South, Las Vegas, NV 89109; ↘ 702 894 7111 or 800 944 7444; web: www.treasureisland.com. *Shows nightly 4.00–11.30pm. Admission free.*

Main Street Station Casino, Brewey and Hotel offers men a once-in-a-lifetime opportunity to express themselves in a way they never dreamed possible – by peeing on a piece of the Berlin Wall. The bathroom, the most photographed men's room in Vegas, has a steady stream of guys standing outside whispering, 'Go on in, honey … it's clear' to their female companions.

German affidavits authenticate the rubble as being a genuine piece of the rock. It's big enough for three guys to express themselves at once. The casino has been used in movies like *Con Air*, *Casino* and *The Hustler*. For a corporation, Main Street Station is eccentric in that they refuse to use voice mail because it's too impersonal.

Main Street Station Casino, Brewery and Hotel, 200 N Main St, Las Vegas, NV 89101; ↘ 800 713 8933; web: www.mainstreetcasino.com

Shows

Master magician **Lance Burton** puts on a show that will have you gasping in disbelief. His strange illusions defy reality and his quirky tricks are unique. Its no wonder the Monte Carlo resort built him a stupendous, multi-million-dollar theater. Even if you don't like magic, you'll love this show.

Lance Burton at the Monte Carlo Resort and Casino, Las Vegas Blvd, Las Vegas, NV; ↘ 702 730 7777 or 888 529 4828; web: www.monte-carlo.com

They're *fabulous*, dahling ... amazing costumes, phenomenal voices and incredible performances. Hosted by Joan Rivers, **An Evening at La Cage** will have you cheering wildly at extraordinary performances by the likes of Cher, Bette Midler and Liza Minelli. You'll completely forget that all the performers are female impersonators.

An Evening at La Cage, 2901 Las Vegas Blvd South, Las Vegas, NV 89109; ↘ 702 794 9433

Cirque du Soleil's Mystère is performance art at its best. The show blends intrigue and entertainment with incredible athletic ability. Acrobats, gymnasts, dancers, singers, musicians and clowns from 15 countries put on a truly amazing show.

Cirque du Soleil's Mystère, 3300 Las Vegas Blvd South, Las Vegas, NV 8919; ↘ 702 894 0711

What does Las Vegas have in store for you in the coming years? How about a skyscraper hotel more opulent than the $1.6 billion Bellagio, and a Mirage casino just for affluent, hip young adults who only want to be around way cool people; a hotel so close to the airport that you step straight off the plane into the lobby; a Titanic resort with an iceberg casino and time share condos in the smokestacks; or City by the Bay, a Vegas version of San Francisco and the Golden Gate Bridge. No idea is too wild, and no plans too grandiose, for one of the most eccentric cities on the planet.

ARIZONA
Festivals and events

Oatman is a real old west mining ghost town. Fewer than 200 folks live there now, but 50,000 visit annually. It's genuinely quirky and full of eccentric characters. In January, during the height of the tourist season, they hold bed races. Five people make up each team – one in the bed and four pushing. Halfway through the figure-eight course they have to stop, change the bedclothes and exchange pajamas with another team member before racing to the finish line.

Also in Oatman, you can answer the age-old question, 'How hot does it get in the desert in July?' You get ten minutes to find out at the July Fourth, high noon, sidewalk egg fry. Hundreds of folks compete for prizes, trying to fry the best-looking, best-cooked egg using whatever they think will speed the sizzle along – tin foil, magnifying glasses, mirrors and a variety of strange contraptions. Since the temperature hovers between 105 and 115 degrees, generating heat isn't too big a problem. That same day, Oatman is witness to dozens of 'gunfights' as groups of staged gunfighters from other western towns converge for a day of competitive shoot outs.

The town is famous for its wandering burros, a legacy of the old mining days. The day ends with a burro-biscuit toss. A burro biscuit is hay that's already made one trip through the burro. They're painted gold, then folks let 'em fly. The record is Oatman to San Diego. It seems one of the biscuits hit the bumper of a moving car and wasn't discovered for 700 miles.

The nearby Gold Road Mine hosts an occasional murder mystery event.

> **Oatman Ghost Town, Egg Fry, Shoot-outs and Bed Races**
> located centrally on Historical Route 66 between Kingman, AZ,
> Bullhead City, AZ, Laughlin, NV, and Needles, CA, approximately 30
> miles from each. Egg Fry part of annual July Fourth celebration. Bed
> Races held annually in January. Contact Oatman-Gold Road Chamber
> of Commerce, PO Box 423, Oatman, AZ 86433; ✎ 520 768 6222;
> fax: 520 768 4274; email: oatmanaz@ctax.com; web:
> www.route66azlastingimpressions.com

Cow Pasture Golf is the zaniest game on the range and it's played each year as a charitable benefit at the Cowboy Golf Tournament. Your horse serves as your caddy, carrying three clubs in a pouch made from the leg of a pair of jeans. The course is full of sage brush, coarse grass, rocks, boulders and cows. To compensate, the holes are coffee-can size and marked with tree branches.

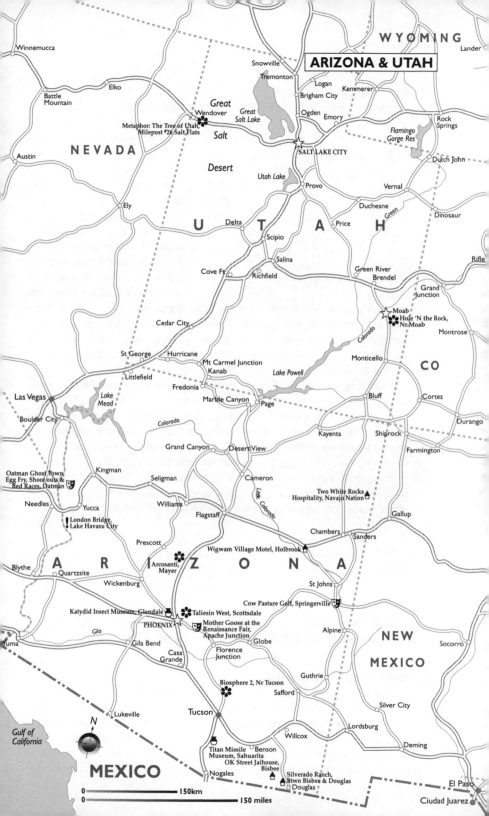

WYOMING

Lander

ARIZONA & UTAH

Winnemucca

Snowville

Elko

Tremonton

Logan
Kemmerer

Brigham City

Great
Salt Lake

Rock
Springs

Battle
Mountain

Wendover

Great
Salt Lake

Ogden
Emory

Flamingo
Gorge Res

Metaphor: The Tree of Utah
Milepost #26 Salt Flats

Salt

SALT LAKE CITY

Dutch John

Austin

Desert

Utah Lake

Provo

Vernal

Dinosaur

N E V A D A

Ely

Duchesne

U   T   A   H

Delta

Price

Green

Scipio

Salina

Rifle

Cove Ft

Richfield

Green River
Brendel

Grand
Junction

Cedar City

Moab
Hole 'N the Rock,
Nr.Moab

Montrose

Colorado

St George

Hurricane

Mt Carmel Junction
Kanab

Monticello

C O

Littlefield

Lake Powell

Bluff

Cortez

Las Vegas

Lake
Mead

Fredonia

Marble Canyon

Page

Durango

Boulder City

Colorado

Kayenta

Shiprock

Farmington

Grand Canyon

Desert View

Oatman Ghost Town,
Egg Fry, Shoot'outs &
Bed Races, Oatman

Kingman

Seligman

Cameron

Little Colorado

Two White Rocks
Hospitality, Navajo Nation

Gallup

Needles

Yucca

Williams

Flagstaff

Chambers

Sanders

London Bridge,
Lake Havasu City

Prescott

Wigwam Village Motel, Holbrook

A   R

Blythe

Quartzsite

Arcosanti,
Mayer

Z   O   N   A

St Johns

Cow Pasture Golf, Springerville

Wickenburg

Katydid Insect Museum, Glendale

Taliesin West, Scottsdale

Alpine

Gila

PHOENIX

Mother Goose at the
Renaissance Fair,
Apache Junction

Globe

N E W

Yuma

Gila Bend

Casa
Grande

Florence
Junction

Guthrie

M E X I C O

Socorro

Biosphere 2, Nr Tucson

Safford

Silver City

Lukeville

Tucson

Titan Missile
Museum, Sahuarita

Benson

Willcox

Lordsburg

Deming

N

Gulf of
California

OK Street Jaihouse,
Bisbee

Nogales

Silverado Ranch,
Btwn Bisbee & Douglas
Douglas

El Paso

M E X I C O

Ciudad Juarez

0   150km
0   150 miles

DIAPERS FOR DUCKS

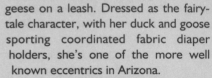

By her own admission Nancy Townsend is hard to insult. This is not at all surprising considering she calls herself Mother Goose and walks diaper-wearing ducks and geese on a leash. Dressed as the fairy-tale character, with her duck and goose sporting coordinated fabric diaper holders, she's one of the more well known eccentrics in Arizona.

Nancy didn't set out to become famous for inventing the world's only known fowl diaper harness. All she wanted to do was bring her pet duck inside to live with the family, which would require some kind of diapering system. After many hits and misses, if you get the drift, she applied for a patent on a comfortable harness that not only allows a ten second diaper change but also provides a convenient leash attachment. Nancy has made is possible to keep ducks and geese as house pets.

According to Mother Goose, ducks are environmentally sound pets, eating bad bugs and leaving the good ones to do their jobs. They'll do your yard work by killing weeds, fertilizing, and keeping your grass and plants healthy. They don't need shelter, never complain about the weather, are free of disease, provide 20% of their own food and can even provide some of yours. Yep, duck eggs are edible. On top of all that, ducks are smart, learning skills and routines in just two to three days. Training requires no discipline, no commands, no orders, and no rewards. Highly social and affectionate, they just want to please. When reared from birth, they imprint

At one hole, you have to hit right off a high cliff. With luck, your ball lands in the wading-pool-sized bucket 500 feet below. The event is held in the fall at Bar Flying V Ranch east of Springerville. A similar event is held near Holbrook.

Cow Pasture Golf, Cowboy Cow Pasture Golf Association, PO Box 31, Springerville, AZ 85938; ☏ 520 333 2123; fax: 520 333 5690

Eccentric environments

Mary Lou Gulley hardly knew the father who built her a castle, yet she's spent the last 53 years living there and leading tours of his off-kilter creation. The **Mystery Castle** began in the late 1920s when Boyce Gulley had to leave his family and coastal home and head to the desert for health reasons. Remembering how his precious little daughter became dismayed when the waves washed away her sandcastles, he vowed to build her a real on humans and, according to Nancy, 'expect to wear clothes and sit on chairs like everyone else. Treat them like well behaved children from a foreign country who do not speak the language', she says, 'and they'll be quite happy.'

Matilda the Duck and Maggie the Goose are Nancy's constant companions, becoming concerned if she's away for more than four hours. Her incredibly tolerant husband, Alan, joins her for their public appearances dressed as – who else? – Father Goose. They all have quite a wardrobe, dressing appropriately for the season and holidays. People are so surprised by the sight of them sipping coffee with Matilda and Maggie on their laps or shoulders that they often blurt our really dumb questions such as 'Is it real?' or 'Is it tame?' 'No', Nancy thinks but does not say, 'I was sitting here minding my own business when this wild duck came out of the sky and sat in my lap all dressed up! Incredible!' Instead, she invites you to pet her pets, telling you all about her life with these fascinating creatures. Maggie the Goose will even hug you, wrapping her silky long neck around yours in a gesture of affection.

Once, while eating lunch on ritzy Rodeo Drive in Los Angeles, a lady from England gently told Nancy, 'You do know, dear, you're just a tad left of center'. Not at all offended, this delightful eccentric agreed.

Look for Nancy's pavilion at the **Renaissance Fair** in Apache Junction each season. You can see Matilda 'hop-walk' on a leash and Mother Goose herself reciting rhymes about her life with ducks. You're welcome to photograph and videotape; tips are appreciated.

Renaissance Fair held every weekend in February and March in Apache Junction, AZ. Fairgrounds are located 9 miles east of Apache Junction on US route 60; ⟍ 520 463-2700; web: www.thegoosesmother.com. *Admission charge.*

one that could never be swept away. He found the perfect place in the Arizona desert.

For 18 years he toiled building the castle, enduring ridicule, poverty and hardship. The result, an odd, pueblo-style structure, has bell towers, shrines, 18 rooms and 13 fireplaces, all built of bottles, throwaway bricks, railroad ties, box cars, river rock and granite. Undulating snakes, usually made from river rock, are set into the walls and floors because Boyce believed they were symbols of protection, wisdom, and defiance. A fold-out bar is made of tequilla bottles cemented into the rock.

His family didn't know about the castle until after his death when they moved here to care for it. The castle didn't get running water and electricity until 1971.

Mystery Castle, 800 East Mineral Rd, Phoenix, AZ 85040; ⟍ 602 268 1581. *Open 11.00am–4.00pm Thur–Sun. Admission charge.*

Sunnyslope Rock Garden is a prime example of dementia concretia constructed over a 22-year period by one Grover Thompson. His vivid imagination propelled him to make 200 sculptures out of concrete set with broken Fiestaware, a popular 1950s pottery. Even more peculiar is why the property appealed so instantly to Marion Blake who fell in love with it at first sight in 1979. She doesn't mind a bit if you stop by to take a look at her purchase.

> **Sunnyslope Rock Garden**, 10023 N 13th Pl, Phoenix, AZ.
> Directions: take Squaw Peak Freeway to Glendale exit, west to 7th St, north to Dunlap, north on Cave Creek, then right on Cinnabar and 13th Pl. ✆ 602 997 4627. *Open 1.00–5.00pm first Sunday of each month.*

You'd have to be a few clowns short of a circus to volunteer to live inside a human terrarium with eight other people for two years, even if it was done in the interest of science. In a case of life imitating art, the experiment at **Biosphere 2** wasn't much more congenial than those survivor-type television shows. The $150 million, privately funded venture turned out to be a cult experiment by a group supposedly hoping to colonize Mars.

The whole thing was supposed to be a sealed, controlled environment with air, food, water and waste being endlessly recycled. Unfortunately, the project ran low on oxygen and high on carbon dioxide, so all the birds, animals, and plants died and the pioneers finally stumbled out, heading for the nearest McDonalds.

Now being operated by Columbia University, the biosphere is open for tours so you can see for yourself what they were trying to accomplish inside this biosphere designed to mimic conditions on earth. The giant, three acre, enclosed glass terrarium is now being used to study the greenhouse effect along with a dozen other scientific projects.

> **Biosphere 2** located on Hwy 77 about 20 miles north of Tucson, AZ; ✆ 800 828 2462; web: www.bio2.edu. *Open daily 8.30am–5.00pm except Christmas Day.*

Looking somewhat like Tinker Toys on steroids, **Arconsanti** hopes to become a model for how the world will build its cities in the future. Unlike most of the eccentric visionaries who dream up similar schemes, Paolo Soleri is a world-renowned architect. Using the concept of arcology (architecture + ecology), he hopes his prototype demonstrates that urban conditions don't have to be destructive to the planet or stressful to the psyche.

Volunteers and students from around the world take a five-week workshop, learning how to build the three-dimensional, pedestrian-oriented city which has been under construction since 1970. When complete, the facility is meant to house 7,000 pioneers, all hoping to avoid rush hour forever. Can a new Starbucks be far behind?

Arcosanti located in Central Arizona, 65 miles north of Phoenix, just off I-17, exit 262 (Cordes Junction). Contact HC 74, Box 4136, Mayer, AZ 86333; ↘ 520 632 7135; fax: 520 632 6229; web: www.arcosanti.org. *Open daily 9.00am–5.00pm except Thanksgiving and Christmas. Donations suggested.*

He was, in his opinion, the greatest architect who ever lived – or who would live in the future. A boast like this usually has little substance, but Frank Lloyd Wright did indeed have enormous talent, along with an enormous ego, to back up his contention. At Wright's desert home at **Taliesen West** in Scottsdale, you can see evidence of both his genius and his eccentricity.

The home was used as a teaching facility for his foundation as well as his part-time residence. Taliesen West, literally created from the rocks and sand of the desert, demonstrates his philosophy that buildings be appropriate to the site; in this case, he believed the finished house 'looked as if it had existed in the desert since creation'. He also believed that architects should experience the building process first-hand, so they lived in a variety of strange on-site structures while learning from the great one.

He allowed no interference or suggestions from his clients, insisting that all his buildings be built exactly as he dictated, including the furnishings. Unfortunately, he minimized the importance of the humans who would inhabit his spaces and a great many of his buildings were difficult or impossible to inhabit comfortably.

Taliesin West, 12621 N Frank Lloyd Wright Blvd, Scottsdale, AZ; ↘ 602 860 2700; tour info: extension 494 or 495. *Open daily except major holidays 9.00am–4.00pm. Admission charge.*

Just plain weird

London Bridge isn't in London any longer. It's in **Lake Havasu City** and it's been there since 1970 when Robert McCulloch, founder of the city, bought it from the British government for $2.5 million. The falling down bridge was disassembled in London, shipped 10,000 miles by boat, then trucked to the desert site. A civil engineer from England reconstructed it over the water, and another tourist destination was born.

London Bridge in Lake Havasu City. Contact Lake Havasu Area Visitor and Convention Bureau; ↘ 800 242 8278 or Lake Havasu Area Chamber of Commerce; ↘ 520 855 4115; web: www.lakehavasucity.com.

Museums and collections

Nedra Soloman's kids say she's easy to shop for. Just buy her a bug that she can display at her **Katydid Insect Museum**. She and her family have been in the pest control business for two decades, but the 62-year-old's passion for bug collecting has been relatively recent – just six years. One of her favorite insects is the $200 Mongolian walking stick, a very skinny insect with a body up to a foot long. She's planning on having a colony of them at the museum, which draws both the curious and the studious. Once you get over the 'Ewu-u!' and 'Ick!' stage, you'll find her hobby quite fascinating. The museum is kid-friendly with plenty of creepy-crawly activities to keep them busy while you try to look cool.

> **Katydid Insect Museum**, a division of Heritage Pest Control, 5060 W Bethany Home #4, PO Box 1702, Glendale, AZ 85311-1702; ↘ 623 931 8718; fax: 623 931 0266; web: www.insectmuseum.com

At the **Titan Missile Museum** you'll follow a retired veteran down into the control bunker of this restored missile silo and see how easy it would have been to start World War III.

> **Titan Missile Museum**, 1580 W Duval Mine Rd, Sahuarita, AZ; ↘ 520 625 7736; web: www.pimaair.org/titan_01.htm. Directions: approximately 25 miles south of Tucson. From Tucson take I-19 south to Green Valley, exit 69 west 10 miles past La Canada to entrance. *Open daily 9.00am–5.00pm Nov 1–Apr 30 except Thanksgiving and Christmas; Wed–Sun 9.00am–5.00pm May 1–Oct 31. Admission charge*

Quirky cuisine

If you look closely at Juan Delgadillo's business card, you'll notice 'dead chicken' listed along with shakes, sundaes and cheeseburgers with cheese. At least he gave you the legit **Snow Cap** card; his other one reads simply 'My card: eat here and get gas. Slightly used napkins and straws'. The drive-in restaurant itself has handles on doors that don't open, a menu offering hamburgers without ham', and a sign that says 'Sorry, we're open'. Juan, who's in his mid-eighties, shares the eccentric spotlight with his younger brother, Angel, who greets the public each day from his barbershop next door. Angel is likely to consult a barbering textbook just as he takes a razor to your chin. The two are well known along the route for their quirky humor and practical jokes.

> **Delgadillo's Snow Cap** located on Route 66 in Seligman, AZ; ↘ 520 422 3291

Quirky quarters

You'll feel like you've been transported back in time at the **Shady Dell Trailer Park** in Bisbee. Here you can sleep in one of seven restored aluminium travel trailers from the 1940s and 1950s, while listening to reproduction radios playing your favorite oldies. Each trailer comes with a refrigerator and propane stove and features the original blonde wood or shiny aluminium interior. Owners Rick and Rita are sticklers for details: your cookies are stored in an old cookie jar, your drinks are mixed in vintage shakers, and old *Life* magazines are scattered about for your reading pleasure.

> **Shady Dell RV Park and Campground,** I Douglas Rd, Bisbee, AZ 85603; ↘ 520 432 3567; fax: 520 432 4858

Documentaries and a movie have bene made at **Wigwam Village**, the famous Route 66 landmark motel. Renovated in the late 80s, the teepees have the original tile baths and hickory furniture. Color TV has replaced the old coin-operated radios that gave you an hour of sound for ten cents. Classic cars are dotted around the village.

> **Wigwam Village Motel,** 8II W Hopi Dr, Holbrook, AZ; ↘ 520 524 3048

Two White Rocks Hospitality is a cultural experience in an eight-sided native hogan (hut) with a dirt floor. Located on the Navajo Reservation, the Hogan Bed and Breakfast has sheepskin sleeping rugs on the dirt floor and a potbellied stove for heat. You can listen to stories around the campfire and take a traditional sweat-lodge bath.

> **Two White Rocks Hospitality,** Navajo Nation, Arizona. Contact: Navajo Tourism Department; ↘ 520 871 6436

The **OK Street Jailhouse** in Bisbee has a jacuzzi in a former upstairs cell and a kitchen and living room in the former drunk tank. The heavy metal cell doors still make a satisfactory clank when they shut.

> **OK Street Jailhouse,** 9 OK St, Bisbee, AZ; ↘ 520 432 7435

Belle Starr, 74 years old, runs the **Silverado Ranch**, a wildlife preserve, bird sanctuary and botanical gardens with old-west-style cabins and RV hookups. There's a real Indian hogan and sweat lodge for purification sweats and meditation. She'll take you on a hayride tour and sing for you by the fire pit. You can pet her miniature horses, mules, and donkeys and meet Lobo, her pet wolf. Star has created this ranch almost entirely on her own and she shares it freely with you, asking only for a donation for maintenance. The ranch is located between Bisbee and Douglas.

Silverado Ranch, Hwy 80, Milepost 353 between Bisbee and Douglas, AZ; 9132 Washboard Rd, 1–40 Adamana exit 303, Holbrook, AZ 86025; ↘ 520 524 9127; web: www.bellestarr.org

UTAH

Utah is a few pews short of a church when it comes to humor; in fact, they're so eccentrically challenged here that it's hard to believe they're American. This state takes itself way too seriously, and wins the Eccentric America award for being the state least likely to poke fun at itself.

Eccentric environments

At least they have a cave dweller, one Albert Christensen, who hand-carved a home for himself out of rock. The place occupies almost 5,000 square feet, and it took 12 years of blasting away to create the 14-room **Hole 'n the Rock**. He and his wife, Gladys, lived there beginning in 1952, even running a diner and gift shop, until Albert took sick. He died in 1957, but his wife kept up the place for 17 more years. When she died, the family left things just as they were, including Harry the donkey, a victim of do-it-yourself taxidermy. Harry stands right next to Albert's painting of Franklin Roosevelt. Roosevelt's head is also carved into the rock near the entrance to the dream home.

Hole 'n the Rock located on Hwy 191, 15 miles south of Moab, UT

The only eccentric burp on the plains of conformity is a strange, contemporary sculpture, **Metaphor: the Tree of Utah**, stuck way out on the Bonneville Salt Flats. Created by European artist Karl Momen, it is meant as a 'hymn to our universe whose glory and dimension is beyond all myth and imagination.' There isn't so much as a place to pull over to contemplate this, however, so maybe Utah doesn't want to encourage anyone to think California-type thoughts.

Metaphor: the Tree of Utah located at milepost 26 on I-80, Salt Flats, UT

The **Hotel Off Center** in Moab is Utah's only vortex of spontaneity. It isn't the least bit upscale, but it sure is bizarre. The place is run by Tim Knouff, an ex-Hollywood prop-maker, who knows the difference between funky and frumpy. It's the hotel of choice among mountain bikers, for Moab is the gateway to the mother of all bike paths in Arches and Canyonlands National parks. You can only book the hotel as part of a Dreamride Tour Package.

Hotel Off Center, 96 East Center St, Moab, UT 84532; ↘ 435 259 4244; fax: 435 259 3366

The **Alien Abduction** is a wild ride of a different sort; a mountain biking vacation quite out of this world. Each day's ride leads you on trails where space craft have supposedly stopped by, parked and picked up people, or sliced up a cow. You decide how far you want to go, both in terms of distance and in terms of courage. Trips range from a few days up to their total imersion, 12-day adventure. The lodgings are so far off the beaten path that you need to plan six months to a year in advance, which is a lot more notice than you'll get from a spaceship. The company also originates tours out of Colorado.

Alien Abduction tours, Dreamride, PO Box 1137, 59E Center St, Moab, UT 84532; ↘ 888 MOAB UTAH (in US); 435 259 6419; fax: 435 259 8196; email: dreamride@mountainbiketours.com; web: www.dreamride.com/alien.html

Quirky quarters
The romantic **Anniversary Inn** in Old Salt Lake City is an all-theme hotel with a variety of unique suites. In the Italian Gondola, you actually sleep in a gondola; in Swiss Family Robinson you sleep in a tree; and in Jackson Hole you sleep in a covered wagon. The Lighthouse has a round bed with an aquarium above it.

Anniversary Inn located 460 South 1000 East, Salt Lake City, UT 84102; ↘ 801 863 4900 or 800 324 4152; and South Temple located 678 East South Temple, Salt Lake City, UT 84102; ↘ 801 363 4950 or 800 324 4152; web: www.anniversaryinn.com

South Central Region

TEXAS
Festivals and events

Oatmeal, Texas is a tiny burg with fewer than a thousand people. But during the **Oatmeal Festival**, its population swells up to around 10,000, with festivities that include an oatmeal cook off and an oatmeal eat-off. The oatmeal sculpture contest is a hoot, as is the Miss Bag of Oats pageant, open only to women over 55. The highlight of the event is when 1,000 pounds of oatmeal is dropped from an airplane on to the crowd. You'll have to find out for yourself whether it's cooked or not.

> **Oatmeal Festival** held annually in September in Bertram, TX; ☏ 512 335 2197

Hormel, the corporate parent responsible for foisting millions of cans of SPAM™ upon an unsuspecting world, is very sensitive about anyone making fun of their potted pork product. You can imagine their reaction, then, when David Arnsberger and Dick Terry held the first **SPAMARAMA™** in Austin back in 1976. Hormel let the guys know, in no uncertain terms, that taking the can's name in vain, without using ALL CAPITALS and the trademark insignia, could have serious legal consequences. That explains why there are so many CAPS and little '™'s in this entry.

Officially called the Pandemonious Potted Pork Festival, the annual SPAMARAMA™ draws 10,000 people with a highly refined sense of humor to one of the wackiest festivals in America. Held each year in Austin on a weekend close to April Fool's Day, the festival is famous for making rollicking good fun of a product folks either love or love to hate.

Entries are divided into two divisions: the open, in which anyone can enter serious or joke dishes; and the professional, which is limited to chefs and restaurateurs. Awards are given not just for the best – and worst-tasting – concoctions, but for showmanship aswell. Past entries have included many flavors of SPAM™ ice cream, Moo Goo Gai SPAM™, GuacaSPAMole™, and SPAMalama™ Ding Dong, made with the pink colored meat, whipped cream, and chocolate. You can even buy a recipe book full of different ways of making this gelatinous pink stuff palatable.

Judges of the SPAM™ cook-off have to actually taste all the dishes entered, although they're allowed three passes during the judging. Additionally, they have the right to require the contestant to take a bite first, minimizing some of the risk. Being thoroughly tanked is also a great help. Imagine how you'd react to SPAMish™ fly, a delightful mix of diced SPAM™, cheddar cheese, mayonnaise and flies of raisins. The creator of this dish was so incensed when he didn't win that he froze it and returned each year with the same entry. That was before they instituted the last-place-even-if-there-were-a-hundred entries award.

Other events include the SPAM™ Cram, a potted pork pig-out with predictable consequences. SPAM™ Carvings often have a pop culture/current events theme such as a SPAMatoyla™, Private Pork by Howard Swine, and Babe II: the Can. Body parts are a popular theme, as are animals such as the SPAMagator™. The SPAM™ calling contest is a riot, as is the SPAM™ toss. One year the showmanship award was won by an artist who carved the word SPAM™ (without the '™') out of a 300-pound block of blue ice with a chain saw.

SPAMARAMA™ gives adults a chance to play with their food, paint their bodies with SPAM™ themes, and sing along to SPAMish™ Eyes and This SPAM™ is my SPAM"!, should they wish to.

SPAMARAMA™ Official Pandemonious Potted Pork Festival held annually in Austin, TX. Contact Austin Convention and Visitors Bureau; ✆ 512 583 7209; web: www.austin360.com

Once u-pun a time (sorry!) a group of courageous pundits came out of the closet, daring to expose their penchant for wretched pun-play to the groans of puns worshipers everywhere. Now in its 23rd year, the **O Henry Pun-Off World Championships** in Austin delight and dismay 2,000 punsters who brave a day of preposterous puns perpetrated by limber linguists who perform this lowest form of humor in high style.

O Henry Pun-Off World Championships held annually in May in Austin, TX. Contact O. Henry Museum, Fourth St at Neches in Brush Park; ✆ 512 472 1903 or 512 453 4431; web: www.puny.webjump.com

Architects, engineers, contractors and a sprinkling of regular folks descend on East Beach in Galveston armed with buckets, pails, rakes, shovels, and wheelbarrows, ready to kick sand in the face of their competitors at the American Institute of Architects annual **Sandcastle Competition**. Like Olympians, they're going for gold, the Golden Bucket award, that is.

Make no mistake, this isn't just a friendly sandcastle contest. These are serious competitors, out to create incredibly complex, multi-part structures that will be judged in five categories: original concept, artistic execution, technical difficulty, carving technique and best use of the site. For five grueling hours, crews battle the elements and race the clock, making such masterpieces as Thinking Outside the Box, Who Cut the Cheese?, Sandtasia, Mount

Schulzmore and How to Bury a Billionaire. Those who don't get the gold still hope to win one of the other category prizes such as Most Hilarious, Most Lifelike, the Public's Favorite, Best Costume, and the Best Team T-Shirt.

> **Sandcastle Competition** held annually in Galveston, TX. Contact American Institute of Architects, 3000 Richmond Ave, Suite 500, Houston, TX 77098; ↘ 713 520 0155; web: www.aiasandcastle.com

Each year in Longview, a local Nissan dealer holds a bizarre competition called **Hands on a Hard Body**. Two dozen quirky contestants, anxious to win a new pick-up, compete to see who can stand the longest with their hand placed firmly on the surface of a new Hardbody truck. They get one five minute break each hour and a 15-minute break every six hours; no leaning is permitted, and no-one gets sleep time. The contest is a test of endurance, stamina and physical, as well as mental, strength, all qualities Texans pride themselves on having in abundance. The previous competition lasted 87 hours, so this isn't for sissies. A very funny documentary, focusing on the contestants' various strategies for winning, was made of the 1995 event.

> **Hands on a Hard Body** held annually in September in Longview, TX. Contact Joe Mallard Nissan, 1201 McCann Rd, Longview, TX; ↘ 903 758 4135 or 800 256 2514; email: mail@joemallardnissan.com; web: www.joemallardnissan.com

The record distance for spitting a watermelon seed stands at 75 feet and 2 inches, a feat recorded in the *Guinness Book of Records*. At the annual **Watermelon Thump** in Luling, 20,000 folks descend on this little town of 4,500 residents to watch the contest, celebrate at the carnival and street dance.

> **Watermelon Thump** held annually in June in Luling, TX. Contact Luling Watermelon Thump, 421 E Davis St, PO Box 710, Luling, TX 78648; ↘ 830 875 3214; fax: 830 875 2082; email: lunlingcc@bsc.net.net; web: www.bscnet.net/lulingcc/thump.htm

It's as much fun as a roll in the mud. The annual **Hogeye Festival** in Elgin pays tribute to porkers by staging greased-pig chases, a Pearls Before Swine art show, a children's costume and pet parade, a hog calling contest, a BBQ cook-off, and the crowning of King Hog or Sowpreme Queen. The cow patty bingo event has a big payoff as the downtown street is painted with 1,500 one-foot-by-one-foot squares. Three cows are let loose, and the owner of the square where the first one plops wins the jackpot.

> **Hogeye Festival** held annually in October in Elgin, TX. Contact City of Elgin, Texas 78621; ☎ 512 281 5724; web: www.elgintx.com

Thirty thousand people show up to hunt rattlesnakes and then eat them at the annual Sweetwater Jaycee's **Rattlesnake Round-up and Cook-off**. In the 40 years since the event was organized as a way to control the deadly snake population, more than 220,000 tons of rattlesnakes have ended up deep fried, barbecued, or otherwise recycled into less-threatening form. There are demonstrations of snake-handling, snake-milking, and a Miss Snake Charmer Queen contest. The squeamish might want to sit this one out.

> **Rattlesnake Round-up and Cook-off** held annually in March in Sweetwater, TX. Contact: Rattlesnake Roundup, PO Box 416, Sweetwater, TX 79556; ☎ 915 235 5488 or 915 235 8938; email: rattle@rattlesnakeroundup.com; web: www.rattlesnakeroundup.com

It's an evening of wacky fun at the **Corn Dog Festival**, a styling competition designed to bring out the hidden nature of this cornbread-wrapped hot-dog-on-a-stick. The decorated doggies compete for the titles of the biggest, best dressed, weirdest, most traveled and celebrity look-alike. You can eat the less fortunate corn dogs who've been deprived of the opportunity to express themselves.

> **Corn Dog Festival** held annually in October in Dallas, TX. Contact email: cdogefest@aol.com; web: www.corndogfestival.com

Play Lucy and Ethel at the annual **Grape Stomp and Harvest Festival** at the Fall Creek Vineyards. You can actually climb into a vat and stomp grapes while watching a video of the famous television episode in which Lucille Ball and her comic cohort did the same. You can even buy a personalized T-shirt with your footprints on it.

Grape Stomp and Harvest Festival held annually in August in Fall
Creek Vineyards on the northwest shores of Lake Buchanan, 2.2
miles north of the Tow post office, on FM 2241 in Llano County, TX.
Contact Fall Creek Vineyards; ↘ 512 467 4477; web: www.fcv.com

Eccentric environments

When it comes to weird, Houston does more than its part as far as the sheer
number of ultra-eccentric people, places and objects it champions is
concerned. The **Orange Show Foundation**, named after the environment
described below, keeps a nationwide database of eccentric artists and their
creations. As sponsors of the Art Car Weekend, it keeps track of the hundreds
of art cars (see page 9) around the country. Folk art educational programs and
projects are held at the Orange Show Monument. The city itself is the only
large city in the country that doesn't have the kind of zoning requirements that
normally discourage budding building eccentrics.

The Orange Show itself is an outlandish place, handmade over a period of
25 years of intense, single-handed labor by Jeff McKissack. McKissak used to
deliver oranges in the south during the Depression, becoming fond not only
of their taste, but of their attributes as well. Believing them to provide a long,
healthy, productive life, he worked obsessively to build a monumental tourist
attraction, hoping that the whole city would turn out to honor his creation.
When he finally did throw open the gates, the expected crowds failed to
materialize and he died just a few months later, possibly of a broken heart.

Now an established site covering an area large enough for two houses, the
Orange Show is a riot of color, especially orange. Made from concrete, brick,
steel, gears, tiles, wagon wheels, mannequins, tractor seats and statuettes, it
lurches maze-like from the arena to the stage, from the pond to the gift shop.
Lettered tiles spell out his philosophy and urge visitors to watch their step, love
oranges and enjoy the show. The site serves as a chapel for weddings and as a
venue for funky dances, art workshops, films, multi-media events and – once –
for McKissak's funeral. His ashes were scattered there.

The Orange Show Foundation Art Car Weekend held in August
in Houston, TX. Contact The Orange Show, 2402 Munger St,
Houston, TX 77023. Directions: take Interstate 45 off the Telephone
Rd exit; ↘ 713 926 6368; fax: 713 926 1506; email:
orange@insync.net; web: www.orangeshow.org

Eighteen years ago Cleveland Turner, the **Flower Man**, had hit bottom. In
despair, he asked God for help, vowing to build a thing of beauty if He would
help him stay sober. God did his part, and Turner did his. His yard and house
are bursting with color. Shiny blue is painted everywhere, even on the curb
that has vegetables growing out of it. Flowers made from scrap materials grow
in a garden of carpet squares.

Flower Man's House located near the University of Houston at
Sampson and Francis Sts, one block off Elgin.

John Milkovisch was blessed with a very patient wife who put up with his compulsion to cover the exterior of their house with beer cans. Beginning in 1968, and working at a rate of a six-pack a day for 18 years, **John Milkovisch's Beer Can House** has long, beer can garlands hanging from the eaves, garlands made from pull tabs, can tops, and can bottoms. The fencing uses the whole can, the siding is made from riveted sheets of flattened beer can labels, while concrete and marble sculptures use the seams of the cans. His handiwork stopped at the door; he wasn't allowed to decorate inside. When the wind blows, you can hear the house before you see it. Fourteen thousand marbles are set in concrete in the garden. Ripley's Believe It or Not estimated that Milkovisch drank 50,000 cans while working on his eccentrosity.

John Milkovisch's Beer Can House, 222 Malone St, north off Memorial Dr between Shepherd Dr and Loop 610, Houston, TX 77007; ✆ 713 862 3238

Ira Poole's yard in Austin stops people in their tracks; a thousand pound sphinx tends to do that. The big guy is resting on a slab the shape of Texas, surrounded by the Statue of Liberty, a relief map of the United States and Mexico, and another Texas map with a yellow rose bush growing from the heart of it. Poole's yard is a convenient stop on the way to or from the airport.

Ira Poole's yard, 2400 E Martin Luther King Blvd, Austin, TX

Just plain weird
It's hard to resist the urge to play hide-and-seek among the 'stones' at **Stonehenge II**, a retirement project that kept Doug Hill and Al Shepperd busy for nine months building it. Using steel posts, rebar, mesh, concrete and plaster, the pals created a smaller-scaled version of the real thing in a field by the highway, causing many a car to slam on its brakes – and its occupants to stare in disbelief – at the totally unexpected sight. They did it just for the fun of it and you're welcome to walk through an opening in the fence and play for a while among the ten-year-old ruins. The site also contains two replicas of the statues found on Easter Island.

Stonehenge II located in Hunt, TX; web:
www.alfredsheppard.com/stonehenge/untitled.html

In honor of Route 66, the American Mother Road, millionaire Stanley Marsh III, planted ten Cadillac cars, fin ends up, noses down, into the ground on a Texas plain west of Amarillo. The spectacle, known as **Cadillac Ranch** has become a shrine to the open road, accessible for worship in Amarillo day and night. All the 1949–1964 cars came from junkyards or used-car lots and had their hubcaps and wheels welded on to minimize vandalism. Graffiti artists have their way with them, which only adds to their charm. In 1977, Marsh had to dig them up and move them a mile further away from the fast encroaching city.

Cadillac Ranch located near Love's Truck Stop at Arnot Rd in Amarillo, TX

You can hock your gun, buy your fiancée a diamond ring and marry her, all in the same place at the same time. **Ted Kipperman** runs the only pawn shop/wedding chapel in the world. A mail-order chaplain, Kipperman will rent you everything you need for a memorable ceremony under a plastic flower canopy.

Ted Kipperman's Pawn Shop/Wedding Chapel on East Bellfort near Mykawa, Houston, TX

Attractions

There are probably as many dinosaurs in Moscow, Texas as there are people. A lonely attraction, **Dinosaur Gardens** has 11 of the fiberglass beasts laid out along a woodsy trail behind Donald Bean's home. He saved up for 20 years to build his dinosaur dreamland, much to the dismay of his wife who has to work to support his obsession, since the attraction has failed to attract many visitors. Bean spends all his time playing in his garden, creating sound effects, hiding speakers in trees and experimenting with environmental settings like jungles and swamps.

Dinosaur Gardens located on US 59 near intersection of FM 62, Moscow, TX. *Open daily Jun–Labor Day 10.00am–6.00pm; weekends Sep–Oct and Mar–May 10.00am–6.00pm; closed Nov–Feb. Admission charge.*

Most everything is larger than life in Texas, and Billy Bob's is no exception. Known as the **World's Largest Honky Tonk** (dance hall), the Fort Worth attraction has 40 bar stations, real bull-riding, a photo 'bull' for the less adventurous and a dance floor big enough to hold a several jumbo jets full of foot stompin' folk. Besides hosting rodeos, livestock auctions and country music concerts, all held inside the enormous facility, Billy Bob's has served as a setting for numerous movies and television shows. Six thousand people can fit inside.

Billy Bob's World's Largest Honky Tonk, 2520 Rodeo Plaza, Fort Worth, TX 76106; ↘ 817 624 7117; fax: 817 626 2340; web: www.billybobstexas.com

The last thing you'd expect to see in Texas is a scaled-down version of ancient China, but **Forbidden Gardens**, an outdoor cultural center in Katy, is just that. Complete with zither music and koi fish, the garden has remarkable replicas of the Forbidden City and the 7,000 terracotta soldiers of Emperor Qin's army, modeled in fiberglass at about one-third the size of those in Xi'an. Highlights of China's history are portrayed throughout the 40-acre garden, with intricately detailed people and buildings.

Financed by a reclusive Hong Kong millionaire living in Seattle, the project gets a new exhibit every year or so, built in China and installed by the Chinese artisans who make it. That's about the only contact park employees have with their eccentric benefactor who's only visited the park a few times since its opening in 1996.

Forbidden Gardens, 23500 Franz Rd, Katy, TX 77493; ↘ 281 347 8000; email: fgarden@btc.net; web: www.forbidden-gardens.com

Texans do everything up B-I-G, and the **Buckhorn Hall of Horns** in San Antonio proves it. If you counted, you'd find 4,000 antlers in just one of their chandeliers.

Buckhorn Hall of Horns, 318 E Houston St, San Antonio, TX 78204; ↘ 210 247 4000; fax: 210 247 4020; web: www.buckhornmuseum.com

Museums and collections

Old Sparky is the star attraction at the **Huntsville Texas Prison Museum**, having played host to 361 condemned prisoners over a 40-year period. The electric chair, now retired, is a stark reminder that Texas executes more prisoners than any other state in the union, and that Texas has the country's second largest prison population after California. The inmate who built the chair never had to test it out; he was eventually released, un-fried.

The museum paints a fascinating portrait of prison life, showcasing the peculiar, often bizarre, ways inmates coped with the culture inside the walls. Confiscated weapons, fashioned from anything from forks to toothbrushes, could be amazingly deadly. Toilet-paper art helped pass the time, as did lifting weights, visiting the chapel and working in the laundry. One inmate carved a sculpture with 20 different animals and faces, completing it during several prison stints interrupted by periods of parole. The prison hardware, such as whips and balls and chains, make you glad you followed the path of righteousness.

A letter from gangster Clyde Barrow, of Bonnie and Clyde fame, written to Henry Ford, praises the V8 engine as an excellent choice for a getaway car. You can try on a 9-foot by 6-foot cell for size, and pick up a copy of the Prison Driving Tour so you don't miss anything, like the arena used for prison rodeos until insurance difficulties shut it down in 1986.

Huntsville Texas Prison Museum, 1113 12th St, Huntsville, TX; ↘ 936 295 8113 or 800 289 0389. *Open Tue–Fri 12.00noon–5.00pm; Sat 9.00am–5.00pm; Sun 12.00noon–5.00pm. Admission charge.*

Today it's against the law to collect or sell bird eggs, but that wasn't the case back in 1880 when D A Cleveland collected and preserved hundreds of eggs representing hundreds of North American species. The collection of eggs from water birds, game birds, birds of prey and song birds can be seen at the **Texas Bird Egg Collection** at Waggoner Ranch in Vernon.

Texas Bird Egg Collection, Waggoner Ranch, 1905 1/2 Wilbarger, Vernon, TX 76384; ↘ 817 552 2506

The **Devil's Rope Museum** is dedicated solely to barbed-wire fencing, the invention that finally tamed the American West. Exhibits containing almost 700 different kinds of barbed wire explore the evolution of the cowboy, the history of brands and branding, the kinds of wire used in range warfare and demonstrations in the art of making barbed wire. Strangely enough, barbed wire is collectible. In order to get a patent, every wire manufacturer had to submit a design that included a completely original 'twist' to the barb. Collectors are a determined bunch, seeking to locate hundreds of unique specimens. They even have a magazine, the *Barbed Wire Collector*. Barbed-wire people may also want to turn to page 305.

Devil's Rope Museum, PO Box 290, McLean, TX 79057; ↘ 806 779 2225; email: barbwiremuseum@centramedia.net; web: www.barbwiremuseum.com. Located in McLean, Texas, 75 miles east of Amarillo, on I-40 and Old Route 66. Directions: take exits 141, 142 and 143 to 'The Heart Of Old Route 66' at 100 Kingsley St.

Every red-blooded boy in America dreamed of being a Texas Ranger when he grew up. At the **Texas Ranger Hall of Fame and Museum** in Waco, you'll see the allure as the Ranger's proud history of fightin' the bad guys is displayed in all its glory. They always got their man, and have gone down in history as the heroes of the frontier. Today they're still catchin' 'em, but the job is substantially less romantic.

Texas Ranger Hall of Fame and Museum, 100 Texas Ranger Trail, Waco, TX 76706; ➘ 254 750 8631; fax: 254 750 8629; web: www.texasranger.org. Located at Interstate 35 Exit 335-B

Presenting the Dr Pepper story as an example of how wonderful the free enterprise system is, the **Dr Pepper Museum and Free Enterprise Institute** in Waco is a strange mix of capitalism and patriotism. The cherry-flavored cola beverage was introduced in 1904, the same time as the hamburger, the hot dog and the ice-cream cone. In true American fashion, the product went through many advertising incarnations, including a stint in the 1920s when it was billed as the 'drink a bite to eat at 10, 2, and 4' beverage, referring to new research which shed light on sugar's ability to give you an energy lift.

The museum, which defines free enterprise as 'the freedom of individuals and businesses to operate and compete with a minimum of government interference or regulation', aims its exhibits at school-age children, hoping to plant the seeds of entrepreneurial initiative and libertarianism early on in life. Part of the museum's mission is to use the soft drink industry to show how Americans do business.

Dr Pepper Museum and Free Enterprise Institute, 300 South Fifth St, Waco, TX; ➘ 254 757 1024; web: www.drpeppermuseum.org. Directions: take IH35 into Waco, exit at the 4th and 5th Sts exit, turn West on 4th Street, go to Mary Ave, turn left on Mary. The museum is on the corner of 5th St and Mary.

Pest control specialist Michael Bohdan, aka Cockroach Dundee, has one heck of a show-and-tell exhibit. He's appeared with his **Cockroach Hall of Fame** on every major television and news channel in the country and is the author of *What's Buggin You*, a book covering his 20 years spent chasing down creepy-crawlies. With four-inch-long roaches that hiss on command, a safari hat covered with roaches and roaches dressed up in costumes, Michael makes for an entertaining guest.

Look for Liberoachi, a roach (dead, of course) wearing a white mink cape and sitting at an itty-bitty piano. Or a spike-heeled, blonde-wigged Marilyn Monroach. Each August he has a contest that draws 2,000 entries for the largest roach of the year as well as the most sensational roach of art. The winners get a cash prize while the bugs get to reign on a throne in the Hall of Fame. The museum is located in Plano.

Cockroach Hall of Fame, The Pest Shop, 2231-B West 15th St, Plano, TX 75075; ➘ 972 519 0355; web: www.pestshop.com

DOTCOMGUY

On New Year's Day, 2000, Mitch Maddox, 26, legally changed his name to DotComGuy, moved into a completely empty townhouse and lived totally off the internet for an entire year. All his necessities, as well as his luxuries, were obtained online, including his food, his furnishings, his clothes and his pet, DotComDog. Two dozen cameras tracked his (almost) every move, so he's learned to think out loud, verbalizing the random thoughts running through his head so viewers won't get bored.

Even though DotComGuy's financing now comes partly from corporate sponsorships, he initiated the plan entirely on his own, ignoring the 'yea, right!' yuks and scoffs from family and friends. He keeps a daily journal, which you can follow on his website, along with his daily schedule, website reviews and DotComGuy chats. Besides the fact that he doesn't venture further than his back yard, he lives a somewhat normal life, entertaining friends, reading, working on the computer, 'meeting' new people, and forming deep bonds with Federal Express and UPS. He even served as a 'big brother' for the Big Brother, Big Sister mentor program. A Dallas radio station reported that he intends to marry a woman he met in his chatroom.

web: www.dotcomguy.com

An eye-opening look at the American funeral customs is graphically presented at the **National Museum of Funeral History** in Houston. From icebox caskets, which kept the body 'fresh' in pre-embalming days; to bizarre caskets, such as the casket built for three; to the ostentatious, like the all-glass casket which proved too heavy for even ten pallbearers to lift, the museum is a fascinating look at the history of burial customs. Mourning attire, jewelry made from the deceased's hair, memorabilia of the funerals of the rich and famous, death wagons and hearses, along with a video on the Value of the Funeral, make this a memorable place to spend a few hours dealing with the inevitable. The entrance to the museum has a 'Find a Famous Grave' kiosk which leads you electronically to the remains of the previously famous.

A recent addition is the collection of fantasy coffins from Ghana, where elaborate coffins are designed to capture the essence of the dead they contain. On display are coffins depicting a KLM airplane, a Mercedes car, various boats, animals and even an outboard motor. You can pass the time on the next long leg of your journey trying to imagine what would happen if this custom caught on here.

National Museum of Funeral History, 415 Barton Springs Dr, Houston, TX 77090; ☏ 281 876 3063; fax: 281 876 2961; web: www.nmfh.org

TEXAS ART

Two guys from Texas, known as the **Art Guys**, personify wackiness, With deadpan humor, wildly inventive concepts and peculiar performances, they tickle the country's funny bone – assuming you're sophisticated enough to get the joke. One recent project, SUITS, had them proposing to sell advertising space on specially tailored suits and then making spectacles of themselves by wearing the things. On their website, they explain they will use the suits to further the image of anyone who wishes to advertise on them. Another project had them producing an innocent little box with the words 'Do Not Open' on the lid. When curiosity prevailed, you'd find yourself looking at words printed on the underside of the lid: Do Not Close'. Their most recent stunt has billboards that get a new coat of paint every day. If one goes up in your neighborhood, it's entertaining to watch the billboard change colors, and the counter going up, on a daily basis. Their website keeps you up to speed on their shenanigans.

web: www.theartguys.com.

Tours

For a truly macabre ride, take the **JFK Presidential Limo Tour** in Dallas. Riding in a restoration of the slain president's 1962 open-air Lincoln limo, complete with presidential trimmings, you travel the motorcade route, hearing historically correct surround sound enhancements along with the narration. Very spooky.

> **JFK Presidential Limo Tour**, 5942 Abrams Rd, #127, Dallas, TX 75231; ↘ 214 348 7777; fax: 214 750 0303

Austin's **Graveyard Chronicles tour van** goes out once a month to explore four cemeteries filled with history and intrigue from Austin's past. And every weekend, **Austin Promenade Tours** offers Ghosts, Murder and Mayhem, a walking tour of the sinister side of Austin.

> **Graveyard Chronicles tour van** goes out once a month, Austin, TX; ↘ 512 498 4686; email: reserve@promenadetours.com; web: www.promenadetours.com

> **Austin Promenade Tours**, ↘ 512 498 GOTO; email: reserve@promenadetours.com; web: www.promenadetours.com

Quirky quarters

Gretchen Asbury and her husband, Roddy, moved from the Big Apple to the quirky little town of Hund. After restoring a hand-hewn log cabin, they decided to open **Roddy Tree Ranch Bed and Breakfast**. They now have 13 cabins, each decorated with a different theme. Husband Roddy, an Elvis impersonator, is restoring an old 1969 summer-of-love psychedelic bus into a rock 'n roll museum. The Stonehenge replica is right up the road (see page 278).

Roddy Tree Ranch Bed and Breakfast, PO Box 820, Hunt, TX 78024; ❧ 830 367 2871 or 800 309 9868; fax: 830 367 2872; email: cabins@roddytree.com; web: www.roddytree.com

At **Cibilo Creek Ranch** you can experience what it was like to live in a fort designed to protect its inhabitants from Indian attacks. The luxury ranch, just north of the Mexican border, manages to let you experience the rugged isolation of the Texas frontier despite its five-star reputation for quality, pampering and price. Restoration of the three-fort complex was meticulous, with no visible evidence of modern conveniences anywhere; some bathrooms even have to be entered through a fake armoire.

Cibilo Creek Ranch, Box 44, Shafter, TX 79850. Located 32 miles south of Marfga on Hwy 67; ❧ 915 229 3737; web: cibilocreekranch.com

NEW MEXICO

Californians pride themselves on their weirdness, putting it out there for the whole world to see. New Mexicans are equally weird, only nobody knows about it. They keep pretty much to themselves and it can be quite a surprise to find yourself face-to-face with some mighty strange people doing mighty strange things. The state is a freaky place, home to secret government projects, ghost towns, UFO fanatics and an extra-terrestrial communication facility. And that's only for starters.

Festivals and events

He's big, he's ugly and he gets bigger and uglier with each passing year. Volunteers spend 1,500 hours creating the monster, only to see their efforts go up in smoke at the culmination of the annual **Burning of Zozobra Fiestas de Santa Fe**.

The gruesome effigy is ceremoniously strung up then set aflame, taking with him all of Santa Fe's troubles for another year. The festival, celebrated since 1712, is America's oldest civic celebration. The puppet became a symbol of the Fiestas de Santa Fe in 1926; the community service club, the Kiwanis, has sponsored the burning since 1963.

It takes two weeks to build Zozobra. He waits behind city hall, illuminated by green fires, for the procession of Kiwanians dressed in black robes and hoods. The mayor proclaims the death sentence, the green fires change to red and Zozobra is toast. The Kiwanis throw off their robes and emerge in costume, leading a torch light parade to the tune of 'La Cucaracha'.

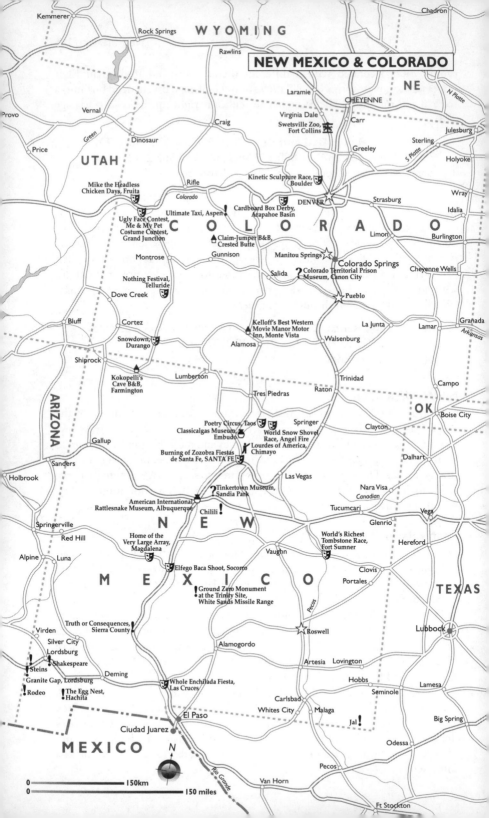

Burning of Zozobra Fiestas de Santa Fe held annually in
September in Santa Fe, NM. Contact Santa Fe Convention and
Visitors Bureau; email: scenter@ci.santa-fe.nm.us; web:
www.santafe.org

If riding a snow shovel down a slope sounds like child's play, think again.
Shovel racing is a daredevil sport and shovel athletes have been clocked going
more than 60mph. The **World Snow Shovel Race** in Angel Fire has three
race categories. Basic production is where you simply nestle into the scoop of a
standard shovel, place the handle between your feet and legs, and shoot down
the 1,000-foot course, desperately flailing and dragging your hands to gain
some semblance of control. The modified class attaches the shovel to a
contraption such as a modified bobsled, luge or dragster framework, while the
modified unique class is supremely wacky. An entire living room has gone
down the 1,585-foot slope at 40mph, followed by a doghouse, only to be beaten
by a chicken sandwich. These contraptions are built to entertain and amuse.

World Snow Shovel Race held annually in February in Angel Fire,
NM. Contact Angel Fire Resort, Angel Fire, NM; ↘ 505 377 4237;
email: events@angelfireresort.com; web: www.angelfireresort.com

The **Taos Poetry Circus** is a nine-day extravaganza of poetry competitions.
Readings are scored competitively and there are both individual and team
events. The audience is invited to hoot and holler at the dramatic
presentations, attracting folks who normally would prefer root canal surgery to
a poetry reading.

Taos Poetry Circus held annually in June in Taos, NM. Contact
World Poetry Bout Association, 232 Paseo del Pueblo Sur, 5275
NDCBU, Taos, NM 87571; ↘ 505 758 1800; email:
spha@laplaza.org; web: www.poetrycircus.org

America's obsession with the paranormal is abundantly evident at the **Roswell
UFO Encounter Festival and Intergalactic Fashion and Food
Extravaganza**. This event celebrates the mysterious crash of an unidentified
flying object (UFO) in Roswell on July 8, 1947. At first, the government
claimed that the fallen debris was really a spaceship. Days later, it retracted its
story, claiming it was really a weather balloon. Fifty years later, in 1997, it
changed its story once again, claiming it was really a secret spy satellite.

Regardless of what the government says, thousands of people believe it was
really a spaceship. Countless documentaries claim that space creatures were
killed in the crash and that the government has been covering it up all these
years.

At the festival, you'll hear all about breeding experiments and alien autopsies
and see the world's largest UFO Parade. An alien costume contest, a

trade show and homemade spaceships will keep your camera snapping at the atmosphere. The Intergalactic Fashion and Food Extravaganza caps off the activities. The event draws thousands of abductees, conspiracy theorists, skeptics, believers, and just plain folk who gather to enjoy the weirdness.

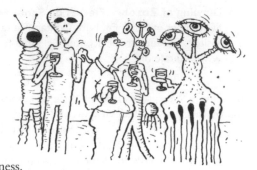

Be prepared to shed some of your skepticism; the evidence and hype can be pretty persuasive.

> **Roswell UFO Encounter Festival and Intergalactic Fashion and Food Extravaganza** held annually in June in Roswell, NM. Contact Roswell UFO Encounter, PO Box 2587, Roswell, NM 88202; ✆ 505 624 6860; fax: 505 6224 6863; email: info@RoswellUFOEncounter.com; web: www.roswellufoencounter.com

The infamous outlaw, Billy the Kid, is buried behind the old Fort Sumner Museum. During its annual festival, the museum puts on the **World's Richest Tombstone Race**. Since Billy the Kid's tombstone has been stolen three times, once spending 27 years in a Texas boxcar, the Fort gives each entrant a replica of the actual tombstone, weighing 80 pounds. They have to carry the thing up to an obstacle, throw it over to the other side, jump the obstacle themselves, pick up the tombstone again and come back. Women get to race with a 20-pound stone. Entrants are really motivated to win – the prize is $1,000 cash.

> **World's Richest Tombstone Race** held annually in June during Old Fort Days in Fort Sumner, NM. Contact Fort Sumner Chamber of Commerce, De Bacca County Chamber of Commerce, 707 N 4th St, Fort Sumner, NM 88119; ✆ 505 355 7705

Robert Estrada gives new meaning to the expression 'the whole enchilada'. The **Whole Enchilada Fiesta** in Las Cruces is a three-day event centered around the making of the world's largest enchilada. Estrada designed the technique and equipment needed to make the monster tortilla. Two-hundred-and-fifty pounds of dough is pressed on a tray which it takes 14 men to carry to a cooking vat. The tortilla is cooked in 550-degree oil in a trampoline-size vat. Then Robert ladles on the three layers of chili sauce, cheese and onions. Two-and-a-half hours later, the enchilada is ready to be shared by hundreds of spectators.

> **Whole Enchilada Fiesta**, PO Box 8258, Las Cruces, NM 88006; ✆ 505 524 6832; email: info@twefie.com

The **Elfego Baca Shoot** is long-distance golf played from a mountain top with the starting hole on a 7,280 foot peak. Each golfer gets ten specially painted balls at the start along with a scorekeeper and three spotters who attempt to keep track of their golfer's balls. Since the average distance to a hole is two-and-a-half miles as the crow flies, the spotter's role is crucial. During play a ball can be moved up to 50 feet laterally from the hole to improve position. All in all, it takes about two-and-a-half hours to play the 'course' and the players move from hole to hole in 4WD vehicles. A low gross score and the lowest ball count determines the winner.

> **Elfego Baca Shoot** held annually in June in Socorro, NM. Located on I-25 approx 65 miles south of Albuquerque. Contact New Mexico Institute of Mining and Technology;➘ 505 835 5725; to register ➘ 505 835 1550

Just plain weird

Only in America would a town hold an election for the sole purpose of deciding whether to change its name to that of a television show. In a previous incarnation, the town was named Palomas Springs, later changed in 1914 to Hot Springs. Then along came television and a silly game show, hosted by a man named Ralph Edwards, called **Truth or Consequences**.

Mr Edwards offered a challenge to any city willing to change its name to Truth or Consequences: he'd broadcast a show from that city or town. A special election was held here and the yeas had it. But 295 residents challenged the results, so another election was held, this time with even more yeas than before. In the 50 years since the name was changed, the issue has been on the ballot two more times, each time retaining the strange name wins.

> **Truth or Consequences**, Sierra County, NM. Contact Truth or Consequences/Sierra County Chamber of Commerce and Visitors Center, PO Box 31, Truth or Consequences, NM 87901; ➘ 800 831 9487; email: cofc@riolink.com; web: www.village.golaldrum.com/sierra_newmexico

The arid desert plains near Magdalena are home to the **Very Large Array** near Socorro, the most powerful radio telescope in the world. Its 27-dish antennas, ten stories high and spread out over 22 miles in a 'Y' formation, can detect extremely faint radio transmissions from distant stars. Astronomers and other scientists apply each year for observing time. UFO types hope the first 'ET, phone home' signal will come through here. The visitor center offers a slide show, displays, and a self guided tour.

> **Very Large Array** located in Magdalena in southwest New Mexico along US Hwy 60. Contact National Radio Astronomy Observatory Public Information Office, PO Box O, Socorro, NM 87801; web: www.nrao.edu

The **Ground Zero Monument** at the Trinity Site is a sobering reminder of the horrors of war. It was here that the United States, on July 16 1945, unveiled the terrifying power of the atom bomb, changing the course of history with a thundering roar. Aside from the black-and-white photos of the event, there isn't much to see except desert, some green 'trinitrite', which is what you get when you melt sand, and a replica of Fat Man, the code name for a bomb casing similar to the ones used a few weeks later to drop atomic bombs on Japan. The monument itself, a lava stone and concrete obelisk, is a strange, grim photo op.

> **Ground Zero Monument** at the Trinity Site located on the northern end of the 3,200 square mile White Sands Missile Range, NM, between Carrizozo and Socorro, NM. Contact White Sands Missile Range Public Affairs Office; ☏ 505 678 1134 or 505 678 1700; web: www.wsmr.army.mil/paopage/Pages/Trinst.htm. *Open to visitors twice annually; first Sat in Apr and Oct.*

Chilili boasts a cemetery in which dozens of the tombstones are made of tin sheets mounted on marble pedestals. The memorials were made by Horace McAfee, today a cemetery resident, who laboriously punched out the entire wording on the tins using just a nail. McAfee was also responsible for the tin angels and the tin sheet explaining his own views on the afterlife.

> **Chilili, NM.** Directions: from Albuquerque take NM I-40 west to Tijeras then south on 337. Contact Albuquerque Visitors Bureau, PO Box 28666, Albuquerque, NM 87125; ☏ 800 733 9918 or 505 842 9918; web: www.abqcvb.org

New Mexico is home to several ghost towns, relics of the short lived boom towns that flourished during the silver rush of the 1870s. The Hill family gives weekend tours of **Shakespeare**, where Billy the Kid supposedly worked as a dishwasher. The place feels eerie, like a movie set waiting for folks to come back and pick up their lives where they left off. **Steins**, an old railroad town of the 1900s, lies just off the highway. In 1988, Larry Link stopped by and found an old coot with a shotgun keeping looters away. Larry and his wife, Linda, ended up buying the town; the whole place is like a museum. Meanwhile, **Granite Gap**, owned by Klondike Mike and Jackass Jill, provides a look at the turn-of-the-century tunnels that honeycomb through Granite Mountain. In Hachita, the **Egg Nest** is a restaurant and shop featuring museum-quality music boxes made out of unfertilized eggshells. Marlene and Pat Harris have been making them for 15 years. The ghost town of **Rodeo** boasts a collection of 2,000 license plates at Kathy's gift shop. And, owner Lois Bernard doesn't print a menu at the Rodeo's tavern restaurant. She'd rather stand there and talk to you. Now that's really eccentric.

Shakespeare, NM located in Hidalgo County, NM. Contact Lordsburg-Hidalgo Chamber of Commerce, 208 E Motel Dr, Lordsburg, NM 88045; ↘ 505 542 9864; email: lordsburgcoc@gilanet.com; web: www.gilanet.com/lordsburgcoc

Steins, NM along Interstate 10 in Southern New Mexico near the Arizona border. Contact Lordsburg-Hidalgo Chamber of Commerce, 208 E Motel Dr, Lordsburg, NM 88045; ↘ 505 542 9864; email: lordsburgcoc@gilanet.com; web: www.gilanet.com/lordsburgcoc

Rodeo, NM located in Hidalgo County, NM, along US Hwy 80 between Douglas, AZ and Road Forks, NM. Contact Lordsburg-Hidalgo Chamber of Commerce, 208 E Motel Dr, Lordsburg, NM 88045; ↘ 505 542 9864; email: lordsburgcoc@gilanet.com; web: www.gilanet.com/lordsburgcoc

Granite Gap located on NM 80, 17 miles north of Rodeo, west of Lordsburg, NM; ↘ 505 557 2266

Egg Nest, Hachita, NM. Contact Lordsburg-Hidalgo Chamber of Commerce, 208 E Motel Dr, Lordsburg, NM 88045; ↘ 505 542 9864; email: lordsburgcoc@gilanet.com; web: www.gilanet.com/lordsburgcoc

You see them way off in the distance: cowboys driving cattle across the barren, desolate landscape. As you get closer to **Jal**, a dusty place with 2,000 hearty souls, you notice that the horses and cows aren't moving. That's because they're made of steel: 17 enormous silhouettes created by artist Brian Norwood. Each of the cowboy, horse and cow silhouettes was cut from a ten-foot by 40-foot piece of steel, weighing 4,000 pounds apiece. Jal raised the funds to install the 400-foot sculpture, hoping to encourage tourists to stop in the town.

Brian also created an 80-foot by 100-foot map of the United States on an elementary school playground. Each state is outlined in parking-lot white paint; the states themselves are painted in color. Alaska alone required over a gallon of red paint.

Jal, located in Lea County, southeast corner of New Mexico. Contact City of Jal, 523 Main St, Jal, NM 88252; ↘ 505 395 2222

Attractions

Tinkertown Museum in Sandia Park started off as a hobby almost 40 years ago when Ross Ward began carving an animated, miniature western town. When he'd finished the town, he built an entire three-ring circus, a circus parade, a menagerie and a side-show. But he still wasn't done. He needed a place to put all this. Fifty thousand recycled bottles later, he had his buildings.

Ward got the inspiration for his first creations as a nine year old, visiting Knott's Berry Farm and coming home with a desire for an old west town of his very own. The bottle idea came while visiting Grandma Prisby's Bottle Village, a famous Simi Valley, California, site. Ross is just a born tinkerer; he even tinkered as a profession, painting carnival rides and fun houses all over the country. When he and his wife Carla retired, they built the kind of place that had always attracted them in their own travels.

Tinkertown Museum, Sandia Park, NM; ↘ 501 281 5223; web: www.tinkertown.com Directions: take I 40 and NM I4 on NM 536, 17 miles east of Albuquerque to the Turquoise Trail.

In 1910, Father Abeyta saw a glowing light that led him to a crucifix buried in the ground. The next day a group of men carried the crucifix to the church. The day after that it was gone, only to be found back where the good Father had originally found it. Again it was carried to the church and again it ended up back in the ground. Church leaders took this as an omen and built a chapel on the site preferred by the traveling crucifix.

Today, the chapel at El Santuario is called the **Lourdes of America**. People come from all over to meditate and to seek a cure for whatever ails them. The prayer room is filled with discarded crutches and handmade memorials to the personal miracles that have occurred there. During Holy Week, several hundred thousand people make a pilgrimage to the shrine.

Lourdes of America located at the chapel at El Santuario, Chimayo, NM. Contact Santuario de Chimayo, PO Box 235, Chimayo, NM 87522

Museums and collections

Before the bald eagle was adopted as America's symbol, the rattlesnake had that honour. During the revolution, soldiers waved flags at the British that pictured a big rattlesnake with 13 rattles and the phrase, 'Don't Tread On Me'.

You can see this flag, and more than 30 kinds of rattlesnakes, at the **American International Rattlesnake Museum** in Albuquerque. Bob Meyers, a former biology teacher, opened the museum to promote a kindlier, more gentle attitude toward this much maligned snake. The museum dispels the myths that rattlesnakes go after people, that you'll die from a rattler bite and that the number of its rattles tells a snake's age.

All those statements are false: these snakes only attack when they're threatened and their warning rattle has been ignored. Only a handful of deaths result each year from their venom, and the number of their rattles has nothing to do with their age. In fact, the most dangerous rattlesnakes are the immature ones that haven't developed rattles yet and have very little experience making objective judgements. Remind you of anyone you know?

American International Rattlesnake Museum, 202 San Felipe NW, Suite A, Albuquerque, NM 87104; ↘ 505 242 6569; web: www.rattlesnakes.com. *Open daily 10.00am–6.00pm; closed major holidays. Admission charge.*

Both the **UFO Enigma Museum** and the **International UFO Museum and Research Center** claim to have authentic debris found at this well-known UFO crash site. Photos, re-creations, videos, books and displays – some compelling and some ludicrously unbelievable – provide you with an entertaining look at the whole UFO phenomenon. The gift shops are equally amusing. (See also Roswell UFO Encounter Festival, page 287.)

UFO Enigma Museum Roswell located near the entrance of Walker Air Base; ℡ 505 347 2275

International UFO Museum and Research Center, 114 N Main St, PO Box 2221, Roswell, NM 88202; ℡ 505 625 9495; fax: 505 625 1907; web: www.iufomrc.com. *Open daily Oct 1–Apr 30; 10.00am–5.00pm; May 1–Sep 30; 9.00am–5.00pm. Admission free; donations accepted.*

After a decade of collecting old gas-station stuff, Johnnie Meier built the **Classicalgas Museum** in Embudo near his home, using old materials so the building would look like an old gas station. The three pumps out front are from an old Route 66 station. Inside you'll find pumps, globes, advertising signs, oil cans and other memorabilia honoring America's love affair with the car.

Classicalgas Museum, 1819 Hwy 68, Embudo, NM 87531; ℡ 505 852 2995; email: classicalgas@crosswinds.net; web: www.crosswinds.net/~classicalgas

Quirky quarters

Kokopelli's Cave Bed and Breakfast in Farmington is a luxury cliff dwelling north of Farmington near Mesa Verde National Monument. Located 70 feet below the surface, you reach this subterranean B and B by way of a sandstone path, steps carved in the rock and a short ladder. The 1,600-square-foot cave was originally built to house a resident geologist. It's completely furnished with carpeting, southwestern furnishings, plumbing, electricity, a full kitchen and laundry, a waterfall shower and a flagstone hot tub. The

setting is unique – isolated and spectacular – but you really have to want to stay there since the climb can be somewhat arduous and you need to carry your own luggage.

Kokopelli's Cave Bed and Breakfast, 206 W 38th Street, Farmington, NM 87401; ℡ 505 325 7855; fax: 505 325 9671; email: koko@cyberport.com

The **Lightning Field** is like a giant garden of lightning rods. The remote, isolated art installation consists of 400 stainless steel poles arranged in a rectangular grid about a mile long. To fully appreciate the impact of the project, you need to view it over an extended period of time. Thus, up to six visitors can reserve the three-bedroom log cabin located on the site. It's the only way you can see it.

> The **Lightning Field**, c/o Dia Center for the Arts in Quemado, NM, off Route 117 South. Directions: the Dia office is a three-hour drive from Albuquerque. Contact ➤ 505 773 4560 or 505 898 3335; web: diacenter.org/ltproj/lf

COLORADO
Festivals and events

Organizing an event around a headless chicken may sound odd to anyone outside of Fruita, Colorado, but as history shows, festivals arise out of many unusual occurrences.

Mike the Headless Chicken Days celebrates the 1945 story of farmer Lloyd Olsen and the chicken that refused to become his dinner. The saga began when Lloyd, who was particularly fond of chicken neck, lopped off the head of a rooster up near the base of its skull. To Lloyd's astonishment, losing his head didn't seen to affect the bird. Fluffing up his feathers, he went right on doing what he'd done all his life: pecking for food. True, he could only go through the motions, but that didn't stop him one bit. It didn't even stop him from crowing, although the sound that came out was more like a gurgle. When Lloyd found the rooster still alive the next morning, he used an eye dropper to put food and water directly down its gullet. After a week of successful feedings, he took the bird, now named Mike, to a university where they determined Mike had just enough brain stem left to continue acting like a chicken.

Lloyd, knowing a good thing when he spotted it, signed on as Mike's public relations agent and took him on the road for personal appearances. The decapitated bird gained fame and fortune, posing for *Life* magazine and making it into the *Guinness Book of World Records*. He lived two profitable years before choking to death on a kernel of corn in 1947. Others tried to create their own Mikes, but the best of the copybirds lived only eleven days. A statue of Mike, made from rakes, axes and other sharp implements, now stands proudly in town, providing an especially weird photo op.

The events at Mike the Headless Chicken Days include a Run Like a Headless Chicken race, egg tosses, Pin the Head on the Chicken, a Cluck Off,

Rubber Chicken Juggling and, of course, the Chicken Dance. Chicken bingo is played with chicken droppings on a grid and great quantities of chicken are enjoyed by all. You can even buy a bar of headless chicken soap.

Mike the Headless Chicken Days held annually in May in Fruita, CO; ↘ 877 680 7379; email: mike@miketheheadlesschicken.org; web: www.miketheheadlesschicken.org

Toss it, hurl it, launch or drive it. One way or another, you'll get rid of that dreadful fruitcake during the January **Fruitcake Toss**. You've got several ways to get the inedible mass out of your life: launching requires some kind of mechanical device capable of thrusting the thing into the air; tossing involves throwing it; and hurling gets you one fling on the official catapult. If you're a golfer, you get one swing to see who can drive their cake the furthest without hitting it out of the park. There's a fruitcake carving event, a fruitcake relay race and recognition for the fruitcake that traveled the most miles to take part in the festivities. If you think you have the ugliest or the most beautiful fruitcake, you might want to save it for the glamour competitions

If you weren't lucky enough to get your very own concoction of glacé fruit, nuts and flour during the holidays, you can rent one for a quarter. Ditto the golf club. Parking tip: fruitcakes travel from west to east, so don't park on the east side of the event.

Fruitcake Toss held annually in January in Manitou Springs, CO. Contact Manitou Springs Chamber of Commerce, 384 Manitou Ave, Manitou Springs, CO 80829; ↘ 800 642 2567 or 719 685 5089; web: www. manitousprings.org

The legend of Emma Crawford lives on in Manitou Springs when coffins, complete with Emmas riding inside, race up the town's main street during the **Emma Crawford Coffin Races** in October. The races are the legacy of one Emma Crawford, an 1800s spiritualist who thought she saw her Indian guide waiting for her on a mountaintop. When she died of illness at a tragically young age, she was buried on the mountain top where she remained until a powerful storm washed the coffin down into town and a tradition was born. A team of four mourners pulls each coffin that is mounted on tiny wheels; the fastest and most creative coffins and teams get a prize. That evening 'ghosts' lead a tour of Emma's favorite haunts, telling tall tales and spinning yarns.

Emma Crawford Coffin Races held annually in October in Manitou Springs, CO. Contact Manitou Springs Chamber of Commerce; ↘ 719 685 5089 or 800 642 2567; web: www.manitousprings.org

Thirty thousand people are on hand each spring to witness human-powered, hand-made machines conquer the deep water and muddy beaches of the Boulder Reservoir at the **Kinetic Sculpture Race**. Prior to the race itself, a parade is held to judge the strange crafts for popularity and style, and the participants for costumes and theme creativity. The course is three miles long, two thirds of it on water. A few craft sink right off the bat, leaving the rest to flounder and splash while trying to sink a competitor's vessel. If they make it across the water, they face an obstacle course, with the final challenge being a plunge down a water slide.

> **Kinetic Sculpture Race** held annually in May in Boulder, CO.
> Contact Boulder Visitor Bureau; ✆ 303 442 2911 or the sponsors,
> KBCO radio; ✆ 303 444 5600; web: www.kbco.com

Telluride, an immensely popular resort town, has some sort of festivity going on every weekend during the summer. Every weekend, that is, except one. During the **Telluride Nothing Festival** they celebrate peace and quiet by doing well ... absolutely nothing. A blank banner hangs across the main street and distinctive commemorative T-shirts sell for $20 if you have no sense of humor; $15 if you do. They have a nothing parade, held nowhere and watched by no-one, although they're considering closing Main Street for this in the future. This is a nada-festival for folks who want to revel without a cause. The website thanks you for not participating. No charge.

> **Telluride Nothing Festival** held annually in July in Telluride, CO.
> Contact Telluride Visitor Services, 700 West Colorado Ave, Telluride,
> CO 81435; ✆ 888 605 2578; fax 970 728 6475; email:
> dennis@telluridenothingfestival web: www.telluridenothingfestival.com

At the July **Rolling River Raft Race** in Pueblo, contestants build their rafts out of recycled materials, then try to race them three-and-a-half miles down the river. Racers with the best speed, best costumes, best use of materials, and most creative raft are awarded prizes.

> **Rolling River Raft Race** held annually in July in Pueblo, CO.
> Contact Pueblo Chamber of Commerce, 302 N Santa Fe, Pueblo,
> CO 81003; web: www.pueblo.org

To beat the midwinter doldrums, Durango locals indulge in some pretty weird behavior at their January **Snowdown** festival. The five days of shenanigans take place all over town and involves 60 events, give or take a few, that range from the ridiculous to the absurd.

One of the most popular is the Grand Mashers Cream Pie Hit Squad. A 'contract' is placed, for a fee, on your intended victim. The squad then notifies the target, offering 'protection' for a price. Anyone whose protection has lapsed, or who is uninsured on hit day, will get his or her just desserts.

At the Golf Tournament, bars round town each set up their own miniature indoor golf holes. Golfers, four to a team and dressed in costume, make their way from watering hole to watering hole with predictable results. Bribery is

encouraged to improve your score. Down at the river, there's a portable steam room. To take the Animas River Plunge, you jump into the icy waters, then scramble up the bank to a warm reception. Shop Til You Drop involves a shopping scavenger hunt sponsored by local stores. For the infamous Follies production, townspeople try out in December, hoping their silly, goofy act will survive the final cut.

The Grocery Games involve SPAM™ carving contests, timed shopping-cart events, and frozen turkey bowling. The local hotels sponsor the Bed Races, providing two twin beds on casters. Contestants compete in bed-making speed and bed racing competitions. Guys have their own beauty contest, the Male Review, at which they strut their stuff in beach wear. If there's enough snow, you can join the Snow Sculpture Contest.

Other events include a waiters-waitress race, a bartender's contest, a dos and don'ts fashion show, a jokedown, a snow shoveling contest, skijoring (where a horse and rider pull the skier through an obstacle course), a pet fashion show, and an owner/pet look alike contest. Although it's hard to imagine, they also play ski softball and race kayaks and mountain bikes downhill. Indoors there's a spelling bee, a dance contest and a blackjack freeze out tournament.

The events are numerous and you can sign up for most of them right then and there. Snowdown culminates with the explosion of a single firework left over from July Fourth festivities.

Snowdown held annually in February in Durango, CO. Contact SNOWDOWN Durango, Inc, PO Box 1144, Durango, CO 81302; ☎ 970 382 3737; web: www.snowdown.org

The February **Cardboard Box Derby** at Arapahoe Basin ski resort brings 10,000 people to the slopes to watch a derby of wacky crafts made solely out of paper, string, glue, tape and cardboard. The event has grown so popular that entries are limited to the first 150 folks who sign up. Prizes are given for originality, costumes and construction. The Empire State Building that won last year was more than 30 feet high and crashed about ten feet from the starting line. Another, King Kong, came complete with screaming movie star on the monster's 35-foot 'sky scrapper' entry.

Cardboard Box Derby held annually in February in Arapahoe Basin, CO. Contact: Arapahoe Basin Resort, Arapahoe Basin, CO 80435; ☎ 970 468 0718; email: abasin@colorado.net

Every August the Grand River Renaissance and Fantasy Festival in Grand Junction holds an **Ugly Face and Me and My Pet Costume Contest.** The winner of the ugliest face contest is crowned King of Fools for the year. (You may want to hide family members who might be mistaken for contest entrants!) The pet contest rewards the best pet/human combo.

> **Ugly Face Contest and Me and My Pet Costume Contest** part of the Grand River Renaissance and Fantasy Festival held annually in August in Grand Junction, CO. Contact Grand Junction Jaycees; ↘ 970 523 7841 or 970 241 8706; web: www.faires.com/GrandRiver

Eccentric environments

It's not easy being God's tool. Even Jim Bishop has trouble understanding why he was chosen to work up to 72 hours a week chopping down trees, making his own timbers, and hauling 1,000 tons of rock and concrete up to his elaborate, ten story high, medieval style castle. Constructed by hand, his only assistance is a system of winches, pulleys, and ropes that he operates with the aid of his pickup. He refuses any outside help.

According to Jim, his is the 'world's biggest – with the help of God – one man, physical project. Always open, always free to the public. It's a place of liberty, freedom, and justice. A poor man's Disneyland.'

He's been building **Bishop's Castle** for 30 years now and has big plans for the future, like adding an orchestra balcony, a tunnel through the mountain, a moat and drawbridge, and maybe a second castle for his long-suffering wife. His massive stone and iron structure is, as he says, a monument to hard working people – a castle to satisfy every man's desires. At 55 years old he's still going strong, driven by voices only he can hear.

> **Bishop's Castle**, 1529 Claremont Ave, Pueblo, CO 81004; ↘ 719 564 4366; fax: 719 564 6704; email: pmbishop@gateway.net; web: www.castlecollectables.com

Just plain weird

By his own claim he's the **Ultimate Taxi**: the only recording studio, theater, nightclub, planetarium, toy store, internet connected taxicab in the world. Jon Barns' theater on wheels has been rolling since 1990 and you can join this colorful character most evenings between 7.30pm and 1.00am. You schedule a ride by emailing him or calling his cell phone. He won't drop you at the dentist but he will show you around Aspen in a style to which it would be difficult to become accustomed.

> **Ultimate Taxi**, Aspen, CO; ↘ 970 927 9239; email: jon@ultimatetaxi.com; web: www.ultimatetaxi.com

Attractions

Bill Swets builds funny, strange critters out of litter. His bizarre menagerie in Fort Collins, called the **Swetsville Zoo**, has 160 insects, birds, dinosaurs and robots, all made from scraps of metal, car parts, farm equipment tools, and machinery. His zany roadside stop is world famous for its dinosaurs, dragons, bugs and other odd creatures. It's a labor of whimsy and Bill's just in it for the love of it; it doesn't cost you anything to enjoy his obsession.

Swetsville Zoo, 4801 East Harmony Road, Fort Collins, CO 80525; ⟍ 970 484 9509. *Open daylight hours. Admission free.*

That strange, submarine-looking thing sitting out front of the **Museum of Colorado Prisons** is a real gas chamber. Thirty-two of the 77 men executed at this notorious prison met their maker in that chamber. Known as the 'Hell Hole', this prison had the distinction of housing the only man ever convicted of cannibalism in the United States. You can sit in his cell and wonder about his unique brand of take out.

Thirty-two cells are filled with exhibits and life sized models that bring life behind bars in the old west all too alive. One of them belongs to an 11-year-old convicted murderer. If the gruesome artifacts and stories get to be too much for you, lighten the mood with the photo ops the museum thoughtfully provides.

Museum of Colorado Prisons, PO Box 1229, Canon City, CO 81215; ⟍ 719 269 3015; email: curator@prisonmuseum.org; web: www.prisonmuseum.org. *Directions: Hwy 50 to 1st St, 2 blocks to museum and signs for parking. Museum is next to the prison. Open summer daily 8.30am–6.00pm; winter Fri–Sun 10.00am–5.00pm. Admission charge.*

Finding the elves at the **Denver Museum of Natural History** is like looking for Waldo. The artists who painted the museum's murals weren't allowed to sign their names, so they painted elves into the pictures to serve as their signatures. The museum's 'Oh, ick' exhibit, Edge of the Wild, displays casts of animal excrement to teach visitors all about the eating and digestive processes of various mammals. There are a dozen unusual, innovative experiences guaranteed to elicit 'wows' from both kids and parents.

Denver Museum of Natural History, 2001 Colorado Blvd, Denver, CO 80205; ⟍ 800 925 2250 or 303 322 7009; web: www.dmnh.org. *Open daily 9.00am–5.00pm. Admission charge.*

Quirky cuisine

You can't miss it from the road. A statue of an Aztec King, on top of a bell-shaped tower, on top of a Spanish mansion, is certain to make heads turn. But this is nothing compared to the dining experience awaiting you inside at **Casa Bonita**. Ten themed dining areas, including a mine shaft with a snoring miner and a cavern with water dripping off stalactites, serve up Mexican food in a setting that can only be described as incredible. But the bizarre part is yet to come, for the restaurant is famous for its indoor cliff divers. The divers, often in strange costumes, execute a variety of jumps and spins while hurling themselves off 15- and 30-foot platforms into 14 feet of water. If you tire of this, Black Bart's Hideout awaits; this a set up geared for children and for adults brave enough to act like one. Add in the puppets and the pinatas and you can see why you'll never get bored. You may even forget to eat.

Casa Bonita, 6715 West Colfax Ave, Denver, CO; ❯ 303 232 5115; web: www.casabonitadenver.com

Game is on the walls as well as on the menu at the **Buckhorn Exchange**. This famous restaurant serves real guy food, like rattlesnake, rocky mountain oysters, fried alligator tail, buffalo and elk. Deceased relatives of the animals that contribute to your eating pleasure line the walls. Almost 500 of them give you glassy eyed stares as you dine.

Buckhorn Exchange, 1000 Osage St, Denver, CO; ❯ 303 534 9505; email: info@buckhorn.com; web: www.buckhorn.com

Quirky quarters

Kelloff's Best Western Movie Manor Motor Inn is a movie motel with 54 rooms facing a giant outdoor movie screen. Sound is piped into your room and you have a good view of the screen through a large picture window. If you feel like climbing out of bed, you can visit the snack bar for popcorn and other goodies. Open from mid-May through September, the motel shows new G, PG, and PG-13 releases. You can also drive your car to the movies, listening through drive-in style speakers.

Kelloff's Best Western Movie Manor Motor Inn, 2830 W US Hwy 160, Monte Vista, CO 81144; ❯ 719 852 5921 or 800 771 9468

Jerry Bigelow, owner of the **Claim-Jumper B and B** in Crested Butte, can't let an empty space stay empty for long. Claiming he never throws anything away, the six guest rooms at his inn are decorated with all manner of unexpected stuff. Soda Creek boasts 300 Coke bottles from 50 countries along with a working Coke machine. Prospector's Gulch looks just like a miner's cabin complete with helmets, lamps and pickaxes hanging about. In Captain Corrigan's Cabin you'll sleep with a mounted marlin named Brando. In Ethyl's room you'll discover the fabulous 1950s with automobile memorabilia, including a gas pump and a Studebaker sign. You enter Jack's Cabin through a secret bookcase door. The sporty Fanatic Room houses Jerry's lifelong sporting collection with many autographed items. The dining area has a couch made from the back end of a 1957 De Soto, a biplane hanging from the rafters and mannequins of Presidents Nixon and Gorbachev.

Claim-Jumper B and B, 704 Whiterock Ave, Crested Butte, CO 81224; ❯ 970 349 6471; email: claimjumperjerry@yahoo.com

KANSAS
Festivals and events

Cuba, Kansas really rocks – that's rocking as in chairs. This tiny hamlet raises funds for civic improvements by holding an annual **Rock-a-thon**. Dozens of folks rock 24 hours a day for a week in two rocking chairs, avoiding boredom by being fed and entertained around the clock. They add 30 minutes each year to their rocking good time.

> **Rock-a-thon** held annually in Cuba, KS. Contact Cuba Chamber of Commerce, 515 4th, Cuba, KS 66940; ↘ 913 729 3000

In an event shared with the town of Olney, England, the annual **International Pancake Race** in Liberal commemorates a centuries old legend that began when an English housewife rushed to the Shrove Tuesday shriving service with her pancake skillet still in hand. For 50 years the race has been held on both sides of the pond with an international winner declared after transatlantic comparisons.

> **International Pancake Race** held annually on Fat Tuesday in Liberal, KS. Contact International Pancake Day, PO Box 665, Liberal, KS 67905

Just plain weird

Talking of monuments, they don't get much bigger, at least in cemeteries, than the gargantuan grave memorial left by John Davis, a childless eccentric determined to spend his every dime rather than see his wealth go to his deceased wife's children.

The **Davis Memorial at the Mount Hope Cemetery** in Hiawatha contains ten, life-sized, Italian marble statues depicting Davis' life with his beloved wife who predeceased him in 1930. The statues portray the early years of their marriage, then progress to their life together as they aged, finally ending with Mr Davis seated next to a 'vacant chair', symbolizing his loneliness after his wife died. At his sparsely attended funeral, the preacher commented, 'Everybody has their peculiarities ...' As for John himself, he defended spending his fortune by stating, 'It's my money; I spent it the way I pleased.' Amen.

> **Davis Memorial at the Mount Hope Cemetery**, Hiawatha, KS. Contact Hiawatha Chamber of Commerce, 602 Oregon, Hiawatha, KS 66434; ↘ 785 742 7136

Quench your thirst at a quirky little bar in Hunter run by a little old lady who doesn't know the meaning of the word 'stranger'. You'll have to sign the guestbook and, if you're willing and able, the ceiling as well. Vera sings for her patrons and shoots pool with her cane. To find her, just find Hunter and head for the center of town. **Vera's Bar** is on the main corner.

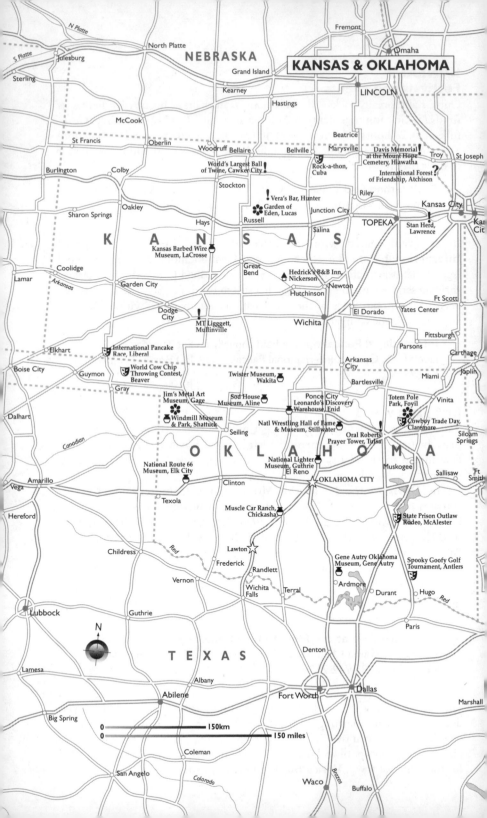

KANSAS & OKLAHOMA

NEBRASKA

N Platte
S Platte
Julesburg
Sterling
North Platte
Fremont
Omaha
Grand Island
Kearney
Hastings
LINCOLN
McCook
St Francis
Oberlin
Woodruff
Bellaire
Bellville
Beatrice
Marysville
Troy
St Joseph
Burlington
Colby
Stockton
World's Largest Ball of Twine, Cawker City
Rock-a-thon, Cuba
Davis Memorial at the Mount Hope Cemetery, Hiawatha
International Forest of Friendship, Atchison
Vera's Bar, Hunter
Riley
K A N S A S
Sharon Springs
Oakley
Hays
Garden of Eden, Lucas
Russell
Junction City
Salina
TOPEKA
Kansas City
Kan City
Stan Herd, Lawrence
Kansas Barbed Wire Museum, LaCrosse
Coolidge
Lamar
Arkansas
Garden City
Great Bend
Hedrick's B&B Inn, Nickerson
Hutchinson
Newton
Ft Scott
Elkhart
Dodge City
MT Ligggett, Mullinville
Wichita
El Dorado
Yates Center
Pittsburgh
Carthage
Boise City
International Pancake Race, Liberal
World Cow Chip Throwing Contest, Beaver
Arkansas City
Bartlesville
Miami
Joplin
Guymon
Gray
Jim's Metal Art Museum, Gage
Twister Museum, Wakita
Sod House Museum, Aline
Ponce City
Leonardo's Discovery Warehouse Enid
Totem Pole Park, Foyil
Vinita
Dalhart
Windmill Museum & Park, Shattuck
Seiling
Natl Wrestling Hall of Fame & Museum, Stillwater
Cowboy Trade Day, Claremore
Siloam Springs
Amarillo
O K L A H O M A
Oral Roberts Prayer Tower, Tulsa
National Route 66 Museum, Elk City
National Lighter Museum, Guthrie El Reno
Muskogee
Sallisaw
Ft Smith
Vega
Clinton
OKLAHOMA CITY
Texola
Hereford
Muscle Car Ranch, Chickasha
State Prison Outlaw Rodeo, McAlester
Childress
Lawton
Frederick
Randlett
Gene Autry Oklahoma Museum, Gene Autry
Spooky Goofy Golf Tournament, Antlers
Vernon
Wichita Falls
Terral
Ardmore
Durant
Hugo
Red
Paris
Lubbock
Guthrie
Marshall
T E X A S
Denton
N
Lamesa
Albany
Abilene
Fort Worth
Dallas
Big Spring
0   150km
0   150 miles
Coleman
San Angelo
Colorado
Waco
Brazos
Buffalo

Vera's Bar, Hunter, Mitchell County, KS; web:
http://skyways.lib.ks.us/counties/MC

The idea of using the land as his canvas just cropped up one day for **Stan Herd**. Stan is a crop artist, meaning he uses plants, rocks, flowers and vegetables to create giant earthworks best appreciated from the air. Given the geography of Kansas, you'll see he couldn't have chosen a better place.

Using a tractor as his brush, he's completed 15 images in 20 years. Some of his work, such as the Absolut vodka bottle he did for a liquor distributor, is for commercial clients, which helps pay the bills. Some is just for the challenge of it, like the landscape image he created on a vacant Trump property in Manhattan.

It was strange to work in the shadow of skyscrapers instead of in the open air of a field, but he had help from an unusual source: the homeless. The vegetables he used in his 'painting' also served as a free supermarket for the needy who harvested the vegetables as they ripened. Better yet, he didn't have to be in a plane to appreciate his efforts; eight stories up worked just fine.

Usually his art lasts for just a single season; occasionally for up to three. But the Amelia Earhart Earthwork is his first attempt at a permanent work of art. An entire acre in size, it's on a hillside near Atchison's International Forest of Friendship (see page 304). He also created a five-acre, interactive corn maze in the shape of a turtle for Pendelton's Country market. The 'Stalk of the Town', 5,000 visitors had played in the turtle maze by the time it closed at harvest.

Stan Herd, 716 Arkansas, Lawrence, KS 66044; ↘ 785 843 3197;
fax: 785 343 3197; email: stan@stanherd.com; web:
www.stanherd.com

What's 40 feet around its middle and weighs 17,000 pounds? The **World's Largest Ball of Twine**. This blob has been part of Cawker City since 1960 when Frank Stoeber, the man who had been working on it for seven years, brought it in. They gave it a spot on Main Street and each year, around Labor Day, the townsfolk add pure twine from hay bales, the only kind of twine allowed.

World's Largest Ball of Twine, Cawker City, KS. Contact the
Cawker City Community Club, PO Box 178, Cawker City, KS 67430;
↘ 785 781 4713 or 785 781 4723; email: twinetown@nckcn.com

M T Liggett of Mullinville uses the fields along Highway 154 to make his opinions known. He's planted dozens and dozens of kinetic, wind-powered, junk sculptures, called 'totems', that mock local and national politicians. His field has become a three-dimensional editorial page, with strange figures such as the Stool Brothers, who have a toilet bowl for a head, and Monica's famous blue dress made out of scrap metal painted blue with dabs of white. The figure of a joker represents a judge with whom he disagrees.

With a never-ending supply of current events to fuel his imagination, this irascible artist continues to add figures to his crop. If he's around when you arrive, he'll happily take you on a highly opinionated tour of his sculptures. Liggett, who isn't afraid of speaking up, is fond of saying, 'A man is never remembered for the words he didn't say.'

M T Liggett, Mullinville, KS 67109; �‾ 316 548 2597. Located along Hwy 154 on west edge of Mullinvlle

Eccentric environments

The **Garden of Eden** in Lucas is frontier eccentricity at its most splendid: the history of the world according to one Samuel Dinsmoor who was gripped by a severe case of concretia dementia in 1905 at the age of 64. Almost defying description, the garden represents Dinsmoor's love of freedom, hatred of big government and big business, and his literal interpretation of the Bible.

At the front of his faux log cabin, in actuality limestone carved to look log-like, Adam and Eve greet you with outstretched arms, forming a gateway to his weird world. A concrete serpent coils in a tree above the pair while a concrete devil watches from a nearby rooftop. A concrete apron, placed there to appease the neighbors, discreetly covers Adam's genitalia. An American flag made of red, white and blue concrete flies above.

Everywhere you look is concrete; 113 tons of it formed into primitive sculptures over a period of 22 years before his death. Dinsmoor's garden has 40-foot trees, huge flags mounted on ball bearings, and hundreds of figures, from bugs to birds to the eye of God. Storks with babies under their wings have light bulbs in their mouths to light their way; children run from demons.

More modern history includes Indians, soldiers, and his quirky tribute to the food chain. Big business and government are lambasted in the Crucifixion of Labor, featuring a doctor, lawyer, banker and preacher nailing the Christ-like figure of Labor to a cross-like tree.

Dinsmoor died in 1933, fully prepared for this event. His mausoleum is in a 40-foot tall building in a corner of his garden; he, himself, is in a glass-sided coffin for all the world to see.

Garden of Eden, 305 East 2nd St, Lucas, KS 67648; �‾ 785 525 6395. *Open daily 10.00am–5.00pm Apr–Oct; 1.00–4.00pm Nov–Mar. Admission charge.*

Attractions

A life-like and life-size bronze statue of Amelia Earhart marks the location of the **International Forest of Friendship**. Atchison, Amelia Earhart's birthplace, is a fitting location for the forest that is made up of trees from all 50 states and from 40 countries around the world. Each tree has its own flag. A tree, grown from a seedling that was taken to the moon on Apollo 14, represents the moon. The forest was a 200th birthday present to the country by the Ninety-Nines, an organization of women pilots.

International Forest of Friendship, Atchison, KS. Contact Atchison Area Chamber of Commerce, PO Box 126, Atchison KS 66002; ꛑ 800 234 1854; fax: 913 367 2485; email: atchcham@journey.com; web: www.atchison.org

Museums and collections

Barbed wire changed the course of western history and the **Kansas Barbed Wire Museum** in La Crosse explains it all for you. The west was nothing but wide open spaces when the settlers arrived. Over time, farmers and ranchers – who got along about as well as oil and water – divided up the land. When barbed wire was invented, farmers fenced their land to prevent herds of livestock from trampling it. Whenever the wire went up, a range war usually ensued. The museum has 700 varieties of the stuff and barbed wire is now a collector's item, fetching up to $400 per section of strand. Also see page 281.

Kansas Barbed Wire Museum, 120 West 1st St, La Crosse, KS; ꛑ 785 222 9900; web: www.rushcounty.org/barbedwiremuseum/

Here's a bank with a quirky sense of humor. In the tiny town of Norton, the First State Bank houses the **Also-Ran Museum**, a collection dedicated to those who ran for president, but didn't win. You'll see a portrait of each loser, along with a description of the election they didn't win.

Also-Ran Museum, First State Bank, 105 West Main St at Hwy 283, Norton, KS 67654; ꛑ 785 877 3341

Quirky quarters

Hedrick's Bed and Breakfast Inn in Nickerson is part of an exotic animal farm that hand-raises giraffe, zebra, llamas, kangaroos, camels, ostriches and emus. Each of its seven rooms is decorated after an animal and its country; you can pet, feed, and even kiss, the animals.

Hedrick's Bed and Breakfast Inn, 7910 N Roy L Smith Rd, Nickerson, KS 67561; ꛑ 316 422 3245 or 888 489 8039; fax: 316 422 3766

OKLAHOMA

Oklahoma has an abundance of weirdly named towns: Gene Autry, Maude, Bowlegs, Romulus and Remus, Trash Hills, Slapout, Hooker, Rain, Snow and Cloudy and, a favorite, Nowhere – located you-know-where.

Festivals and events

A chip is the part of a bovine's meal that goes 'plop' as it hits the ground. Early settlers discovered that buffalo chips, and later cow chips, left by the animals after summer grazing made excellent cooking fuel. So the chips were collected each fall, with whole communities setting out in wagons to load up with their winter fuel. Tossing the chips into the wagon evolved into friendly competitions and today the **World Cow Chip Throwing Contest** in Beaver celebrates this strange art of slinging dung.

Contestants get two chips each, the goal being to throw the chip the farthest. If the poop pops in mid air, the piece that goes the farthest counts. The chips are provided by the county, have to be at least six inches diameter, and can't be altered in any way. The variety of throwing styles will vary depending upon wind direction and speed. Some toss underhanded, others use a Frisbee fling or an Olympic-style shot-put. The record of 182 feet, 3 inches has been standing for 22 years.

> **World Cow Chip Throwing Contest** held annually in April in Beaver, OK. Contact Beaver County Chamber of Commerce, PO Box 878, 33 W 2nd St, Beaver, OK 73932; ↘ 580 625 4726

At the Antlers Springs Golf Course in Antlers, they hold a **Spooky Goofy Golf Tournament** that has you teeing off from the first nine holes on weird things like bed springs, toilets, and cola cans, and using brooms, baseball bats and cue sticks as clubs. The second nine holes are played after dark with glow balls.

> **Spooky Goofy Golf Tournament** held annually in October in Antlers, OK. Contact Antlers Springs Golf Course, Antlers, OK 74523; ↘ 580 298 9900

Shop where the cowboys do at the **Cowboy Trade Day** in Claremore. It's the biggest cowboy swap meet, cowboy craft and western trade show in the country. No yard sale or flea market junk allowed; only cowboy, western and old west merchandise and artifacts. Stock up on spurs, horses, mules, wagons, saddles, hats, chaps, trucks, stock dogs, trailers and hay; Native American art, western wear, boots and farm gear. Cowboy music, poetry and storytelling let you take a load off yer feet; it's an open mike, so you're invited to share if you have something to contribute. You even git in free if you bring your guitar and know how to play it.

Cowboy Trade Day held twice annually in May and October in Claremore, OK. Directions: north of the city on Historic Route 66, watch for the Git 'N Go Store, turn east on to Blue Starr Drive, go 1 mile to Round Up Club. Contact Cowboy Trader; web: www.cowboytrader.com

You've got to be on your good behavior to participate in this rodeo; one screw-up and you're not only off the team, you could be sent to solitary. The Oklahoma **State Prison Outlaw Rodeo** in McAlester is the world's only rodeo that takes place behind prison walls, and the only time every seat in the prison's 12,000-seat arena is filled.

It's not just for state prison inmates either. Inmates from other correctional facilities participate, as do free cowboys from the outside. Real life, tough-as-nails cowpokes go up against real life, tough-as-nails felons, and it isn't always a pretty site. Calf-roping, bull-riding, steer-wrestling, and barrel-racing keep you on the edge of your seat, as does an inmate-only event which involves grabbing a $100 bill(four months' salary in prison currency) from between the horns of a very irritated bull. At least you can count on the crowd to be reasonably well-behaved; it's just you and the prisoners, no alcohol allowed.

State Prison Outlaw Rodeo held annually in September at Oklahoma State Penitentiary in McAlester, OK; �‛ 918 423 2550; fax: 918 423 1345; web: www.icok.net/~macok/

Eccentric environments

Ed Galloway spent his retirement years building a unique monument to the American Indian known as **Totem Pole Park**. The totem poles inside don't look like any you've seen before. These are made from stones and concrete, lumpy but colorful, ranging in size from petite to over 90 feet tall. The largest pole sits atop a giant turtle and served as an observation tower from which to look out over the plains. Birds, coyotes, and squirrels cavort on these brightly colored poles.

Totem poles, however, weren't Ed's only obsessions. So were violins. This unlikely duo shared Ed's imagination and you'll be astounded when you see inside the 11-sided Fiddle House. Violins line every wall, hundreds of them. Some are works of art, delicately inlaid with designs and patterns. Others are made from hundreds of tiny pieces of wood. These delicate instruments are quite a contrast to the chunky totem poles outside.

Totem Pole Park, SH 28A, 4 miles E of Foyil, OK; �‛ 918 287 4803. *Open daily. Admission free, donations accepted.*

Powers Salvage in Gage isn't your ordinary junkyard. It's got **Jim's Metal Art Museum** and metal's the medium of choice for junk artist Jim Powers who creates gigantic insects, animals, and dinosaurs out of scrap metal from junked cars. Powers, 67, refers to himself as a 'happy scrap-yard man who likes to do art.' He says he 'just sits in a daze' and soon his next project materializes. He's put a door in the tail of his dinosaur so kids can climb inside the belly of the monster. Ripley's has bought some of his pieces for their Believe It or Not Museums. You can see some of his work by just driving by, but if you want to meet Jimmy and see his museum, you'll have to call first. He's 'un-busy' since retirement and would be happy to see you.

Jim's Metal Art Museum, Hwy 15 and 46 South, Gage, OK 73843;
☏ 580 923 7935. *Open 1.00–6.00pm Sun, 9.00am–5.00pm Tue–Sat
May 15–Sept 15. Tours by appointment only.*

Just plain weird

Located in the center of evangelist Oral Roberts University is the **Oral Roberts Prayer Tower** in Tusla, an oddly shaped structure meant to symbolize the importance of prayer as the center of life. The upward spiral represents man's relationship with God; the outward thrust of the observation deck represents the crown of thorns. An eternal flame sits on top. At the bottom – surprise, surprise – a gift shop, along with a 'Journey into Faith' video. What's the gospel according to Oral? 'No second-class buildings for God.'

Oral Roberts Prayer Tower located at Oral Roberts University,
7777 S Lewis Ave, Tulsa, OK 74171. Directions: take I 44, exit 227,
south on Lewis Ave to 81st St; web: www.oru.edu

Republicans should love this place. Located on the campus of Oklahoma Christian University of Science and Arts in Oklahoma City, **Enterprise Square** is a celebration of free enterprise and a warning of the dangers of government intervention. After watching a slide show introducing you to the great American consumer way of life, head on in to the Great American Market Place, not to shop but to see the world's largest cash register and giant, paper money that sings. Icons of free enterprise are commemorated in the Hall of Giants, then the government is taken to task for daring to interfere with a free economy by regulating commerce. Finally the remarkable Donut Shop for Demanding Donut Dunkers teaches how supply and demand can result in a beer belly.

Enterprise Square located on the campus of Oklahoma Christian
University of Science and Arts, 2501 E Memorial Rd, Oklahoma City,
OK 73136; ☏ 405 425 5030; email: info@esusa.org; web:
www.esusa.org

Attractions

The **Holy City of the Wichitas** is the site for an Easter Passion Play that was first put on in 1926 when the late Reverend Wallock took his Bible studies class up a mountain to present a tableau of the Resurrection. It's become an annual event, attracting hundreds of cast members and tens of thousands of worshipers. The site has a chapel built by the Works Progress Administration (WPA), a government project that provided work for the unemployed during the Depression.

Holy City of the Wichitas, Wichita Mountain Wildlife Refuge, Lawton, OK 73501; ☎ 580 248 4043 or 580 429 3361. Located off I-44 near Lawton; take Hwy 49 West for 10 miles.

Museums and collections

Oklahoma is tornado territory and it's where the movie *Twister* was filmed. It's inevitable, this being America, that some enterprising soul would find value in the debris and memorabilia left over after the filming. At the **Twister Museum** in Wakita, they saved some furnishings from Aunt Meg's home, the Elm Street sign used in the movie and a windmill sculpture from Aunt Meg's front yard. Residents have plans to develop a Twister Park across the street, but for now you'll have to be content with pictures of the storefronts and houses used as sets for the movie. They're displayed on pedestals in front of the now mostly empty lots.

Twister Museum, 101 Main St, Wakita, OK 73771; ☎ 580 594 2312.

Leonardo's Discovery Warehouse in Enid is an unusual museum devoted to hands-on experiences in the arts and sciences. You can build your own castle in the carpentry shop, get lost in a warren of tunnels, bridges, and mazes, fly to the moon in a simulated space shuttle, dig for fossils and plunge down a three-story-high slide.

Leonardo's Discovery Warehouse, 200 E Maple, Enid, OK 73701; ☎ 580 233 2787; fax: 580 237 7574; web: www.leonardos.org. *Open 9.30am–5.30pm Tue–Sat; 2.00–5.00pm Sun. Admission charge.*

A 70-acre, open air museum in Chickasha, **Muscle Car Ranch**, is devoted to souped up cars, antique auto signs, vintage motorcycles and classic Mack trucks. The Ranch hosts a huge annual Car Swap Meet that attracts collectors from all over the world. The site itself is an early 1900s dairy farm with all the original barns providing a novel backdrop for the cars and trucks.

Muscle Car Ranch, 3609 S 16th, Chickasha, OK 73108; ↘ 405 222 4910; web: www.musclecarranch.com. *Open 8.00am–5.00pm Mon–Fri or by appointment. Admission free, donations accepted.*

Almost every American over the age of 40 can remember movie stars flicking open their Zippo lighter in such a way that its flame illuminated the emotion of the moment. The **National Lighter Museum** in Guthrie has hundreds of old lighters, from table models to pocket ones; from Zippos to Ronsons, and from 85,000-year-old fire-starters to modern plastic flicks. The museum's mission is to preserve the history of the evolution of lighters, and to that end they've given the plain old lighter a more politically correct name: the 'mechanical pyrotechnic apparatus'.

Twenty-thousand such apparatuses are in the museum owned by Ted and Pat Ballard; they live upstairs of the biggest collection of fire-starters in the world. If Ballard can't convince someone to keep their lighters, then he wants to buy them for his collection. If he had his way, he'd have everyone looking through their basements and attics for the things, especially the ones used for advertising or to commemorate special occasions. Years ago, lighters were as common as pens and pencils, and Ted thinks their heritage is too important to lose.

National Lighter Museum, 5715 South Sooner Rd, Guthrie, OK 73044; ↘ 405 282 3025; web: www.natlitrmus.com. *Scheduled to reopen Fall 2001 after remodeling.*

Besides the museums described above, Oklahoma is home to a variety of other off-the wall collections and halls-of-fame. The **Percussive Art Society Museum** in Lawton displays only percussion (striking) instruments from around the world. The **Gene Autry Museum** in the town that bears his name honors the famous Old West cowboy movie and television star. College and Olympic wrestling is the theme at the **National Wrestling Hall of Fame and Museum** in Stillwater. The original sod house built in 1894 is furnished and preserved at the **Sod House Museum** in Aline. In Shattuck is an outdoor display of rare and restored windmills at the **Shattuck Windmill Museum and Park**. The **99s Museum of Women Pilots** in Oklahoma City honors past and present female aviators. A museum that focuses on the people who lived, worked, and traveled America's mother road, the **Route 66 Museum** in Elk City, takes you along the road through eight states. The **National Four String Banjo Hall of Fame Museum** in Guthrie is for and about nothing but banjos, banjo recordings and banjo players.

The Percussive Art Society Museum, 701 NW Ferris Ave, Lawton, OK 73507-5442; ↘ 580 353 1455; fax: 580 353 1456; web: www.pas.org. *Open 8.00am–5.00pm Mon–Fri; 1.00–4.00pm Sat–Sun. Admission charge.*

Gene Autry Oklahoma Museum, 601 Praire St, Gene Autry, OK 73436; ↘ 580 294 3047; web: www.cow-boy.com/museum.htm. *Open 10.00am–4.00pm Mon–Sat. Admission free.*

National Wrestling Hall of Fame and Museum, 405 W Hall of Fame Ave, Stillwater, OK 74075; ↘ 405 377 5243; web: www.wrestlinghalloffame.org. *Open 9.00am–4.00pm Mon–Fri. Admission free.*

Sod House Museum, State Hwy 8 South, Aline, OK 73716; ↘ 580 463 2441. *Open 9.00am–5.00pm Tue–Fri; 2.00–5.00 Sat–Sun. Admission free.*

Shattuck Windmill Museum and Park, 1100 S Main, Shattuck, OK 73858; ↘ 580 938 2818. *Open daily, outdoor exhibit.*

99s Museum of Women Pilots, 4300 Amelia Earhart Lane, Oklahoma City, OK 73159; ↘ 405 685 9990; web: www.ninety-nines.org/museum.html. *Open 10.00am–4.00pm Tue–Sat. Admission charge.*

National Route 66 Museum, US 66 and Pioneer Rd, PO Box 542, Elk City, OK 73648; ↘ 580 225 6266. *Open 9.00am–5.00pm Tue–Sat, 2.00–5.00pm Sun. Admission charge.*

National Four String Banjo Museum and Hall of Fame, The International Banjo College, 116 E Oklahoma Ave, Guthrie, OK 73044; ↘ 405 260 1323; email: info@banjomuseum.com; web: www.banjomuseum.com

MISSOURI
Festivals and events

St Louis has its own version of **Mardi Gras**, the third largest in the world behind New Orleans and Rio. The parade put on by the Mystic Krewe of Barkus is a favorite, with pooches parading in their Mardi Gras finery through the streets of the Soulard district. On Bastille Day, the same district sees Marie Antoinette and her hubby lose their heads during a three-day Bastille celebration. Marie and King Louis are paraded through the crowds to the faux guillotine; the cries of 'off with their heads' have the desired results.

St Louis Mardi Gras held annually. Contact St Louis Regional Chamber and Growth Association, One Metropolitan Square, Suite 1300, St Louis, MO 63102; ↘ 314 231 5555; fax: 314 206 3277, web: www.st-louis.mo.us

Mark Twain made Hannibal, Missouri famous. On **Tom Sawyer Days**, they have fence painting contests for pre-teens and adults, a Tom and Becky competition that is only for pre-teens and, of course, frog-jumping contests.

Tom Sawyer Days held annually in July in Hannibal, MO. Contact Hannibal Convention and Visitors Bureau, 505 N Third St, Hannibal, MO 63401; ↘ 573 221 2477; fax: 573 221 6999; web: www.hanmo.com

Attractions

St Louis has found a way to corral the energy and talents of graffiti artists by offering them a mile of legal concrete on which to express themselves. The **Miracle Mile** is now the longest, continuous graffiti art mural in the world. When the city first made the offer a few years ago, it expected, maybe 20 to 30 artists. Instead, 200 wall bombers, as the artists are called, showed up, toting 2,000 cans of spray paint, plus brushes and rollers, to do their thing. The project is quite remarkable, giving you a chance to really study some very eccentric graffiti in a secure setting.

Miracle Mile, St Louis, MO. Contact St Louis Regional Chamber and Growth Association, One Metropolitan Square, Suite 1300, St Louis, MO 63102; ↘ 314 231 5555; fax: 314 206 3277, web: www.st-louis.mo.us

Collectors of the angelic Precious Moments bisque porcelain figurines will be enchanted by the **Precious Moments** chapel complex near Carthage. If you're not a collector, you'll be astonished by this shrine to the work of artist Sam Butcher who combines art and ministry while producing the world's most popular collectibles. The Chapel Center has overtones of Las Vegas; it's an eccentric attraction designed to part you from your money while making you feel good about doing it.

The chapel itself has 52 biblical murals, 30 stained-glass windows, and bronze relief panels all done in the Precious Moments art style. The Fountain of Angels Show is pure glitz, with one of the world's largest show fountains featuring 252 bronze sculptures made by Butcher. Victorian Wedding Island sits on a lake in a storybook setting that would give any Vegas chapel a run for its money. A honeymoon mansion and bridal cottage nestle nearby. To make you feel really, really romantic, the aroma of freshly baked bread and pastries

APRIL FOOL?
An annual tradition in Kansas City used to be the **Mike Murphy Cattle Drive**. Murphy, host of a local AM radio show, started driving cattle through the streets on April Fool's Day to make people proud of their 'cow town' heritage. Around a hundred head of cattle were herded through downtown to obey a state senate resolution proclaiming a full day of festivities to celebrate cattle and the great steaks they provide.

SOUTH CENTRAL REGION

emanate from the Royal Delights Café and Sammy's Sweet Shoppe. Naturally, there's a convenient gift shop.

You can even sleep in the complex at the Best Western Precious Moments Hotel decorated, of course, with Precious Moments art. The place is so large that it offers a shuttle service to take you from place to place. With half a million collectors worldwide, it's obvious that art, ministry and manufacturing can go well together.

Precious Moments, 4321 Chapel Rd, Carthage, MO 64836; ↘ 800 543 7975; web: www.preciousmoments.com

Museums and collections

The latest news from the **Elvis is Alive Museum** in Wright City is that, well, Elvis is alive. How can they prove it? DNA, of course. It seems that samples from Elvis don't match up with samples from the body they buried in his place. It also seems that the real Lisa Marie Presley was placed in a foster home and a fake Lisa Marie brought in, at age 18, to sign over her wealth to Priscilla. The fake Lisa also married Michael Jackson. Don't quibble about details. Just accept the facts.

Bill Beeny, curator of the museum, has several theories as to why Elvis is alive and why he's hiding from the world. Prime among them is that Elvis was a secret FBI informer who had to fake his death and/or that he was working undercover for the Drug Enforcement Agency exposing a mob drug ring and had to fake his death. Yea, that Elvis certainly could blend right into a crowd.

The museum is a shrine to Beeny's convictions, loaded with evidence that the King lives. Elvis sightings are well documented, and Elvis' wax figure, lying in a coffin, suggest that a dummy was buried in the King's place.

Elvis is Alive Museum, I 70 exit, Wright City, MO; ↘ 636 745 3107

One of the museums most likely to produce a cringing-at-the-very-thought-of-it response, the **Glore Psychiatric Museum** in St Joseph uses full-sized replicas of such delights as the Bath of Surprise, a gallows-like contraption that plunged patients into icy water, supposedly to make them more co-operative. The Tranquilizing Chair was a grisly device into which a difficult patient could be strapped, naked, for months at a time; a bucket was placed beneath the seat to handle waste. Back in the days before pharmaceuticals, tortures like these were used to drive out the evil spirits thought to cause mental illness. Be grateful for Freud and Prozac.

The Glore Psychiatric Museum, 3406 Frederick Ave, St Joseph, MO; ↘ 816 387 2310 or 877 387 2310. *Open 9.00am–5.00pm Mon–Sat; 1.00–5.00pm Sun. Admission free.*

Back before cameras could record family history, it wasn't unusual for family hair to be woven into keepsakes like rings, necklaces, bracelets, brooches, hatpins, bookmarks, and cuff links. Multiple generations, as well as happy occasions, were memorialized in elaborate hair wreathes and woven hair art. Sometimes a hair ring would be sent to a friend or relative who couldn't attend the funeral of a loved one.

Leila's Hair Museum in Independence displays the collection that the cosmetology school owner has been collecting for 40 years. Once she got hooked on hair art, now a lost craft, she had to stash her purchases out of sight of her husband so he wouldn't know how much she was spending. Coming out of the closet with the museum in 1992, she doesn't regret the time or money she's spent. It's been a labor of love.

Leila's Hair Museum, 815 W 23rd, Independence, MO; ↘ 816 252 4247; web: www.hairwork.com/leila

Bowling might not be the most exciting spectator sport, but it is one of the oldest. The **National Bowling Hall of Fame** in St Louis is the keeper of the frames, recording bowling history as it's made. Its collection of 1,000 bowling shirts, some 90 years old, would make a retro store buyer hyperventilate. With 50,000 square feet, it even has room for a bowling-pin car. Believe it or not, more than a hundred million people around the world go bowling. The thought of all those monogrammed league shirts is enough to bowl you over.

National Bowling Hall of Fame, 111 Stadium Plaza, St Louis, MO 63102; ↘ 800 966 BOWL; web: www.bowlingmuseum.com. *Open Oct–Mar 11.00am–4.00pm; Apr–Sept Mon–Sat 9.00am–5.00pm; Sun 12.00noon–5.00pm. Admission charge.*

It's hard to know where to begin in a place that has no end. The **City Museum** in St Louis is – all at once – an outrageous environment, an innovative event, a madcap museum and a provocateur of preposterous pursuits that have everyone behaving as if they're kids. The museum grabs children at the entrance and lets them loose only when they've reluctantly admitted they've had enough stimulation for the day. For grownups, it's an irresistible opportunity to shed the confines of maturity and just plain play along. It's like a giant erector set; a warehouse of wacky adventures and outlandish events waiting to happen.

Founded by Bob Cassilly, a delightful rebel who needed a bigger playpen for his toys, this three-floor museum gives him the freedom to create whatever his fertile imagination propels him to do. For instance, the entire museum is built with recycled materials, including the concrete, the bricks, the roof tops and even the sidewalks. Two thousand steel squirrel-cages line the exterior bathroom walls. The Brontosaurus staircase banisters are made of conveyor-belt rollers. An enormous whale has ribs of scrap-metal shelving units, while the recycled water from the aquarium comes crashing down into the caves to the delight of squealing children. In the restaurant, mosaics are

FERTHAIRLIZER!

Barber Bill Black has a novel obsession. He's hoping to help feed, clothe, and house poverty-stricken areas of the world using human hair. His vision is utterly unique: to make productive use of the mountains of hair clippings disposed of each day in America in a product he calls FertHAIRlizer, a 20/80 hair-to-soil ratio mix that he claims is superior to other fertilizers on the market today. He'd also use hair in adobe bricks in place of straw, and would even weave it into bolts of cloth. Black's epiphany sprang from observing that the house plants in his shop receiving daily doses of airborne hair clippings were thriving despite being otherwise neglected. After testing his hypothesis and seeing his FertHAIRlizer out perform the competition, he tried to interest investors, without success, in his concept.

His idea sounded so far fetched, however, that he drew the attention of the media, garnering publicity in print, radio, and television, including the Tonite Show and David Letterman. Happy to get anyone to listen to him, he proudly talks about his hair bikini, hair undies, hair clip-on ties, vests, and hair shirts, all of which are lined with cotton for comfort, and all of which are made to pique curiosity about his ideas. While he's quite accepting of the ridicule that often comes his way, he hasn't given up hope that, someday, we'll see the light and turn our obsession with the hair on our heads into one more serving of mankind.

created from springs, plastic watchbands, pencils, shells and floor sweepings from industrial plants.

Aside from this astonishing visual assault, a jumble of startling experiences await. Kids disappear into a whale's mouth only to reappear over the aquarium. A dinosaur with a staircase on its back leads upwards to the upper floors; you come down in a slide shoot, which is a lot more fun. A maze-like network of caves is crawling with kids; in fact, anyone can crawl through anything in this place, as long as you can fit through. There are tunnels, secret passageways, waterfalls, streams, an enchanted forest, a crawl-through bird's nest and a jungle gym of ropes and screens.

Quirky events spring up all around you: an everyday, interactive circus, life-size chess and checkers games, recycled art workshops, an express mini-train, a toddler mini city with chalk and magnetic walls and a youth city where kids from ages three through eight play in gravel pits with trucks, tools, and blocks.

Then there are the special events, like the annual Fiber Day, when hairdressers and pet groomers harvest human and animal hair to weave into rugs and art. The Really Big Shoe Show showcased what happens when you tell 50 artists to have a go at it: a shoe of nails made a political statement about women's footwear; while an 18- foot, one-and-a-half-ton stiletto pump, made of 2,000 cast aluminum pumps, was big enough to stand in.

Every visit is different, stirring up activity and energy you didn't know you had. Interactive without computers or electronics of any kind, the City Museum is an experiential breath of fresh air in a world of entertainment given over to virtual reality. It's the real thing.

City Museum, 701 N 15th St, St Louis, MO; ↘ 314 231 2489; web: www.citymuseum.org. *Open Wed–Fri 9.00am–5.00pm; Sat–Sun 10.0am–5.00pm. Admission charge.*

Uppercrust dogs (no mutts need apply) have their pedigrees on parade at the **Museum of the Dog**, the American Kennel Club's tribute to pedigree pooches. The museum displays paintings, drawings, sculptures and other decorative arts devoted to the dog as well as maintaining an extensive dog library. This is the place to buy jeweled dog dishes and tapestry pet pillows for your purebred best friend.

Museum of the Dog, 1721 S. Mason Rd (in Queeny Park) West St. Louis County, MO; ↘ 314 821 3647; web: www.akc.org/love/museum/index.cfm. *Open Tue–Sat 9.00am–5.00pm, Sun 12noon–5.00pm. Admission charge.*

Shopping

Three Dog Bakery is an American phenomenon, its mission being to bake the world's best dog biscuits. The concept originated here; now more than 32 stores around the country cater to pampered pups everywhere.

Three Dog Bakery, headquarters located at Main St, Suite 700, Kansas City, MO 64108; ↘ 800 487 3287; fax: 816 474 2171; with over 30 bakeries located in various states. Their location can be found at the Bakery's website: www.threedog.com

Quirky cuisine

The hot rolls flying through the air astound people eating at **Lambert's Café** for the first time. It all started back in 1976 when the owner got tired of saying, over and over, 'Would you care for a hot roll?' One day a customer called out to her, 'Just throw the damn thing'. She did, and everyone else joined in. They've been throwin' 'em ever since, an average of more than two million a year. The 'Home of the Throwed Rolls' is also famous for their hubcap cinnamon rolls. There are two locations in Missouri: Sikeston and Ozark. Also located in Foley, AL (see page 170).

Lambert's Café, 1800 W Hwy J, Ozark, MO 65721; ↘ 417 581 7655; fax: 417 485 5830 and 2515 E Malone, Sikeston, MO 63801; ↘ 573 471 4261; fax: 573 471 7563; web: www.throwedrolls.com

ARKANSAS
Festivals and events

Bill Clinton's home state puts on some very strange events, the most notorious of which is the **Yellville Turkey Trot**. To understand this event you need to know that wild turkeys can fly and domestic turkeys cannot. When the festival started 55 years ago, they threw live wild turkeys off the courthouse roof, presumably for target practice. Then someone had the bright idea of tossing the turkeys out of a low-flying airplane and the Turkey Drop was born.

Well, the animal rights people got wind of this and the tabloids had a field day. A popular sitcom TV show of the 1970s, *WKRP in Cincinnati*, did a spoof of the event, the premise being that the fictional radio station would drop Thanksgiving turkeys, domestic of course, as a charitable gesture. The publicity stunt went down in a hail of feathers and screaming children.

Today the event is closely monitored to make sure there's no animal cruelty. The wild turkeys are dropped into the waiting arms of the crowd. What happens to them after the festival is anyone's guess. Parades, bands, and pageants add to the occasion. The Yellville Turkey Trot is famous for its renowned turkey calling contest; while the Miss Drumsticks beauty contest is judged by seeing only the legs of the girls lined up on stage. A Lip Sync contest, a turkey shooting competition, a Turkey Trot race and a turkey dinner round out the festivities.

> **Yellville Turkey Trot** held annually in October in Yellville, AR.
> Contact Yellville Area Chamber of Commerce, PO Box 369, Yellville,
> AR 72687; ↘ 870 449 4676 or 800 832 1414; email:
> chamber@yellville.com; web: www.yellville.com

The highlight of the **Mountain View Bean Festival** in October is the championship outhouse race. Following – appropriately – a free beans, onion and cornbread feed, the bizarrely bedecked outhouse toilets are paraded through the streets. Once the prizes for most original outhouse and best costumes are handed out, the outhouses compete in a drag race by being pulled, not pushed, along the racecourse by two-person teams. The frolic continues with a Tall Tale Telling Contest and a Talent Competition.

> **Mountain View Bean Festival** held annually in October in
> Mountain View, AR. Contact Mountain View Area Chamber of
> Commerce; ↘ 870 269 8068 or 888 679 2859; email:
> mychamber@mvtel.net; web: www.mountainviewcc.org

You only have to know how to swim to compete in the **World Championship Cardboard Boat Festival** in July. The boats, which can be of any shape and design, have to be constructed entirely of cardboard, glue, and duct tape. Then they're painted and waterproofed and the costumed skippers try to stay afloat for 200 yards using any form of human propulsion. The first boat to cross the finish line wins regardless of how much time it takes its crew to get there. The Titanic award is given for the most spectacular sinking. It looks as wacky as it sounds.

World Championship Cardboard Boat Festival held annually in July in Heber Springs, AR; ↘ 501 362 2444; web: www.heber-springs.com

At Conway's **Toad Suck Daze**, the Toad Master, sporting a bright green jacket, jump-starts the festivities with a baby crawl race. Then the toad store opens and it's time to select the your little toad jock for the frog jumping contest. With proper care and training, your toad may win you a fleeting moment of fame. The secret is in the crickets. A few of those tasty morsels before the race gets the old toad blood sugar going. After their tour of duty, all toads are carefully returned to their habitat.

Frog legs aren't on the menu, but food on a stick is. If it can be eaten with your hands, or put on a stick, you'll find someone selling it at Toad Suck Daze. A Tour de Toad bike race and a Mardi Daze parade round out the festivities. Be sure to hear the Toad Suck Drum and Kazoo Corps play 'When the Toads Go Marching In'. The Toad Suck event got its name in reference to the boatmen who refreshed themselves so copiously at the local tavern that they were said to suck on the bottle 'til they swelled up like toads'. Anyone for alligator on a stick? Could be snappy.

Toad Suck Daze held annually in May in Conway, AR. Contact Conway Area Chamber of Commerce, 900 Oak St, Conway, AR 72032; ↘ 501 327 7788; fax: 501 327 7790; web: www.toadsuck.org

In May, Atkins holds a **Pickle Fest**, with a pickle juice drinking contest, a pickle eating contest, and all the fried dill pickles you can eat. Blurp. Obviously there's no shortage of bizarre festivals in Arkansas, which is not surprising for a state famous for its political eccentricities.

Pickle Fest held annually in May in Atkins, AR. Contact Chuck; ↘ 501 641 1993 or People for a Better Atkins, Box 474, Atkins, AR 72823; ↘ 501 641 7210

Eccentric environments

If you think living in a lumber shed with five children is tough, try living in a chicken house. Tired of her husband's procrastination in building her a decent house, Elsie Quigley tore down the shed they were living in when hubby wasn't home and moved the whole family into the chicken house. That got his attention and he started building her the 'castle' she'd designed years earlier.

Elsie was a flower child long before the hippies of the 1960s adopted the name. She had been collecting rocks since childhood and she used those rocks to cover the entire exterior of the abode. Over the next 50 years she added more rocks, covering benches, ponds and bird baths, and planted 400 flower varieties in her garden. Tropical plants grow in the soil on the ground floor inside the house. She even found an ingenious way to sleep in the treetops. By far, **Quigley's Castle** is the Ozark's strangest dwelling; it also houses Mrs

Quigley's extraordinary collections of butterflies, fossils, crystals, arrowheads and glassware.

Quigley's Castle Ark, 23 S Eureka Springs, AR; ℩ 501 253 8311; web: www.quigleyscastle.com. *Open Mon–Wed, Fri–Sat 8.30am–5.00pm Apr 1–Oct 31. Admission charge.*

Just plain weird

Eureka Springs is the town's name; quirky is its game. The town, referred to as 'the place where misfits fit' by the *New York Times*, is where 'Woodstock meets livestock meets Birkenstock meets the stock market'. An authentic 1900 Victorian town nestled in the Ozarks, it plays host to almost a million tourists a year. There are no traffic lights and no streets that cross at right-angles, and there are so many hills that one hotel had a different address for each of its four floors. The town boasts an above-average number of psychics, palm readers, Tarot card readers, white witches, hypnotists, astrologists and other new age types. It's not unusual to see some of the town's 25 massage therapists setting up shop in the city parks.

It's also host to an annual UFO Conference and a Dowser's Convention.

More than 4,000 wedding licenses are issued each year in the 'town that lovers love'. You can get married in a tree house, on horseback, or in an all-glass chapel in the woods. They have more bed and breakfast inns than any other city or town in the country, including San Francisco.

They even elected a dead mayor, a candidate who died before the election. The townsfolk were so disenchanted with the alternative candidates that they voted for the deceased anyway. The current mayor, Beau Satori, is very much alive and will happily tie his below-the-waist ponytail into a bun and take you on a tour of the town. You can also take a historic haunted mansions and cemeteries tour here.

Eureka Springs located in the Ozarks region of Arkansas. Contact Eureka Springs Chamber of Commerce Visitors Information Center, 137 West Van Buren, Hwy 62 West, Eureka Springs, AR 72632; ℩ 501 253 8737; web: www.eurekaspringschamber.com

Attractions

A six-story-tall King Kong, holding a life-size Fay Ray, greets you at **Dinosaur World** near Beaver Dam, the largest dinosaur park in the world. By largest, they're referring to the setting: about 70 acres of meadow and lake. Dotted randomly throughout the park are about a hundred, life-size, concrete dinosaurs along with a few cavemen thrown in for anthropological atmosphere. About the only thing that's 'actual' about these creatures is their size. Their bright colors are a reflection of the theory that dinosaurs could see color and thus might have been colorful themselves. It's a very strange Kodak moment.

Dinosaur World located on Hwy 187, 8 miles west of Eureka Springs, AR; ℩ 501 253 8113. *Open 7.00am–7.00pm daily Apr–Oct ; 9.00am–4.00pm daily Nov–Dec.*

Hen Travolta, Leonardo Duckcaprio, and Kate Wings-let join a piano-playing rabbit and guitar-playing ducks in a continuous show of feathered and furry talent at the **Educated Animals and Petting Zoo** in Hot Springs. More than 120 birds and animals have been trained to perform as thespians to the delight of tourists. Biologist Mark Duncan has been training the animals here for 15 years. Before he took over, the animals were inside cages at a place called the IQ Zoo. You'd drop in quarters and they would start performing in hope of getting a food reward. Mark prefers more personal interaction and creates playlets such as *Star Wars* featuring Luke Skyhopper and Darth Gator. In another he 'shoots' a macaw and the bird pretends to drop dead. After the show, you can visit the petting zoo to meet the performer yourself.

Educated Animals and Petting Zoo, 380 Whittington Ave, Hot Springs, AR 71901;❯ 501 623 4311. *Open 9.30am–4.00pm fall and spring; 9.00am–5.30pm summer.*

All aboard the soul tram for a guided, narrated tour of the New Holy Land in Eureka Springs, complete with the only known, life-sized, fully furnished reproduction of Moses' Tabernacle in the Wilderness. The driver communicates with exhibit guides by walkie-talkie, saying such things as 'Holy Land to Simon Peter, we're nearing the Sea of Galilee.' Costumed guides enthusiastically portray key biblical characters. Each of the 40 exhibits and settings is 'authentically' replicated with historical accuracy, but you'll have to judge for yourself how successful they've been at doing this. A Bible Museum and Sacred Arts Center complete the complex.

New Holy Land Tours, PO Box 471, Eureka Springs, AR 72632; ❯ 501 253 9200 or 800 882 7529; email: drama@ipa.net; web: www.eurekasprings.com/passionplay. *Tours leave every 15 minutes Mon–Sat beginning at 9.00am.*

Riddle's Elephant Sanctuary is a pachyderm paradise. Serving as a cross between an orphanage and a rest home for stray and unwanted elephants, Riddle's takes in any elephant regardless of previous health or behavioral problems. Owners Scott and Heidi Riddle are passionate about protecting and expanding the number of Indian and Asian elephants in the sanctuary. Besides caring for these gentle creatures, they offer a two-week school in elephant management and care, as well as weekend elephant treks through the Ozarks. In between rides you can help feed and care for the elephants.

Riddle's Elephant Sanctuary, PO Box 715, Greenbrier, AR 72058; ❯ 501 589 3291; fax: 501 589 2248; email: elephantfarm@alltel.net; web: www.elephantsanctuary.org

If you're gonna build it, you might as well build it BIG – as in seven stories high. Looking down on Eureka Springs, land of the relaxed and massaged, **Christ of**

the Ozarks was created by Emmet Sullivan, one of the sculptors of Mount Rushmore. Every inch of the monument was made by hand. The foundation required 340 tons of concrete and Sullivan had to build an elevator up the side to work on the higher sections. The face alone is 15 feet high; the hands from wrist to fingertip measure around seven feet. Tip to tip, the arms span 65ft.

> **Christ of the Ozarks** located in Eureka Springs, AR; ↘ 800 882 7529; email: drama@ipa.net; web: www.eurekasprings.com/passionplay

Museums and collections

They're obviously big on frogs in these parts and Louise Mesa has 7,000 of the knick-knack kind at her **Frog Fantasies Museum** in Eureka Springs. This ever-expanding collection represents 60 years' worth of collecting. The Frog Lady even hosts conventions for frog enthusiasts. Fifty to 100 of the country's more than 5,000 frogophiles convene annually to buy, sell and trade their Kermit brethern. It's a chance to show off your finest in frog- wear and jewelry and spend time with peers who share your fascination with these croakers. When you ask her the obvious question – 'Why?' – she'll tell you all about the mythological and literary history of the frog. It has been a symbol of prosperity, wealth and abundance in many cultures; and a symbol of fertility in others. No wonder they're so many frog collectors.

> **Frog Fantasies Museum**, 151 Spring St, Eureka Springs, AR; ↘ 501 253 7227; web: www.frogfantasies.com

At the **Last Precinct Police Museum**, the mannequins are dressed in cop uniforms and displayed in settings that may bring back heart-pounding moments you'd sooner forget. Jim Post, a retired police sergeant, has assembled an astounding collection of vintage cop cars, patches, badges, jail logs, balls and chains, wanted posters, weapons and toy cars. The cars are all in running condition, including a Dick Tracy car and a propane-powered cruiser. Post likes to track down the officers who once drove the vehicles in his collection, so many of the cruisers have their own histories displayed. The badge collection numbers around 10,000. He's a member of Police Car Owners of America, whose 750 members have often held their national convention in Eureka Springs

> **The Last Precinct Police Museum**, 15677 Hwy 62W, Eureka Springs, AR 72632; ↘ 501 253 4948; web: www.policeguide.com/police-museum.htm. Located on US Hwy 62 West 4 miles west of Eureka Springs, AR. *Call for rates and hours.*

The **Stuttgart Agricultural Museum** has one of the most bizarre coats you'll ever see: a coat made entirely of duck heads. That's right, duck heads. The late Ruby Abel, two-time women's world champion duck caller and professional duck dresser, saved 450 of the mallard heads she'd chopped off at work. She painstakingly skinned them, tanned the hides, and hand stitched them together to make a coat. Ruby actually wore the thing while appearing as a contestant on television's *What's My Line* game show in the 1960s. A fetching duck-feather hat completed her ensemble. Not even Madonna could have dreamed this one up.

> **Stuttgart Agricultural Museum**, 921 East Fourth, Stuttgart, AR 72160; ↘ 870 673 7001. *Open Tue–Sat 10.00am–12.00noon and 1.00–4.00pm; Sun 1.30–4.30pm. Closed Mondays, legal holidays and Easter.*

Moving on from dead ducks to dead bucks, **Whitetail World** in Clarksville offers 10,000 square feet of whitetail deer mounts and replicas. The greatest bucks ever are displayed here from the most magnificent to the most unusual. Jordan Buck, Hole in the Horn and Mossy Horns are some of the Hall of Famers in a grandiose tribute to this elusive buck.

> **Whitetail World Museum**, PO Box 40, Clarksville, AR 72830; ↘ 501 754 8620 or 888 456 5051; web: www.whitetailworld.net. Located two blocks off I-40 at Exit 58. *Open Mon–Sat 8.00am–5.30pm; Sun 1.00–5.30pm. Admission charge.*

At 73 years old, Tedna Merritt knows a little something about miniatures. Her **Museum of Merritt**, part of Tiny Town Tours, in the tiny town of Mountain Home, has amassed one of the largest private collections in the world – more than 100,000 items, including a 19-room replica of Tara, the famous *Gone With the Wind* plantation house. Tedna offers her poetry and art work free for the asking.

> **Museum of Merritt**, Tiny Town Tours 2113 Hwy 62B, Mountain Home, AR 71901; ↘ 501 624 4742 or 870 425 4979

Quirky cuisine

Food and fantasy meet in a mad swirl at **Otis Zark's restaurant at Terra Studios** in Fayetteville where the floor tiles, tables, dinnerware, lights and murals are all handmade by local artists. Everything except the cutlery and chairs is art; the effect is a riot of whimsy. The restuarant gets its name from a legend about an elf-like fellow assigned to bring magic back to humans. He did his job so well that the place is overrun with trolls, dragons, elves and dwarves. You might as well succumb to the fantasy and enjoy an innovative menu – perhaps in a fantasy booth – in the most talked-about place to eat in the Ozarks.

Otis Zark's restaurant at Terra Studios, 12103 Hazel Valley Rd, Fayetteville, AR; ℩ 877 866 6689 or 501 643 4063; fax: 501 643 4264; email: otiszark@arkansasusa.com; web: www.otiszark.com. *Open Tue–Thur 11.00am–9.00pm; Fri–Sat 11.00am–11.00pm; Sun 11.00am–3.00pm; Mon 11.00am–4.00pm.*

LOUISIANA
New Orleans

New Orleans is where America kicks off its shoes and lets its hair down. Unlike the corporate eccentricity of Las Vegas, New Orleans is genuinely oddball, with behavior ranging from peculiar to outrageous; from quirky to preposterous; and from madcap to downright loony. Where else can one million people party like there's no tomorrow, face themselves in the mirror the next day, then go out and do it all over again when tomorrow comes?

Even on an ordinary day, New Orleans looks like a carnival. It's the only city in America , besides Las Vegas, with no closing laws. Stay out as late as you like, for you'll always have company. Eat as much as you wish, for good food is cherished and never eaten in a rush. The most European in feeling of American cities, it's a vast stew of curious religions, secretive societies, and delightfully daft characters.

N'awlins, as its properly pronounced, prizes itself on idiosyncrasy. With 3,000 bars, 41 cemeteries, and 700 churches, it's a mixture of Disneyland, Times Square, and a religious tent revival. If America were to select one city as it's national theme park, New ORR-le-ins, the only other correct pronunciation, would win hands down.

Mardi Gras is the biggest bash in North America. Carnival season begins on January 6 and goes through Fat Tuesday, the day before the start of the austere Lenten season. Mardi Gras also refers to the last two weeks of carnival when 60 parades take place morning, noon and night. Two of the biggest parades alone involve 60 marching bands, 250 floats and units and 2,300 'krewe' members throwing, literally, millions and millions of trinkets to the crowd. Spectators jostle for position, crying out 'Throw me something, mister!'

Mardi Gras has its own unique vocabulary. Krewes are private, membership societies that throw elaborate carnival parades and masked balls, many costing upwards of $100,000. The throws they toss include cups, beads and medallions with the krewe's logo and motto. Costumed float riders are called 'masquers'. The strange-sounding krewe names, like Proteus and Bacchus, are mostly taken from mythology. Each krewe goes to great lengths to keep its theme a secret, and being chosen king or queen to reign over a krewe's parade is a great honor. A 200-member krewe might have up to 3,000 participants, including band members, dance teams, clowns and other costumed groups.

A tour of **Blaine Kern's Mardi Gras World** takes you behind the scenes where artists, painters, and sculptors work in full view all year long creating the sensational props, costumes, and giant figures that make the festival so colorfully flamboyant. After seeing a historical video of the spectacle, you can gaze in amazement at the costumes and floats and even dress up in costume yourself. This is a definite Kodak moment.

Blaine Kern's Mardi Gras World, 233 Newton St, New Orleans, LA 70114; ✆ 800 362 8213 or 504 361 7821; email: briankern@mardigrasworld.com; web: www.mardigrasworld.com. Directions: from Downtown/French Quarter, cross Mississippi River Bridge, exit Gen DeGaulle, go east, left on to Shirley to Mardi Gras Blvd, follow signs to Mardi Gras World.

And don't even think of making sense of it all without Arthur Hardy's *Mardi Gras Guide*, an indispensable companion to parade goers for 24 years. You can buy a copy practically anywhere in the city.

New Orleans sits an average of five feet below sea level, which makes being put six feet under an almost impossible task. In the days before they built above-ground tombs, holes would have to be drilled in the underside of a coffin so gravediggers, armed with poles, could push the casket down into the muck before it could float to the surface. This gruesome practice was thankfully dispensed with when elaborate mausoleums began to be constructed topside instead.

A **Cities of the Dead Cemetery Tour** is an absolute must and one of the most fascinating excursions offered in the city. There are 42 cemeteries, with Metairie Cemetery considered the most varied and unique. Home to the tallest privately owned monument in the country, its 85-foot height makes it visible from the freeway. It was built by Daniel Moriarty who wanted his wife buried where she could look down on the blue bloods who had snubbed her during her life.

Cities of the Dead Cemetery Tours. Contact Save Our Cemeteries; ✆ 888 721 7493 or 504 525 3377; fax: 504 525 6677; email: soc@saveourcemeteries.org; web: www.saveourcemeteries.org. Tours depart from Royal Blend Coffee Shop, 623 Royal St, New Orleans, LA. The tour is accompanied through the cemetery by a uniformed security guard.

In the mid-19th century, voodoo was all the rage, much like today's new age movement. Voodoo is an African cult, brought here by the slaves. Once animistic, it has many variations involving strange and exotic ceremonies. Tours take you into the mysterious and secretive world of sorcery, curses and black magic. Mojo hands, dead bits of reptiles, birds, animals and humans, are still used today, along with voodoo charms, to fix that problematic someone or something.

The **Historic Voodoo Museum** offers walking tours guaranteed not to be run-of-the-mill experiences. With names like the Mourning Tour, the Voodoo/Cemetery tour, the Tour of the Undead and the Singing Bones Tour, you're sure to remember these spooky practices. **Haunted History Tours** combine history and fiction, legend and lore, and fact and fantasy, exploring the grim and ghastly past – including some ghosts still hanging around at the present.

Historic Voodoo Museum, 724 Rue Dumaine, New Orleans, LA 70116; ↘ 504 523 5223; web: www.voodoomuseum.com. *French Quarter walking tours depart daily from the museum.*

Haunted History Tours, New Orleans, LA; ↘ 504 861 2727 or 888 6GHOSTS; email: info@hauntedhistorytours.com web: www.hauntedhistorytours.com. *Tours depart from various locations around the city.*

The French Quarter is a magnet for colorful characters who are free to flourish in the eccentric culture. Some characters, such as the Chicken Man, are legendary. He was famous for biting off chicken heads during voodoo rituals. Ruthie the Duck Lady was trailed on her daily rounds, often while on roller skates, by a duck or two. **Big Al Tapilet**, a shoeshine man who paints on old roof tiles, trash-can lids and other street findings, rides around on a slate-covered bicycle. Expect the unexpected as you roam the streets.

Big Al Tapilet, Maison Dupuy Hotel lobby, 1001 Toulouse, New Orleans, LA

New Orleans is famous for music, with jazz, rhythm and blues, new age rock and gospel all playing an important role in its culture. The historic Storyville district got its name from one Sidney Story, a city councilman who proposed zoning the district for houses of ill repute. Mr Storey thought it would be best to keep the red light district all in once place so such businesses wouldn't bring down property values in other parts of the city. Well, it became America's first red-music district; the first place where European brass and African drums mixed it up. The brothels, dancehalls and clubs were filled with the new sound of jazz and Storyville became a notorious night and day hot spot.

You'll hear music coming from most every doorway, even from the bowling alley. At **Mid-City Lanes Rock 'n Bowl**, the air is filled with the sounds of rolling balls, falling pins, crashing drums and honking saxophones.

Rock 'n Bowl started quite by accident. Owner John Blanchard's bowling alley was facing a bleak future when he decided to book a band for the weekend. People started dancing even while they were bowling and John decided that offbeat was the secret. Today, there's a full bar, good food like fried alligator sausage and New Orleans street scenes painted on the walls. On St Patrick's Day he offers Shamrock and Bowl; Thanksgiving is Pluck and Bowl. An Elvis impersonator emerges from behind the pins in a cloud of smoke twice each year, once on Elvis's birthday and once on his 'deathday'.

Mid-City Lanes Rock 'n Bowl, 4133 Carrolton Ave, New Orleans, LA; ↘ 504 482 3133; email: info@rockandbowl.com; web: www.rockandbowl.com. *Directions: located at the corner of Carrolton and Tulane Aves.*

Festivals and events

Bonnie and Clyde, the bank robber lovebirds, met their maker near Gibsland. The town celebrates their infamous fame and couplehood at the **Authentic Bonnie and Clyde Festival and Museum**. You can see re-enactments of both the FBI ambush and the duo's death scene. The FBI and the bad guys are locked in a perpetual popularity contest, with the bandit's memorabilia more in demand than that of the good guys.

> **Authentic Bonnie and Clyde Festival and Museum**, Hwy 154, Gibsland, LA; ↘ 318 843 6141. Held annually on the weekend nearest May 23. *Museum open by appointment.*

The **Office Olympics** in Shreveport pits office workers against one another in manic events such as The Human Post-It Note, Toss the Boss, the Pencil Push, the Scissors Slide, the Water Break Relay and the Office Chair Roll-off.

> **Office Olympics** held annually in August in Shreveport, LA. Contact Melinda Coyer; ↘ 318 865 5173; web: www.shreveport-bossier.org

Five thousand eggs makes for a pretty awesome omelette. At Abbeville's **Giant Omelette Celebration**, they cook up a big one each year to celebrate their French heritage and their membership in a worldwide fraternity of cultural exchange cities known as the confrerie. Every year foreign representatives from member cities are knighted as chefs to help prepare the cajun style omelette that is eaten by happy spectators.

Besides the eggs, the omelette takes 50 pounds of onions, two gallons of parsley, six-and-a-half gallons of milk, 52 pounds of butter, three boxes of salt, two boxes of black pepper, and Tabasco Pepper Sauce 'to taste'.

> **Giant Omelette Celebration** held annually in November in Abbeville, LA. Contact Confrerie d'Abbeville, PO Box 1272, Abbeville, LA 70511; email: giantomelette@hotmail.com; web: www.giantomelette.org.

Attractions

A variety of swamp tours explore the muck and marshes that surround New Orleans. You'll see alligators, egrets and wild animals in moss-covered swamps that once were home to Indians and pirates. Try **Zam's Swamp Tours** in Kraemer, where you can browse alligator skulls in the gift shop.

> **Zam's Swamp Tours**, Kraemer, LA; ↘ 504 633 7881. Directions: 50 miles southwest of New Orleans in Kraemer. Take US 90 to Hwy 307. Contact 135 Kramer Bayou Rd, Thibodaux, LA 70301; ↘ 504 633 7881.

If you prefer your alligators alive, **Bayou Pierre Alligator Park** in Natchitoches has hundreds of them, ranging in size from petite four-footers to huge 1,000-pounders. You can feed 'em, touch 'em and eat 'em all in one place.

> **Bayou Pierre Alligator Park**, 380 Old Bayou Pierre Rd, Natchitoches, LA 71457; ℩ 877 354 7001; email: bpap@alligatorshow.com; web: www.alligatorshow.com. Directions: Old Bayou Pierre Road, about 10 minutes north of Natchitoches on Hwy 1 North. Look for the Alligator School Bus.

Museums and collections

The whimsical **UCM Museum** ('You-see-em Mu-se-um', get it?) in Abita Springs is the work of eccentric curator John Preble. Every day John asks himself, 'What would be fun?', then answers his own question by making whatever strikes his playful fancy. His intricately carved, animated scenes of southern life are impossibly detailed, and made with more than 50,000 found and recycled objects. Rocks, bottle caps, license plates, springs, motors; you name it, John has saved it. A pull tab becomes a taillight; a plastic fork becomes a tractor grill. It's all housed in a clump of old buildings, including a vintage gas station, an old Creole cottage, and the famous House of Shards which is covered with tens of thousands of itty bitty pieces of tiles, pottery, mirrors and glass.

> **UCM Museum**, 22275 Hwy 36, Abita Springs, LA 70420; ℩ 504 892 2624. Directions: one block east on Hwy 36 from town's only traffic light.

Grandmother's Buttons is housed in the vault of an old turn-of-the-century bank building. The vault is only 9 feet square but houses thousands of antique and contemporary buttons. The 'star' button is one of the original buttons hand-minted for delegates to George Washington's first presidential inauguration.

> **Grandmother's Buttons**, 9814 Royal St, St Francisville, LA 70775; ℩ 800 580 6941 or 225 635 4107; fax: 225 635 6067; email: info@grandmothersbuttons.com; web: www.grandmothersbuttons.com

Quirky quarters

The **Dive Inn Guest House** in New Orleans has aquatic themed rooms with toilets situated in outlandish places such as a phone booth or a shower. This six-room, off-the-wall establishment has a swimming pool in the lobby.

> **Dive Inn Guest House**, 4417 Dryades St, New Orleans, LA 70115; ℩ 888 788 DIVE; web: thediveinn.com

Appendix 1

GLOSSARY

Bik	brand name of a cigarette lighter; 'Flick your Bik' is a famous advertising slogan
Blue Book	social register of high-society families
Blue Cross/Blue Shield	huge health insurance companies
Bronx cheer	an obnoxious 'raspberry' sound expressing disapproval
Cheese Whiz	a processed cheese food that squirts out of a can
comfort station	a restroom or bathroom; American euphemism for toilet
Dave Barry	famous newspaper columnist and humorist
Dick Clark	television host of the 1950s' 'American Bandstand' dance show; long-time master of ceremonies at the New Year's Eve countdown in Times Square, New York
doozy	something noteworthy, extraordinary or bizarre
double header	two sports games played as a single event
Drew Carey	a plump, nerdy-looking television comic
Duncan Phyfe	a style of furniture
e-bay	on-line auction site
eccentrocity	eccentric monstrosity
FAC page	term for 'frequently asked questions'
grits	ground meal of dried and hulled corn kernels, boiled, then served as a breakfast food or side dish
gussied up	dressed up way beyond normal for a special event
half and half	a dairy mixture of half cream, half milk
hog	slang name for a Harley Davidson motorcycle
hogan	a round Navajo Indian dwelling hut built with the entrance facing east
honky tonk	a cheap night club or dance hall
hummer	an extremely expensive, indestructible military vehicle favored as a status symbol in wealthy neighborhoods
Jay Leno	host of the long-running, late-night *Tonite Show*; a talk show popularized by Johnny Carson
Julia Child	celebrity chef; originated television cooking shows

Kramer	kooky character in the television situation comedy *Seinfeld*
Lawrence Welk	dance-band leader famous for sentimental songs in the 1950s and 1960s
lazy susan	a round revolving tray
Lazy-Boy	brand name of a reclining chair; sometimes comes equipped with a pocket for the TV guide and a beer
Lily Tomlin	famous comedienne
Looking for Waldo	a busy, complex drawing in which cartoon character 'Waldo' is hiding (in the British version, called Wally)
Lucy and Ethel	zany female characters on the 1950s *Lucille Ball* television series
Martha Stewart	reigning priestess of home economics on television
Matlock	home-spun detective television series
outhouse	a small, enclosed structure with a seat, built over a pit and serving as an outdoor toilet; built as a one-holer or a two-holer
petting zoo	an attraction with baby animals
pinatas	a Mexican paper toy filled with candy, suspended in the air, then hit by blindfolded partygoers with a stick until it bursts and scatters the candy about
RV	abbreviation for a large recreational vehicle such as a camper or motor home
sasquatch	a mythical man-beast supposedly roaming the woods in the Pacific northwest
Seinfeld	famous television situation comedy about nothing that spoofed life's daily routine; starred stand up comic Jerry Seinfeld
souvenir sign	a token of remembrance; a memento sold at tourist attraction gift shops
SUV	a luxury four-wheel-drive vehicle able to be driven off road but seldom leaving city streets
Tim Allen	famous 'handyman' television personality; jokes that duct tape can solve most problems
vaudeville	old-fashioned music-hall entertainment
Wal-Mart	America's most famous 'big box' discount superstore; no-one wants this giant, architecturally ugly box built in their neighborhood but everyone wants one nearby for shopping

American: British terms

bathroom	toilet
billboard	hoarding
blowout	tyre puncture
bomb	in the theatre a great success

boondocks	backwoods
box car	goods wagon
caboose	last wagon on a goods train
checking account	current account
cookie	biscuit
cotton candy	candy floss
cube sugar	lump sugar
dishpan	washing-up bowl
druggist	chemist
glue factory	knacker's yard
jelly	jam
lox	smoked salmon
mononucleosis	glandular fever
night crawler	fishing worm
oatmeal	porridge
paddy wagon	black maria
parakeet	budgerigar
pegged pants	tapered trousers
pullover sweater	jumper
realtor	estate agent
roomer	lodger
Rube Goldberg	Heath Robinson
second floor	first floor
sedan	saloon car
station wagon	estate car
to pinch-hit	to substitute for
undershirt	vest
underwear	knickers/pants
wash up	wash yourself, not the dishes

Appendix 2

FURTHER READING

535 Wonderful Things to do this Weekend: A Guide to Annual Festivals, Fairs and Events in the Mid-Atlantic States, New Jersey, Pennsylvania, New York, Delaware and Maryland, Mitch Kaplan, Middle Atlantic Press, 1999.

America Bizarro: A Guide to Freaky Festivals, Groovy Gatherings, Kooky Contests and other Strange Happenings Across the USA, Nelson Taylor, St Martin's Griffen, 2000.

American Ways: A Guide for Foreigners in the United States, Gary Althen, Intercultural Press, 1988.

America's Strangest Museums: A Traveler's Guide to the Most Unusual and Eccentric Collections, Sandra Gurvis, Carol Publishing Group, 1996.

An American Festival of 'World Capitals' From Garlic Queens to Cherry Parades: Over 300 'World Capitals' of Arts, Crafts, Food, Culture and Sport, Laura Bergheim, John Wiley and Sons, Inc, 1997.

Culture Shock USA: A Guide to Customs and Etiquette, Esther Wanning, Graphics Arts Center Publishing, 1991.

The Darwin Awards: Evolution in Action, Wendy Northcutt, E P Dutton, 2000.

Dear Elvis: Graffiti from Graceland, Daniel Wright, Mustang Publishing, 1996.

The Dream Lives On: The House On The Rock, The House On The Rock, 1991.

Eccentric Britain, Benedict le Vay, Bradt Publications, 2000.

Field Guide to Elvis Shrines, Bill Yenne, Renaissance Books, 1999.

Frommer's Irreverent Guide to Manhattan, 3rd Edition, Ian McMahan, IDG Books Worldwide, 2000.

Frommer's Irreverent Guide to San Francisco, 3rd Edition, Liz Barrett, IDG Books Worldwide, 2000.

The Fun Also Rises Travel Guide North America: The Most Fun Places to be at the Right Time: The Ultimate Vacation Planner to the 50 Best Events and Destinations in the US and Canada, Alan Davis, Greenline Publications, 1998.

Great American Motorcycle Tours, Gary McKechnie, John Muir Publications, 2000.

The Great San Francisco Trivia and Fact Book, Janet Bailey, Cumberland House, 1999.

Holding On: Dreamers, Visionaries, Eccentrics and Other American Heroes, David Isay and Harvey Wang, W W Norton and Company, 1997.

How to Talk American: A Guide to our Native Tongues, Jim 'the Mad Monk' Crotty, Houghton Mifflin Company, 1997.
Idaho Loners Hermits, Solitaires and Individualists, Cort Conley, Backeddy Books, 1994.
LA Bizarro: The Insider's Guide to the Obscure, the Absurd, and the Perverse in Los Angeles, Anthony R Lovett and Matt Maranian, St Martin's Press, 1997.
The Last of the Mountain Men: The True Story of an Idaho Solitary, Sylvan Hart, Backeddy Books, 1969.
Little Museums: Over 1,000 Small (and Not-So-Small) American Showplaces, Lynne Arany and Archie Hobson, Henry Holt and Company, 1998.
The Mad Monks' Guide to California, James Crotty and Michael Lane (The Monks), Macmillan Travel, 2000.
The Mad Monks' Guide to New York City, James Crotty and Michael Lane (The Monks), Macmillan Travel, 1997.
Main Street Festivals: Traditional and Unique Events on America's Main Streets, Amanda B West, The National Main Street Center of the National Trust for Historic Preservation, John Wiley and Sons, Inc, 1998.
Making America: The Society and Cultrure of the United States, edited by Luther Leudtke, University of North Carolina Press, 1992.
Nevada off the Beaten Path: A Guide to Unique Places, Donna Peck, The Globe Pequot Press, 1997.
The New Roadside America: The Modern Traveler's Guide to the Wild and Wonderful World of America's Tourist Attractions, Mike Wilkins, Ken Smith and Doug Kirby, Simon & Schuster, 1986.
New York off the Beaten Path: A Guide to Unique Places, William G and Kay Scheller, The Globe Pequot Press, 1994, 1997 and 1999.
North Carolina Curiosities: Jerry Bledsoe's Guide to Outlandish Things to See and Do in North Carolina, updated by Sara Pitzer, The Globe Pequot Press, 1984, 1990 and 1999.
Northern California off the Beaten Path: A Guide to Unique Places, Mark Williams, The Globe Pequot Press, 1989, 1996, 1999.
Oddball Illinois: A Guide to Some Really Strange Places, Jerome Pohlen, Chicago Review Press, 2000.
Off the Beaten Aisle: America's Quirky Spots to Tie the Knot, Lisa Primerano, Carol Publishing Group, 1998.
Offbeat Museums: The Collections and Curators of America's Most Unusual Museums, Saul Rubin, Santa Monica Press, 1997.
On The Back Roads: Discovering Small Towns of America, Bill Graves, Addicus Books Inc, 1999.
Only In Mississippi: A Guide for the Adventurous Traveller, Lorraine Redd and Jack E Davis, Quail Ridge Press, 1993.
The Outrageous Atlas: A Guide to North America's Strangest Places, Richard D Rogers and Laurine Rogers, Citadel Press, 1993.
Philly Firsts: The Famous, Infamous and Quirky of the City of Brotherly Love, Janice L Booker, Camino Books Inc, 1999.
Radical Walking Tours of New York City, Bruce Kayton, Seven Stories Press, 1999.

The Rhode Island Guide, Barbara Radcliffe Rogers and Stillman D Rogers, Fulcrum Publishing, 1998.

The Ridgerunner Elusive Loner of the Wilderness, Richard Ripley, Backeddy Books, 1986.

San Francisco Bizarro: A Guide to Notorious Sights, Lusty Pursuits and Downright Freakiness in the City by the Bay, Jack Boulware, St Martin's Press, 2000.

Sense of Place: American Regional Cultures, edited by Barbara Allen and Thomas J Schlereth, University Press of Kentucky, 1990.

Slanguage: A Cool, Fresh, Phat, and Shagadelic Guide to All Kinds of Slang, Mike Ellis, Hyperion Books, 2000.

South Dakota, T D Griffith, Photographs by Paul Horsted, Compass American Guides, 1994.

Southern California off the Beaten Path: A Guide to Unique Places, Kathy Strong, The Globe Pequot Press, 1989 and 1995.

Texas Curiosities: Quirky Characters, Roadside Oddities and Other Offbeat Stuff, John Kelso, The Globe Pequot Press, 2000.

Watch it Made in the USA: A Visitor's Guide to the Companies that Make your Favorite Products, Karen Axelrod and Bruce Brumbert, John Muir Publications, 1997.

Way out in West Virginia: A Must-have Guide to the Oddities and Wonders of the Mountain State, Jeanne Mozier, Quarrier Press, 1999.

Wet and Wired: A Pop Culture Encyclopedia of the Pacific Northwest, Randy Hodgins and Steve McLellan, Taylor Publishing Company, 2000.

Appendix 3

THE WEIRD AND WACKY WEB
Highway/Road Trip/Roadside

The American Highway Project (photo gallery of America's vanishing roadside culture): www.highwayproject.org

Explore Route 66 (history in the remaking): www.national66.com/

Hidden America (on the road Americana): www.hiddenamerica.com

Interesting Ideas (roadside art, outsider art, and commentary): www.interestingideas.com

Kitsch Tour USA (Frank Wu's favorite kitschy sites around the country): www.frankwu.com/kitschhome.html

Out West Newspaper ('on the road' quarterly newspaper): www.outwestnewspaper.com

Road Trip America ('Life's a journey... we might as well be taking the scenic route'; web magazine produced from the road): www.roadtripamerica.com

Roadside America (online guide to offbeat tourist attractions): www.roadsideamerica.com

Roadside attractions www.4roadtrips.4anything.com/4/0,1001,6013.00.html

Roadside Online (the latest diner news): www.roadsidemagazine.com

Roadside Peek (an American roadside journey): www.roadsidepeek.com

Society for Commercial Archeology (buildings, artifacts, signs and symbols of the 20th century commercial landscape): www.sca-roadside.org/

Two-Lane Roads (quarterly magazine of off-beat roadside delights): www.two-lane.com

World's Largest Roadside Attractions (photo collection of large roadside attractions): www.infomagic.net/~martince/

Events

Art Cars in Cyberspace: www.artcars.com

The Bad Fads Museum in cyberspace: www.badfads.com

Celebrating Festivals Worldwide: www.festivals.com

The Cosmic Ray Deflection Society of North America (links to outsider art): www.geocities.com/SunsetStrip/1482/links.html

Gallery of the Absurd (collection of weird advertisements, labels, signs): www.absurdgallery.com

Illumination Project (monumental and fleeting works of art):
www.burningart.com
Mural Art (website featuring mural art and mural art culture):
www.muralart.com/
Museum of Bad Art (art too bad to be ignored): www.glyphs.com/moba/
Raw Vision (magazine of outsider art): www.rawvision.com
RetroCulture (retro culture, design and style): www.retroculture.com
Southern Festivals (The South's Festival and Fair Resource):
www.southfest.com/
What's Going On (events countrywide including today's coolest place, Top
Spots, Top 10 Unique Events and Top 10 One of A Kind Events in the
USA): www.whatsgoingon.com
Zenzibar (huge alternative culture directory): www.zenzibar.com

Just plain weird
Amazing Maize Maze (cornfield maze art): www.americanmaze.com
Bananas on the Web (dedicated to bananas and banana label collectors):
www.geocities.com/NapaValley/1702/
Beyond Weird (bizarre websites from conspiracies to UFOs):
www.beyondweird.com
**The BigKid Collection of Bizarre, Funny and Engrossing Weird
Sites**: www.now2000.com/weird/index.shtml
Bizarre food links: www.cvixen.com/bizarre-food.htm
Bizarre links: www.ishouldbeworking.com/bizarre.htm
Bizarre News (spanning the globe for the weird, strange and stupid):
www.bizarrenews.com
Collector Online Club Directory: www.collectoronline.com/club-
directory.shtml
Darwin Awards (Evolution in Action. Commemorates those individuals
insuring the long-term survival of our species by removing themselves from
the gene pool in a sublimely idiotic fashion): www.darwinawards.com
Deuce of Clubs (links to all things eccentric):
www.deuceofclubs.com/map.htm
Directory of Urban Legends and Folklore:
www.urbanlegends.about.com/science/urbanlegends/
Dumb Warnings (dumb warnings and laws): www.dumbwarnings.com
Gallery of Regrettable Foods: www.lileks.com/institute/gallery
Little Museums: www.littlemuseums.com/lm2.html
Museum of Dirt (collection of soils from around the world):
www.planet.com/dirtweb
The Onion (newspaper satire): www.theonion.com
Project Denny's (a trek across country to dine at every single Denny's
Restaurant): www.p7a77.net/dennys/
Real Haunted Houses (ghost hunter clubs): www.realhaunts.com/clubs.htm
The Tackiest Place in America Contest:
www.thepoint.net/~usul/text/tacky.html

Totally Absurd (totally absurd patents and inventions):
www.totallyabsurd.com
Urban Legends (separating fact from fiction): www.urbanlegends.com
USA Centric (strange and interesting places in the USA):
www.webedelic.com/usacentric.html
Web WWWeirdness (the official WWWeirdness repository)
www.randysweb.com/weird/
Weirdlinks (bizarre index of weird websites): www.weirdlinks.com/
What a Collection (unusual collections, shows and events):
www.whatacollection.com

Cities and states

Alabama Live's wacky Alabama website: www.al.com/wacky/wacky3.html
All Things Las Vegas: www.unlv.edu/tourism/vegas.html
The Arkansas Traveler's Roadside distractions:
www.aristotle.net/~russjohn/
Best Read Guide (Las Vegas Facts and Figures):
www.bestreadguide.com/lasvegas/stories/19991007/tri_trivia.shtml
The Boardwalk Catalog (best of the Jersey shore)
www.jerseyboardwalk.com/index.html
Calendar Live (offering information about a variety of events in the Los
Angeles area): www.calendarlive.com
Chicago Entertainment Newsletter: chicagofun.org/list/index.htm
From Walking Tours to Gospel Tours, New York Offers it All
(article): www.suite101.com/article.cfm/new_york_city/31793
Las Vegas Fun Facts and Information:
www.lvstriphistory.com/funfacts.htm
Laughing Squid (art and underground culture in San Francisco):
http://www.laughingsquid.org/
Mississippi Trivia: www.mslawyer.com/trivia.htm
New England for Visitors with Kimbery Knox (New England Oddities
A–Z): www.gonewengland.about.com/travel/gonewengland/library/weekly/
aa081798.htm?COB=home&PID=
San Francisco Chronicle (offbeat news): www.sfgate.com
San Francisco Underground Travel (the good, the bad and the ugly):
www.sftravel.com/
University of Alabama's Southern Culture Resources:
www.lib.ua.edu/Fsmr/Fsouth1.htm
UNLV's Unique Las Vegas Links: www.unlv.edu/toursim/lvmisc.html
Weird New Jersey: www.weirdnj.com
Wisconsin Department of Tourism's list of Quirky Attractions:
www.tourism.state.wi.us/activities/quirky.shtml
Wisconsin Tourism Sites list of Strange Sites:
www.wisconsintourism.com/type/strangesites.htm
World Wide Multi-Media Magazine (scenes and happenings from mainly
Northern California): www.hooked.net/users/cjoga/

Hotels/motels

Haunted Places Directory (guide to haunted hotels, inns and restaurants in the 50 states): www.haunted-places.com
Listing of Unique Hotels in US and Canada:
www.hotels.about.com/travel/hotels/msuboddca.htm

Language

American Slanguages (the hick to hip translation guide):
www.slanguage.com

State Index

Alphabetical Index